S0-BDP-926

Published by Teachers College Press, 1234 Amsterdam Avenue, New York, N.Y. 10027

Library of Congress Cataloging in Publication Data

Johnson, Howard M., 1938–
Planning and financial management for the school principal.

Bibliography: p. 269
Includes index.
1. School management and organization. I. Title.
LB3011.J6 371.2 82-3288
ISBN 0-8077-2719-9 AACR2

Manufactured in the United States of America

87 86 85 84 83 82 1 2 3 4 5 6

CONTENTS

FOREWORD

The principal has come to be recognized as the single most important person in determining the quality of education our children receive. By his or her leadership and example, the good principal can give confidence to teachers and help them understand how important their daily responsibilities are. The good principal can reinforce in the minds of teachers and students alike a respect for learning and a respect for the worth of the individual. Beyond these important duties, the principal can convey the realization that teaching and learning are joyful experiences. These higher aspects of the principalship, however, are most likely to be forthcoming when the principal is confident in the mastery of the position, and to help principals acquire such mastery, Dr. Howard Johnson has written this book. It is a book that is both scholarly and practical.

In *Planning and Financial Management for the School Principal,* Dr. Johnson looks at the principalship from a management perspective. He maintains the view that school management is a cyclical process focusing on and evaluating attainment of goal priorities. Throughout the book, he presents concepts and techniques useful in creating and monitoring constantly changing goal priorities.

Dr. Johnson brings his own background as teacher, principal, and professor of school finance and planning to bear on the material presented in this book. He obviously understands and has used the techniques and strategies included here. This is not a cookbook approach with the usual do's and don'ts of administering schools but rather an encounter with generic skills required in the conduct of planning and evaluation in our schools. Those training for future administrative roles and those who simply desire to improve on current skills will find a wealth of ideas about the practice of administration in schools. The exercises included at the end of each chapter are timely in nature and represent the best in management practice today. This book is a major addition to the training of school leaders in the 1980s.

Charles S. Benson
Professor
Department of Education
University of California
Berkeley

April 1982

INTRODUCTION

This book is an encounter with some of the management skills judged most crucial to building administrators. Many books and articles have been written about the demands of the principalship. In recent years, most of this literature has been directed to perceived role changes for building administrators. Most observers agree that the expansion of collective bargaining into education has tended to alter the traditional decision-making role at the building level, making the principal more of a contract interpreter and conflict resolver than a decision maker. While the existence of this shift in decision-making responsibility is not to be denied, it is still true that the school principal has considerable latitude in guiding the implementation of policies and decisions established at other levels of the school district operation. It is also true that this guiding and interpreting role requires considerable skill in planning and financial management.

If anything, the capacity to develop carefully written plans and to accept the educational and financial responsibility for successful implementation of these plans has never been more important to success as a building principal. Today's principal certainly has to be expert in the areas of human relations and conflict management. The principal must also understand theories of group process and organizational structure. However, these latter understandings and skills must be matched with a capacity to plan, evaluate, and manage the school program. Extensive grounding in theories of organization and concepts of leadership style, while helpful in giving perspective and insight to the job, must be blended with important planning and management skills involved in getting the job done.

Two examples might help illustrate this critical need for planning and management skills on the part of building administrators. The first of these occurred in connection with goal development activity in a school district. Each administrator was required to establish both personal and school goals and to develop some procedure for evaluating the attainment of these goals. The following goal statements were taken verbatim from the lists submitted by the building principals:

1. To refine existing diagnostic tests and to correlate instructional placement, skills units, and teaching strategies with results of diagnostic tests.
2. To design and pilot alternate reading and spelling programs to respond findings of standardized test results of present fifth and sixth grade students.
3. To initiate and follow through on exchange of curricular functions primarily between junior and senior high teachers—emphasis to be placed in core areas of science, math, social studies, and language arts.
4. To personally visit every classroom with the purpose of improving instruction with the Instructional Theory Into Practice (ITIP) method every 60 days, and hold a constructional conference with every teacher after the visitation to assist them to improve their teaching.

Quite obviously, this set of goal statements is poorly written. The related evaluative procedures were equally poor expressions of intent. Not only are these four goal statements lacking in specificity, but the use of such phrases as a "follow through on exchange of curricular functions" and "hold a constructional conference" indicates that the authors of these statements have serious problems with written communication. An administrator who thinks and/or writes in such a vague manner is likely to be minimally effective in guiding the planning process at the building level. Such an administrator will also provide little help to teachers who, in this time of increased accountability, are asked to write and communicate instructional objectives for their classrooms.

The other illustration of this need for planning and management skills occurred in connection with registration and scheduling in a secondary school. In this particular case, both the principal and the vice-principal were new to the building and neither had much prior training or experience in scheduling students. They struggled through preparation of a master schedule. With the help of the school registrar, who was also new on the job, they were set for a walk-around student assignment procedure on the opening day of school. The problem of not having sufficient course offerings for tenth-grade students during selected periods of the day was not discovered until students arrived to begin the walk-around procedure. The problems of unbalanced classes and course conflicts were of such magnitude that school had to be dismissed for two days while the master schedule was completely revised. In this instance, the lack of administrator knowledge and skill in student scheduling procedures caused a serious problem, even before the school year started. A potentially effective administrative team developed a serious credibility problem with their student and parent communities because they failed to implement the generally routine procedures of registration and scheduling.

Other examples could be given; however, the point is simply that those persons training for the school principalship should be exposed in their preparation programs to a number of the more important planning and management skills required by today's school principal. It is evident from the examples cited that many practicing administrators need to update their skills in these same areas. In addressing these skills, this book selects examples from both the elementary and secondary levels and is therefore applicable to administrators at all levels. The format of the book is a presentation of concepts followed by a set of exercises designed to give the reader practice with these same concepts. The presentation of the concepts is generally done within the context of building-level management, thus bringing greater reality to the training experience.

The provision of skill-building practice in relation to the various concepts presented is a special feature of the book. Whatever concept is discussed—goal setting, planning a sequence of school activities, or assessing the financial health of the school—it is presented in the school context and the reader is given an opportunity to apply the concepts and skills involved. This application of important management skills to the building level, along with a clear recognition of modern data processing capabilities, makes the book unique in the field of educational administration. The opportunity to apply the concepts through use of discussion questions and problems is simply not provided in most other books used in administrative training programs.

The three parts of the book represent clusters of responsibilities facing today's building-level administrator. The first part deals with a variety of concepts and tasks associated with establishing and monitoring organizational goals. In the second part of the book, selected skills associated with the implementation of goal priorities are reviewed. The final portion directs attention to management of finances in the school setting. Included here is an examination of the types of financial reporting and budgeting practices found in both public and private schools across the United States.

The book may be used either in its entirety or on a selective basis. It can be used as a basic text for a course on the principalship or as a supplementary reference in courses focusing on planning, evaluation, and financial management at the building level. The final part could be used separately in a unit or course on school finance for the building administrator.

Although the book is intended for building-level administrators and the applications are most generally directed to those positions, many sections are appropriate to administrators in every part and level of the school system. The kinds of planning and management skills covered are important to the daily operation of schools; use of the practice exercises provided in the text can improve performance of both current and future administrators as they strive to meet the challenge of excellence in education.

PART I

ESTABLISHING AND MONITORING DIRECTION FOR THE ORGANIZATION

OVERVIEW

Most researchers of organizational behavior cite the focusing and clarifying of goals as a necessary first step to effectiveness and survival.[1] Yet, schools and school systems have considerable difficulty arriving at a set of goals that is supported both by the various citizen groups and by the school district's employees. Goal priorities seem to shift over time between academic and socialization functions depending on the respondent group and the particular situation or time period under consideration. Some segments of the social system seem to favor a broad-ranging responsibility for both academic and socialization functions; other segments would limit the school responsibility to the academic pursuits, leaving the value-laden socialization functions to other community institutions such as the home, the church, and community recreation centers. Others, though they are not likely to admit it, view the school primarily as a holding station for young people who have no viable alternatives. This latter goal is sometimes called the custodial function and it seems to have gained importance in recent years due to the reduced number of employment opportunities for youth.

With respect to this confusion and uncertainty in the education goal domain, James March in 1974 made the following observation: "The goals [for schools] are problematic. It is difficult to specify a consistent set of goals. Instead, goals seem to shift over time; they seem to vary from one part of the organization to another; they seem to be stated in terms that are hard to translate into action" (March, p. 394).

In Part I of this book, we are most concerned with the latter part of March's observation, namely, the difficulty of translating educational goals into action. Such translation techniques are dependent on some vision of the types of goal statements suitable for educational institutions and the procedures that are needed to translate these goals into statements that guide the school and its component instructional units. With this in mind, two chapters on goals—the first, involving the classification and derivation of goals statements, and the second, dealing with techniques for the translation of goal statements into action programs—are included. In each chapter, attention is given to practical application of alternative strategies for goal and objective development. Questions dealing with these strategies and actual skill development in goal implementation are included at the conclusion of each chapter.

---

[1]Goal clarity is a necessary but not sufficient condition to organizational health and effectiveness. Matthew B. Miles argues that goals must also be accepted and appropriate. These arguments are developed in "Planned Change and Organizational Health," in *Organizations and Human Behavior,* edited by Fred B. Carver and Thomas J. Sergiavanni (New York: McGraw-Hill, 1969), pp. 375–391.

CHAPTER 1
GOAL DEVELOPMENT AND PRIORITY SETTING IN SCHOOLS

Administration is a process of working with and through individuals and groups to accomplish organizational goals. Whether one is referring to a large manufacturing plant, a small accounting firm, or a public agency such as a school system, administration necessarily begins with organizational goals. In some cases, these goals are simply understood and little attention is given to their classification or dissemination. Rarely does the manager of a local department store have to identify the organization's major goal as selling goods at a price that assures a reasonable profit margin for the organization. Neither does the coach of a high school basketball team have to identify winning basketball games as at least one of the major goals for the team. These goals—making a profit and winning basketball games—are inherent in the organization context and require very little explanation, either for those working within the organization or for clients or observers of the organizational activity. Unfortunately, the goals for schools are not as well defined as is the case for the typical department store or basketball team. This lack of clarity in school goals structure can be attributed to several factors, discussed below.

A public school system serves a diverse public under a somewhat compulsory format and must therefore operate with a broader range of goals than most organizations.

In the cases of the department store and the basketball team, there is no expectation that all persons in the public are to be served. A department store may purposely direct its services to a high-income group or to persons who desire only certain types of merchandise. Similarly, the basketball team is generally reserved for athletes who can jump a certain height or exhibit a certain minimum level of coordination. Schools, at least those supported by public funding, depend on the entire community for support and must therefore accept a broad set of goals. Whether the school is or even can be successful in accomplishing these broad-range goals, it must, in order to survive, at least symbolically profess to take seriously the entire set of broad goals existing within the public domain.

The range of school goals often includes conflicting intentions, at least some of which the school is not likely to be capable of achieving.

Most organizations operate with some level of conflict in their goal structure. The basketball team strives to win games and at the same time to encourage good sportsmanship. This latter goal, particularly when it involves developing a feeling of respect and concern for the opponent, may conflict with the goal of winning games. In the case of the department store, the intent of preserving the downtown area by cleaning the streets in front of the store may conflict with the intent of making a maximum profit for the owner. There may also be some disagreement as to whether short-term profit margins take priority over the long-term investments needed for survival in a competitive world. In neither of these cases, however, is the level of goal conflict so evident as in the case of a school or school system. The school that encourages individual choice and self-fulfillment for its students must necessarily realize that this goal, and its related instructional processes, may eventually conflict rather directly with the intent of teaching respect for law and authority. This is nothing more than the conflicting tenets of our democratic society, namely, a respect for individual rights coupled with the often-conflicting tenet of majority rule. Any enterprise like the school that attempts to deal with the total being and to nurture that being to social maturity is likely to face this conflict between the humanistic trust in individual good and the historical reality of man as a selfish being requiring some kind of law and regulation for survival.

In addition, the school may not be equipped to accomplish some of its professed goals. One set of goals called into serious question in recent years is related to a more even distribution of such benefits as income, status, and occupational opportunity. The assumption is that schools and their services are intended to provide young people with increased life chances. While this is an admirable goal, the current high unemployment (or at least downgraded employment) among well-educated groups has led many to question whether the school is really an appropriate vehicle for alleviating such social ills as unemployment, poverty, and crime. The evidence of school success in these areas is not very convincing at present, and this lack of success simply adds to a questioning and uncertainty about the goals themselves.

Difficulty in measuring accomplishment of the several goals or in assessing responsibility for goal attainment tends to reduce concern for the goal identification process itself.

School personnel often claim success in some instructional program only to learn that the evidence is simply teacher hunch or a short test over specific points included in the day's lesson. Rarely do we know with any degree of certainty that the material learned will have any impact on the future livelihood of students. Test results generated from school programs are almost always directed to the short-term cognitive skills and bear a rather unconvincing relationship to such school goals as "develop desire for learning now and in the future" or "understand and practice democratic ideas and ideals."[1] Test technology is simply not equipped to measure progress in relation to these social goals and particularly those that make reference to long-term effects on student behavior.

Even if one were successful in measuring attainment in relation to these long-term goals, attributing success or failure to specific contributing institutions is generally impossible. Many other institutions seek to achieve goals such as those listed above and we can therefore only guess as to the influence of a given school program or teacher. These dual problems of measuring goal attainment and of identifying specific causal agents in relation to goal attainment lead to a lack of concern for the goal identification process itself, a reality faced by any school principal or instructional leader who sets out to clarify the goal structure for a school or school program.

Despite these obstacles, it is important to remember that all organizations, whether private or public, encounter some degree of goal confusion. The effective administrator must accept a certain amount of goal confusion and conflict as inevitable; yet, at the same time, there is an organizational need to achieve greater clarity and understanding of goals and objectives in providing needed direction for organization activities. Drucker put it succinctly:

> Achievement is never possible except against specific limited, clearly defined targets, in business as well as in a service institution. Only if targets are defined can resources be allocated to their attainment, priorities and deadlines set, and somebody be held accountable for results. But the starting point for effective work is a definition of the purpose and mission of the institution, which is almost always intangible. (Drucker, p. 140)

In succeeding sections of this first chapter, we examine both the historical development of goal structures for the public schools and ways in which administrators can build on these historical statements in developing more definitive statements of purpose in their own local school settings.

GOAL STATEMENTS IN AMERICAN SCHOOLS

In the colonial period, schools were primarily directed to maintenance of religion and the salvation of souls. This religious orientation in schooling did include some consideration of the intellectual skills, at least insofar as these skills could be used to further religious aims. The Protestant Reformation in Europe had earlier established the importance of reading as a means of understanding biblical teachings and this served as a prime motivation in American schools, both in New England and elsewhere in the colonies. Many schools in this period were established and supported solely by the church. Separation of church and state was not an issue. Only as mobility in and between the colonies increased and as civil governments were needed to handle problems of trade and land ownership did the religious purpose of learning give way to claims in the social, vocational, and political areas.

This broadened aim or purpose for education became evident immediately following the

[1]These are two of the eighteen goals established in 1972 by the Phi Delta Kappa Task Force. The entire list is presented in Figure 1–3.

American Revolution. Agriculture and trade became important to the new nation and the schools changed markedly in response to these demands. The Latin grammar school with its focus on skills needed to read and interpret the Bible was supplemented with, and in some cases replaced by, the more practical academy, which, with its broader curriculum and concern for agriculture and commercial practices, came into its own in the early 1800s. The regular public school program also reflected this broader goal structure but was still generally limited to grades K–8.

By the time of the Civil War, the shape of American education was reasonably clear. It was intended for all American youth and was designed to play a major socialization function. This intention was clearly evidenced in the first compulsory-attendance statute, passed by the Massachusetts legislature in 1853. One text in the history of education focuses on this socialization theme: "The socialization function took on increasing importance with the large influx of immigrants after 1850. Over five million newcomers arrived in the ten year period between 1880 and 1890 and it was expected that schools would ready this immigrant population, and particularly the younger children, for a full participation in the new country" (Butts, pp. 267–268).

Many of these immigrants in the later part of the nineteenth century came from southern and eastern Europe and they differed from the northern European immigrants of the pre-Civil War period. Particularly important from the standpoint of schools were the lower literacy rates among these southern and eastern European immigrants and their tendency to settle in urban centers rather than in farming communities. Many of these immigrants were employed in unskilled positions in a society that was rapidly becoming more industrialized. It was a monumental task for the schools to teach the language skills required in order for these people to survive in their new country.

In meeting the challenge, school systems became more centralized and statewide direction and control of education was strengthened. The notion of systematic and mandated curriculum could be considered. This move toward more centralized control of education coincided with an expansion of public schooling beyond grade eight. The Kalamazoo decision of 1874 established the right of local government to tax for the purpose of high school education and thus represented the beginning of a major thrust toward public schooling in grades 9–12. This effort to extend education to the high school years was not immediately successful and even as late as 1900 the enrollment in grades 9–12 represented only 11.4 percent of all youth in the 14–17 age group. Nonetheless, there were numerous secondary schools started in the late 1800s and these schools were presumably directed both to meeting the socialization requirements of a large immigrant population and to providing the specialized occupational training demanded by an industrial technology.

The schools that were started during this period of rapid growth were a diverse group and there evolved no clear educational format. The lack of uniformity became bothersome to many elements of society. Colleges were particularly confused by the lack of uniformity and found it difficult to adjust their programs to the varied background of incoming students. This confusion and diversity along with the growing centralization in school organization led to a number of efforts to establish more clearly the mission and purpose of public schooling in grades K–12. Much of the attention in these efforts was directed to the high school level; however, education at the elementary or grammar school level was addressed in at least some of the study efforts.

Among the earliest and most influential of these study groups was the Committee of Ten, which published its report in 1893. Directed by Charles W. Elliott, then president of Harvard University, this committee gave support to the broader curriculum already existing at the college level. Elective programs as outlined in the committee report represented a definite departure from the classical-language programs accepted by many as the only legitimate training for college entrance in the late 1800s.

Further support for a broader goal structure came in the 1918 report of the Commission on the Reorganization of Secondary Education. This report identified what have become known as the "Cardinal Principles of Secondary Education." These principles include: (1) sound health, (2) command of fundamental processes, (3) worthy home membership, (4) vocational preparation, (5) civic education, (6) worthy use of leisure time, and (7) ethical character. This acceptance of a broader set of goals is, perhaps more than anything else, a reflection of the changing school population of the early 1900s.

The two reports mentioned above are representative of a number of national goal-setting efforts since the late 1800s. Some of the more recent national activities receiving attention in education literature include *Education for All American Youth* (Educational Policies Commission, 1944), *The American High School Today* (Conant, 1960), and *Reform of Secondary Education* (National Commission on the Reform of Secondary Education, 1973). A review of these several national reports shows that the goal structure over the past 100 years has responded to both the changing population of students and the changing requirements of the social system. Without this capacity to change direction or goal structure, the public school could not have survived to the present day; similar calls for change must be met in the years ahead if we hope to maintain the school as an essential element of acculturation in our society.

NATURE OF GOAL AND OBJECTIVE STATEMENTS IN SCHOOLS

Whatever the collection of goals associated with a given program, school, or school system, it is certain that constant effort will be required to select and clarify those particular goals needed to give the organization a sense of purpose and accomplishment. The responsibility for developing and clarifying goals statements is a critical administrative or leadership task and involves the ability to work effectively with relevant client groups and to establish reasonable procedures for collecting and interpreting data. An important part of this latter concern is an understanding of the nature of goal statements appropriate for use in today's schools.

Critical to this understanding of the nature of goals is a recognition that the level of specificity in goal statements depends on the level of operation within the school system and the particular audience involved in the consideration of the goals. A goal of "teaching students to successfully add and subtract fractions" may be quite meaningful as a goal or objective for a particular fourth-grade class or even all fourth-grade classes, but it is likely to have little value as a goal statement for an entire school system. As we move from general to specific goal statements, it is important to observe that the most specific performance or behavioral objectives are really nothing more than very specific goal statements. This can best be seen by examining the sequence of goals in Figure 1–1. Notice that each succeeding statement is simply one of the several possible subgoals of the prior goal statement and that the final statement could very well serve as a test question to see if, in fact, the student had accomplished the prior goals or objectives. The point here is simply that goals are appropriately stated at varying levels of specificity, and that administrators and teachers involved in establishing goal priorities must therefore be skilled both in understanding relationships between various goal hierarchies of the type illustrated in Figure 1–1 and in selecting the appropriate level for each type of goal- or objective-development activity.

From Figure 1–1, we observe that the terms *goal* and *objective* are distinguished only by the level of specificity in the statement. In this text, three different types of goal/objective statements—product, process, and organizational—are discussed. The most common type and that most likely to characterize the terminal purposes of the school is the product or outcome goal. At the classroom level, this type of goal is sometimes referred to as an

Figure 1–1 Educational Goals—General to Specific

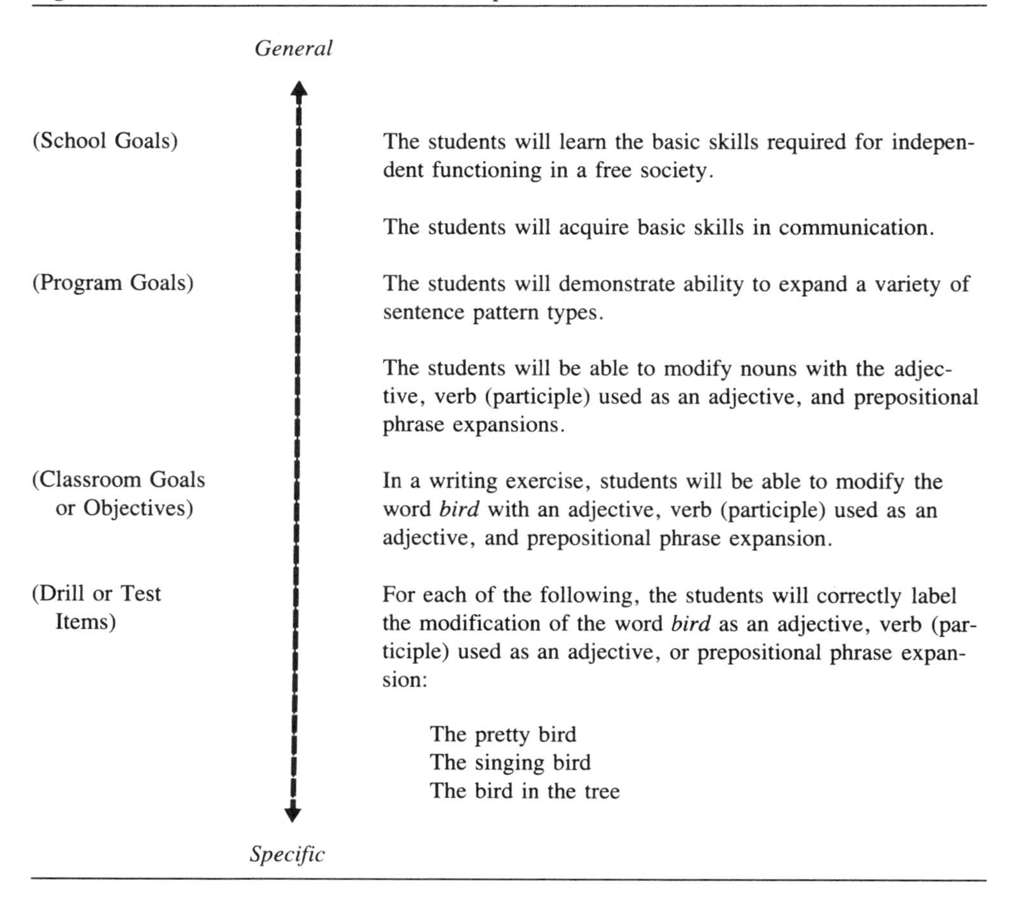

instructional objective in that it represents an intended outcome of instruction.[2] This is the type of goal/objective statement illustrated in Figure 1–1. Note that these statements refer to some capability or knowledge level to be demonstrated by the student.

Sometimes outcome-goal statements refer to an established level of achievement at a particular point in time, and sometimes they speak to change over a given period of time. The goals can also be stated in relation to group attainment or in relation to attainment by individual students. These several options are illustrated in Figure 1–2. Note that the single program goal statement has been written in four different ways in accordance with these options. The appropriateness of each of the four options is determined by the situation. For example, the status-at-given-time statements are appropriate in a situation where the central

[2]As one example, the Instructional Theory Into Practice (ITIP) program as developed by Madeline C. Hunter and her associates at the University of California, Los Angeles, refers to this product-type objective as an instructional objective. The reader should note that the term *product* is being used here in a very limited way and does not include the development of instructional units or materials by either the teacher or the student except as these represent terminal learning gains by students. For example, the arithmetic exercises developed by an elementary teacher or the completed workbook assignment of a student are not generally considered product goals or objectives even though they are physical products or materials. These will most likely be classified as process- or organizational-type objectives, depending on their actual use.

Figure 1–2 Typology of Outcome Goals/Objectives

Program Goal: The students will be able to modify nouns with adjective, verb, and prepositional phrase expansions.

Target Population		*Level of Competence*	
		Status at Given Time	*Increase Over Time*
Target Population	*Individual Students*	The student will, at the end of the school year, demonstrate ability to modify at least 5 out of 6 nouns with advective, verb, and prepositional phrase expansions.	The student will, during the next school year, demonstrate an increased competence in modifying nouns with adjective, verb, and prepositional phrase expansions.
Target Population	*Group of Students*	At least 90 percent of the sixth-grade students will, on completion of the school year, be capable of modifying 5 out of 6 nouns with adjective, verb, and prepositional phrase expansions.	At least 80 percent of the sixth-grade students will, during the next semester, demonstrate increased ability to modify nouns with adjective, verb, and prepositional phrase expansions.

concern is a minimum competence at the end of a given school year. Certainly, statements of this type would be useful in describing expected achievement goals associated with the completion of the primary or intermediate grades. On the other hand, the increase-over-time statement is used in instances where growth over time is the central concern. There exists the option in this latter case of stating a set amount of growth (e.g., the student will, during the next school year, increase *by at least 20 percent* the number of nouns correctly modified with adjective, verb (participial) and prepositional phrase expansions); however, because of known differences in learning rates among students, such specification is primarily useful in relation to the individual-student type of goal statement.

This distinction between status-at-given-time and increase-over-time in relation to goal and objective statements parallels much of the recent discussion of high school graduation requirements. Some people have expressed the concern that high school graduation represents only an exposure to educational experiences over a period of years—and, presumably, at least some growth for each student—without any guarantee of having reached a particular level of competence. People holding this view are essentially concerned that the goal structure of the school has not included the status-at-given-time type of statement and has rather concentrated on the experience of a certain number of years of exposure. In response to this concern, many states and school districts are attaching some type of status-at-given-time criterion as at least a partial condition of granting the high school diploma. This most often takes the form of a required score on some type of competency test taken prior to graduation or teacher verification of competency as demonstrated in a course required for graduation.

Statements of the outcome type as illustrated in Figure 1–2 are clearly the most appropriate in discussion of terminal goals and objectives for school programs; however, other types of goal statements are frequently used in planning and describing educational programs. One of these is the process type, which specifies as a goal or objective the establishment of certain learning processes in the school or classroom. Examples of this type of objective are:

- The students will watch a film describing the hazards of excessive drug use.
- The students will be placed in groups of three for purposes of running the relay.
- The students will discuss the merits of alternative water conservation measures.
- The students will analyze water samples.

Notice that each of these process goals calls for some kind of learning activity or experience. Presumably, these activities are related to some outcome objectives; however, the technology of education is often not sufficiently exacting to make a direct tie between a given activity or process and a specific learner outcome—particularly when the outcome is noncognitive in nature. In some situations the activity-outcome relationship is quite obvious. This is true in relation to the last of the objectives listed above, where students are to "analyze water samples." By changing just a few words, this particular goal statement can be changed into a variety of statements of the product or outcome classification:

- The students will correctly analyze water samples.
- The students will demonstrate the ability to correctly analyze a water sample.
- The students will correctly identify the potassium level of the water sample and will indicate any related limitations for use of the water.

We note here that the process objective is easily shifted to one of the outcome type simply by using such words as "correctly analyze" and "demonstrate the ability to correctly analyze." These latter phrases speak to outcome behavior of a specified type rather than merely going through an activity or process in the classroom.

When the process statement refers to activity apart from the classroom and rather addresses implementing requirements of a particular school program, the goal or objective is sometimes described as organizational in nature. Organizational goals are more generalized types of process objectives and refer to implementing steps that are required by the total school program. Examples of organizational goal/objective statements are:

- By the end of November, the school library will have ready for checkout at least ten books on the subject of water conservation.
- The school bus will be available at 9:00 A.M. to transport students to the wilderness field trip.
- The curriculum department will offer a workshop in environmental education; this workshop will be designed for teachers with minimal science background.

Note that organizational statements can be of a process nature, but the processes in this case describe organizational implementation requirements rather than classroom activities. These organizational objectives are generally critical to the conduct of classroom and school learning, but are not related in a direct manner to student instructional activities or outcomes. As an illustration, none of the organizational statements listed above has a direct tie to the classroom process goal of students' learning how to analyze water samples; however, any one of these organizational goals or objectives could be an essential element of support for the classroom activity. Students may need the library books in order to learn about water pollution levels. Likewise, the bus may be necessary to carry the students to a place where they can test their skill in a real-world situation, and the in-service workshop may be a necessary prerequisite to the entire environmental education class.

The reference to the in-service workshop indicates an important relationship among the three types of goals: that a product goal for the teacher in-service workshop session can very well become a process or organizational goal in relation to the classroom experiences of students. If, as a part of the workshop, a teacher learns to successfully conduct a particular type of presentation on water pollution levels or works to develop a set of instructional materials suitable for use in the classroom or library, he or she is obviously engaged in meeting goals/objectives of a process or organizational type in relation to students, while meeting product or outcome objectives of the in-service workshop. In this same sense, much of the assistance building administrators give to teachers can be viewed as having a product or outcome goal of improving the processes employed in the classroom. The product of the principal's teaching activity or process can be viewed as a process or organizational objective of the teacher who works directly with students in the classroom. While this interrelationship between the several goal/objective types is important in any overview of goal development in schools, it will have only limited application in this text. The focus here is on the development of product or outcome goals for students; we therefore place most other goals in the process or organizational typology, even when they may represent an outcome at some other level within the organization.

After this introduction of the three goal/objective types, it is important to emphasize that for most goal-setting activities, and particularly those involving input from public groups, product-type goal statements at a fairly general level are those most likely to be used. Public and student groups involved in goal-setting activities generally feel much more comfortable limiting their involvement to general product-level goals, leaving the specifics of process and organizational targets to professional educators.

This preference for dealing with product goals at the general level has certain advantages. For one thing, support and agreement on goals are more easily achieved at the general level. Few among us would oppose good highways, nice parks, or responsible citizenship as appropriate goals for society. This level of agreement might very well decline, however, when we start talking about the highway to be built at the end of our own street, the park where delinquent youths have been hanging out, or the teacher at the local school who has been teaching young people about their rights as citizens. Many of our general goals for schools make sense until the specifics contained within those goals are noted.

Recognizing this tendency to support general symbols over the specifics represented by those symbols, it is important in any sort of goal-setting activity that statements of approximately equal generality be selected. This concern regarding specificity level can best be illustrated by looking at the following list of goal statements.

The student will increase in:

1. understanding of personal behavior and the behavior of others;
2. understanding and appreciation of the need for sound physical and mental health;
3. ability to perform the skills of reading, writing, and arithmetic;
4. ability to add and subtract fractions;
5. understanding of the U.S. Constitution and its importance to stability in our social system;
6. understanding of personal rights as guaranteed in the Fifth Amendment to the U.S. Constitution; and
7. willingness to assume responsibility for personal actions.

If you were asked to rank this list of goals in relation to a particular school or to select the three most important in planning for the coming school year, the wide variance in specificity would undoubtedly be troublesome. Statements 4 and 6 are actually subparts of statements 3 and 5 respectively, and are more specific than the others. In the particular context of an entire school, it is probably inappropriate to consider such specific statements as 4 and 6, and we certainly would not want them in the same list as the other, more general, statements. Not only is a list of such varying specificity confusing to the respondent but the result of the ranking effort also becomes suspect when one considers potential differences in agreement likely to be associated with the differing levels of generality.

GOAL CLARIFICATION VERSUS GOAL SETTING

The term *goal clarification* seems preferable to *goal setting* in describing the goal-related activities of the typical public school or school district. This is because schools have inherent and long-established goals that cannot suddenly be erased. The review of several national efforts to write goal statements for the schools provides evidence that goals for the local schools are not new statements but represent a selection from and clarification of goal statements that have existed for many years. The local school or district, in most cases, selects from among these existing goal statements.

This preference for the term *goal clarification* is illustrated by looking at the set of goals presented in Figure 1–3. These eighteen goal statements were distributed in 1970 by a Phi Delta Kappa (PDK) task force, and have been used by many districts as a basis for goal clarification work. The PDK goal statements, for the most part, parallel those in some of the national study efforts. For example, each of the eighteen goals can be mapped onto one or more of the "Cardinal Principles of Secondary Education" posited in 1918. It is doubtful that any would be eliminated as being unreasonable goals for school programs today. When we ask a given group of citizens, staff, or students to consider this list of goal statements, it is done not with the intent of eliminating any of them, but rather of clarifying their meaning and establishing possible goal priorities for some future time. Again, the likelihood of eliminating any of these goals is minimal because the school, like any other public institution, has a long history that includes, at any given point, a particular group of competing goal priorities. This particular group of goals is not going to change dramatically except in the face of a major societal upheaval. Even then, the goal preferences existing in the supporting public are not likely to be changed quickly.

Despite the fact that most goal clarification activities deal with product-type statements, many people view processes as extremely important and feel that they cannot be totally neglected in goal clarification activities. This is true for at least two reasons. First, there has always existed a conflict as to whether schooling is work and preparation for work, or whether schooling is an enjoyable and natural growth experience with certain intrinsic values of its own. These two concepts of education constantly compete for our attention as we think about learning and schooling. They were certainly central to the progressive education debates of the early 1900s and have probably existed as long as formal schooling itself. To the extent that the second view—namely, that education is a natural process with intrinsic values—holds our attention, we are likely to place at least as much importance on the processes of instruction as on the outcome or product. We will, at such times, have strong views as to the appropriateness of certain techniques or processes. For example, most adults would disapprove of physically chaining a student to the desk, even if it could be shown that such chaining were an effective short-term technique for teaching the multiplication tables. Many oppose corporal punishment of students and feel it is simply an inappropriate way to deal with human beings. In most cases, preferences for or against certain processes relate to the weight given to these competing viewpoints on education, and the process decisions will, therefore, vary as one or the other viewpoint dominates our collective preference.

A second reason for dominant concern about processes of instruction is related directly

Figure 1–3 Phi Delta Kappa Goals

1. Learn How to Be a Good Citizen
   - A. Develop an awareness of civic rights and responsibilities.
   - B. Develop attitudes for productive citizenship in a democracy.
   - C. Develop an attitude of respect for personal and public property.
   - D. Develop an understanding of the obligations and responsibilities of citizenship.

2. Learn How to Respect and Get Along with People Who Think, Dress, and Act Differently
   - A. Develop an appreciation for and an understanding of other people and other cultures.
   - B. Develop an understanding of political, economic, and social patterns of the rest of the world.
   - C. Develop awareness of the interdependence of races, creeds, nations, and cultures.
   - D. Develop an awareness of the process of group relationships.

3. Learn About and Try to Understand the Changes That Take Place in the World
   - A. Develop ability to adjust to the changing demands of society.
   - B. Develop an awareness of and the ability to adjust to a changing world and its problems.
   - C. Develop understanding of the past, identify yourself with the present, and the ability to meet the future.

4. Develop Skills in Reading, Writing, Speaking, and Listening
   - A. Develop ability to communicate ideas and feelings effectively.
   - B. Develop skills in oral and written English.

5. Understand And Practice Democratic Ideas and Ideals
   - A. Develop loyalty to American democratic ideals.
   - B. Develop patriotism and loyalty to ideas of democracy.
   - C. Develop knowledge and appreciation of the rights and privileges in our democracy.
   - D. Develop an understanding of our American heritage.

6. Learn How to Examine and Use Information
   - A. Develop ability to examine constructively and creatively.
   - B. Develop ability to use scientific methods.
   - C. Develop reasoning abilities.
   - D. Develop skills to think and process logically.

7. Understand and Practice the Skills of Family Living
   - A. Develop understanding and appreciation of the principles of living in the family group.
   - B. Develop attitudes leading to acceptance of responsibilities as family members.
   - C. Develop an awareness of future family responsibilities and achievement of skills in preparing to accept them.

8. Learn to Respect and Get Along with People with Whom We Work and Live
   - A. Develop appreciation of and respect for the worth and dignity of individuals.
   - B. Develop respect for individual worth and understanding of minority opinions and acceptance of majority decisions.

9. Develop Skills to Enter a Specific Field of Work
   - A. Develop abilities and skills needed for immediate employment.
   - B. Develop an awareness of opportunities and requirements related to a specific field of work.
   - C. Develop an appreciation of good workmanship.

10. Learn How to Be a Good Manager of Money, Property, and Resources

Figure 1–3 (continued)

A. Develop an understanding of economic principles and responsibilities.
B. Develop ability and understanding in personal buying, selling, and investment.
C. Develop skills in management of natural and human resources and man's environment.

11. Develop a Desire for Learning Now and in the Future

A. Develop intellectual curiosity and eagerness for lifelong learning.
B. Develop a positive attitude toward learning.
C. Develop a positive attitude toward continuing independent education.

12. Learn How to Use Leisure Time

A. Develop ability to use leisure time productively.
B. Develop a positive attitude toward participation in a range of leisure time activities—physical, intellectual, and creative.
C. Develop appreciation and interests which will lead to wise and enjoyable use of leisure time.

13. Practice and Understand the Ideas of Health and Safety

A. Establish an effective individual physical fitness program.
B. Develop an understanding of good physical health and well-being.
C. Establish sound personal health habits and information.
D. Develop a concern for public health and safety.

14. Appreciate Culture and Beauty in the World

A. Develop abilities for effective expression of ideas and cultural appreciation (fine arts).
B. Cultivate appreciation for beauty in various forms.
C. Develop creative self-expression through various media (art, music, writing, etc.).
D. Develop special talents in music, art, literature, and foreign languages.

15. Gain Information Needed to Make Job Selections

A. Promote self-understanding and self-direction in relation to student's occupational interests.
B. Develop the ability to use information and counseling services related to the selection of a job.
C. Develop a knowledge of specific information about a particular vocation.

16. Develop Pride in Work and a Feeling of Self-Worth

A. Develop a feeling of student pride in his achievements and progress.
B. Develop self-understanding and self-awareness.
C. Develop the student's feeling of positive self-worth, security, and self-assurance.

17. Develop Good Character and Self-Respect

A. Develop moral responsibility and sound ethical and moral behavior.
B. Develop the student's capacity to discipline himself to work, study, and play constructively.
C. Develop a moral and ethical sense of values, goals, and processes of free society.
D. Develop standards of personal character and ideas.

18. Gain a General Education

A. Develop background and skills in the use of numbers, natural sciences, mathematics, and social sciences.
B. Develop a fund of information and concepts.
C. Develop special interests and abilities.

Source: Education Goals and Objectives, a workshop packet describing a model goal-setting program that utilizes both staff and community involvement (Bloomington, Ind.: Phi Delta Kappa Commission on Educational Planning, 1970).

to conflict among the goal statements. To illustrate this conflict and its consequent shift to process concerns, let us look at two goals from the list of Figure 1–3: "develop skills in reading, writing, speaking, and listening;" and "develop pride in work and a feeling of self-worth." Notice that the first goal statement addresses cognitive learning and the second affective or feeling-type learning. Both are stated as product or outcome statements; however, because educators have not isolated a single best method or process to teach reading or to assure positive feelings of self-worth, the processes themselves can easily become a matter of intense interest. If a given teacher places greater weight on the first of the goals and feels strongly that a particular method or process is superior for its accomplishment with a given group of students, the teacher may very well face opposition—both from those who share the goal preference but question the process as being best for teaching reading, and from those who would emphasize the second goal and feel the teacher's preferred process for teaching reading is damaging to feelings of self-worth.

This confusing state exists, in large part, because of the uncertainty of educational technology. We simply do not know the precise impact of certain processes and have even found that the same processes can have a different impact on different groups of students.[3] This uncertainty about process-product connections in education makes it inevitable that goal clarification procedures will, to some extent, spill over into the process domain. While concern for process is not stressed in the goal clarification activities presented in this text, it is considered an important part of the overall task, and one that, to a limited extent, should be shared with the community. The several procedures outlined in Appendix 1 include a strategy for allowing the community to make its process preferences known to the educators.

GOAL CLARIFICATION PROCEDURES FOR SCHOOLS

It is useful now to apply some of the ideas on the nature of goal statements and the complexities of their use in a school setting to the process of establishing goal priorities in a school or school district. As one develops a process for establishing or clarifying goals, it is helpful to look on the goal clarification process as an initial step in the overall operation of a school or school system. Such a viewpoint is inherent in Figure 1–4. This idealized schematic presents a way to relate goal clarification activities to the ongoing school operation. It is particularly important in this text because it portrays the goal-setting process as a basic foundation for implementation and evaluation activities and indicates appropriate groups to be involved in these several component activities. The first three steps presented in Figure 1–4 coincide with the general flow of material to be presented in subsequent chapters of this text.

In this first chapter, we have been concerned primarily with Step I of Figure 1–4. Note that this is the step in which the community is most directly involved. It is here that citizens at large can play a significant role in determining and clarifying priority statements for the school or school system. What happens in this first step is crucial in determining the degree to which serious attention is given the priority goals articulated by the citizens. A number of considerations should aid the administration involved in the goal clarification process. The

[3]There exists some evidence that methods of instruction most effective with elementary school students of low socioeconomic status differ from those most effectively used with students of higher socioeconomic status. For a description of these differences and a general review of research on process-product relations in schools, see Thomas L. Good, Bruce J. Biddle, and Jere E. Brophy, *Teachers Make a Difference* (New York: Holt, Rinehart, & Winston, 1975), pp. 54–85.

Figure 1–4 Schematic for Translating Goals Into Action Programs

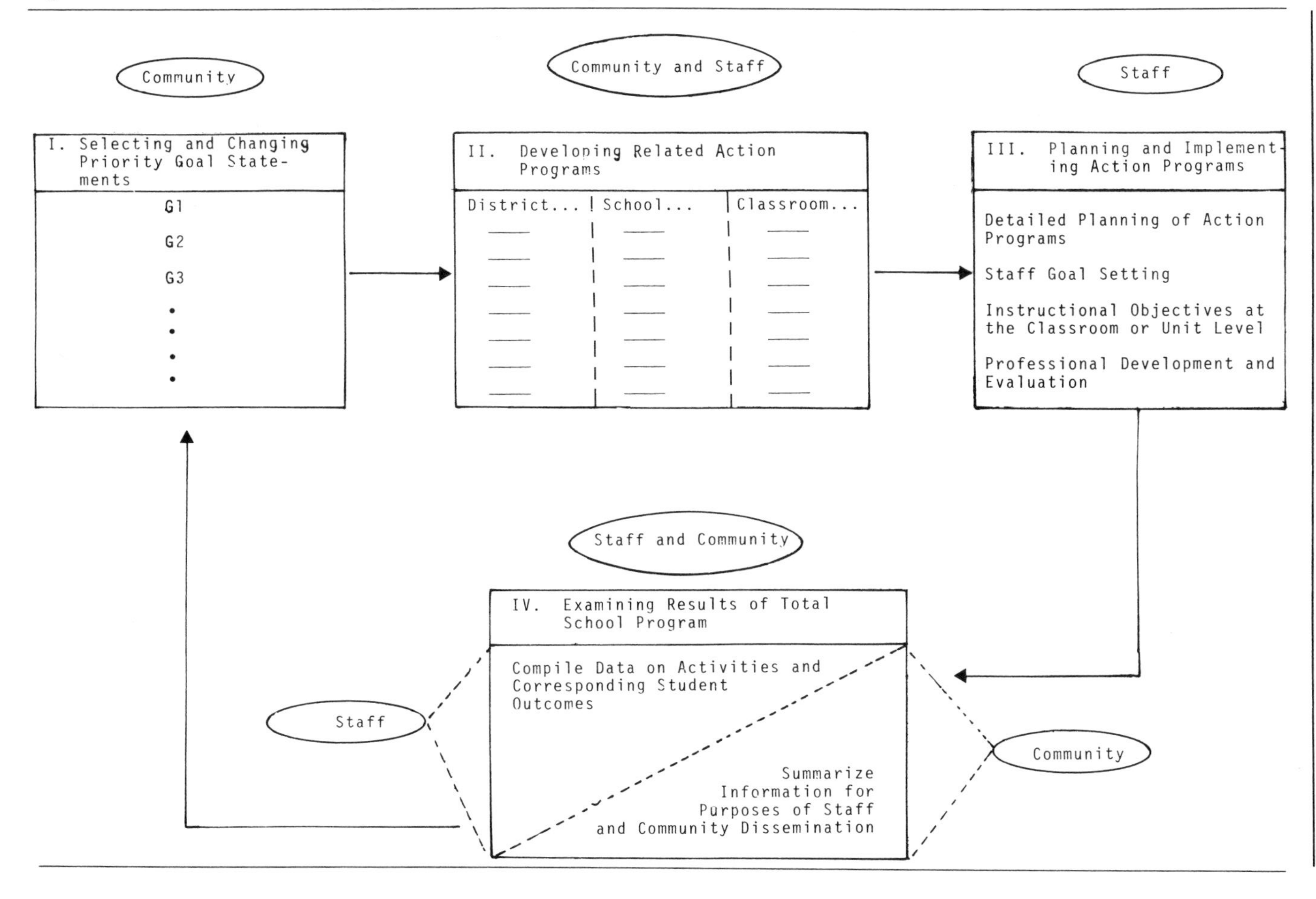

specific techniques discussed in relation to these considerations should help in developing an appropriate goal clarification model for any particular school or school district.

Purposes of Goal Clarification Activity and Persons to Be Involved

As a first step and even prior to embarking on the goal clarification process, it is essential that the leadership of the school or school district isolate the reasons for doing so. Is the purpose simply to get many citizens involved in a school-related activity? Is it intended to create needed interaction among various school groups such as parents, teachers, and administrators? Is it to apply to the entire school district or is it designed for only some part of the district—for example, a single region, school, or department? Is it to be a genuine effort to establish direction for school programs as implied in Figure 1–4? Answers to these questions are essential in order to decide who is to be involved in the goal clarification process and in what manner.

The first of the above-mentioned reasons—getting citizens involved—is not the most-often cited reason for embarking on a goal clarification project, but it can be a legitimate reason. All too often it appears to be the only reason, as those directing the effort seem to desire little more than a lot of activity at the schoolhouse. It is hoped that some of the other reasons will prevail and those involved in providing leadership at the school or district level will want to involve a cross section of individuals in at least some phase of the activity. A more open feeling is generally obtained when organizations and groups are allowed to select their own representation to the goal clarification study group, and the total time commitment and type of activity required should be stipulated at the time the invitation is issued.

Those leading the goal clarification process should strive to represent all people and interest groups in the community and should see that major factions within the community are represented in proportion to their membership. Such guidelines for representation will add credibility to the results. If the goal clarification and follow-up planning activities are to be beneficial in achieving direction for the organization, it is important that the board of directors of the school district or the board of the school Parent-Teacher Association take an active and supportive role right from the start. The "Model Program for Community and Professional Involvement," a goal development process promoted by Phi Delta Kappa in the early 1970s, calls for including one school board member on the steering committee for the project.[4] This is an excellent suggestion and establishes from the beginning a sense of importance for the goal clarification activity.

Selection and/or Identification of Goal Statements

Early in the goal clarification process and preferably before involving large numbers of lay citizens, it will be helpful to identify a set of goal statements to be used as the basis for the clarification process. Many samples are available and some of these have been mentioned earlier. Figure 1–5 presents a summary of several goal profiles that have been used as a basis for goal development. All of them could be stated in terms of student outcomes or products. Most of the statements already suggest a particular behavior, feeling, or attitude to be

[4]Program Development Center of Northern California at Chico State University in Chico, California, prepared a series of materials describing a model goal-setting activity for schools and school districts. These materials were later distributed by the Commission on Educational Planning of Phi Delta Kappa and have been used in numerous school settings over the past few years. Details of the program along with sample results from one school district are presented in Appendix 1. The materials have been modified slightly since their development and are still available through the Center for Dissemination of Innovative Programs, Phi Delta Kappa, Bloomington, Indiana 47402.

Figure 1–5 Selected Sets of Educational Goal Statements

Task of Public Education (1958)
(Developed by L.M. Downey as part of a national goal study)

A. Intellectual Dimensions
   1. Possession of Knowledge
   2. Communication of Knowledge
   3. Reasoning Abilities and Creative Thinking
   4. Desire for Learning

B. Social Dimensions
   1. Ability to Get Along with Others
   2. Understanding of Rights and Duties of Citizenship
   3. Loyalty to America
   4. Appreciation of People From All Lands and Cultures

C. Personal Dimensions
   1. Physical Health and Development
   2. Emotional Stability
   3. Moral Standard of Behavior
   4. Enjoyment of Cultural Activities

D. Productive Dimensions
   1. Awareness of Jobs and Preparation Needs
   2. Training and Placement for Jobs
   3. Home and Family Jobs and Responsibilities
   4. Consumer Skills and Managing Finances

School Planning, Evaluation, and Communication System (1972)
(A special project at the Center for the Advanced Study of Educational Administration, University of Oregon)

A. Basic Skills Development
   1. Conceptual Skills (memory, creative inquiry, logical processes)
   2. Communication Skills (writing, reading, verbal)
   3. Quantitative Skills (numerical properties, operations, measurement)

B. Intellectual Development
   1. Science (physical, social, and life)
   2. Humanities (arts, literature and language, history)

C. Social Development
   1. Personal (moral and spiritual, health and recreation, productive)
   2. Interpersonal (human relations, civic responsibility)

Reform of Secondary Education (1973)
(A goal structure suggested by a special study group working under sponsorship of the Charles F. Kettering Foundation)

Content Goals:
- Achievement of Communication Skills
- Achievement of Computation Skills
- Attainment of Proficienty in Critical and Objective Thinking
- Acquisition of Occupational Competence
- Clear Perception of Nature and Environment
- Development of Economic Understanding
- Acceptance of Responsibility for Citizenship

Process Goals:
- Knowledge of Self
- Appreciation of Others
- Ability to Adjust to Change
- Respect for Law and Authority
- Clarification of Values
- Appreciation of the Achievements of Man

Purposes of Education in American Democracy (1938)
(A proposed goal structure made by Education Policies Commission of National Education Association, Washington, D.C.)

Self-Realization (including fundamental skills, inquiring mind, and formation of character)

Human Relationships (including respect for others and appreciation of the family)

Economic Efficiency (including respect for good workmanship and occupational selection and training)

Civic Responsibility (including observance of law, tolerance of others, and world citizenship)

Interlake High School, Bellevue, Washington (1969)
(A set of goals established by the school faculty and in cooperation with the Northwest Association of Secondary and Higher Schools)

Awareness of Personal Strengths and Limitations
   (help the student acquire an awareness of strengths and limitations so that he/she can project a reasonable set of goals and plans for adult life)

Figure 1–5 (continued)

Responsible and Productive Citizenship
(help the student become a responsible and productive citizen, capable of contributing to the development of a better society)

Knowledge About Life and Living
(help the student become knowledgeable and understanding in his/her relationships with family, community, nation, and world)

Cardinal Principles of Secondary Education (1918)
(Goals identified by the Commission on Reorganization of Secondary Education of the National Education Association, Washington, D.C.)

1. Sound Health Knowledge and Habits
2. Command of Fundamental Processes
3. Worthy Home Membership
4. Vocational Preparation
5. Civic Education
6. Worthy Use of Leisure Time
7. Ethical Character

Montgomery County Public Schools, Rockville, Maryland (1965)
(A set of educational goals developed for the Montgomery County Schools)

1. Competence in the fundamental skills of listening, observing, speaking, reading, writing, spelling, mathematics, and the arts.
2. Recognition of and respect for the worth of each individual.
3. Appreciation for and power in logical, critical, and creative thinking.
4. Understanding and acceptance of the responsibilities and appreciation of the privileges inherent in the American way of life.
5. Understanding and evaluation of the cultures and contributions of other peoples.
6. Understanding of scientific truths of the universe and man's relationship to them.
7. Effective human relationships for democratic living, as they apply to the individual in the family, in the school and community, in the country and in the world.
8. Wise use of human, natural, and material resources.
9. Competence in choosing and pursuing a vocation.
10. Respect for and pride in good workmanship.
11. Values in aesthetic appreciation and creative expression.
12. Ethical behavior based on moral and spiritual values.

demonstrated by the student. In some cases, for example, with the four-part breakdown used by the Task of Public Education survey, there is a definite hierarchy to the goal presentation. In other cases, as with the Montgomery County Public Schools list, there is no particular effort to develop a sequencing or hierarchical structure.

It is possible to establish a reasonably good match between goal statements. Such a match between the *Reform of Secondary Education* (1973) and the *Cardinal Principles of Secondary Education* (1918) was completed in the more recent of these two reports and is summarized in Figure 1–6 of this text. The fact that such a matching process is possible suggests that the overall goal structure of public education is relatively stable, and that we tend to vary the level of specificity of the goal statements and their relative emphasis over time. This reinforces the earlier contention that the activity in Step I of Figure 1–4 is one of clarifying goal statements and their relative emphasis in relation to future planning rather than setting entirely new goals for the institution.

For some situations, and particularly in those cases where maximum citizen input is desired, the group may choose to develop its own set of goal statements from within. Even here, however, it is helpful to check against prepared lists for possible omissions. Whatever method is employed in generating an appropriate goal listing, it is important to remember that some checking against existing lists is helpful in clarifying both the wording and the meaning of the goal statements to be used. Developing subgoals within each of the broad

Figure 1-6 Contrasting Goal Statements for Secondary Schools

Cardinal Principles of Secondary Education (1918)	*Reform of Secondary Education Goals (1973)*
Health (physical fitness)	Adjustment to Change (mental health)
Command of Fundamental Processes	Communication Skills Computation Skills
Vocation	Occupational Competence
Civic Education	Responsibility for Citizenship Respect for Law and Authority Appreciation of Others
Worthy Home Membership Worthy Use of Leisure Ethical Character	Knowledge of Self Critical Thinking Clarification of Values Economic Understanding The Achievements of Man Nature and Environment

– – – – – Broken Line Separates Interrelated Goals
——— Solid Line Separates Unrelated Goals

Source: The National Commission on the Reform of Secondary Education, *The Reform of Secondary Education* (New York: McGraw-Hill Book Company, 1973), p. 188.

goal statements (as was done with the Phi Delta Kappa listing in Figure 1–3) can also assist in this initial clarification or discovery process.

The critical point is that one should not involve large numbers of people in any kind of goal-selection task without a set of reasonably distinct and clear goal statements. The steering committee should plan to spend sufficient time early in the process to achieve this clear and distinct listing of school or school district goals. Some kind of independent validation process in which the meanings of selected goal statements are compared among a diverse group of citizens may be useful in avoiding problems at a later point. All too often, a given goal receives a high rating but it later becomes apparent that persons rating it as such had widely varying interpretations of its meaning.

Manner of Analysis to Be Used

The manner of analysis depends on the purposes of the goal clarification activity. If the purpose is simply to list a set of broad goals for the school district and to disseminate these goals to patrons of the community, the manner of analysis can be relatively simple. Some type of ranking (selecting the top ten from a list of twenty, checking all that are deemed important, etc.) is sufficient in this instance, since the only intent is to eliminate those goal statements that are inappropriate or have little community support. If, on the other hand, the school or school district intends that the goal-selection activity result in some kind of action program for the next five years, a more comprehensive program of goal discovery and/or clarification is needed. Ideally, the process will include (1) examination of goal preferences, (2) analysis of current goal satisfaction, and (3) development of action statements relating to goal preferences. A discussion of alternative strategies available for accomplishing each of these three phases is provided in Appendix 1.

The action statements developed out of this three-phase process must, at some point, be assigned to various organizational units or departments within the school or school district. This is usually done only after selecting from among many possible action programs those that are judged to be most critical for accomplishing goal preferences and that have some chance of being accomplished with the resources available. Procedures for selecting action programs and for building them into an overall program of school improvement are detailed in Chapter 2; the reader is reminded that this need to select a reasonable number of action programs is founded on the recognition that the school staff simply cannot do everything at once. Far too many school districts have ended up with so many goals and action-program statements that they have no possible means to accomplish an otherwise well-intended program for educational improvement. The advice of Alan Lakein, a time-management consultant, is worth considering on this point: "In my opinion, no list is complete until it shows priorities. Whenever you make a list, finish the list by setting priorities" (Lakein, p. 28). Surely this advice, given initially to individuals planning for better time utilization and effectiveness, applies no less to the planning of school improvement programs.

Sharing Goal Priorities and Action Statements with the Community

There are at least two important reasons for communicating to the public both the processes and the results of goal clarification work. First, it serves as an excellent way to provide credibility with citizens who will eventually decide whether the goal-selection activity results in any long-range benefits to the system. The majority of these citizens, many of whom are not parents, have a rather detached relationship to the school system and register their support or lack of support only in occasional elections and fund drives. It is important that these people have the feeling that the school personnel are supporting preferences that have been identified by the total community. Reporting results and progress in relation to goal clarification activities can add to this needed credibility with both the parent and the nonparent populations. It also gives the organization, at least in a symbolic way, a greater sense of purpose; and this unity of purpose or mission may be helpful in rallying needed support for the organization. A second related reason for communicating with the broader public about the goal clarification process is its importance in the planning that follows. Staff members are much more likely to engage in the needed goal-directed planning if they have the feeling that those involved in the goal clarification process gave serious attention to the needs of the total community and are willing to share that work with the total community.

The concern with needs as they are reflected by the community leads to a specific suggestion that the total community be involved in providing at least verification of priorities as developed by representative groups of citizens, parents, and students. Such verification can be achieved to some extent by distributing, through mailings and local press releases, the results of the goal clarification activities. Better still might be some kind of random sample verification of both the goal priorities and the related action statements developed by representative citizens, staff, and students. High-speed data processing permits such sampling with a minimum of delay in the total project and the verification process can only encourage greater staff commitment to the planning and implementation phases to follow.

The importance of this goal focus in school organizations has been highlighted by much of the recent research on school effectiveness. In those schools which are judged most effective, the principal consistently conveys a vision or purpose for the school. Mannasse underscores this point in a recent review of school effectiveness research: "To be successful in setting goals, the principal first must have a vision of where the school is going, based on values that can be, and are, publicly articulated and explained" (Mannasse, p. 14).

SUMMARY

Establishing useful goal structures for school organizations is not an easy task, but the fact that gaining community and staff agreement on goal structure is difficult is no reason to abandon the effort, particularly in a time when governmental organizations of all types are being challenged to justify programs on the basis of results. Several prior efforts to identify goal structure for the public schools have identified goal statements that can be used as a starting point for local school districts and schools.

A schematic for translating goals into action programs is presented in Figure 1–4. This goal-based model for school improvement serves as an overall organizer for this text and should be helpful to both administrators and teachers in understanding the important relationship among goal/objective statements, action programs, and the ongoing planning and evaluation functions of schools. There are a number of important considerations that should be used in working on the goal-definition process in local school districts. These considerations are based on the assumption that schools operate best and with greatest support from their public constituency when they incorporate a sense of mission or purpose and take visible steps to accomplish this purpose.

QUESTIONS AND PROBLEMS ON CHAPTER 1

1. The following statement, taken from the Harvard report *General Education in a Free Society* (Cambridge, Mass.: Harvard University Press, 1945), suggests that the mission of our public schools is a limited one: "The schools cannot do everything. When they attempt too many tasks, they sometimes fail to do any of them well. Other social institutions are concerned with helping the individual develop personal competence, while the schools have the special and major responsibility of furthering the growth of intellectual abilities" (p. 170).
   a. Do you agree or disagree that the mission of the schools should be primarily directed to the intellectual domain? Why?
   b. What practices in the curriculum and organization of today's schools suggest that this limitation is or is not followed?
   c. Which of the Phi Delta Kappa goal statements listed in Figure 1–3 would have to be eliminated or at least minimized if the above limitation were in effect?
2. A possible matching between the *Cardinal Principles of Secondary Education* (1918) and the *Reform of Secondary Education* goals (1973) is presented in Figure 1–6. Develop a similar matching between the *Cardinal Principles of Secondary Education* and the "Ten Imperative Needs of Youth" (listed in *Education for All American Youth,* pp. 225–226). What goal statements, if any, on either list appear to have no corresponding statement on the other list?
3. Bereiter, in *Must We Educate,* proposes that schools abandon "education" (which, to Bereiter, includes the many social and value components of education) and limit their role to training in the basic skills.
   a. Which of the Phi Delta Kappa goal statements would be eliminated, or at least minimized, if we were to subscribe to Bereiter's model of education?
   b. What obstacles are likely to be experienced in implementing Bereiter's goal limitation?
4. In a publication entitled *Behavioral Goals of General Education in High School* (New York: Russell Sage Foundation, 1957), Will French and his associates list

over 100 pages of goal statements for secondary school students. A sample list of these statements follows:

(1) Uses books, maps, globes, charts, timetables, and graphs of all kinds to find needed information.
(2) Shows interest in learning more about world affairs.
(3) Sees the application of the basic principles of science to daily living.
(4) Accepts democracy as a force of government and a way of life.
(5) Avoids exposing self or others to colds or other diseases during the period when they are infectious; disposes promptly of used paper handkerchiefs and napkins.
(6) Will adjust personal interests for the sake of the group.
(7) Follows directions intelligently.
(8) Has a system of values in which altruism takes a high place.

a. These goal statements are at a slightly more specific level than statements identified for the Montgomery County Public Schools (Figure 1–5). Identify for each of the above goal statements the single need from the Montgomery County list that is most closely related. Are there any in the above list that seem related to more than one of the Montgomery County goal statements?
b. The first of the goal statements listed above deals with skills in acquiring information. Using this statement as a starting point, write two related outcome goals for individual students, one that reflects a status-at-given-time orientation and one that stipulates a certain increase-over-time. (It may be helpful to review the examples in Figure 1–2 in preparing this response.)
c. The second goal statement listed above refers to showing "interest in learning more about world affairs." Explain why a test of knowledge about world affairs would not be an adequate test of this goal and what alternative measures of goal attainment you might suggest.
d. The third goal statement listed above refers to seeing "the application of the basic principles of science to daily living." Write two different outcome statements that are more specific than this particular goal statement and then write a related process or organizational goal statement for each.

5. The goal orientation approach to education has sometimes been criticized by those who feel that it overlooks the more important question of the control of education. Evaluate this criticism.

6. Following are two goal statements that might be used to give direction to a school program:
- The students will demonstrate ability to multiply and divide numbers.
- The students will demonstrate loyalty to democratic ideals.

Both of these statements are written at the program or school level as defined in Figure 1–1. For each statement, generate at least three more goal or objective statements and place these statements in order of increasing specificity.

7. Design a goal-setting procedure for your own school or school district, briefly outlining each of the considerations identified in the text and listed below:
- Reasons for Goal Setting and Persons to Be Involved
  (including brief description of how various persons are selected and how they will contribute to the process)
- Selection of Goal Statements to Be Used
- Manner of Analysis to Be Used
  (including scaling methods, analysis of data, and procedures for developing action statements, if any)
- Sharing Goal Priorities with the Total Community

8. A particular junior high school conducts a goal clarification activity using the *Reform of Secondary Education* goal statements presented in Figure 1–5. This activity shows that "acquisition of occupational competence" and "development of economic understanding" are high priorities for the immediate future. Write at least three suitable action-program statements for each of these goal areas and outline a procedure that might be used to set priorities for these several action programs.

CHAPTER 2
TRANSLATION OF GOALS INTO ACTION PROGRAMS

The processes of clarifying and ranking goal statements are essential first steps but unless these goals are translated into organizational change, little will actually be accomplished. Accomplishing organizational change is more difficult and time-consuming than the clarification activities described in Chapter 1; for most goal statements, it involves initiation of change at several levels within the organization. Because of the basically decentralized format for delivering educational services at the classroom level, change as related to a given goal priority cannot be accomplished without at least some level of support by building administrators and classroom teachers; hence, the action programs emanating from specific goal priorities should involve staff input at the developmental stage and these action programs must then be included as part of the program and personnel evaluation systems of the total organization.

This staff involvement at the developmental stage is best seen by referring to Figure 1–4. In this schematic, the community is primarily responsible for selecting the priority goal statements (Step I) but community and staff work together in developing the related action programs (Step II). In Chapter 1, emphasis was given to the processes for encouraging the community to make initial suggestions for action programs that relate to priority goal statements. The staff must then take these suggested action statements, refine and add to them, and develop an overall plan of action for the school and/or school district. Following development of this overall plan (Step II), the more detailed planning and implementation process can begin. This implementation process (Step III) flows naturally into the review of results (Step IV), which provides useful background data for the next cycle of goal-related action programs. This chapter is concerned most directly with selected skills needed to accomplish Steps II and III of Figure 1–4. Particular attention will be given to the development of unit and classroom objectives and the way in which these objectives can reasonably be tied to the ongoing staff development and evaluation procedures of the school or district. While the compilation, analysis, and summary of results generated by the school program (Step IV) are essential to completing the cycle of goal-related organizational change, these final steps receive limited attention in this text. It is hoped that some of the skills addressed in later chapters of the text along with course background and experiences in evaluation and testing can aid the reader in dealing with these final steps in the change or improvement cycle.

Because of the complexities associated with the goal-development model as defined in Figure 1–4, it is well to caution that these planning processes are not likely to be completed successfully in an annual cycle. Most schools and school districts involved in this type of goal-management approach are well advised to think in terms of at least a 2–5 year cycle. Working within a shorter time frame is likely to be frustrating to both community and staff and is not likely to result in the deliberate and structured change inherent in the model. Obstacles to use of this goal-based model for organizational change can be expected and the longer time frame permits greater opportunity for dealing with problems that will inevitably occur during its implementation.

OBSTACLES TO DEVELOPING ACTION PROGRAMS FOR SCHOOLS

In Chapter 1, a number of purposes for goal clarification activities in a school district were discussed. As part of that discussion the reader was advised that genuine organizational change would result from such activities only if this intent to change was planned in advance. Too many school districts involve citizens in massive goal-priority surveys and workshops with no particular plans for how these should have an impact on the educational programs that operate on a daily basis in the schools of the district. This absence of follow-through on the part of school districts has led some states to mandate minimal follow-up procedures.[1] While it is unfortunate that such a mandate is necessary, it is useful before discussing specific procedures for the follow-up itself to examine some of the factors making such mandatory measures necessary.

At least part of the problem stems from a failure to recognize that goal priorities are not always easily translated into action programs. It is common for the administration to

[1]For example, the state of Washington in its "Basic Education Act of 1977" requires local school districts to publish an annual descriptive guide, which includes program objectives and test results for various schools within the district. A general discussion and summary of state accountability measures is found in Frederick M. Wirt, "What State Laws Say About Local Control," *Phi Delta Kappan* 59 (April 1978): 517–520.

distribute goal priorities as defined by some community effort to the school principals and teachers without realizing that the translation is itself a complex and challenging task. It is complex partly because the goals are often stated in broad generalities and in ways that give very little indication of implied program changes. As an example, suppose one of the priority goals is that "students should develop good character and self-respect." A first reaction is, "Who could disagree with this as an ultimate aim for education?" Unfortunately, such statements of aim or purpose are rarely of much help in prescribing change in the school system. "Good character" to some tends to translate into docility and acceptance of authority while to others it may suggest a willingness to speak up for individual rights, even when such action may be viewed as uncooperative by those in authority positions. Both behaviors are of course to be encouraged in selected circumstances but there is, unfortunately, no single action program that will be likely to maximize growth on either of these conflicting dimensions of good character; nor is there any educational program that has been shown to achieve a desired balance between the two.

The point here is that in dealing with long-range or ultimate impact in the affective domain, the mere statement of goals or objectives is of limited help in determining needed change within the system. These goal/objective statements must be accompanied with specifics as to process or action. Peters suggests that "the crucial question to ask when men wax enthusiastic on the subject of their aims, is what procedures are to be adopted in order to implement them. We then get down to moral brass tacks" (Peters, p. 86). It is this need for specific discussion of desired processes that led to the earlier suggestion (Chapter 1) that the community goal clarification process include some preliminary attention to suggested action programs. These discussions are essential to an accurate reading of the goal statements themselves and the absence of such action-program statements restricts the follow-up by the staff.

When the goal clarification activities include reference to action-program suggestions from the community, they sometimes lack sufficient focus. This occurs both with respect to the content of the suggested processes and the failure to stipulate the center of responsibility for the various action programs. Both of these problems could be remedied by a perceptive building or unit administrator but so often they are used instead as a reason to do little or nothing to follow up on goal priorities established by the community.

Lack of focus can best be illustrated with a specific example. Assume that as a building principal at the elementary school level you are informed about the particular set of goal statements and action programs listed in Figure 2–1. Notice that there is no specific reference to the grade levels where the various action programs are to be emphasized. Are the exchange programs of reference in Action Program 1.2 to be at the elementary or secondary level or both? How about the required course in speech mentioned in Action Program 3.3? It would be nice to know something more of the citizen and/or central-office preference as to whether this requirement is to be added at the elementary, junior high, or high school level and what personnel are responsible for designing the course. In addition to the omission of grade-level designation, some of the action-program statements are inadequate for other reasons. Action Program 3.4 seems more a restatement of the goal priority than a specific action program. In the case of Action Program 3.1, the statement is more a suggested area of study than an action program ready for implementation in the classrooms of the school district.

Many of these problems are corrected in the more focused list of Figure 2–2. Notice that specific schools and/or units of the district are identified, as are the specific individuals having responsibility for the action program. The statements themselves identify target grade levels for many of the action programs, making it easier for each building principal to identify areas of immediate concern. In our specific example of the elementary school

Figure 2–1 Sample Set of Goal Priorities and Related Action Programs (without focused content and responsibility)

Goal Priority 1: The students will show appreciation of peoples from other ethnic groups and cultures.

Suggested Action Programs:

1.1 School programs should include more material on major ethnic groups living in the community.
1.2 Schools should encourage exchange programs involving students of different ethnic groups and cultures.
1.3 Schools should select books that more adequately reflect the ethnic and cultural diversity of the community.

Goal Priority 2: The students will show a desire for learning both now and in the future.

Suggested Action Programs:

2.1 Schools should encourage greater use of "free exploration" learning.
2.2 Schools should stock a greater diversity of learning material and should see that students are exposed to them.

Goal Priority 3: The students will demonstrate competence in the basic skill areas of reading, writing, speaking, and listening.

Suggested Action Programs:

3.1 The current practice of social promotion is unsatisfactory and should probably be replaced by demonstrated competency in the basic skill areas.
3.2 Schools should add special tutors for those students reading below grade level.
3.3 A required course in speech should be added to the school curriculum.
3.4 Students should develop skills in oral and written language.

principal, it is clear from Figure 2–2 that only Action Programs 2.1, 2.2, 3.2, and 3.4 are likely to be of immediate importance. The greater clarity and focus of these statements along with the reduced number of statements relating directly to the elementary school level make it more likely that the elementary principal will give serious attention to the overall improvement program.

A discussion of reasons for limited follow-up of goal-ranking activities would not be complete without indicating the resistance to change that is a recognized part of both organizations and individuals. Almost any of the action programs listed in Figure 2–2 will serve to threaten someone in the organization. The addition of a required course in speech at the high school level (Action Program 3.3) may reduce enrollments in foreign languages and art to a point that teacher reductions are required in these elective areas. Fifth- and sixth-grade teachers throughout the district may be required to change their current social studies curriculum in order to accommodate the pilot materials on blacks and Chicanos (Action Program 1.1). The extra effort required to make these changes will trigger opposition, particularly among those who do not support the goal itself. In both cases, one can expect some administrators and teachers to resist the interference with their current way of doing things. Even under the most benign circumstances, one can expect a certain skepticism toward the citizen and district planners; given a real threat to livelihood or position, one can expect this skepticism to be replaced with mistrust and open hostility. Only by recognizing the dynamics of organizational change and by employing suitable change strategies can the school administrator hope to accomplish a program of the kind outlined in Figure 2–2.

Figure 2–2 Sample Set of Goal Priorities and Related Action Programs (with focused content and responsibility)

Goal Priority and Suggested Action Programs	*Target School or Units*	*Person Responsible for Planning*
Goal Priority 1: The students will show appreciation of peoples from other ethnic groups and cultures.		
1.1 Social studies units at the fifth and sixth grades should be revised to include units on blacks and Chicanos and these units should be tried out in at least four elementary schools in the district.	Curriculum Dept. for Development Work and Pilot Schools to be Selected Later	H. Herman, Social Studies Coordinator
1.2 Each senior high school should establish an exchange program such as those provided through the American Field Service and should strive for participation of at least four students per academic year.	Totem and Maple Senior High Schools	D. Danner, Principal of Totem, and J. Botter, Vice-Principal of Maple
1.3 The instructional materials division of the school district, working with an appropriate citizen committee, should inventory current library materials in all schools and move as rapidly as possible to provide a more adequate reflection of ethnic and cultural diversity.	All Schools	E. Cornish, Dir. of Instructional Materials
Goal Priority 2: The students will show a desire for learning both now and in the future.		
2.1 The elementary schools of one zone will try out the use of a "free exploration" learning program and will attempt to discover whether this program leads to more positive views toward school learning.	Oakleaf and Mann Schools of Central Zone	R. Tanner, Dir. of Research and Evaluation
2.2 The librarian of each school should attempt to diversify learning material collections with particular emphasis on expanding nonbook materials such as pictures, slides, and tapes.	All Schools	E. Cornish, Dir. of Instructional Materials
Goal Priority 3: The students will demonstrate competence in the basic skill areas of reading, writing, speaking, and listening.		
3.1 A study committee of citizens and staff should be appointed to review current policies of grade-to-grade promotion with the intent of recommending changes that might increase basic skill competencies among students..	None	R. Marshall, Dir. of Pupil Personnel
3.2 Elementary schools should be encouraged to design and implement special reading tutorial programs for students in the intermediate grades who are reading one or more years below grade level. Each school will receive a financial allocation to aid in establishing the programs.	All Elementary Schools	D. Salyer, Reading Coordinator, and R. Tanner, Dir. of Research and Evaluation

Figure 2–2 (continued)

Goal Priority and Suggested Action Programs	*Target School or Units*	*Person Responsible for Planning*
3.3 A special committee with representation from each of the senior and junior high schools should study the feasibility of adding a required course in speech at the high school level.	All Senior High Schools	J. Sabol, Lang. Arts Coordinator
3.4 Teachers at all levels should provide students more opportunities for developing skills in oral and written communication and the curriculum division should supply the required training and materials to see that this is accomplished.	All Schools	A. Clark, Dir. of Curriculum, and J. Sabol, Lang. Arts Coordinator

GAINING CONSENSUS ON ACTION PROGRAMS

Now that several prime factors that slow the goal clarification follow-up process have been reviewed, it is important to examine a set of procedures that might be used with good result in arriving at consensus on a set of action programs. The following steps represent a good overview of this suggested process:

Step 1. Develop a list of possible action programs relating to each of the goal priorities previously identified by the community.
Step 2. Edit this list into a form that can be reviewed by a representative community and staff group (or groups).
Step 3. Collect preferences on action programs from representative group (or groups).
Step 4. Gain consensus on those action programs that show the greatest promise of achieving goals and of being implemented in the school or district.

Much can be said about the options available in relation to these four steps. One can gain a better understanding of the intended process by applying these steps to a specific school situation and commenting on some of the major options in the context of that situation. With this in mind, let us outline accomplishment of the above steps in relation to the Gooding Elementary School, which serves grades K–6 in a large suburban district.

Begin by assuming that a set of general goal priorities of the type listed in Figures 2–1 and 2–2 have been identified through some type of community goal-selection exercise. (Several options available for this type of activity are presented in Appendix 1.) Assume that these goals were identified at the school district level and that each elementary school has been asked to develop a procedure for implementing the four goal priorities:

A. Students on completion of elementary school will understand and practice skills of family living (including communication, acceptance of family responsibilities, and financial affairs).
B. Students at all grade levels will show pride in their work (including work completed inside and outside the classroom).

C. Students will increase their skills in mathematical computation, with emphasis on both speed and accuracy.
D. Students at all grade levels will develop a more positive self-image.

Before proceeding with Step 1 (the listing of possible action programs), it is important to note certain characteristics of the four goal priorities. They are all stated in terms of products or outcomes of the school experience. As currently stated, both A and B address the status of accomplishment at a particular point in time; C and D, on the other hand, speak of increase or growth over time. This does not necessarily alter the selection of possible action programs but it does suggest that accomplishment of the first two will require some preset criterion of acceptability whereas evaluation of C and D, if done properly, will involve pre- and post-treatment measures of student gain. We also observe that the first two goal priorities include a parenthetical reference to subobjectives. This information should be helpful in generating possible action programs for Gooding Elementary School.

Steps 1 and 2, developing and editing a list of action programs, are probably best handled by a staff committee. The committee might find it helpful to involve the entire faculty and a representative group of parents in the brainstorming associated with Step 1. An initial list of possible action programs for Gooding Elementary School is presented in Figure 2–3. Any list of this type is likely to require at least some editing (Step 2) before collecting preferences from a cross section of relevant school groups. Although the major consideration in the editing process is the clarification of wording, it is also important that each of the proposed items is, in fact, an action program bearing some relationship to the goal priority of reference. It is quite possible that certain items that are not relevant programs will creep into the brainstorming process. This appears to be the case in relation to Statements B5 and C6 of Figure 2–3.

Statement B5 is reasonably clear, but it is not action to be taken by the school. Earning higher ratings or grades could very well represent increased student pride in work, but what specifically is the school to do to encourage students to earn these higher ratings or grades? How do we really know the higher grades were earned and even then what action by the school caused them to be earned? Unless teachers become involved in the highly unethical practice of giving higher grades just so the criterion or indicator of success can be accomplished, nothing can be found in this particular statement that can be called an action program initiated and carried out by the school or its personnel. Statement C6 refers to an activity relating to the measure or evaluation of goal attainment and not to the goal attainment itself. It, too, should probably be dropped from the list at this point in the editing process.

Other items, such as B4, C5, and D3, while stated as action programs, seem to have only a distant relationship to the attainment of the goal priority of reference. Those persons involved in the editing process will want to satisfy themselves of a necessary goal priority–action program tie as a condition for leaving these particular items on the list. Some rewording of these statements may help to clarify this goal-to-action-program tie.

Returning to the concern over the clarification of wording, a number of statements in Figure 2–3 need special attention in the editing process. The editing begins by noting that certain of the action-program statements of Figure 2–3 can be made clearer just by indicating the specific grade levels to be covered. This is true in such cases as A5, B1, and D1. For example, several options might be considered for A5:

Option 1 (Action Program A5)
Students in grades 5 and 6 will study about family living in cultures other than their own.

Figure 2–3 List of Action Programs for Gooding Elementary School (before editing)

Goal Priority A: Students on completion of elementary school will understand and practice skills of family living.

A1 – – – A special unit on family responsibilities will be incorporated into the regular fifth-grade social studies program.
A2 – – – Special units on consumer skills will be added to the K–3 curriculum.
A3 – – – Instruction in family budgeting will be added to the social studies program in grades 4–6.
A4 – – – Exchange visits will be encouraged among students.
A5 – – – Students will study about family living in cultures other than their own.

Goal Priority B: Students at all grade levels will show pride in their work.

B1 – – – Students will be assigned definite work responsibilities as part of the school program.
B2 – – – Teachers will more frequently utilize bulletin boards.
B3 – – – Students in grade 6 will be used as custodial assistants around the school and will be given encouragement for successful service in these assistant roles.
B4 – – – Guest speakers from industry will present descriptions of occupational requirements in various fields of work.
B5 – – – Students will earn higher ratings or grades on their written work, thereby indicating a greater degree of pride in high achievement.

Goal Priority C: Students will increase their skills in mathematical computation.

C1 – – – A mathematics laboratory will be established and will be open before and after school for students who need help with their mathematics problems.
C2 – – – Two sets of pocket calculators will be purchased and these sets will be available for classroom use.
C3 – – – Parents will be encouraged to help their children with their mathematical computation skills.
C4 – – – Teachers at all grade levels will spend more time on mathematical computation.
C5 – – – Teachers will attend workshops on the teaching of mathematics.
C6 – – – The comprehensive test of basic skills (CTBS) will be given to all students in grade 3 and grade 6.

Goal Priority D: Students at all grade levels will develop a more positive self-image.

D1 – – – Assignments will be more individualized, thereby permitting each student to receive positive feedback on his/her work.
D2 – – – Teachers at all grade levels will attend at least one of the human relations workshops being run by the district.
D3 – – – Information on student rights and responsibilities will be distributed to students in grades 4–6 and follow-up discussions will be held in the classrooms.
D4 – – – Students will be given more opportunities to perform before groups of people.
D5 – – – Competition between students at all grade levels will be minimized in order to avoid giving students negative feelings about self.

Option 2 (Action Program A5)

Students in grades 5 and 6 will study about family living in at least three cultures different from their own.

Either of these options would be preferable to the original wording of Figure 2–3 simply because they specify grade levels to be affected by the program and therefore communicate more clearly the intent of the program.

The choice between Option 1 and 2 will depend on the degree to which teachers at the two grade levels want to specify the number of cultures to be considered. Option 2 has the advantage of communicating a clearer reference to those involved in ranking action programs but its selection would be a mistake if planning had not already narrowed the focus to the extent indicated.

This concern for specificity is a critical one in the overall editing process and appears to be a real problem with such statements as A4, B2, C3, and D4. For purposes of illustration, notice the lack of specificity in relation to the first two of these action programs. In the case of Action Program A4, the statement as presented in Figure 2–3 does not provide much of an idea as to how this encouragement of exchange visits is to occur or at what grade levels it will be encouraged. Both factors appear to be corrected in the following alternative wording:

Action Program A4 (alternative wording)

> Students in the intermediate grades will be formed into groups of three or four members and students in each of the groups will be encouraged to visit in the homes of other group members.

Notice that the alternative wording makes the nature of the exchange program under consideration clearer, thereby making it much easier for the respondent to establish his or her level of support for the action program.

In Action Program B2, there is a rather clear statement of action to be taken but its relation to the goal priority is not as clear as it might be. How is the more frequent use of the bulletin board to improve the student's pride in work? This would have little chance of happening unless student work was placed on the bulletin board. Should this not be indicated in the statement itself? A preferred alternative to Statement B2 follows:

Action Program B2 (alternative wording)

> Teachers at all grade levels will set up bulletin boards for the purpose of displaying student work and teachers will see that the best pieces of work for every student are displayed on these boards.

Note that both the grade level and the goal–action program ties are designated more clearly than in the original statement of Figure 2–3. Again, this clarity will be helpful to those who become involved in setting priorities for action programs and will give the school staff greater confidence in the overall planning process.

The results of this editing process are summarized in Figure 2–4. The original list of twenty-one statements has been reduced to eighteen action programs having a relationship to one or more of the goal priorities that were identified earlier in the planning process.

Before proceeding with the ranking process (Step 3), some assessment of resource requirements associated with each action-program statement should be accomplished. This is best done by the school staff; however, the information should be available to any citizen or citizen-staff group involved in ranking action programs. In relation to the eighteen statements in Figure 2–4, it is useful to note that some of them do have definite cost implications. This is particularly true of Statement A2, which involves summer developmental work by staff, and Statements C1 and C2, which call for sizable space and equipment allocations. Increased staff time may be involved in several of the other statements.

Whatever the list of action programs, it is important that this cost information, at least in rough form, be available because any activity of a school district is justified to individual patrons on some kind of cost-benefit rationale. Agreement on the precise benefits to be

Figure 2–4 List of Action Programs for Gooding Elementary School (after editing)

Goal Priority A: Students on completion of elementary school will understand and practice skills of family living.

A1 – – – A special unit on family responsibilities, already developed at the district level, will be incorporated into the regular fifth-grade social studies program. (Indication of unit availability added to original statement)

A2 – – – Special units on consumer skills will be developed over the summer months and will be added to the K–3 curriculum for the next school year. (Indication of timing of development and implementation of units added to original statement)

A3 – – – Instruction in family budgeting will be added to the social studies program in grades 4–6. (No change)

A4 – – – Students in the intermediate grades will be formed into groups of three or four members and students in each of the groups will be encouraged to visit in the homes of other group members. (Statement revised to specify format for exchange visits)

A5 – – – Students in grades 5 and 6 will study about family living in at least three cultures different from their own. (Indication of grade level and number of cultures added to the original statement)

Goal Priority B: Students at all grade levels will show pride in their work.

B1 – – – Each student in grades K–3 will be assigned individual responsibilities or tasks to be completed and positive feedback will be given at the point of successful task completion. (Statement expanded beyond the mere assignment of responsibilities to reflect the provision of positive feedback and grade-level designation added)

B2 – – – Teachers at all grade levels will set up bulletin boards for the purpose of displaying student work and teachers will see that the best pieces of work for every student are displayed on these boards. (Grade-level designation added; also the intent to display best work for each student specified)

B3 – – – Students in grade 6 will be used as custodial assistants around the school and will be given encouragement for successful service in these assistant roles. (No change)

B4 – – – Omitted because of lack of relationship to goal priority.

B5 – – – Omitted because of not being an action program to be generated by the school.

Goal Priority C: Students will increase their skills in mathematical computation.

C1 – – – A mathematics laboratory will be established for the purpose of helping students with math problems before and after school. (No change)

C2 – – – Two sets of pocket calculators will be purchased and these sets will be available for classroom use. (No change)

C3 – – – A special parent-orientation program will be initiated in the fall and parents at that time will be informed of the mathematical computation emphasis and will be encouraged to assist their children. (Clarification of the way in which parents will become involved in assisting their children in mathematical computation)

C4 – – – Teachers at all grade levels will use at least two Science Research Associates (SRA) drill sheets or the equivalent during each week. (Specification of how increased time on mathematical computation is to be accomplished is added to original statement)

C5 – – – At least one-third of the teachers in the intermediate grades will attend a workshop designed to aid in the teaching of mathematical computation skills. (Clarification of the number of teachers participating and some indication of relationship to goal priority)

C6 – – – Omitted because of not representing an action program related to the goal priority.

Goal Priority D: Students at all grade levels will develop a more positive self-image.

D1 – – – Assignments at all grade levels will be more individualized, thereby permitting each student to receive positive feedback of his or her work. (Indication of grade level added to original statement)

Figure 2–4 (continued)

D2 – – – Teachers at all grade levels will attend at least one of the human relations workshops being run by the district. (No change)

D3 – – – As a way of showing students that they do have societal status, information on student rights and responsibilities will be distributed to students in grades 4–6 and follow-up discussions will be held in the classrooms. (Clarification of relationship between activity and the goal-priority statement)

D4 – – – In order to give individual students an opportunity to perform in unique skill areas, at least one talent show and one play will be presented by the school each year. (Clarification of the exact way in which student performance before groups is to be accomplished)

D5 – – – Competition between students at all grade levels will be minimized in order to avoid giving students negative feelings about self. (No change)

The degree and nature of the editing is indicated in parentheses following each statement. The original action-program statements are presented in Figure 2–3.

gained from any given activity will most assuredly be difficult to achieve and the benefits may not always be viewed by certain patrons in terms of student growth and development gains. Nonetheless, these benefits, however they may be viewed by a given observer, will ultimately have to be compared with the dollar cost of their realization. It stands to reason that the enthusiasm one has for any given action program will be influenced by the dollar cost of initiating that program.

It is important to realize that use of cost information in ranking action programs for a given school is quite different from deciding on possible expenditures within a family or household unit. Both the costs and benefits related to most items in the family budget are associated with the same fixed group of persons and are usually relatively easy to identify. Not only are benefits difficult to measure and quantify in schools, but those persons realizing most of the direct benefits are often not the same group as those paying the bill. It is difficult for a parent or teacher in Gooding Elementary School to turn down a chance to obtain two classroom sets of pocket calculators (Action Program C2 of Figure 2–4) from a federal or state grant even when the expected benefits from such an acquisition as viewed by persons in the Gooding Elementary School community are minimal. If the total cost were to come from local tax funds, it is likely that the priority given to this particular action program would be somewhat less. The point here is that persons involved in setting priorities at the local level should focus attention on total costs of various programs, regardless of the source of the funds, and should give high priority to those items that they personally judge will yield the highest benefit for the least overall cost. Because people often want the greatest benefit for the least personal cost, this more global approach to viewing the merit of possible action programs is extremely difficult to accomplish. Yet it is the only way that planning for improvement at the local school level can be built on actual preferences existing within the local school community.

Because of the complexity of the cost-benefit analysis in the context of public agencies like schools, it is probably best to present an analysis of additional costs showing both local and outside funding components associated with each of the action programs under consideration. This information, coupled with a word of encouragement to look at total cost rather than just that part to be paid locally, is probably all that can be done by the administrator directing the priority-setting activity. At least the group is encouraged under these conditions to look at its own preferences without being unduly influenced by outside factors. In addition to this information on costs, it is useful to supply those involved in this activity with any available information on probable benefits. This information may not always be convincing or even reliable, but those making the decisions should nonetheless provide a maximum of information and an opportunity to question experts on the limitations of the information provided.

Having completed the editing and the cost computations, we are in a position to move ahead with the actual collection of preferences (Step 3) and the development of a consensus plan of action (Step 4). These two steps will often be accomplished in sequence with the same group of staff and community representatives but can also be done as two separate activities. The strategy used in any given situation will depend on the preferences of local school personnel and the time and resources available.

Whatever strategy or option is used, it is important that all persons participating in Steps 3 and 4 be given a complete orientation to the goal-development and action-program-development work already completed. It is also important that these persons spend some time initially discussing the goal priority–action program relationships. Some attention should be given to the analysis of cost data, and discussion about possible conflicts between various goal priorities and/or action programs is quite appropriate background to the priority–setting effort.

This matter of possible goal conflict is evident in comparing Action Programs D4 and D5 for Gooding Elementary School (see Figure 2–4). Even though both action programs relate to the maintenance of positive self-image, note that the two programs have considerable potential for conflict. How can a talent show or play (Action Program D4) be presented without some element of competition or at least comparison between students (Action Program D5)? Some level of competition between students can probably also be expected in relation to the bulletin board displays associated with Action Program B2. These conflicts should be understood by persons involved in the ranking of action programs. Life itself is a set of conflicting values and goals and these conflicts must be recognized as a very natural part of the school community. Indicating this to those persons involved in developing goal priorities and related action programs tends to lessen the possibility of looking for simple solutions to complex public policy problems and brings an element of reality to the overall planning process.

After the required orientation is completed, it is time to move ahead with the actual collection of preferences. One suggested instrument for collecting preferences of individual group members is presented in Figure 2–5. This particular survey instrument gives each member of the group a similar weighting of forty-five points in the ranking process and encourages each to consider the approximate cost data as part of the rating process. This format is similar to that used with the Phi Delta Kappa Goals discussed in Chapter 1. Note that it does force choices between action programs, at least in the sense that any person choosing an above-average rating in one program area is automatically required to rate at least one other program with a below-average score. The administrator faced with designing a process for reaching agreement on a set of action programs may want to consider methods other than the survey approach. If the group is small, it is likely that a brief discussion of the options as presented in Figure 2–5 could lead to establishment of a reasonable set of action programs. More sophisticated techniques such as the Charrette or Delphi approaches may have merit in selected situations.[2] Whatever the method used, it is important that the administrator and/or steering committee be prepared to put the resulting consensus plan into a written statement that can be shared with the entire school community.

---

[2]The Charrette is a structured brainstorming technique applied most often in the architectural and building field; the Delphi involves reaction to a sequence of surveys by a selected group of persons, and has been used frequently in educational planning activities. For a more detailed discussion of these two techniques, the reader is referred to Harold L. Cramer and Robert J. Wehking, *Charretting the Planning Process* (June 1973); and Harold A. Linstone and Murray Turoff, eds., *The Delphi Method* (1975).

Figure 2–5 Survey of Action-Program Preferences

Listed below are eighteen possible action programs that might be used to improve education at the Gooding Elementary School over the next few years. These programs have been grouped in accordance with goal priorities established at the district level. An estimate of additional cost is provided with each item.

You are to assign a score of 0–5 for each of the items with 5 indicating a very positive rating and 0 indicating no support for the program in question. You are asked to use exactly 45 points in the rating process. This of course represents an average score of 2.5 points per item.

Goal Priority A: Students on completion of elementary school will understand and practice skills of family living.

____ 1. A special unit on family responsibilities, already developed at the district level, will be incorporated into the regular fifth-grade social studies program. (No additional cost)

____ 2. Special units on consumer skills will be developed over the summer months and will be added to the K–3 curriculum for the next school year. ($6,000 cost to develop materials)

____ 3. Instruction in family budgeting will be added to the social studies program in grades 4–6. (No additional cost)

____ 4. Students in the intermediate grades will be formed into groups of three or four members and students in each of the groups will be encouraged to visit in the homes of other group members. (No additional cost)

____ 5. Students in grades 5 and 6 will study about family living in at least three cultures different from their own. (No additional cost)

Goal Priority B: Students at all grade levels will show pride in their work.

____ 1. Each student in grades K–3 will be assigned individual responsibilities or tasks to be completed and positive feedback will be given at the point of successful task completion. (No additional cost)

____ 2. Teachers at all grade levels will set up bulletin boards for the purpose of displaying student work and teachers will see that the best pieces of work for each student are displayed on these boards. (No additional cost)

____ 3. Students in grade 6 will be used as custodial assistants around the school and will be given encouragement for successful service in these assistant roles. (No additional cost)

Goal Priority C: Students will increase their skills in mathematical computation.

____ 1. A mathematics laboratory will be established for the purpose of helping students with math problems before and after school. ($800 for materials and $1,800 for paraprofessional time for a total additional cost of $2,600)

____ 2. Two sets of pocket calculators will be purchased and these sets will be available for classroom use. ($1,250 cost for the calculators)

____ 3. A special parent-orientation meeting will be initiated in the fall and parents at that time will be informed of the mathematical computation emphasis and will be encouraged to assist their children. (No additional cost)

____ 4. Teachers at all grade levels will use at least two Science Research Associates (SRA) drill sheets or the equivalent during each week. (No additional cost)

____ 5. At least one-third of the teachers in the intermediate grades will attend a workshop designed to aid in the teaching of mathematical computation skills. ($400 to pay for substitute teachers)

Goal Priority D: Students at all grade levels will develop a more positive self-image.

____ 1. Assignments at all grade levels will be more individualized, thereby permitting each student to receive positive feedback on his or her work. (No additional cost)

____ 2. Teachers at all grade levels will attend at least one of the human relations workshops being run by the district. ($800 to pay for substitute teachers)

Figure 2–5 (continued)

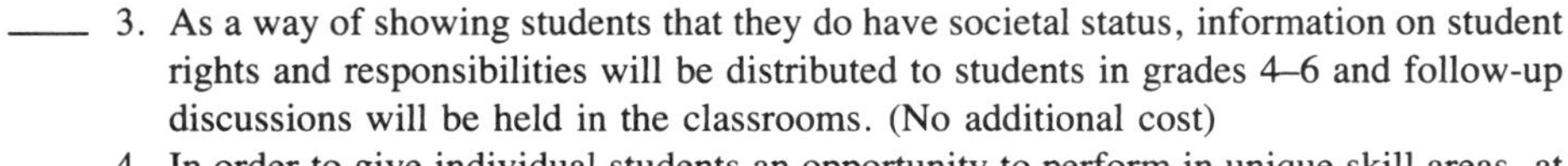

____ 3. As a way of showing students that they do have societal status, information on student rights and responsibilities will be distributed to students in grades 4–6 and follow-up discussions will be held in the classrooms. (No additional cost)

____ 4. In order to give individual students an opportunity to perform in unique skill areas, at least one talent show and one play will be presented by the school each year. (No additional cost as costumes, props, etc., will be donated by parents)

____ 5. Competition between students at all grade levels will be minimized in order to avoid giving students negative feelings of self. (No additional cost)

IMPORTANCE OF TRANSLATING ACTION PROGRAMS INTO CHANGE AT THE CLASSROOM LEVEL

In the previous section, a particular process for gaining consensus on action programs was explained. These action programs were directed to previously developed goal priorities and were intended for use as part of a general plan of school improvement over a 2–5 year period. In the form presented in Figure 2–5, it is clear that many of the action-program statements are directed at the school level and say very little about actions to be taken in individual classrooms. Yet, if many of these action programs and related goal priorities are to be realized, they must be translated into change at the classroom level. For example, it is unlikely that students in grades five and six at the Gooding Elementary School will "study family living in at least three cultures different from their own" (Goal Priority A, Action Program 5 of Figure 2–5) unless there exists a definite commitment on the part of the several teachers involved at those grade levels. There may even be a need for these teachers to receive staff development assistance in preparing materials appropriate to the task. The completion of this particular action program should also be established as part of the overall evaluation for teachers of grades five and six at the Gooding Elementary School.

In essense, this planning of action programs at both building and classroom levels is Step III of the goal model presented in Figure 1–4. Some part of this detailed planning of action programs was covered earlier in discussions of the need for clarifying intent of action-program statements and for assessing costs and benefits associated with implementation of selected action programs. In the succeeding sections of this chapter, the important processes of staff goal selection and preparation of classroom objectives are considered.

In dealing with both of these component processes, the assumption is made that little progress in the implementation of action programs will be achieved without the support of the building administrator.[3] It is further assumed that the process of aiding teachers in the development of goals and objectives to be used as a basis for classroom instruction is the single most important task of the building principal. For these reasons, emphasis throughout is given to the support role to be played by the administrator in supervising the implementation of goal-related action programs.

One may argue that much of the material included in this chapter is more appropriately covered in teacher training programs and need not be repeated in a book designed for the training of building administrators. While certain of the skills relating to objective writing

[3]Administrator support and authority are judged essential to task accomplishment by numerous researchers. For specific documentaton, see Peter F. Drucker, *The Effective Executive* (New York: Harper & Row, 1967), p. 1; and Andrew W. Halpin and Don B. Croft, *The Organizational Climate of Schools* (Washington, D.C.: U.S. Office of Education, 1962), pp. 122–142.

are included in teacher training programs, rarely do such programs consider the broad range of product, process, and organizational goals and objectives utilized in the school goal selection situation as described here. Further, recent experience in schools indicates that both administrators and teachers continue to struggle with the task of establishing objectives at an appropriate level of difficulty and teaching to those objectives.[4] Adding the additional requirement that at least some of these objectives relate to community-determined goal priorities and related action-program statements further complicates this process for school personnel. If instructional leadership is, as we so often claim, central to the role of the building administrator, there is little question but that these materials on action-program implementation at the classroom level are appropriately included in this book dealing with the administrator's role in the planning process. Only as administrators develop greater skill in this staff development and evaluation area will goal development and action programming be implemented at the classroom level.

STAFF GOAL SETTING AND EVALUATION

Education to most people refers to the development of persons mentally, physically, and morally. Educational development in the context of a school involves bringing about intentional change in the learner. It is assumed that this intentional change, even when not clearly understood or agreed on by all participants, represents the very basis for the school's existing as a separate institution. It is further assumed that this intentional change will occur only when it guides activities in all parts of the school organization. Certainly specific instances of change will have little chance of being accomplished unless they are in some way transformed into activities at the classroom level.

This transformation to the classroom level is not likely to occur unless the goal setting and staff evaluation program of the school and school system encourages direct teacher implementation of the action programs. Whether teachers establish classroom goals and objectives in direct relation to action-program statements or conduct some kind of comparison between existing classroom activities and action-program statements, the connection must at some point be made. Our purpose here is to examine techniques and understandings to be used by principals and other unit managers in seeing that this connection is made.

Without going into detail on alternative systems for staff evaluation in schools, it is important to note that the connection between classroom goals and objectives and action-program statements is not likely to be realized using the traditional checklist form of staff evaluation. Such checklists, while required in many school systems, look for the same teacher and student indicators (e.g., existence of preplanning, bulletin boards, empathy with students, and clear voice) in all teacher-learner situations and hence are not adaptable to action-program statements, which may change annually. Further, it is assumed that action-program statements of the type presented in the previous chapter apply differently to teachers of different grade levels and of different subjects.

The kind of implementation called for here will necessarily involve a much more individualized form of teacher goal selection and evaluation. Some of the Management by Objective (MBO) evaluation plans, in which goal and objective selection for each indi-

[4]This conclusion is based on observations from several consultants involved in implementing the Instructional Theory Into Practice (ITIP) program developed at University Elementary School of the University of California, Los Angeles. This program is designed to give teachers greater skill in selecting appropriate objectives and in teaching to those objectives. Most consultants working with the program indicate that many teachers need help with both of these areas.

vidual employee is a key element, have potential for accomplishing this connection between action-program statements and teacher objectives for a given classroom cycle.[5] As part of this activity, the individual teacher and the supervisor spend considerable time discussing the priority needs within the classroom unit. In addition, the teacher's role with respect to the total school and the high-priority action-program statements must be reviewed. All of this discussion depends on a prior understanding of the purposes of the evaluation process.

The professional staff evaluation process in most schools has the dual purpose of improving the delivery of educational services and encouraging professional growth of the staff. It does not have as its basic purpose the removal of weak or incompetent persons from the system. In those few cases where this latter purpose must be involved in the evaluation system (and there are indeed some situations where removal of personnel may be the only sure way to improve the learning situation for students), implementation of action programs probably will not even come into the picture. Goal setting for this latter group of probationary employees will concentrate on those standard behaviors required for minimal performance (e.g., ability to communicate expectations to students and parents, evidence of planning, effective student discipline, and attention to the learning task) and will not require specific attention to action-program implementation.

The overall staff evaluation program will undoubtedly operate at a much higher level of trust and cooperation if this threat of removal from the system is specifically omitted as a purpose of evaluation except for a very few probationary employees. It is recommended, therefore, that a clear separation be made between the probationary employees and those involved in the regular evaluation and professional-improvement program of the school or school district. The action-program implementation procedures presented here apply almost exclusively to this much larger group of professional personnel who are in absolutely no danger of removal from the system, at least for reasons of professional performance.

Once the purpose of evaluation has been established as furthering the improvement of school programs and the professional growth of employees, it is important to focus on the establishment of goals and objectives for the next cycle of evaluation. Because of state and school district policies, this evaluation cycle most generally coincides with the school year, but this need not be the case. It is sometimes appropriate to establish longer-range objectives that span a period of 2–3 years and some objectives involve periods considerably less than a year. It is helpful to begin consideration of goals and objectives for a given evaluation cycle by looking at the following categories of concern:

- Carry-over objectives
- General role expectations (including both classroom and nonclassroom areas)
- Action-program statements
- General professional growth

Carry-over objectives are items from a previous evaluation cycle that need further attention even if only in the sense that additional evaluative data is to be collected and analyzed. General role expectations are those behaviors and expectations that are established on a district or school basis for selected professional roles. They will generally include any standards against which all teachers are to be evaluated on an annual basis. Action-program statements were discussed in the previous chapter and cover a wide range

[5]For a comprehensive presentation of Management by Objectives models for staff evaluation, see Dale L. Bolton, *Selection and Evaluation of Teachers* (Berkeley, Calif.: McCutchan, 1973); John D. McNeil, *Toward Accountable Teachers* (New York: Holt, Rinehart, & Winston, 1971); and George B. Redfern, *How to Evaluate Teaching* (Worthington, Ohio: School Management Institute, 1972).

of goal priorities that have been identified by representatives of parent, staff, and student groups. These have presumably been presented to the teachers prior to the initial goal-setting conference. General professional growth includes those areas of personal and professional development that are of interest to either the school or the teacher and that may relate to future change in assignment, for example, from classroom teacher to curriculum consultant. All four of these categories must be considered in developing a plan that maximizes both improvement of school programs and professional growth of employees.

Factors to consider in the goal-setting process are covered at length in other text sources.[6] At this point, it will suffice to suggest that the following five questions be raised as a guide to effective and realistic goal selection by professional personnel:

1. Does the list of goal statements reflect an adequate balance of organizational and personal needs?
2. Is the list of goal statements reasonable within the time and resource constraints of the education setting?
3. Do any of the goals require coordination with other personnel and how is this coordination to be accomplished?
4. Are the goals and/or objectives stated clearly and in a manner that permits evaluation of goal attainment?
5. Which goals should be evaluated and in what manner will the evaluation be accomplished?

Considering these five questions early in the planning process can do a great deal to avoid misunderstandings later and can provide needed direction to the evaluation process. All too often, evaluation is viewed as a process where the principal or supervisor spends a set number of minutes observing the teacher in the classroom. This is apparently the view that encourages state legislatures and local school boards to establish time-based systems of personnel evaluation. Such a vision of evaluation is unfortunate and serves only to perpetuate the mistaken notion that classroom visitations are the sole basis for evaluating school personnel.

The data collection associated with evaluation of some teachers, at least those not on probationary status, may require little or no classroom visitation time on the part of the school principal. This determination should be based on the goals established in the initial conference and the actual types of data required to make judgments regarding their accomplishment. If goals and objectives are clearly stated and if those directed to classroom instruction are to be measured in terms of changes in students (i.e., product-type objectives), it is possible that the required data collection can be accomplished by the teacher, perhaps with some assistance from an evaluation specialist. This will free the principal, department chairperson, or unit leader for the more creative activity of assisting in the clarification of goals and the development of appropriate evaluation plans and data collection procedures.

PREPARING OBJECTIVES FOR USE AT THE CLASSROOM LEVEL

Certain teacher goals developed as part of the detailed implementation of action programs will involve student outcome or product measures. If these goals stated in terms of student

---

[6]For a more detailed treatment of advantages and disadvantages of using goal and objectives as part of the instructional planning process, the reader is referred to D. Cecil Clark, *Using Instructional Objectives in Teaching* (1972); and Hildreth H. McAshan, *Writing Behavioral Objectives: A New Approach* (1970).

outcome are to be taken seriously, they must at some point be translated into measures that capture the desired behavior and/or attitude change in a reasonably objective and reliable manner. The design of tests and other measurement techniques is not our concern here, but it is appropriate to address the problem of stating classroom objectives in a clear and concise manner.

Product or instruction objectives were discussed in some detail in Chapter 1. Ideally, such objective statements should make reference to (1) the behavior, attitude, or capability to be demonstrated by the student; (2) the subject matter or object at which the learner behavior is to be directed; and (3) the conditions under which the activity or attitude is to be shown and, when possible, some indication of criteria of acceptability.[7]

The first referent, namely, the description of the behavior or attitude to be demonstrated by the student, is essentially a means of checking that the objective statement is a product or outcome to be demonstrated by the student and not something done by the teacher. Of the three referents, this is clearly the most important. This is so because any attempt to assess student growth depends on identification of behaviors, attitudes and competencies to be changed. As Anderson observed, "Without well-stated objectives there is no basis for making any judgment as to whether or not the program has achieved the desired goals" (Anderson, p. 20).

Experience indicates that many goals established by teachers are stated as teacher actions and must therefore be revised to a product form prior to any serious evaluation of their impact on students. As one example, take the teacher goal of "incorporating a unit on careers into the junior year required course in American history." This goal is stated as a teacher process rather than as a student behavior to be demonstrated on completion of the career unit. Samples of possible product or outcome statements (which include at least some degree of attention to the referents mentioned above) related to the career unit are:

1. Students completing the unit will demonstrate awareness and understanding of worker trait groups as presented in the text and will demonstrate this awareness by correctly listing at least three jobs within each of the groups.
2. Students will correctly identify the relative importance of data, people, and things in a variety of jobs.
3. Students completing the unit will be capable of listing the five basic steps of good career planning.
4. Students will understand positive and negative rewards associated with various types of work and will demonstrate this understanding by scoring at least 75 percent on a written test matching jobs and rewards.
5. Students completing the unit will show greater personal interest in jobs stereotyped for the opposite sex. This greater interest will be shown by a pre-post-unit selection of jobs from a prepared list.
6. On completion of the careers unit, students will give more attention to the relationship between careers and basic skills and will be more likely to choose careers that require a basic skill profile consistent with their own.

Note that each of these statements refers to some behavior, attitude, or capability to be exhibited by the student on completion of the career unit. In relation to the typology of

[7]Various writers have stated these conditions in alternative forms and some have stressed certain of the conditions more than others. For example, the well-publicized ITIP model developed by Hunter at the University of California, Los Angeles, calls for objectives that specify the content or thought process, the covert and overt behavior demonstrated by the learner, the conditions under which the demonstrated behavior is to be completed, and the criteria of acceptable performance. These four specifications provide a close match for the three stated here.

product objectives presented in Figure 1–2, observe that these objective statements are presented in terms of individual student accomplishments rather than group aims. Objectives 1–4 address the status of accomplishment at a given point in time (in this case, on completion of the program) and Objectives 5 and 6 refer to growth or increased accomplishment as a result of participation in the career unit. While the teacher or teachers involved in monitoring these objectives may desire to test all students on all six objectives both before and after the unit is taught, this is required only in the case of the last two statements, which call for increased accomplishment.

This determination of whether to state the objective statements in terms of "status on completion of program" or "increase between pre- and post-periods" is based on the likelihood that at least some students would have competence in the area prior to participation in the program. In the case of the career unit under discussion here, it would probably make little sense to test students on their knowledge of worker trait groups (Objective 1) or data, people, and things (Objective 2) as these are terms to which students would have had little or no exposure prior to the instructional unit on careers. On the other hand, students would no doubt have interests in jobs (Objective 5) and knowledge of their basic skill competencies (Objective 6) prior to beginning the unit; hence, the before/after comparison is a reasonable approach in relation to these latter objectives.

In relation to the second referent—stating the subject matter to which the learner behavior is directed—it is important to note that this will be addressed to varying degrees depending on the level of specificity desired by the teacher and supervisor. In the above list of objective statements, observe that the subject matter is at least mentioned in each case; however, the level of specificity varies across the several statements. For example, the subject matter in Objective 1 (understanding of worker trait groups as presented in the text) seems more specific than the subject matter in Objective 2 (identifying the relative importance of data, people, and things in a variety of jobs). The subject matter or topic to which this second statement is addressed could, of course, be made considerably more specific if desired, for example:

- Students will correctly identify the relative importance of data (words and numbers), people, and things (tools and machines) in a variety of jobs.
- Students will correctly identify the complexity of the use of data (words and numbers), people, and things (tools and machines) in a variety of jobs.

In the first example, we observe that the meaning of data, people, and things is made more specific than in the original statement. The second provides added clarification about the meaning of "identify the relative importance of." Based on this second statement, we know that the relative importance is dependent mainly on the complexity rather than the amount of involvement. Thus, a typical grocery store manager will rank higher in terms of involvement with people than the checkout clerk even though the latter probably spends more time in actual contact with people. Without this clarifying statement, the correct identification of involvement with people might very well have gone the other way.

Up to this point, the topic or subject matter of the objective statement has been easy to identify. When talking about skills such as swimming, skiing, and sawing, the topic and the action verb can often be viewed as the same thing. In the statement "The student will correctly saw the materials," the emphasis, if it is truly an objective statement, is on the demonstration of proper sawing techniques and this demonstrated behavior is, therefore, the topic or subject of the objective statement. With this in mind, the objective statement might be presented as "The student will properly complete the sawing of the materials." Note that the topic or subject matter of sawing is more clearly identified as such. It is also stated in a way that permits the attachment of criteria for acceptable performance.

The third reference to conditions under which the activity is to be shown has been a subject of considerable debate in educational circles over the past few years. Many writers on instructional or behavioral objectives have argued that no objective is clear unless it includes both the conditions under which the behavior is to be demonstrated and a rather specific standard or criterion of acceptable performance. This requirement seems fairly easy to satisfy when referring to such well-defined skill areas as reading, arithmetic, and spelling. As the behavior becomes more complex, the specification of conditions and standards of acceptable performance is much more difficult. Teachers have quite properly questioned the detailed level of specification suggested by some writers. How does one express criteria of acceptable performance for such areas as "accepting persons of other ethnic groups" or "appreciating music of a particular time period"? Many would argue that such behaviors are much too attitudinal to be measured in precise operational or behavioral terms.

Even in skill areas like mathematics we sometimes utilize rather specific language that is not all that meaningful in describing the desired behavior. Two examples of this tendency to overspecify will suffice:

- The student will demonstrate competence in adding and subtracting fractions by correctly solving nine out of ten problems presented on a written test.
- The student will graph the linear equation with 90 percent accuracy.

In both cases, the writer has embellished the objective statement with criteria of acceptance; however, the criteria, without some additional explanation, are not at all helpful and may even be deceptively precise to those not trained in mathematics. In the first case, the significance of the criteria as stated must necessarily depend on information that is missing from the statement, namely, the degree of difficulty of the fractions to be added and subtracted. Successfully adding nine of ten fractions like $1/2 + 1/4 = 3/4$ is not nearly as significant an accomplishment as the same success rate with fractions like $5/3 + 7/8 = 2\ 13/24$. The 90 percent success rate is therefore virtually meaningless without some specific reference to the level of difficulty of the problems.

Even more serious difficulties are encountered in the second case, where we are to decide whether a student has demonstrated 90 percent accuracy in graphing a linear equation. What does this 90 percent accuracy represent and how would we go about measuring it? No mathematics teacher with whom I have spoken has been able to give a satisfactory answer to this question and most confess that it would be exceedingly difficult to get agreement on any such measure. While there may be certain key components to the graphing process (e.g., the point where the graph cuts the *y* axis, the slope of the line, or the exact point where it intersects with some other function), there is not much point in pretending that such graphing can be so precise as to judge it as being more or less than 90 percent correct.

In relation to tendency to attach false precision to statements of instructional objectives, a recent school policy adopted in Pearland, Texas, is of interest. The new policy asks teachers to indicate whether students have achieved 80 percent mastery of a list of eighty skills. One of the skills is appreciation of poetry. A fifth-grade teacher in the district commented, "I think I can tell who in my class understands poetry but I frankly haven't figured out how to handle the 80 percent part" (*NOW*, p. 4). This teacher's frustration is well-founded. When we have trouble attaching operational meaning to 80–90 percent accuracy in skill areas like mathematics, we can expect even greater problems in such areas as "appreciation of poetry" or "acceptance of students from other cultures or races." It is my contention that some of those involved in the behavioral objectives and competency movements have gone overboard in their efforts to quantify levels of acceptable performance, and in doing so have greatly oversimplified the schooling process. McAshan and others have written on this oversimplification and observe that teachers can be expected to oppose excessive specificity in writing objectives, particularly when such specificity results in unreal, impractical, or trivial objectives.[8]

Most recently, this teacher opposition has surfaced in relation to certain requirements of P.L. 94–142, the Education for All Handicapped Children Act. Some districts, in attempting to implement the Individualized Educational Program (IEP) requirements of P.L. 94–142, have pushed for a level of specificity that is almost certain to bring strong opposition from teacher groups.[9] Recognizing the likelihood of such opposition, it is important that this third referent of specifying conditions and criteria for acceptable performance be handled with considerable caution and with full consideration of the instructional context. The conditions and criteria should be specific enough to fit the situation but not so specific that the topical matter of the objective is distorted. This decision as to the proper level of specification is a complex judgment and is best made by those most familiar with the topic to be learned and the instructional setting.

The reasons for using instructional objectives of the type examined here are many. D. Cecil Clark describes seven advantages to their use:

1. The teacher will have a method by which to measure, at least partially, important objectives not measured in the past.
2. The teacher and student will have greater visible evidence that the objectives have been achieved.
3. The student will experience considerably more freedom in achieving an objective.
4. The student will feel greater focus and direction on what is important, on what to study for, and on what he will be evaluated.
5. In the long run, both the teacher and student will save energy.
6. The student will participate more in his own instruction.
7. The teacher will feel greater security with this more direct evidence of "teaching effectiveness." (Clark, p. 27)

Clark cautions that most of these advantages have not as yet been proven in a careful evaluative sense. Most are defended on the basis of teacher opinion and there currently exists little or no evidence that students attending classes that use product-type instructional objectives learn more than those attending classes not using them. Much more careful research is needed before we can accept as true all seven of the advantages listed above.

SUMMARY

This second chapter dealt with the procedures used in translating goal statements into action programs at the school-building level. The product of this activity is a plan of the type presented in Figure 2–2. Such a written consensus of action-program statements, including

[8]A brief summary of teacher resistance to overspecificity in objective writing is found in McAshan, *Writing Behavioral Objectives*, pp. 6–7. Also, an interesting critique of the military's early emphasis on the 90–90 proficiency level (90 percent of learners to obtain 90 percent proficiency) is found in W. James Popham, *The Uses of Instructional Objectives* (1973), pp. 6–7.

[9]One of the components of the IEP, as required under P.L. 94–142, is a statement of annual goals, including short-term instructional objectives. The development and monitoring of these short-term instructional objectives, even when stated in fairly general terms, can be very time-consuming. When considerable specificity is required, the IEP process is just that much more likely to be viewed by teachers as an unrealistic expectation.

the designation of persons responsible for detailed planning, becomes the basis for implementation of program-development work at both building and classroom levels.

Little implementation of this written consensus statement will be achieved unless the goals and action-program statements have an eventual impact on the staff goal-setting process. This is accomplished through teacher preparation of reasonably specific statements of intent. Such statements, if carefully prepared, have the potential for giving direction to both the teaching act and the evaluation of that teaching. When the teacher and the supervisor can agree on instructional objectives early in the evaluation cycle, both parties are freed for the challenging tasks of collecting information related to those objectives and of searching for modes of instruction that maximize objective attainment.

For the majority of teachers who are clearly performing above the probationary level, it is a willingness to become involved in this search for the best methods of objective accomplishment, rather than the objective accomplishment itself, that forms the real focus of evaluation. This striving activity on the part of staff members at all levels of the organization cannot help but lead to improved instructional programs for students.

QUESTIONS AND PROBLEMS ON CHAPTER 2

1. In discussing procedures for developing action programs, mention was made of the fact that certain goal statements have conflicting elements when translated into more specific terms.
   a. Demonstrate this problem by writing at least two specific and at least partially conflicting product or outcome statements relating to each of the following general goals:
      - Develop loyalty to American democratic ideals
      - Develop ability to use leisure time constructively
      - Establish sound personal health habits
      - Become knowledgeable about life and living
      - Make wise use of natural resources
   b. Assume that a teacher has presented any one of the above as a general goal for the coming school year. As the supervisor of this teacher, outline key points you would want to include in a conversation aimed at gaining clarification of this particular goal.

2. Listed below are three pairs of action-program statements. The second in each pair is an edited version of the first. For each pair, indicate the nature of the editing and why this editing is likely to be important to any ranking of the action-program statements. (The reader may want to review the action-program statements in Figures 2–3 and 2–4 as background for this response.)
   a-1. A special unit on computers will be added to the junior high school curriculum.
   a-2. A special unit on computers will be developed by the mathematics and science department chairs over the summer months and will be tried out in five eighth-grade science classes during the next school year.
   b-1. Human relations will be emphasized in all elementary classrooms next year.
   b-2. All elementary teachers will attend one of the district-sponsored human relations workshops next year and will be encouraged to apply selected techniques from the workshop in their own classrooms.
   c-1. Instruction in family budgeting will be added to the junior high program.

c-2. Beginning in the 19X5–19X6 school year, a unit of family budgeting will be added to the grade-nine social studies curriculum. This unit will be developed by a team of social studies teachers from all junior high schools of the district and will include practice in group decision making.

3. The following action statements are lacking in specificity. In most cases, the statements need greater clarification as to grade-level placement and/or focus of responsibility for goal accomplishment. In others, the statements can be sharpened. Place yourself in the position of a school administrator and, following the general format of Figure 2–2, rewrite the statements in a manner that would be acceptable. You may want to present your response in the context of a specific school district.

Goal Priority 1: The students will understand scientific truths of the universe and man's relation to them.

1.1 The science curriculum units will be updated.
1.2 Teacher in-service activities will be provided in science concepts.
1.3 Additional books on science will be purchased for all school libraries.
1.4 Science laboratory facilities will be added at the junior high school.

Goal Priority 2: The students will demonstrate competence in choosing a career.

2.1 Career resource rooms will be added in selected schools.
2.2 All students will take Holland's Self-directed Search (1970) as part of a career unit.
2.3 A required course in career selection will be added to the school curriculum.

4. Discuss the problems that are likely to be experienced by an elementary school staff in attempting to set priorities among the following action-program statements and suggest how the statements might be revised to minimize these problems.

Goal Priority 1: Students will increase their skills in writing.

1.1 Writing kits will be ordered from the state department of education.
1.2 Teachers will spend more time on writing instruction.
1.3 Parents of elementary school students will be encouraged to work with the students on writing.
1.4 The teachers will develop a diagnostic writing program to be used by teachers throughout the school.

Goal Priority 2: Students will respect the worth of each individual.

2.1 Students will treat one another as equals.
2.2 Students at the junior high school level will study a variety of persons who have contributed to our welfare as a nation and will show respect for the contribution made by each.
2.3 Students will be forced in a classroom exercise to identify positive traits for each of their classmates.

Goal Priority 3: Students will demonstrate good health practices.

3.1 Several health films will be shown in the primary grades.
3.2 The sixth-grade classes will develop a program on health to be presented to the rest of the school.
3.3 A physical fitness program will be developed for all students, complete with expected proficiencies for grade level.
3.4 Students will brush their teeth regularly.
3.5 Students will take a field trip to the County Health Clinic.

5. For some school setting with which you are familiar, describe a procedure you might use, as the school principal, to gain consensus on a set of action programs of the type presented in Questions 3 and 4. Be sure to identify the groups to be working on each step of the process.
6. A number of possible action-program statements are listed below:
   (1) Instruction in family budgeting will be added to the social studies program in grades 4–6.
   (2) Teachers at all grade levels will set up bulletin boards for the purpose of displaying student work and teachers will see that the best pieces of work for each student are displayed on these bulletin boards.
   (3) Greater emphasis will be placed on physical fitness at all grade levels and each teacher will develop grade-level expectations for basic exercise routines.
   (4) Each staff member will identify parents who do not attend the regular open house and will seek alternative methods of communicating with the families so identified.
   a. Write two different teacher goals for each of the above statements. Write these goals in a manner acceptable to you as a principal, if the goals were written by a sixth-grade teacher. These goals are to be used as a basis for staff evaluation during a single school year.
   b. For each of the goal statements, indicate the type of measurement you might propose to assess goal attainment.
7. Assume that you are interested in developing test measures to be used in relation to the family budgeting unit referred to in Question 6–Statement 1 above. As a guide to the test developer, it would be useful for the teacher and/or administrator to specify product-type objectives that indicate student behaviors to be demonstrated as a result of participating in the unit. With this intent, write three such outcome statements and classify each with respect to the typology identified in Figure 1–2.
8. Assume that you are a district curriculum director.
   a. Write two product-type goal statements for each of the following action-program statements:
      (1) Each school in the district will have a curriculum advisory committee consisting of community representatives and staff members. Community representatives are to be selected by the elected officers of the Parent-Teacher Association and the staff members are elected by the faculty. At least one community representative must be a person having no children attending school.
      (2) A unit in punctuation will be added to all tenth-grade English classes throughout the district.
      (3) A special committee of parents, staff, and students will review current practices regarding the sale of food within the school district and make recommendations for improvement of the present programs.
      (4) A special program for employer-based career education experiences will be developed cooperatively by the counseling and business education departments.
   b. These goal statements are to be shared with an immediate supervisor and will be the basis for the year's evaluation. For each of the goal statements, indicate the type of measurement you might propose.
9. In the section of the text on staff goal setting and evaluation, it is suggested that

at least four types of objectives be considered in developing a given staff member's program for professional development in any given evaluation cycle. These four categories were carry-over objectives, general role expectations, action-program statements, and general professional growth.

a. From the administration's perspective, what is the rationale for considering all four types of objective statements?
b. Are there other categories of objective statements that might be useful as a part of the staff evaluation process?
c. Why would an employee on probationary status probably be asked to concentrate on the first two categories only?

PART II

IMPLEMENTATION OF GOAL PRIORITIES

OVERVIEW

In Part I, a particular set of procedures for translating goal priorities into action programs at the school and classroom levels was presented. Special attention was given to the way in which this translation process relates to the ongoing staff development and evaluation programs. Little was said about the planning and evaluation strategies needed to guide this translation process or the day-to-day scheduling processes required to assure timely completion of various tasks. Several of these implementation techniques are examined in this second part of the book. Sample applications of various planning and evaluation techniques are presented in the next four chapters of the text and practice exercises and problems are included at the conclusion of each chapter.

Chapter 3 deals with planning and scheduling strategies (including network scheduling and Gantt charting) and shows how these strategies can be helpful in implementing long-term projects at the school level. Chapters 4 and 5 deal with different aspects of time allocation and scheduling. Chapter 4 will be especially important for those preparing for administration at the secondary school level, though some scheduling applications at the elementary level are also included. This chapter addresses both the master-schedule and student-assignment components of the scheduling task. In Chapter 5, potential time management problems for the school administrator are discussed and specific guidelines for improving time utilization are presented.

Chapter 6 presents an overview of evaluation issues to be considered in guiding the development and implementation of action programs in schools. Obviously, the detailed procedures to be used in developing and implementing comprehensive evaluation plans cannot be included in this brief treatment; the intent here is rather to emphasize the importance of various types of evaluation in guiding decision making in school organizations.

The importance of these several planning and evaluation techniques must not be underestimated as these are the things that are almost always noted in a given administrator's behavior. They are skills that give confidence to fellow workers and they are critical in assuring the accomplishment of organizational goals and related action programs. These are at least some of the skills needed in accomplishing Steps III and IV of the goal implementation model of Figure 1–4; without them, there is little chance of moving the organization toward goal attainment or of maintaining that sense of direction and momentum so important in the learning environment. The planning and scheduling concepts included here are essential in communicating direction within any organization and in responding appropriately to the many pressures that face those persons charged with administering today's public and private schools.

CHAPTER 3
NETWORK PLANNING OF PROJECTS

At least some of the action programs identified through the goal-selection activities described in Part I of this text will entail projects that involve a careful sequencing of activities over a considerable period of time. Examples include such projects as design and implementation of a new program for gifted students, implementation of a follow-up procedure for high school graduates, and a program for orienting new students to the school. In cases such as these, there is a need to sequence many interrelated tasks and to make certain that the final project is completed at a particular time.

This same type of scheduling problem is faced in the private sector where business leaders, engineers, and scientists are often expected to meet deadlines on projects that require close sequencing and coordination. One of the early scheduling techniques used in the private sector was Gantt Charting as developed by Henry Lawrence Gantt in the late 1800s. This technique involves placing the tasks for a given project on a chart in such a way

Figure 3–1 Gantt Chart for School-Funding Issue

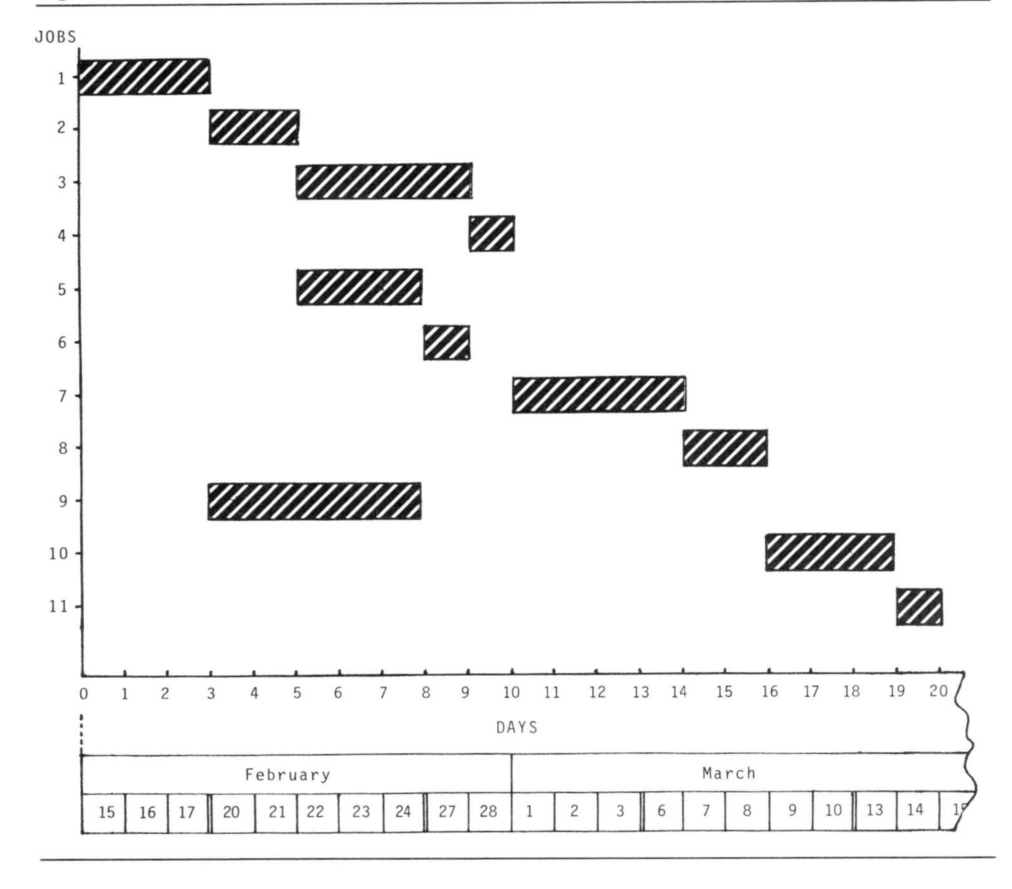

that the scheduled time for completion can be identified quickly by the reader. Figure 3–1 illustrates this charting approach in relation to the vote on a school-funding issue. Note that the total project or task is scheduled to take twenty days and consists of eleven different jobs or activities. These activities along with their respective times for completion are identified in Figure 3–2.

A Gantt schedule of this type can be extremely helpful both for the school principal and for the many staff members and parents who become involved in the project. Such a chart can build confidence among those involved in the project, whether it is a vote on school funding, planning for a new school, production of a new student handbook, or any other project involving the coordination of several people over an extended time period. The very act of establishing this kind of a schedule forces those managing the project to think through the several jobs involved and the interrelationships between these jobs. Such careful thought in the initial stages can be most helpful in assuring timely completion of the project.

One limitation of the Gantt chart is the absence of any definite sequencing requirements that might be associated with the several jobs. While such sequencing may indeed have been considered in development of the Gantt chart in Figure 3–1, we have no guarantee of this just by looking at the chart. We do not know, for example, how long Job 9 (prepare and publish materials for distribution) can be delayed without extending the project completion time of twenty days. Neither do we know from looking at the chart whether Job 9 could be

Figure 3–2 Sequencing Relationships for School-Funding Issue

Activity Code	*Activity*	*Days Required*	*Immediate Predecessors*
1	Select Chairperson for Funding Program	3	—
2	Identify Suitable Block Groups Within Attendance Area	2	1
3	Select Block Captains for Each Block Group	4	2
4	Orient Block Captains	1	3
5	Develop Block Maps	3	2
6	Make Copies of Block Maps	1	5
7	Block Captains Recruit Distributors	4	4
8	Block Captains Hold Meetings to Give Maps to Distributors and to Explain the Funding Issue	2	6,7
9	Prepare and Publish Materials for Distribution	5	1
10	Deliver Materials to Homes	3*	8,9
11	Vote on Funding Issue	1	10

*The actual delivery is to take only one day but since it is to be completed two full days prior to the voting day, the time is listed here as three days.

started prior to Day 3, its scheduled starting point in Figure 3–1. Both of these questions can be answered only when we consider the type of information presented in Figure 3–2. Note here that certain sequencing requirements are indicated. Observe that Job 9 cannot start until Job 1 is completed; it has apparently been scheduled in Figure 3–1 at its earliest possible starting time. Since, according to Figures 3–1 and 3–2, Job 9 is a predecessor only to Job 10 and Job 10 is scheduled to start on Day 16, we note that Job 9 could start as late as Day 11 (the latest starting time to assure completion by Day 16) without delaying the total project. Hence, the start for Job 9 could be delayed eight days (from Day 3 to Day 11) beyond that shown in Figure 3–1.

These kinds of sequencing relationships can best be handled using network techniques. This text considers both the Critical Path Method (CPM) and the Program Evaluation and Review Technique (PERT), both of which were developed in the late 1950s and have been applied to numerous scheduling tasks in both private and governmental agencies. The CPM approach to network planning grew out of an effort by the DuPont Company to control maintenance of its several chemical plants. This work was accomplished in concert with the Univac Division of Remington Rand Corporation (now Sperry Rand Corporation). PERT was developed in 1957 as a means of controlling the U.S. Navy's Polaris Project, an extremely large endeavor involving approximately three thousand separate contracting units. It was developed within the Navy Office of Special Projects and with the assistance of the Booz-Allen and Hamilton Company and the Missile Systems Division of Lockheed Aircraft Company. Both CPM and PERT are most useful in large, one-time projects involving sequential tasks whose duration can be reasonably predicted. In succeeding sections, we look more specifically at the two approaches and the way in which they might be used in a school setting.

NETWORK DESIGN IN PERT AND CPM

Both PERT and CPM involve the sequencing of activities. One key difference in the two approaches (but one that proves to be of little functional importance) is the network structure utilized in sequencing the activities. This difference is best seen by looking at a

Figure 3–3 Sequencing Relationships for School-Funding Issue (shortened version)

Activity Code	*Activity*	*Days Required*	*Immediate Predecessors*
1	Select Chairperson for Funding Program	3	—
2	Identify Suitable Block Groups Within Attendance Area	2	1
3	Select Block Captains and Complete All Planning for Distribution of Materials	11	2
4	Prepare and Publish Materials for Distribution	5	1
5	Deliver Materials to Homes and Vote on Funding Issue	4*	3,4

*The actual delivery of materials and the final vote will take one day each but since two full days are to be scheduled between these two subactivities, the total time is listed here as four days.

simplified version of the school-funding project defined in Figures 3–1 and 3–2. Instead of the eleven tasks or activities, this project can be viewed as consisting of only the five steps identified in Figure 3–3.

With the nodes as activities and the arrows connecting the activities, this project can be described in the CPM network of Figure 3–4. Notice that the total project will take the same twenty days as indicated in Figure 3–1 for the more detailed breakdown. This twenty days represents the longer of the paths through the network and this path (including Jobs 1–2–3–5–T where T represents the terminal point) is known as the critical path for the project. This path is called critical simply because a delay in the start of any job or activity on this path would delay the scheduled overall project completion time of twenty days. Of all the jobs or activities in Figure 3–4, only Job 4 can be delayed without delaying completion of the entire project. More specifically, the start of Job 4 can be delayed as much as eight days beyond its earliest start without delaying the total project. For this reason, Job 4 is described as having eight days of slack time.

Before proceeding with a closer analysis of slack time, let us look at the contrasting PERT network in Figure 3–5 for the same project of five jobs. In this network, the nodes represent the beginning and completion points for the jobs or activities with the activities themselves designated by arrows. Here again, the critical path consists of Jobs 1–2–3–5 and the total time for project completion is twenty days. Note that exactly the same set of sequential task relationships has been described by the two different approaches. The selection of network approaches historically may have depended on the particular analysis

Figure 3–4 CPM Network for School-Funding Issue (shortened version)

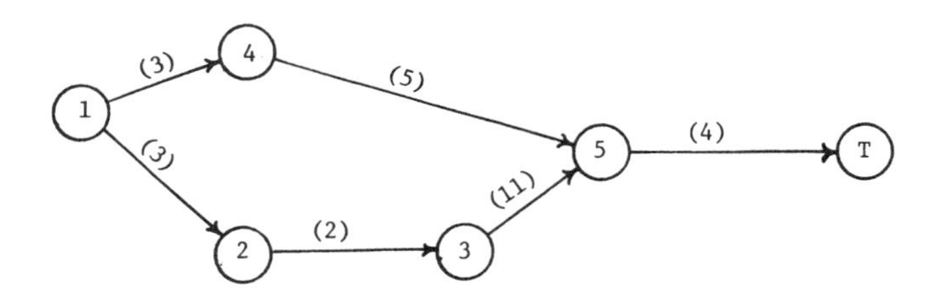

Numbers in parentheses represent the estimated time required to complete the respective activities or jobs.

Figure 3–5 PERT Network for School-Funding Issue (shortened version)

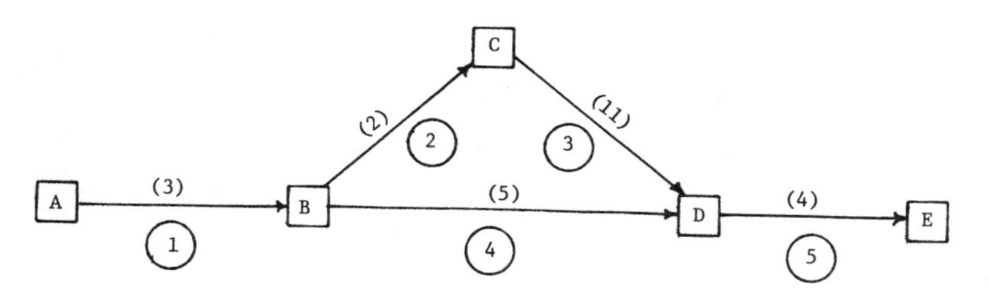

Numbers in parentheses represent the estimated time required to complete the respective activities or jobs.

desired by the user; however, since both network approaches yield exactly the same results, the selection of the network approach for this particular example is strictly a matter of user preference. Certain historical reasons for using one or the other of the network methods will be discussed later in this chapter; suffice it here to mention that, for most of today's applications in education, either method of networking is quite adequate.

OPTIONS AVAILABLE IN PROJECT SCHEDULING

Up to this point, the sequencing of tasks into a network design has been our focus. The real analytic power to be gained through use of network planning stems not from the mere sequencing of tasks but from the examination of alternative starting times for activities and the interaction of these alternatives with resource requirements of the project. This is best introduced by reviewing basic steps to the two versions of our school-funding issue.

Identification and Sequencing of Activities

This is the critical first step to any network planning activity. Without such identification by the user, no analysis of options can be considered. One cannot even be sure that the project conforms to a network design where each and every activity has at least one immediate predecessor.

From the examples given in Figures 3–2 and 3–3, we observe that the user has considerable latitude in deciding on the specific tasks identified in the project. The longer version of the funding issue (Figure 3–2) involved eleven distinct tasks whereas the shorter version (Figure 3–3) utilized only five separate tasks or activities. While the longer version would probably be more useful to the school administrator (primarily because it does a better job of separating activities to be completed by different combinations of resources), there is no set specificity level required for use of network planning. The potential user groups are in the best position to identify tasks or activities and they could even be defined on a more specific level than that presented in the longer version of Figure 3–2. As just one example, it might be useful to break down Job 9 (Prepare and Publish Materials for Distribution) into subtasks, particularly if the preparation and publication subtasks are to be completed sequentially and by different resource configurations.

The sequencing of tasks is generally a part of the identification process and is made evident in network designs of the type presented in Figures 3–4 and 3–5. If the project does not involve precedence relationships of the type described in these networks but is rather a priority list or conditional sequence of some type, the user will have to abandon the network application in favor of other approaches.[1]

Estimation of Time Required to Complete Each Activity

Very little analysis of schedule options can be considered without knowing with some degree of certainty the time required to complete tasks. Making such estimates requires persons who are reasonably familiar with the techniques and methods to be employed in accomplishing the several activities. In the examples of Figure 3–3, someone had to estimate that it would take exactly two days to accomplish Job 2 (Identify Suitable Block Groups Within Attendance Area). This activity may very well involve the study of area maps, a drive through the designated area, and perhaps even a visit to the city planning office; but, whatever the combination of subactivities involved, it is likely that the person most knowledgeable about the technology of the situation will be in a position to make the best estimate of probable completion times.

In many cases, it will probably be useful to consider options with respect to subactivity times. Consideration of multiple options has been enhanced in recent years by use of high-speed computers. Later in this chapter, a specific probabilistic model for determining the expected completion time based on optimistic, pessimistic, and most-probable conditions is presented. The important point here is that network planning does rely on some reasonable estimate of time required for the several tasks of the network.

Examination of Options with Respect to Starting and Ending Times for Each Activity

Having time estimates, or at least optimal time estimates, the planner is now ready to utilize these estimates to arrive at reasonable starting and ending times for activities. It is in this area that one begins to realize the potential advantages of network planning. Understanding the impact of delaying the start of certain activities or of applying additional resources to completion of a particular activity is very much a part of network planning.

This third step is best explained by returning to the shortened version of the funding issue. Using the network of Figure 3–4, earliest starting (ES) times for each of the activities are computed. This is simply a matter of moving from left to right through the network and indicating the time beyond the zero starting point that each job or activity can be initiated. These times for our shortened version of the funding issue are presented in Figure 3–6. Notice that the ES = 20 associated with the terminal point, T, represents the minimal completion time for the entire project.

Using this earliest completion time (ES = 20) and working backward through the network, we are able to establish latest starting (LS) times for each of the activities. Observe in Figure 3–7 that the ES and LS times coincide in all cases except Job 4. This means that a delay in the start of any job except 4 will result in a delay of the total project. In the case of Job 4, the difference of eight days between its ES and LS times indicates a slack time of eight days for that job. The job could be started at any point between Day 3 and Day 11 (assuming a beginning point of zero) without delaying the entire project beyond Day 20.

Applying this same process to the longer version of the school funding project as defined in Figure 3–2, we arrive at the network and tabular presentations of Figures 3–8 and 3–9.

[1]For those interested in descriptions of these other types of planning problems, consult Ronald L. Graham, "The Combinatorial Mathematics of Scheduling," *Scientific American* 238 (March 1978): 124–132.

Figure 3–6 CPM Network Showing Earliest Start Times for School-Funding Issue (shortened version)

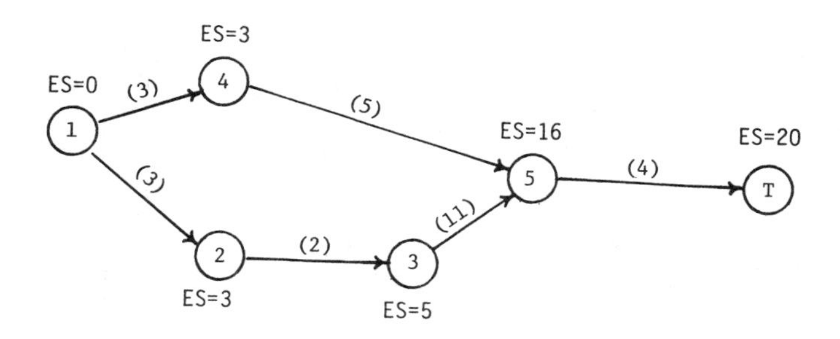

This is the CPM network for tasks identified in Figure 3-3 and is simply the network of Figure 3-4 with the addition of earliest start times. Numbers in parentheses represent the estimated time required to complete the respective activities or jobs.

Figure 3–7 CPM Network Showing Earliest and Latest Starting Times for School-Funding Issue (shortened version)

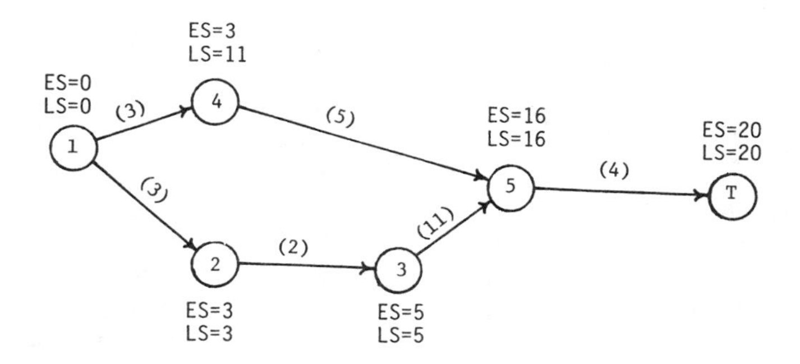

This is the same network as in Figure 3-6 with the addition of latest starting (LS) times for each activity or job.

Figure 3–8 CPM Network for School-Funding Issue (longer version)

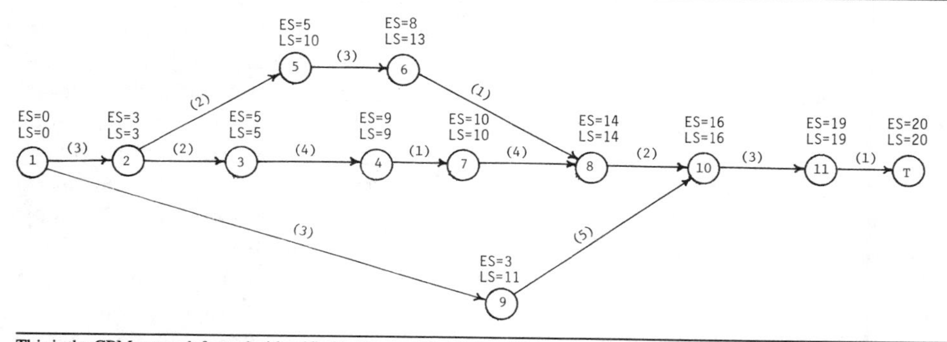

This is the CPM network for tasks identified in Figure 3-2 with the addition of earliest and latest start times. Numbers in parentheses represent estimated time required to complete the respective activities or jobs.

Figure 3–9 Analysis of Slack Time for School-Funding Issue (longer version)

Job or Activity	*Earliest Start*	*Latest Start*	*Slack Time**
1	0	0	0
2	3	3	0
3	5	5	0
4	9	9	0
5	5	10	5
6	8	13	5
7	10	10	0
8	14	14	0
9	3	11	8
10	16	16	0
11	19	19	0

*Slack time as presented here is simply the difference between the earliest and latest times for the respective jobs.

With this longer and more useful version of the funding issue we see that three jobs—5, 6, and 9—have slack time with all other jobs having zero slack and therefore being on the critical path for the project. Slack time associated with Job 5, if used, causes a delay in the starting time for Job 6. On the other hand, all slack time for Jobs 6 and 9 can be used without delaying any other jobs in the network. This latter type of slack time is known as free slack in the sense that it does not affect any other jobs. Jobs 6 and 9 are said to have five and eight days respectively of free slack whereas Job 5 has five days of slack, none of which is free slack.

Monitoring and Adjusting Project Schedule

Once the sequencing of activities and the earliest and the latest starting times have been established, it is important to establish some kind of system for monitoring progress. The best of schedules is of little value unless those in charge of the project take it seriously. This serious attention and concern by those directing the work is an absolute prerequisite of effective monitoring of the project. For those activities having slack time, it is important to decide on the most appropriate start and finish times. This is usually dependent on the availability and cost of resources needed to accomplish the task.

As the monitoring progresses, it is necessary to check on the timely completion of activities located on the critical path. Any delays of tasks on the critical path will involve either a delay in the total project completion date or an equivalent reduction in the time required for one or more of the remaining critical tasks.

In the example of the school-funding issue, monitoring is essentially the task of seeing that all tasks are started and completed according to the Gantt Chart of Figure 3–1. Those activities or jobs having slack time must be identified and a definite schedule must be established for each. For example, we must decide for Job 5 whether it should start at the beginning of the fifth day (ES for Job 5), at the beginning of the tenth day (LS for Job 5), or at some point between the two. Essentially, we are referring to Figure 3–1 and are asking how far to the right to shift the bar representing Job 5. The earlier computation of five days slack time for Job 5 of course tells us the outer limit of that shift to the right. With more complicated networks, the job of monitoring is obviously more demanding. This is particularly true when large numbers of individual tasks have slack time. The advent of computers permits the planner to assess options and to make adjustments in a much more efficient manner than was previously possible.

Before we proceed to examine some additional differences between PERT and CPM and to comment briefly on more detailed analyses made possible by the use of the two approaches to network planning, it is useful to remind the reader that network planning is intended to assist the administrator in management and should not be viewed as an exacting set of procedures always to be used in a prescribed manner. As Van Dusseldorp and his associates have cautioned recently,[2]

> PERT-CPM is a flexible tool. The way in which it is used will depend on the needs and methods of the user. Just as different users will come up with different activities, networks, and time estimates for a given project, different users will use PERT-CPM in different ways. The only correct way to use PERT-CPM is the way it best suits the needs and methods of the user. (p. 132)

The presentation in succeeding sections of this chapter will provide additional insight into the ways in which network planning can be used by the skilled administrator and/or planner.

PROBABILISTIC NETWORK METHODS AND PERT

PERT, as mentioned earlier, was developed in connection with the Polaris Project of the U.S. Navy. Because of the complexity of this project and the frequent lack of control over the accomplishment of certain jobs, it was possible to develop only most-probable times for many of the tasks. The development of most-probable times utilized an approximation to the so-called Beta distribution. This distribution has certain useful properties and its application to PERT requires that the user establish three time estimates for each task in the project:

- The *optimistic time,* which is the shortest possible time in which the activity may be accomplished if all goes well (estimate based on the assumption that the activity would have no more than one chance in 100 of being completed in less than this time)
- The *pessimistic time,* which is the longest time that any activity should take under adverse conditions but barring acts of nature (estimate based on the assumption that the activity would have no more than one chance in 100 of being completed in a time more than the time estimate in question)
- The *most-likely time,* which is the modal value of the distribution of the possible time estimates

These three time estimates are used to compute a single time estimate, t_e, which is both the single best guess as to the time for the activity in question and the best estimate of the mean of the relevant Beta distribution. If A, B, and M are our estimates of optimistic, pessimistic, and modal times for a given activity, the following formulas are then used as estimates of the mean and variance for the Beta distribution:

$$t_e = \frac{A + 4M + B}{6} \quad \text{and} \quad S^2 = \left(\frac{B - A}{6}\right)^2$$

[2]Ralph A. Van Dusseldorp, Duane E. Richardson, and Walter J. Foley, *Educational Decision Making Through Operations Research* (Boston: Allyn & Bacon, 1971). This book contains several PERT applications, most of which refer to school system rather than school-building problems.

Certain computer programs designed for use with network planning permit the user to submit the three time estimates described above. Slack time analysis, earliest and latest start times, and critical paths are then all based on the t_e values, which are usually referred to as the expected times for the various jobs.

As an illustration of the use of these optimistic, pessimistic, and modal time estimates in a specific PERT application, return to the short version of the funding issue shown in Figure 3–5 but substitute the time estimates as indicated below:

	Time Estimates (in days)		
Activity	*Optimistic*	*Pessimistic*	*Most Likely*
1	1	5	3
2	1	4	1.5
3	3	23	10
4	2	8	5
5	2	10	3

No longer is a definite assignment of time to each task made but the time for each task is viewed as a variable with each time estimate—optimistic, pessimistic, and most likely—having a certain probability of occurence. Obviously, of the three estimates, the greatest probability should be assigned to the most-likely category. The Beta distribution approximation formula for t_e does give greatest weight to this most-likely estimate and is therefore useful in the network analysis.

Applying the previously stated formula to Activity 1, we find the best estimate to be

$$t_e = \frac{A + 4M + B}{6} = \frac{1 + 4(3) + 5}{6} = 3$$

This same formula, along with the related formula for variance, applied to other activities in the project yields results as shown in Figure 3–10.

Figure 3–10 PERT Network Showing Estimated Times and Variances for Each Activity

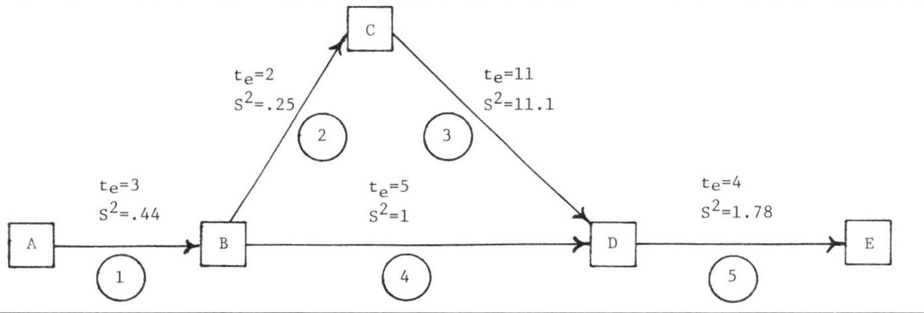

This is the same network format as that used in Figure 3–5; however, the time (t_e) and variance (S^2) estimates are based on the formulas:

$$t_e = \frac{A + 4M + B}{6}$$

$$S^2 = \left(\frac{B - A}{6}\right)^2$$

While the total project time remains twenty days as it was in Figure 3–5, the gain is a set of task variance estimates that can be used to make probability statements about finishing individual jobs and/or the total project within a specified number of days. For example, notice that the actual time required for Activity 2 in Figure 3–10 will fall within one-half day of the estimated time of two days about two-thirds of the time. This is so because the standard deviation is the square root of the computed variance of .25 and two-thirds of the cases fall within a single standard deviation of the mean. Readers interested in this type of analysis are referred to more detailed presentations on the subject of PERT.[3] In concluding this summary, it must be stressed that these multiple time estimates required by the original PERT, that is, the optimistic, pessimistic, and most-likely estimates, may not be appropriate to some projects. In some cases, it is no easier to come up with three time estimates than it is to arrive at a single best estimate of task duration. This underscores the principle that no network planning technique can be better than the time estimates supplied by the user.

OTHER ASPECTS OF NETWORK PLANNING

Just as users of PERT typically were involved with multiple time estimates and statements regarding the probability of completing jobs by certain times, those using CPM tended to utilize single estimates of completion time and focused rather on resource allocation and methods of reducing project time by altering resources. Early users of CPM recognized that there were basically three ways of shortening a given project. First, one could replan the project, using a different method for one or more activities. For example, in relation to the tasks identified for the longer version of the school-funding issue (as listed in Figure 3–2), we could find an alternative method of selecting block captains (Activity 3). Using the telephone to recruit the block captains rather than making personal visits in the home may reduce the activity from four days to a single day, thereby reducing the critical path of the network in Figure 3–8 by three days. A second way to shorten projects involves the resequencing of tasks so that operations previously done in sequence are now done in parallel. Using the same example of funding issue (as sequenced in Figure 3–8), we could perhaps "select block captains for each block group" (Activity 3) at the same time we "identify suitable block groups within the attendance area" (Activity 2). We observe in Figure 3–11 that such a change can potentially reduce the time for project completion from the original twenty days to eighteen days. Other changes in network design could achieve even greater savings in overall project time; however, it is often not possible to place operations in parallel and such a procedure is also accompanied by certain risks. In the example cited, selecting block captains (Activity 3) prior to or during the establishment of boundaries for the block groups (Activity 2) may mean that certain block captains will live outside the areas serviced. It may be harder to recruit some of the block captains without a promise of serving in the vicinity of their own residence. A third approach to shortening activity and project time is the application of additional resources such as personnel or equipment. We could, for example, shorten the development of block maps (Activity 5 in Figure 3–11) by simply assigning three persons instead of one to the task. Similarly, the selection of block captains (Activity 3 in Figure 3–11) could be reduced from its current allotment of four days if additional persons were assigned to help with the task. Since this

[3]More detailed presentations on PERT time estimates are found in Albert Battersby, *Network Analysis for Planning and Scheduling* (1970), pp. 261–269; and Joseph Horowitz, *Critical Path Scheduling* (1967), pp. 150–158.

Figure 3–11 Revised CPM Network for School-Funding Issue (longer version)

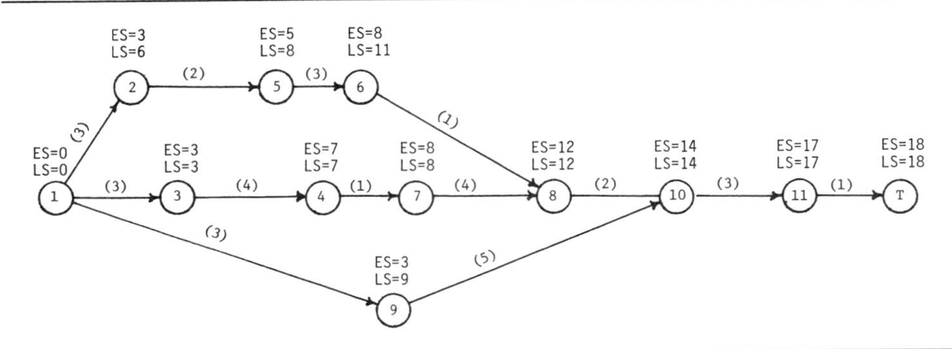

This is a revised version of the CPM network in Figure 3-8. Activities 2 and 3 of that network have been placed in parallel here, thereby reducing total project time to 18 days.

latter task is on the critical path, the additional help would represent an actual savings in total project time.

This approach of shortening project time through application of additional resources is closely related to least-cost scheduling, a technique often used in industrial applications of CPM. This involves the selection of tasks to be shortened based on getting the greatest reduction of time with the minimum in additional cost. Such analysis is most often applied in areas where technology is sophisticated and where time/cost relationships are reasonably precise; applications of least-cost scheduling in the educational domain are judged to be very limited.

One aspect of network planning that does have application in education is the modified bar chart. This technique parallels Gantt Charting but incorporates the presentation of slack or float time in a visible manner. A modified bar chart for the longer version of the school-funding issue is shown in Figure 3–12. Notice that this modified bar chart is very similar to the Gantt Chart of Figure 3–1. Its advantages are the illustration of precedence relationships existing within the project and the indication of slack time associated with each of the activities. Neither of these factors is evident in the Gantt Chart presentation.

Figure 3–12 Modified Bar Chart for School-Funding Issue

Jobs on Critical Path
Jobs not on Critical Path
Slack Time

0 5 10 15 20

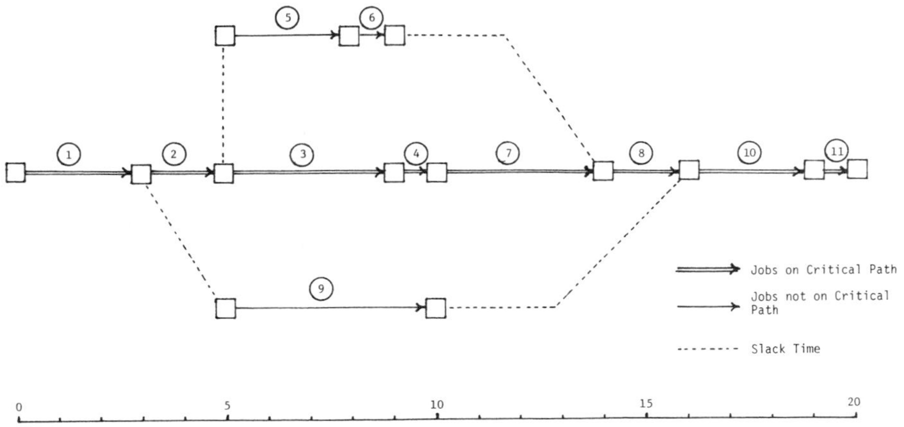

This is based on the CPM network of Figure 3-8 but utilizes arrows as activities rather than nodes. For this reason, it most closely parallels the PERT network pattern. The start and finish times for each activity are as indicated but can be changed to the extent indicated by the slack time.

APPROPRIATE APPLICATION OF NETWORK PLANNING

All too often, administrators think that a new planning device like CPM or Gantt Charting will suddenly solve all their time and scheduling problems. Some even think that the planning techniques will tell them what jobs have to be done and the order in which they should be done. Those familiar with network planning realize, of course, that such expectations are totally unrealistic. The several network and charting devices discussed in this chapter require a good deal of input from the user and cannot be appropriately applied to every school planning activity. This limitation to the application of network planning techniques is evident in discussing several conditions required for a satisfactory application.

The project must be subdivided into a set of predictable, independent activities.

Predictability is not always present in school planning. Yet, if network planning is to be useful in guiding progress, such predictability is desirable. Without reasonable estimates for completing tasks, there is little value in the scheduling process.

In general, predictability of time increases with understanding of the actual processes to be employed in the activity. In activities such as research and development or negotiations, the understanding and/or control of the processes may not be sufficient to merit the use of network analysis. It makes little sense, for example, to schedule a certain number of days for negotiating a particular issue with the local teachers' association without first gaining agreement from the teachers as to a suitable decision deadline. Since this itself is likely to be negotiable, it may be counterproductive to try to build such decisions into a network planning effort. This lack of predictability in the negotiations arena is of course one of the reasons many school systems find themselves in sometimes unavoidable problems with respect to timely decision making and planning.

Independence as called for in this condition refers to the separation of activities included in the project. Essentially, network planning can be accomplished only where clear beginning and ending points exist for the several activities and where activities can be started and stopped independently of one another.

The precedence relationship of project activities exists in such a way that each activity connects directly into its immediate successor.

The precedence relationship is sometimes missing in school planning, particularly in those areas where the next activity is in some way contingent on results of prior activities. Consider the planning for an addition to a building where it is necessary first to gain voter approval for a bond issue. To plan the entire project (including both voter approval and construction phases) in a single network would be difficult as the immediate successor to the vote would be conditional on the outcome. The traditional forms of network planning do not permit either cyclical or conditional routes through the network. All activities in the network must be performed in the order shown.

Another difficulty in meeting this condition stems from the problems in anticipating all the precedence relationships involved in a project. This is particularly true of research and development projects, which usually involve unknown problems. For example, it may be necessary to conduct an extensive search of a particular street address directory prior to picking the sample for a house-to-house survey simply because the computer file (which was originally to be used) has been lost or does not include names of parents as required in the sampling procedure. Such problems are often unknown at the beginning of the planning stage and consequently interfere with developing an accurate network of the project at that time.

Administrators and others involved in the planning must show a willingness to think seriously about maximizing use of time and resources.

Successful application of network planning techniques depends more than anything else on the attitude of those involved in administering school programs. If planners and administrators are not particularly interested in accomplishing goals and/or projects according to scheduled deadlines but are rather satisfied to watch the school or school system run itself, there is little reason to engage in PERT, CPM, Gantt Charting, or other forms of network planning. Network planning is a technique for helping administrators and planners accomplish goals and do so with efficient use of time and resources.

It is not enough to establish a planning department and to expect that department to complete all aspects of network planning. There must be involvement of line administrators at several levels if time estimates are to be reasonable. These line administrators must themselves be interested in goal accomplishment and must be willing to think seriously about the planning process. Without this commitment, the application of network planning will never go beyond the drafting table.

There must be a commitment by administrators at all levels to monitor the time schedules developed in the network planning process and to meet the time deadlines established as part of that process.

Network diagrams and computer programs are often impressive to review and they can give a sense of forward motion to those inside and outside the formal organization. If, however, these charts and network designs are not used in actually monitoring the starting and ending times for activities, their potential value to the organization has not been realized.

This monitoring will usually cut across several levels of the organization and cannot therefore be accomplished by a single department or person. Support must exist from the top management on down through the school organization. All persons involved must watch to see that jobs on the critical path are completed according to the scheduled time. Neither can extra slack time be used in connection with noncritical jobs. Where slippage is allowed to enter the system, the schedule must be updated promptly to reflect the effects of delays and/or changes in the plan.

SUMMARY

Network planning is primarily useful in connection with long-term projects in which component activities relate in a sequential manner and have predictable completion times. In education, these conditions are likely to exist in, for example, planning a school bond issue or a new school, scheduling tasks associated with implementation of a new reading program, or revising a student or faculty handbook. Much of the gain achieved through use of network planning results from the process of thinking through component tasks of a project prior to its initiation. This thinking process alone can save considerable time in the implementation of long-term projects.

Network applications covered in this chapter are PERT and CPM. Alternatives such as Gantt Charting and modified bar charts were discussed as was the use of slack time in analyzing alternative starting and ending times for tasks. The importance of administrator commitment in assuring the successful application of network planning has been stressed throughout. Unless the administrator is concerned with meeting project deadlines and is willing to monitor project schedules accordingly, little is likely to be gained from the use of network planning techniques. More than anything else, network planning is an aid to the administrator in seeing that organizational activity is managed effectively and in the accomplishment of organizational priorities.

QUESTIONS AND PROBLEMS ON CHAPTER 3

1. The CPM network shown as Figure 3–13 describes precedence relationships for a particular project.

Figure 3–13

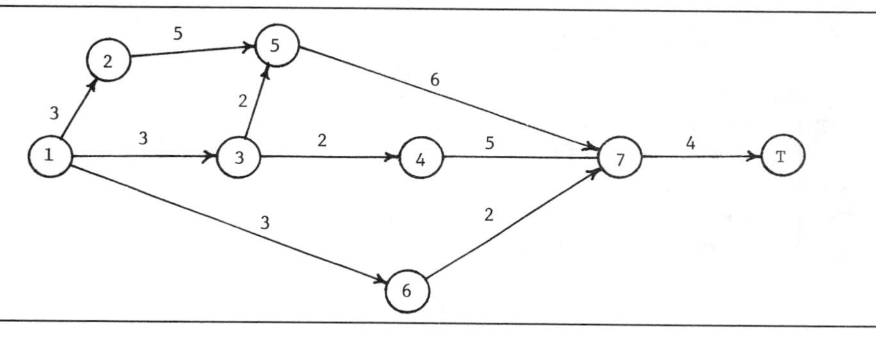

   a. Find the critical path for the network.
   b. How much slack time is associated with Job 3?
   c. Draw an alternative PERT network where the jobs are arrows and the nodes are simply connections between jobs.

2. Draw a CPM network for each of the following sets of sequence requirements (tasks or activities are indicated by letters):
   a. In this network
      A must precede B
      B must precede C and D
      C must precede E
      D must precede F
      E must precede F
   b. In this network
      A and B must precede D
      A must precede C
      D must precede E and F
      C must precede E
      E and F must precede G

3. A small maintenance project consists of the jobs or activities indicated in the PERT network shown in Figure 3–14.
   a. Identify the jobs on the critical path.
   b. How much slack or float time is associated with Jobs 4 and 10?
   c. Do any jobs in the network have free slack (i.e., slack time that affects no other jobs in the network)?

Figure 3–14

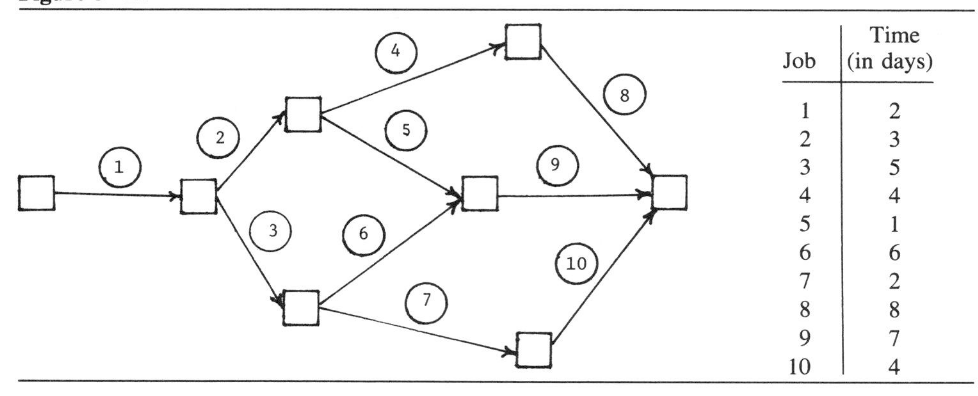

Job	Time (in days)
1	2
2	3
3	5
4	4
5	1
6	6
7	2
8	8
9	7
10	4

d. If Job 2 were to take six days instead of three, how would the project completion time be affected?
e. Draw a CPM network for the same project.

4. Plans call for building a combination running track and exercise equipment area adjacent to a particular elementary school building. This is part of a new commitment to physical fitness and will involve a major change in the physical education program of the school. Bids will be taken on the running track construction and the contractor will put in the running track prior to the time the parents install the special equipment. The tasks and times for each are listed in Figure 3–15 along with the connecting nodes for a PERT network.

a. Using the connecting nodes, task descriptions, and times listed above, develop a PERT network for the project.
b. Identify the critical path through the network and determine the minimum time for project completion.
c. Complete the chart by deriving the earliest and latest starts and slack time for each task.
d. Is the slack time for any of the jobs considered to be free slack?

5. As part of a simplified budget-planning process, we might envision the following steps and times:

Step 1 Complete enrollment projections (5 days)
Step 2 Estimate local tax and nontax revenues (2 days)
Step 3 Obtain briefing from state and federal officials regarding funding changes (3 days)
Step 4 Estimate state revenues (1 day)
Step 5 Estimate federal revenues (2 days)
Step 6 Estimate total revenues (1 day)

The sequence of these steps (identified as circled numbers) is presented in the PERT network shown as Figure 3–16.

a. Redraw the PERT network in a way that eliminates the need for the Dummy-2 arrow and explain why it is not possible to remove the Dummy-1 arrow.
b. What tasks are on the critical path and what is the shortest time for completing the entire budget-planning process?
c. Show how using the CPM network (nodes rather than arrows are activities) for this process can eliminate the need for any dummy jobs.
d. Make a modified bar chart for the budget planning process.

Figure 3–15

Nodes		Description of Task	Time (in days)	Earliest Start	Latest Start	Slack Time
i	j					
1	2	Architect Develops Plans	7			
2	3	Plans Approved by School Board	5			
3	4	Select Parents to Install Equipment	2			
3	5	Raise Funds for Equipment Purchase	10			
3	6	Bids Taken on Track Construction	5			
3	7	District Crew Prepares Area for Equipment	3			
4	7	Orient Parents on Installation	1			
5	7	Purchase Equipment and Take Delivery	22			
6	7	Construction of Track	9			
2	8	Staff Curriculum Committees Formed	3			
7	9	Install Equipment	6			
8	9	Develop Curriculum and Grade Level Goals	25			
9	10	Conduct Pilot Test of Program	6			

Figure 3–16

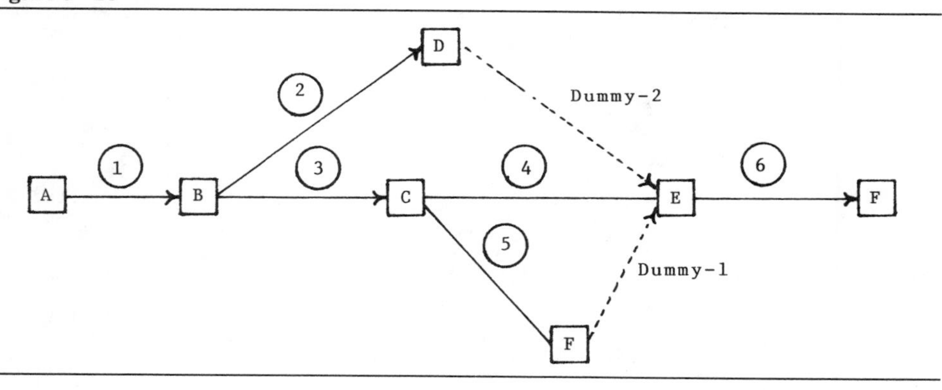

6. In relation to the same budget-planning process described in Question 5, assume we have only estimates of the times for each activity, as indicated in Figure 3–17.
   a. Determine the expected time for each activity using the regular PERT formula and use these expected times to determine the overall time required to complete the budget process.

Figure 3–17

Nodes		Time Estimates		
Start	Finish	Optimistic	Most Likely	Pessimistic
A	B	2.0	5.0	8.0
B	C	1.5	2.0	3.7
B	D	2.0	3.0	5.2
C	E	.5	.9	2.5
C	F	1.0	2.0	3.0
E	G	1.0	1.2	2.0

Figure 3–18

Activity Number	Description of Activity	Days Required	Immediate Predecessors
1	Select an orientation coordinator	2.0	-
2	Review prior orientations with coordinator and establish priorities for this year's program	1.0	1
3	Select student guides from senior class roster	1.0	2
4	Meet with counseling staff and administration to set exact time and format for parent/student meetings	2.0	2
5	Secretaries prepare student files for incoming students and assign them to advisory teachers	7.0	1
6	Call to invite student guides two days prior to the training session	2.0	3,4
7	Prepare letters notifying teachers of students assigned to their advisory rooms and of the exact times for the parent/student meetings	2.0	4,5
8	Prepare orientation invitations to parents and students new to the school	3.0	4,5
9	Prepare student orientation handbook	6.0	1
10	Prepare signs to direct incoming students and their parents	1.0	4
11*	Little League banquet scheduled 14 days after project starting point	12.0	1
12	Post signs in hallway areas	1.0	10,11
13	Publish 200 copies of orientation handbook	3.0	9
14	Hold training session for student guides	1.0	6
15	Arrange for refreshments with the PTSA	1.0	2
16**	Students, parents, and teachers receive letters announcing meeting times at least five days prior to the meetings (add one day for mailing)	6.0	7,8
17	Orientation meeting	1.0	12,13,14,15,16

*This is not specifically an activity but is necessary to make certain that the signs are not posted (Activity 12) until after the banquet is held.

**This is not an activity but is necessary to assure that all letters are received well in advance of the orientation meeting.

b. Which activities have slack time and how much of this slack time is considered free slack?

7. Listed in Figure 3–18 are activities associated with a proposed program for orienting new students and their parents to a senior high school. Both precedence relationships and times are as indicated.

a. Draw a CPM network for the project.

b. Use this network and the indicated times to supply the information requested in Figure 3–19.

Figure 3–19

Activity Number	Days Required	Earliest Start	Latest Start	Slack Time	
				Total	Free
1	2.0				
3	1.0				
7	2.0				
10	1.0				
13	3.0				
15	1.0				
17	1.0				

c. If available, utilize a computer program to derive the information requested in the chart.

d. Explain an alternative method of assuring that the conditions indicated in Activities 11 and 16 are preserved and the advantages and disadvantages associated with this alternative.

8. Listed below are a number of projects that may reasonably lend themselves to some type of network planning:

- Develop and implement a new grading procedure.
- Conduct a self-study accreditation process involving the entire school staff.
- Open a new school.
- Develop and implement a new staff evaluation system.
- Plan and carry out a major in-service training program for the school staff.

Select any one of the above projects and complete the following steps related to that project:

a. Identify seven to twenty-five tasks associated with the selected project.

b. Develop a network showing the sequence of tasks.

c. Supply time estimates for each of the tasks.

d. Determine the critical path through the network and the amount of slack time associated with each task.

e. Present a Gantt Chart or some other visual representation for the project.

CHAPTER 4
SCHEDULING SCHOOL PROGRAMS

In Chapter 3, we reviewed a number of techniques used in the control and scheduling of specific projects operating within the school setting. We now look at the scheduling of the regular, ongoing school program. The secondary school scheduling problem, because of its complexity, receives major attention here; however, some application of these skills to the elementary school level is provided in practice exercises at the end of the chapter. While some consideration early in the chapter is given to reviewing types of schedule formats most often used in secondary schools, this text focuses on the understandings and skills needed in the actual management of the scheduling process.

Adminstrative trainees often find themselves inadequately equipped in this area when they assume their first administrative assignment as principal or assistant principal; yet, they are sometimes forced to learn quickly because the job places them directly in charge of the student registration and scheduling processes. Few textbooks on the principalship give the administrative trainee anything more than a general exposure to the types of schedules used in schools and a brief listing of the steps involved in building a master schedule. Consequently, many have had almost no exposure to the myriad analytic procedures associated with good schedule building, nor have they had firsthand experience with the schedule-building process. Both concerns are covered here, especially for those who take time to complete the several practice exercises.

VARIATION IN SCHEDULING FORMATS

Although the traditional school day of five, six, or seven periods is still the practice in the vast majority of secondary schools today, there have been, over the past twenty years, several efforts to provide greater variation in scheduling formats in secondary schools. Experimentation with the so-called flexible-modular schedules in the 1960s and the more recent attempts to implement daily teacher-demand scheduling, student-structured programs, and minicourse options are evidence of this willingness to look at alternatives to the more conventional formats.[1] A review of the history of scheduling in secondary schools indicates that most schedules can be classified as utilizing a fixed or a variable time pattern. The fixed-time patterns include the traditional, floating, and rotating types; frequently used variable-time patterns include the dual-track and modular-schedule types. We look briefly at sample student schedules for each of these schedule formats prior to examining steps required in their development.

In Figure 4–1, we see sample student schedules for three of the more frequently used fixed-time patterns. Fixed time as used here refers to the fact that all courses are structured to meet for a fixed time period during each meeting of the course. Classes may vary in size or nature of activity from one class period to the next, but the time of each class meeting is fixed. Note that in the traditional pattern in Figure 4–1, each class meets daily for the same time period. Assuming a six-hour (or 360-minute) school day and 30 minutes for lunch, we find that each of the six classes meets 55 minutes (330/6) less whatever time may be lost passing between classes. Obviously, many schools using this traditional schedule do vary slightly the length of the several class periods, often for purposes of taking attendance or reading the bulletin in certain class periods; but generally the variance in class meeting time (except for days of special assemblies or activity arrangements) is minimal.

The second pattern in Figure 4–1 is known as a floating pattern because one of the classes (in this case English) floats to different periods as the week progresses. Note that the student takes the same six classes as in the traditional pattern and all classes are still of fixed-time duration whenever they meet. Since only five class periods are scheduled each day with this pattern, the length of each class period, using a given school day configuration, will be longer than in the traditional pattern. Assuming again a six-hour school day and 30 minutes for lunch, we would anticipate a period of 66 minutes (330/5) less the passing time. This longer period is used to compensate for the fact that classes meet only four times a week under this pattern. Advantages cited by one school using this floating-pattern schedule were the provision of a longer period without actually reducing the number of class registrations

[1]A description of the flexible-modular schedule can be found in D. W. Allen, "First Steps in Developing a Master Schedule" (1962), pp. 34–36. Daily teacher-demand scheduling is described in Glen F. Ovard, "Daily Computer Scheduling" (1974), pp. 113–118. A Model of student-structured scheduling is presented in Howard M. Johnson, "Flexibility in the Secondary School" (1969), pp. 62–72, and a plan for minicourse options is found in Vernon Potts and Ray Kemper, "Micro-Mini Units for Junior High Schools" (1974), pp. 530–532.

Figure 4–1 Sample Student Schedules for Selected Fixed-Time Patterns

A. Traditional Pattern

PERIOD \ DAY	MONDAY	TUESDAY	WEDNESDAY	THURSDAY	FRIDAY
1	Geometry	Geometry	Geometry	Geometry	Geometry
2	Spanish	Spanish	Spanish	Spanish	Spanish
3	Art	Art	Art	Art	Art
4	Biology	Biology	Biology	Biology	Biology
5	P.E.	P.E.	P.E.	P.E.	P.E.
6	English	English	English	English	English

B. Floating Pattern

PERIOD \ DAY	MONDAY	TUESDAY	WEDNESDAY	THURSDAY	FRIDAY
1	English	Geometry	Geometry	Geometry	Geometry
2	Spanish	English	Spanish	Spanish	Spanish
3	Art	Art	English	Art	Art
4	Biology	Biology	Biology	English	Biology
5	P.E.	P.E.	P.E.	P.E.	Activity Period

C. Rotation Pattern

PERIOD \ DAY	D_1	D_2	D_3	D_4	D_5	D_6
1	Geometry	English	P.E.	Biology	Art	Spanish
2	Spanish	Geometry	English	P.E.	Biology	Art
3	Art	Spanish	Geometry	English	P.E.	Biology
4	Biology	Art	Spanish	Geometry	English	P.E.
5	P.E.	Biology	Art	Spanish	Geometry	English
6	English	P.E.	Biology	Art	Spanish	Geometry

for each student and the ease of floating the activity period to different times of the day as needed.[2]

Variations of the rotation pattern presented in Figure 4–1 have been used by a number of schools to avoid the monotony of the same class meeting at the same time each day of the

[2]A sample student schedule for Cobre Consolidated High School, Bayard, New Mexico, is presented in David B. Austin and Noble Gividen, *The High School Principal and Staff Develop a Master Schedule* (1960), p. 30. This particular school changed from a six-period, traditional schedule to a five-period, floating schedule and was able to maintain the student option for six class registrations.

week. Note that in the particular pattern presented in Figure 4–1, a schedule cycle of six days has been used, as this is the only way to complete a full rotation of classes with a six-period day. Some schools have developed rotation schedules with the standard one-week cycle by using scattered drop periods or by utilizing only a partial rotation within the schedule. One example of the partial rotation is the rotating of morning and afternoon classes separately, thereby making it possible for part-time students to hold down morning or afternoon jobs without having to drop out of school. Some schools have utilized a form of the rotation schedule to permit a longer class session for each course during each schedule cycle. For example, we could, by increasing the length of second period in the rotating pattern of Figure 4–1, give each class a longer period once every six days (Spanish on D_1, Geometry on D_2, English on D_3, etc.). This longer period for each class can be used on a scheduled basis for field trips, films, or other activities suited to the longer time frame.

Once we have begun to alter the time frame in this manner, we are moving into a variable-time pattern as described earlier. Several samples of student schedules using variable-time patterns are shown in Figure 4–2. The first of these is known as an alternate-day pattern. Note that this schedule is similar to the traditional pattern except for the double periods on Tuesday and Thursday. Each class meets only four times a week; however, the double period on either Tuesday or Thursday results in the same total class time per week. An eight-period variation of this schedule was used for a number of years in the high schools of Eugene, Oregon. Several teachers in that district cited the longer period as a real bonus for instruction, but others had problems keeping student interest for the longer time period. The schedule was dropped in the mid-1970s in favor of a more traditional schedule pattern.

The dual-track pattern shown in Figure 4–2 gets its name from the dual set of period formats operating within the schedule. Note that the day is divided into six shorter periods on one schedule and four long periods on the other. Assuming the 330 minutes of instructional time mentioned earlier, this represents a period length of 55 minutes on Schedule A and 82.5 minutes on Schedule B. Both of these period lengths include the time needed to move between classes. While the dual-track plan has the obvious advantage of matching time in class more closely with learning activity, it has been rejected by most schools. Reasons often cited for this rejection are difficulties in handling credit arrangements for the differing amounts of instructional time allocated to short- and long-period courses, the loss of instructional time for students as they move from one schedule to the other, and the difficulties in supervising students during the time when they are not assigned to class. This loss of instructional time in moving from one schedule to the other is evident in our sample in Figure 4–2. Because of the instructional time loss in this particular case, we observe that the student is able to complete only five courses rather than the six accommodated under most of the other plans.

The final sample in Figure 4–2 is the modular pattern. In this particular case, the student takes six classes but time configurations both between and within courses vary widely. We think of this modular pattern in Figure 4–2 as accommodating twelve modules of time per day. If we continue to operate from our total instructional time base of 330 minutes (including passing time), each module consists of 27.5 minutes. Applying these same figures to the sample class schedule of Figure 4–2, we arrive at the profile of course structures at the bottom of the following page. Comparing this time allocation with that achieved under the traditional- or alternate-day patterns (where each class meets for five periods of 55 minutes each per week for a total of 275 minutes), we observe that only in the case of P.E. is the total course-time allocation of the traditional pattern equaled. Out of the sixty modules per week in the modular pattern of Figure 4–2, a total of thirteen (or 21.7

Figure 4–2 Sample Student Schedules for Selected Variable-Time Patterns

A. Alternate-Day Pattern

PERIOD \ DAY	MONDAY	TUESDAY	WEDNESDAY	THURSDAY	FRIDAY
1	Geometry	Geometry	Geometry	Spanish	Geometry
2	Spanish		Spanish		Spanish
3	Art	Art	Art	Biology	Art
4	Biology		Biology		Biology
5	P.E.	P.E.	P.E.	English	P.E.
6	English		English		English

B. Dual-Track Pattern

PERIOD A	PERIOD B	MONDAY	TUESDAY	WEDNESDAY	THURSDAY	FRIDAY
1	1	Geometry	Geometry	Geometry	Geometry	Geometry
2						
3	2	Art	Art	Art	Art	Art
4	3	P.E.	P.E.	P.E.	P.E.	P.E.
5		Spanish	Spanish	Spanish	Spanish	Spanish
6	4	English	English	English	English	English

C. Modular Pattern

PERIOD \ DAY	MONDAY	TUESDAY	WEDNESDAY	THURSDAY	FRIDAY
1	Geom. Lecture	Art Lab.	Eng. Lecture	Art Lab.	
2			Geom.Lab.		
3					Geom. Class
4			Biol. Lec.		
5	P.E.	P.E.	P.E.	P.E.	P.E.
6					
7	Spanish	Spanish		Spanish	Spanish
8					
9	Eng. Sem.		Eng. Sem.		Eng. Sem.
10		Biology Lab.		Biology Lab	
11			Geom. Class		
12					

Course	Modules per week	Total Instructional Minutes per Week (including passing time)
Geometry	7	192.5
Spanish	8	220.0
Art	8	220.0
Biology	7	192.5
P.E.	10	275.0
English	7	192.5

percent) represents unassigned time for the student. This unassigned time accounts for the fewer minutes of total instructional time usually associated with the modular pattern. A school's lack of success in getting students to use this unassigned time in an appropriate manner is often used as a major reason for not considering use of the modular pattern.

Most people experienced in the implementation of modular schedules permitting a reasonable level of course-structure variation (i.e., permitting different courses to be taught under differing time configurations) suggest that, on the average, 40 percent of student time must be unassigned in order to make the course requests fit. That this high a percentage of the school day must go into unassigned time is a surprise to many people, but it is somewhat akin to trying to pack objects of various sizes and shapes into a rectangular box—the more varied the shapes and sizes, the less efficient the packing exercise. So it is with modular scheduling—the more varied the course structures, the more unassigned time required to make a proper fit.

It is appropriate to note that the dual-track schedule of Figure 4–2 is actually a special case of the modular pattern. This is seen by viewing the A and B tracks respectively of the dual-track pattern as consisting of two- and three-module classes. Many of the other patterns, including the traditional, can conceivably be viewed as special cases of the modular pattern; however, in this presentation we think of modular schedules as actually utilizing a variable course structure at least approximating that illustrated in Figure 4–2.

The presentation to this point has emphasized some major differences in schedule patterns used in the secondary schools. The differences in the procedures and skills required in implementing these different schedule patterns are minimal. For example, we know that exactly the same set of procedures can be used both in building the master schedule and in assigning students to classes in all three patterns shown in Figure 4–1 and in the alternate-day pattern of Figure 4–2. Even for the dual-track and modular-schedule patterns of Figure 4–2, many of the same tools of analysis (e.g., simple tally, conflict matrix, average class size per period or module) are utilized in accomplishing the scheduling task.

These same scheduling tools are sometimes applied at the elementary school level in sectioning students or in the establishment of mini-elective programs. Both of these applications are illustrated in problems at the end of the chapter. In subsequent sections of the chapter, we examine several of these scheduling procedures and gain practice in the analysis of scheduling options frequently used in the schools.

DEVELOPING A SCHEDULING PROCEDURE

Scheduling is, by its very nature, a set of compromises and/or choices. The administrator often has to decide whether to admit one more student to the class over the objection of a teacher, or to create another section of the class, thereby using one more segment of a limited teacher allocation. Another frequent decision is whether a teacher should be assigned a class he or she is only marginally equipped to handle, or whether the students should be told to select another elective. These are illustrative of the types of compromises inevitably involved in the scheduling process.

Quite obviously, if there is surplus classroom space in the several course areas and a group of teachers each of whom is proficient in teaching all or most of the subject offerings, there will be fewer compromises involved in the scheduling process. In the typical school setting, however, there are limited space and human resources, making compromise inevitable; we must therefore develop a system for collecting and analyzing information to make these compromises effectively. The system must assure that they are made in a manner that maximizes benefits to students and yet meets the many state and local guidelines impinging on the school curriculum.

It seems reasonable to assume that such a system will have four essential characteristics. First, school staff will be encouraged to evaluate the scheduling procedures on a continuing basis. Since both curricula and student needs are constantly changing, there is need for the staff to continually examine the effectiveness of its scheduling pattern and related registration processes. The custodial staff, cafeteria crew, and office help should not be discounted in this evaluation effort. They may have helpful suggestions for coordinating the activities of the school.

Second, a clear understanding of the scheduling procedures is a reasonable right of all who are likely to be affected. The administrator cannot do the job alone. The cooperation of the school staff, parents, and students is essential to a satisfactory schedule. Such cooperation is not likely to be achieved without adequate communication. School personnel will undoubtedly be more understanding of a temporary failure when they are personally identified with the scheduling process. The authority for certain scheduling decisions must rest with the school administrator, but the wise administrator will share many of the decisions with an informed faculty.

Third, the schedule and related implementing procedures must service a curriculum that is acceptable to a significant majority of the faculty. The administrator who desires to add flexibility to the school program must encourage genuine faculty participation from the beginning. The added flexibility cannot be achieved by an administrative decree adding ten minutes to every class period. Any such addition of time must be preceded by a definite commitment on the part of faculty members to alter their classroom procedures. The schedule must be seen as a device to help the school achieve its goals and it should be defended on no other terms.

Fourth, the interest of the student must be the primary consideration of those involved in the scheduling process. Those charged with responsibility for scheduling must make many decisions involving the personal interest of school staff. The business of assigning teachers and students to classes often results in irresolvable conflict between the two. Teachers sometimes object to inequities in load or extracurricular assignments, claiming they violate contractual agreements. The custodial staff may be unhappy with certain activities scheduled outside the regular school day. These decisions involving strong personal preference must be decided with maximum possible attention to the interest of students. Only then can the basic purpose of the school be served.

BUILDING THE MASTER SCHEDULE

Whatever the schedule pattern involved, the process of building and implementing the school schedule will almost always consist of two major tasks—building the master schedule and assigning or sectioning students into that master schedule. Beginning with the task of building the master schedule, we identify four major steps to be accomplished.

Establish listing of possible classes to be offered with indication as to students eligible for each class.

This first step is part of the continuous evaluation referred to in the previous section; if properly done, it requires involvement of the entire faculty. Changes in grouping practices, new elective course offerings, and shifts in the grade levels when certain required courses are to be taken must all be considered as part of this evaluation activity. There should be opportunity to review requests for new electives and to assess faculty availability to teach these proposed elective courses. Policies regarding the number of required and elective courses to be taken by students at the several grade levels should be clearly established during this step; without such policies, data collected in the prepregistration process will be of limited value.

Some administrators simply reestablish the schedule from the previous year rather than initiate the type of evaluation being proposed here. Unfortunately, this mechanical approach to building the master schedule has little chance of improving the school curriculum, nor is it likely to build understanding and trust in the overall scheduling process. Recognizing these factors, the school principal is urged to view this first step as an ongoing form of evaluation and to use it creatively as an opportunity for needed faculty and student involvement in school decision making.

Conduct a preregistration of student interest in the classes that can be offered.

This step should be accomplished well in advance of the beginning of the school term and during a time when students are in school. For the fall term, we are therefore thinking of preregistration sometime during the preceding spring and at a time when students have access to both teachers and guidance counselors. Students should be asked during this preregistration period to compare course requests for the coming term or school year with both graduation requirements and long-range schooling plans. Involvement of parents, if not required, should at least be encouraged.

The result of this registration activity is both a simple tally of projected course enrollments and a cross-tabulation or conflict matrix showing the number of students signing up for each pair of course offerings. Samples of these two listings are presented in Figures 4–3 and 4–4, respectively.

That this preregistration information should represent an accurate projection of actual enrollments cannot be overemphasized, as establishing a schedule based on a distorted picture of student preferences is of little value. Teachers and students must be encouraged to give serious attention to this preregistration step in schedule building.

Analyze the preregistration information and decide on the number of sections of each course to offer.

Critical to this analysis phase is the establishment of guidelines with respect to class size. Using sample data from Figure 4–3, we must decide whether Anthropology and Psychology

Figure 4–3 Simple Tally of Course Requests (partial listing only)

	Grade Level			
Course	*10*	*11*	*12*	*Total*
English 10	175	—	—	175
Creative Writing	1	38	14	53
American Literature	2	15	10	27
Typing 1	47	18	14	79
U.S./World History	—	143	2	145
Anthropology	—	4	5	9
Psychology	2	2	7	11
German II	—	18	2	20
Physics	—	5	19	24
Electronics	4	7	6	17
Math Analysis	—	2	21	23

Figure 4–4 Conflict Matrix for Selected Courses

	English 10	Creative Writing	American Literature	Typing 1	U.S./World History	Anthropology	Psychology	German II	Physics	Electronics	Math Analysis
English 10	175	1	2	47	—	—	2	—	—	—	—
Creative Writing		53	1	4	37	—	1	2	1	2	3
American Literature			27	1	15	1	1	1	1	1	1
Typing 1				79	18	2	2	3	4	2	2
U.S./World History					145	3	2	18	3	6	1
Anthropology						9	—	1	1	1	1
Psychology							11	—	—	1	—
German II								20	7	—	5
Physics									24	2	19
Electronics										17	3
Math Analysis											23

with preregistration enrollments of nine and eleven respectively should be offered. Similarly, we need some guidance as to whether two or three sections of Creative Writing (with a preregistration enrollment of fifty-three students) should be established in the master schedule. There is obviously no universal set of answers to questions of this type and the answers will depend on staffing allocations available within a given building, preferences of staff as to how those allocations should be used, and, in some cases, restrictions existing within state guidelines or local contractual regulations.

In Figure 4–5, we review, based on data from Figures 4–3 and 4–4, a particular decision on the number of sections offered. Note that seven sections of English 10 are needed. Creating only six sections results in an average class size of 29.2, which clearly exceeds the established limit of 28 students. We also observe that the Anthropology class with a preregistration enrollment of only nine students was canceled. These students will be reassigned to other classes at a later time. The Psychology class with an estimated enrollment of eleven students was maintained, with the hope for some increase prior to the opening of the term. In most situations, it is necessary to make projections (based on past

Figure 4–5 Number of Sections Required in Selected Courses

Course	*Preregistration Enrollment*	*Number of Sections*	*Estimated Class Size*
English 10 (28)	175	7	25.0
Creative Writing (28)	53	2	26.5
American Literature (28)	27	1	27.0
Typing 1 (30)	79	3	26.3
U.S./World History (28)	145	6	24.2
Anthropology (28)	9	—	—
Psychology (26)	11	1	11.0
German II (24)	20	1	20.0
Physics (26)	24	1	24.0
Electronics (24)	17	1	17.0
Math Analysis (30)	23	1	23.0

These data are based on the simple tally in Figure 4-3. Numbers in parentheses represent the maximum class size established for each course.

history) of preregistration data, as the actual enrollments rarely match preregistration information no matter how carefully the process is handled.

The administrator charged with scheduling responsibility must work closely with staff in establishing enrollment limits for the different courses and the criteria used in making decisions in this area must be communicated to the entire faculty. It usually works best if departments are given some latitude in setting minimum and maximum class-size figures as sometimes allowing a larger class in one course within a given department can be offset by a class or two with smaller enrollment, thereby more adequately serving the needs and desires of students and faculty.

An additional dimension of deciding on the number of class sections in each course is the availability of faculty to teach the sections as provided. In schools where faculty turnover and/or growth are limited, this dimension can be an essential part of the decision making as it relates to the scheduling process. Often, final decisions on providing certain sections cannot be made until the staff selection process is completed; however, it is necessary during this analysis of preregistration data to make at least tentative decisions as to whether staff will be available for the number and type of sections desired and needed.

Build the master schedule, including at least tentative teacher and room assignments.

With at least a tentative count of sections for the several courses accomplished, the schedule builder is now prepared to begin plotting sections onto a master schedule for the school. A starting point for this process is some kind of schedule board or paper on which to plot the teachers on one axis and the periods provided in the schedule pattern on the other. A suggested format for such a master-schedule board is shown in Figure 4–6.

The information already compiled on conflicts must now be examined carefully, as this information is helpful in deciding the order for plotting sections on the master-schedule board. We observe in Figure 4–4 the conflict matrix for the same eleven courses for which

Figure 4–6 Illustration of Master-Schedule Board (starting to plot sections)

TEACHER NAME	PERIOD					
	1	2	3	4	5	6
Cook						
Estep				24 - Physics 5 (Rm.E-6) 19		17 4 Electron. 7 (Rm.E-7) 6
Hall						
Kuehn					23 - Math.An. 2 (Rm.A-8) 21	
Morgan						20 - Ger.II 18 (Rm.B-5) 2

numbers of sections were established in Figure 4–5. This conflict matrix plots each pair of courses, indicating the number of students registering in both courses. For example, we observe in Figure 4–4 that only 1 of the 175 students registered in English 10 is also registered in Creative Writing. Similarly, 47 of the students registered in English 10 are also signed up for Typing 1.

Although most computer programs used to generate the conflict matrix provide this type of conflict analysis for all pairs of courses included as part of the preregistration, we are most interested in the level of conflict existing for those courses that have only one or two sections to be placed on the master-schedule board. Looking just at the single-section courses (sometimes referred to as "singletons"), we observe in Figure 4–5 that six of the eleven courses must be considered: American Literature, Psychology, German II, Physics, Electronics, and Math Analysis. In examining the conflicts associated with these six courses, we quickly establish that the larger number of conflicts is associated with the German II, Physics, Math Analysis, and Electronics courses. As examples, we see the following as possible conflict problems in scheduling:

German II/Physics	7
German II/Math Analysis	5
Physics/Electronics	2
Physics/Math Analysis	19
Electronics/Math Analysis	3

Since these are all singleton courses and since each pair involves more than one student as a potential conflict, it makes sense to begin the master-schedule board by plotting these sections first.

The Physics, Math Analysis, German II, and Electronics classes are plotted in Figure 4–6. Note that the Physics, Math Analysis, and German II sections have been placed in periods 4, 5, and 6, respectively, and we are debating the placement of Electronics in either the fifth or the sixth period. Based on the information obtained from the conflict matrix, namely, that Electronics/Math Analysis generates three conflicts and Electronics/German II generates no conflicts, it makes sense to plot the Electronics section in the sixth period rather than the fifth.[3] Placement of the other two singleton sections, Psychology and American Literature, is based on similar reasoning. Since American Literature has one conflict with each of the other courses already plotted on the master-schedule board, it is probably best to assign it to period 1, 2, or 3 and at a time different from Psychology. Psychology could be placed in either the fourth or fifth period at this point, as it has no conflicts with either Physics or Math Analysis.

It is easy to see from this brief introduction that some trial and error is involved in the schedule-building process. Despite this, it is possible to suggest some general guidelines to be used in filling out the master-schedule board:

1. Prior to placing any sections on the schedule board, it is good to block out any special, nonteaching assignments for teachers. These might include periods when a teacher is assigned to lunch supervision or counseling. It is also appropriate to block out time periods when a teacher is assigned to some other building or is otherwise unavailable for a teaching assignment.
2. Begin by assigning those classes that simply must be assigned to a particular period of the day. Examples include a course being taught by a teacher who is in the building only

[3]At this point in the scheduling process, Electronics could, of course, be placed in period one, two, or three as no other sections have been assigned into any of those periods.

one period and that period is specified in advance, or a need to have a particular class, such as distributive education, assigned to the last period in the day due to its partial location out in the community.

3. Next, work with singleton classes, particularly any that meet for more than a single class period. In plotting the singleton classes, attempt to minimize the number of student conflicts in essentially the same manner described previously. When it is necessary to schedule conflicting singletons in the same period of the day, it is usually best to do this in a way that minimizes conflict choices for students enrolled in the highest grades of the school. These students will presumably have no future chance to register in courses at the school and should therefore experience fewer conflicts in the scheduling process.

4. Next, deal with doubleton classes (those for which only two sections are to be offered in the schedule) and attempt to minimize conflicts with the singleton classes already in the schedule. It is also important to begin watching the distribution of students by grade level per period. Both of these concerns—elimination of conflicts with doubleton classes and the distribution of students by grade level—are likely to be particularly important in smaller secondary schools. They may not need special attention in larger schools where the number of doubleton classes tends to be small and the distribution of students by grade level seems to take care of itself.

5. Finish the assignment process, being careful to watch the enrollment figures, both total and for individual grades, by modules or class periods. Particularly in small schools, it is possible to build a schedule that is without conflicts but does not provide sufficient seats for students during specific periods of the day. Severe enrollment imbalances can be avoided by periodically checking the enrollments of sections already placed on the schedule board. This checking procedure can be illustrated with reference to Figure 4–6, where both the total and grade-level enrollments are recorded. In checking enrollments on a period-by-period basis, the schedule builder must watch for special circumstances that may call for an uneven distribution of seats in the several periods, for example, a school with a large number of students on early dismissal may need to schedule fewer sections, and hence class enrollments, in the later periods of the school day. The enrollment figures used in building sections of a multisection course should reflect the total enrollment in the course; thus, if twenty students in Grade 10 are signed up for a course with four sections, five students in Grade 10 should be allocated to each section of the course.

As the schedule is built according to the steps outlined above, two additional factors must be considered. First, it is important to observe the facility requirements of the sections as they are assigned. One cannot schedule three typing classes in a single class period if, in fact, only two typing rooms are available for use. Also, it is preferable to avoid the assignment of academic classes, such as English or history, to the home economics kitchen; however, compromises are sometimes required in meeting the needs of the maximum number of students. Potential room problems can usually be avoided by noting the room number on the section entry as it is assigned to the master schedule. This type of notation is illustrated in the master-schedule board of Figure 4–6.

A second and very important factor to consider throughout the master-scheduling process is the qualifications of teachers. Compromises will no doubt have to be made on occasion and some teachers may be assigned to classes for which they are marginally qualified. Insofar as possible, however, teachers should be assigned to courses corresponding to their own training, interest, and expertise. In some instances the administrator may want to check on the feasibility of additional preparation for a teacher prior to assigning him or her to a given course; this may be preferable to eliminating the course.

Readers interested in following through with a reasonably complete sample of the master-schedule building process are referred to Appendix 2, in which a specific set of preregistration data for a school of 325 students is presented along with information on potential teacher assignments. Those interested in trying their skill at building a complete master schedule are invited to compare their result with the one developed as part of the presentation in Appendix 2.

ASSIGNING STUDENTS ACCORDING TO THE MASTER SCHEDULE

Having reviewed the key steps involved in building the master schedule, we now proceed to the second phase of the scheduling process. This is the assignment or sectioning of students into the master schedule. This process is generally handled either through computer assignment or through some form of individual selection. Certain advantages can be seen for each of these approaches and the school administration and the teaching faculty must make a choice based on local circumstances.

Computer Assignment

The computer assignment process is available through numerous school district computer centers and computer service bureaus. Essentially, the user inputs both the master schedule and the student course requests and the computer makes the assignment to sections in accordance with specified class-size limitations. The student-course requests can be those obtained in preregistration or they can be based on a registration process completed following development of the master schedule.

Advantages of this assignment method are its speed and objectivity. No one can legitimately claim that certain students or parents have received special attention in the assignment process and the computer can be expected to do a reasonably good job of balancing class size, particularly in those cases where the master schedule was developed with careful attention to balancing seats by grade level.

Individual Selection

Under the individual-selection plan, some person actually assigns the student to individual classes. One very common form of this plan is the "walk-around," in which the student selects class cards and essentially makes the assignment himself or herself. In other cases, a counseling secretary or registration clerk may pull the class cards. Whatever the method, there is usually a set of judgments made in completing the class assignment for each student. Students may consider the teacher variable in making some selections; faculty may encourage or avoid certain combinations of students being assigned to the same section of a particular course. In short, the very kind of individualized judgments discouraged under the computer assignment method are encouraged (or at least permitted) under the individual-selection format.

As one might expect, the major advantage claimed for this method is the capacity to make individual judgments when desired. Many teachers feel strongly that students are likely to be more satisfied with a given class if they have some choice of teacher and time of day. For many administrators, the walk-around is preferred simply because it can be accomplished with ease at a time just prior to the beginning of the school term. This tends to give students less excuse to change course requests between the time of assignment to classes and the first meeting of these classes; hence, at least in theory, the schedule-change requests should be minimal.

Whichever method is used, the computer can print multiple copies of teacher and student schedules. Most secondary schools today utilize at least this high-speed printing feature of the computer as part of the total scheduling process.

Dealing with Schedule Changes

No discussion of scheduling is complete without some comment on the procedures used in handling student requests for schedule changes. The change procedure is an extremely important part of the overall scheduling system and, if not adequately understood in advance, it can lead to unnecessary frustration on the part of both faculty and students. Earlier in this presentation, it was mentioned that the specific method or procedure used in assigning students to sections can sometimes influence the number of schedule-change requests. Even when assignment to sections is made immediately prior to the beginning of the term and is based on the very latest course registration preferences of students, there will be some requests for change. A system for handling these requests, both reasonable and unreasonable, must be developed. Obviously, those requests judged to be reasonable must be resolved as quickly as possible after the beginning of the school term.

COMPUTER ASSISTANCE IN THE SCHEDULING PROCESS

Computer assistance in various aspects of the scheduling process has all but replaced the tab and marginal card systems used previously.[4] Despite the increase in computer use, there still exists no idealized computer program that begins with student requests, teacher preferences, room specifications, and class characteristics and results in a finalized master schedule with the student assignments all completed. Some of the heuristic computer programs such as the Generalized Academic Simulation Program (GASP), developed by Robert Holz of M.I.T., or the programs developed as part of a five-year scheduling project at Stanford University approximate this ideal by simultaneously building the master schedule and assigning students to it.

Unfortunately, the data input requirements on most of these programs are so extensive and the heuristics so involved that it is not practical to use them except on fairly complex variable time schedules.[5] Even then, the benefits may be greatest in those situations where the scheduler is trying a new set of course structures or an otherwise distinctly different set of scheduling configurations.

For the vast majority of schools, computer assistance will most likely continue with the analysis of registration data (simple tally and conflict matrix generation), the assignment of students to a hand-developed master schedule, and the printing of teacher and student schedules. The actual development of the master schedule is an extremely complex endeavor, even in schools with fairly traditional schedule patterns. It is both difficult and time-consuming to input the myriad conditions regarding teacher competence and preference, room availability, minimum and maximum enrollment levels, and student need into a single computer program. Even the administrator building the master schedule by hand often changes priorities as the need for compromise is realized. The computer has trouble

[4]A complete description of the tab card system appears in John J. Herbert, "Class Scheduling and Grade Reporting Aided by Marginally Punched Card System" (1963), pp. 129–137.

[5]A description of variable-time schedules and an introduction to the problems faced in building master schedules for them can be found in Robert N. Bush et al., "The High School Schedule" (1961), pp. 48–59.

simulating this complex decision-making process and is perhaps best reserved for the three time-saving tasks mentioned above.

For the reader interested in the logic involved in computer generation of simple tally and conflict matrices, a simple version of such a program written in the BASIC computer languge is included in Appendix 3. Programs designed to assign or section students to a master schedule can be obtained from most school district computer centers and programs for listing teacher and student schedules are likewise available at almost all public and private computer centers servicing school accounts.

IMPLICATIONS OF ALTERNATIVE SCHEDULING PATTERNS

Most school faculties can find problems with the scheduling system in use. This is true in part because the processes involved in designing and implementing any schedule involve compromise. The schedule that provides the longer periods desired by art and shop teachers may not be ideal for the foreign-language teacher who desires a short daily period of instruction. Some students may be stretching a bit to take the five subjects and study period provided with the traditional six-period day, but others want to fit in another elective that they see as essential to their future plans. While some internal scheduling adjustments can be made to alleviate selected concerns of this type, the creative faculty will nonetheless always be searching for a better way.

The administrator charged with scheduling responsibilities must be capable of examining the implications of proposed changes in the schedule pattern. Too many school staffs have become excited about a particular schedule change only to find that, when implemented, the change either did not do anything to solve the problems or resulted in some other undesirable result such as large class sizes or less controlled study time for students.

Schedule patterns vary in relation to the staffing and facility resources of the individual building, and cannot be covered comprehensively here. It is useful, however, to outline briefly the type of analysis that should be completed by any building administrator considering change in the schedule pattern of a school.[6] At the very least, the administrator charged with scheduling responsibility should be capable of assessing with reasonable precision the facility, teacher load, and class-size implications of a basic change in schedule pattern.

For example, let us consider a secondary school with an enrollment of 1,000 students that is currently operating on a six-period traditional schedule. We further assume that teachers teach five of the six class periods and all students take either six classes or five classes and a study period. The faculty is allocated to the building on the basis of one full-time-equivalent teacher (a teacher teaching five classes) for every twenty students. The faculty is exploring the possibility of changing to a seven-period traditional schedule and is interested in assessing the implications of that change.

The analysis of this alternative schedule begins with a clear understanding of the current schedule pattern. The 20:1 student-teacher allocation ratio generates a total of 50 teachers for the building. Since each teacher is involved with exactly five class sections and each student takes six classes, we conclude that the present average class size including study period is $(6 \times 1000) \div (5 \times 50)$, or 24.0 students. Alternatively, looking at it on a single-period basis, we can see that, because all students are in class each period and 5/6 of the 50 teachers are assigned to class each period, the average class size is $1000 \div 5/6(50)$, or 24.0 students. Facility demands with the current schedule average 5/6(50) or approximately 42

[6]A more detailed discussion of techniques for analyzing schedules, especially relating to teacher load, can be found in Anthony Saville, *Instructional Programming* (1973), pp. 89–99.

classrooms per period. Obviously, this will vary some according to the specific class size distribution existing during the several periods.

Now, in looking at the proposed change to a seven-period day, we must make additional assumptions regarding number of class assignments for teachers and the number of classes in which students will be enrolled. For purposes of this illustration, we assume that teachers continue under the new plan to teach just five periods a day and students will take a full load of seven classes or six classes and a study period. With these assumptions, one can examine with reasonable accuracy the major changes involved in the proposed schedule. First, it is clear that classes under the revised plan will be a bit shorter unless the faculty adopts one of the patterns that involves dropping one period each day of a seven-day cycle. With respect to class size, we note that classes will be distinctly larger than with the current pattern. Since each student now takes seven classes and faculty still teach only five class sections, the average class size will now be $(7 \times 1000) \div (5 \times 50)$, or 28.0 students. Relating this new class size figure to the previous 24.0, we observe that the new figure is exactly 28/24 or 7/6 of the original. This larger average class size suggests a lesser demand for classroom stations under the proposed schedule. Specifically, since on the average only 5/7 of the faculty is teaching in any one period, we need only 5/7(50) or approximately 36 classrooms each period of the day. In this case, we note that the exact multiple for classroom demand is 6/7, with the requirement under the proposed schedule being 6/7 that of the existing schedule.

Quite obviously, differing results in this example would be obtained under a different set of assumptions. Perhaps under the proposed schedule teachers would plan to teach six out of seven class periods. Students under either the original or proposed schedule could be released from school rather than assigned to study classes within the school.

Whatever the assumptions, the administrator must be able to spell out implications both for the school program and for such important indices as teaching load, class size, and facility requirements. Only then can the faculty as a whole hope to make informed and intelligent decisions as to the most desirable schedule patterns for a particular school setting.

SUMMARY

Schedules used in most secondary schools today can be viewed as being built on either fixed- or variable-time patterns. Examples of the two types of schedules were illustrated in this chapter and their advantages and disadvantages discussed. This review of basic schedule formats was followed by a suggested set of guidelines to be used in developing schedules for individual schools. Although these guidelines are intended for the secondary level, they also apply to the less complicated scheduling tasks associated with elementary school administraton. Scheduling at whatever level can be viewed as a compromising activity and it was suggested in this review that prime consideration in resolving these compromises be given to the interests of students.

Following the general review of guidelines to be used in developing the schedule, two major aspects of the scheduling task, namely, building the master schedule and assigning students to the classes defined by that master schedule, were discussed. Specific techniques for minimizing conflict and for assuring the availability of classes to all students were presented, as was a summary of how the computer can be used to aid in the scheduling process. In a concluding section, the reader was provided assistance in anticipating implications of alternative scheduling formats. This latter material should be helpful to those who, in advance of implementing a specific schedule change, want to predict its impact on such variables as class size, teaching load, and facility requirements.

QUESTIONS AND PROBLEMS ON CHAPTER 4

1. Consider the specific rotation schedule of Figure 4–1 in responding to each of the following:
   a. What advantages does this rotation schedule have? Explain how the schedule could be adjusted to give each course one longer period during each schedule cycle.
   b. Design an alternative rotation schedule format with a five-day cycle and indicate its probable advantages and disadvantages in any school situation of your choosing.
2. Examine the alternate-day pattern of Figure 4–2.
   a. This pattern could conceivably result in slightly more in-class time than the traditional schedule of Figure 4–1, even though both call for the same number of individual class periods per course per week. Explain why this is so.
   b. Building a master schedule for the alternate-day model involves a procedure similar to that used in the traditional schedule of Figure 4–1, but building the master schedule for the dual-track program of Figure 4–2 introduces an added dimension of difficulty. Explain the added difficulty introduced by the dual-track schedule.
3. Show how a dual-track schedule with eight shorter periods and six longer periods can permit inclusion of all six subjects rather than the five used in the illustration of Figure 4–2 and explain the advantages or disadvantages that might be associated with the revised dual-track schedule.
4. Consider the enrollments and numbers of sections presented in Figure 4–5.
   a. What would be the average class size of the English 10 classes if we added an eighth section of the class?
   b. What would be the average class size of the U.S./World History sections if those students who signed up for Anthropology but not U.S./World History on the preregistration were to make that switch to U.S./World History on learning that Anthropology was not being offered? (The conflict matrix of Figure 4–4 should help in arriving at your response.)
   c. What is the overall average class size for all sections presented in Figure 4–5 assuming inclusion of the switch outlined in Part b above?
5. The faculty of Imagination Elementary School decides to set up a special elective program during the afternoons for a six-week period. A three-period schedule (with each period of forty-five-minute duration) is established and the twenty students to be involved are each asked to sign up for three different electives. The conflict matrix shown in Figure 4–7 is developed from this registration process.
   a. Assuming a class section limit of eight students, how many sections of each of the above-listed elective classes should be offered?
   b. What will be the average class size for the elective program?
   c. If Batik is to be offered during the first period, what other classes could be scheduled the same period with one or fewer conflicts?
6. In relation to the elective program in Question 5 above, assume that five teachers and/or parents are to be involved in instruction. Figure 4–8 indicates the number and type of assignments that can be given to each. Assume both photography sections are taught in Period 3, as indicated in Figure 4–9, and that Jones must have Period 2 for planning. Develop a master schedule that minimizes conflict, being certain to use the conflict matrix of Figure 4–7.

Figure 4–7

	Batik	Basketry	Drugs/ Alcohol	Indian Culture	Jazz	Map Reading	Music Appreciation	Photography
Batik	8	0	3	1	4	0	2	6
Basketry		7	4	1	2	0	3	4
Drugs/Alcohol			7	0	0	0	2	5
Indian Culture				7	5	0	2	5
Jazz					11	0	5	6
Map Reading						0	0	0
Music Appreciation							7	0
Photography								13

Figure 4–8

Teacher/Parent	Number of Sections	Classes for Which a Section Can Be Assigned
Jones	2	Batik, Map Reading, Photography
May	2	Indian Culture, Jazz, Music Appreciation
Reff	2	Drugs/Alcohol, Map Reading, Music Appreciation
Smith	2	Basketry, Batik, Jazz
Welch	1	Photography

7. Consider the conflict matrix shown in Figure 4–10 for Imagination Junior High School. This particular school has a traditional five-period schedule pattern and an enrollment of twenty students. Assume that all classes as listed meet for a single period each day.
   a. If Science is scheduled during the first period of the school day, which foreign language—German or French—should probably not be offered that same period? Why?
   b. Are there any courses that are apparently required of all students? Explain your reasoning.
   c. Assuming all twenty students sign up for either five classes or four classes and an early release period, how many total students are on early release? Explain your reasoning.
   d. Specify a set of registration requests for each of the twenty students that could have generated the conflict matrix of Figure 4-10. Is this the only set of

Figure 4–9

Teacher/ Parent	Period		
	1	2	3
Jones			Photo-graphy
May			
Reff			
Smith			
Welch			Photo-graphy

Figure 4–10

	English	Science	German	French	History	Math	P.E.	Speech	Band	Art
English	20	6	5	6	14	15	8	3	9	7
Science		6	5	-	3	5	1	3	-	-
German			5	-	3	5	-	2	-	-
French				6	5	4	2	-	1	5
History					14	10	5	-	6	6
Math						15	3	2	7	5
P.E.							8	1	5	3
Speech								3	-	-
Band									9	2
Art										7

course requests that could generate this particular conflict matrix? (This is a difficult trial-and-error process and the request list will be used in connection with Question 11.)

8. Consider a 1,000-student secondary school with a six-period traditional schedule. Assume that each of the fifty teachers is teaching five of the six periods and students are taking six classes. As indicated in the text, this results in an average class size of twenty-four students.
   a. How many teachers on the average will be on their planning time each period of the day?
   b. Suppose four of the fifty teachers were given nonclassroom assignments for one period each in addition to their planning time. How would the average class size of twenty-four be affected by such a change?
   c. Suppose the school decided to go to a five-period, traditional schedule pattern with students taking five classes and teachers teaching four out of five periods. What would be the average class size under such a change?
   d. Suppose that when the change in Part c was implemented, it was decided to go to a trimester (three terms of sixty days) rather than the present semester (two terms of ninety days). What impact would such a change have on both the number of courses taken each year by the student and the length of classroom instructional time committed to each class?

9. Assume that, in a 1,000-student junior high school with a seven-period, traditional schedule, the English department proposes a team-teaching situation in which 110 ninth-grade students would be assigned to a four-teacher team in each of three periods of the day. This would accommodate the 330 ninth graders taking English and would presumably permit the teachers to do more grouping for the purposes of instruction. What facility and scheduling factors should be examined by the administration before approving this plan?

10. Assume that a particular secondary school receives teaching staff at a ratio of one teacher for every 25 students. The current enrollment is 900 students and the school is thinking of switching from its present seven-period, traditional schedule to a five-period, traditional pattern. Each student under the current plan takes six classes and under the proposed plan each would be expected to take five classes.
   a. What is the average class size under the current schedule, assuming each teacher teaches six of the seven class periods?
   b. How would the class size in Part a change if 100 students were permitted to sign up for a full load of seven classes?
   c. What is the average class size under the proposed schedule, assuming each teacher teaches four of the five class periods?
   d. How much would the average class size in Part c increase if one of the teachers is assigned to a math resource center for two periods each day? (This math resource assignment is considered noninstructional in nature.)
   e. In relation to the proposed schedule in Part c, how many students would have to opt for a reduced load of four classes in order to bring the average class size down to twenty-eight?

Questions 11–13 are to be answered by students with background or interest in learning about computer programming procedures.

11. Using the set of registration requests in Question 7d or some similar set of enrollment data:
   a. Employ the BASIC program steps of Appendix 3 to develop a conflict matrix using the computer.

   b. Generate this same matrix from the course-registration requests using the MULT RESPONSE function of the Statistical Package for the Social Sciences (SPSS).

12. Explain the function of each series of program steps in the program of Appendix 3. (This may be accomplished by simply adding additional REM statements to the program as written.)

13. Rewrite the computer programs of Appendix 3 to accomplish one or both of the following:

   a. User can specify that courses in the output be listed in order of registration size rather than in the sequence of the input data set. (This may be useful in placing singleton classes together on the conflict matrix.)

   b. The program can be utilized for up to 100 separate course offerings instead of the ten currently specified. (This primarily involves changing and extending the print formats on the conflict matrix.)

CHAPTER 5
TIME AND STRESS MANAGEMENT IN SCHOOLS

Our focus thus far in Part II has been on skills of planning and scheduling. The discussion has been limited to techniques for the planning and evaluation of activities designed to further organizational aims; we have not concerned ourselves with the way in which school principals and other administrators organize and schedule their personal affairs to accomplish these many important activities. It seems fitting at this point to direct attention to the administrator's interface with the school organization and to suggest techniques for handling the many organizational and personal stresses found within today's school environments.

The stresses placed on professionals working within schools are indeed great. A report on violence in the schools documents much of this potential for stress.[1] Not only do

[1]Although school violence has apparently leveled off since the early 1970s, there is still a considerable problem with both vandalism and personal violence. Crime and vandalism in schools is still listed as one of the top fifteen problems in George H. Gallup, "The Thirteenth Annual Gallup Poll of the Public's Attitude Toward Public Schools," *Phi Delta Kappan* 63 (September 1981): 34–35; however, its ranking as a problem area has dropped in the past three years. National Institute of Education, *Violent Schools—Safe Schools,* vol. 1 (Washington D.C.: U.S. Government Printing Office, January 1978), reported serious problems with crime in fully 8 percent of the nation's schools.

principals and other middle-management personnel in schools face more pressure in relation to student behavior, but the fact that teachers and parents both claim a larger role in school decision making has led to greater demands for good record keeping and for careful evaluation of school personnel and programs. These demands are evidenced by the generally increased regulation from state and federal government sources. Although the planning and control mechanisms and skills discussed in other chapters of this text can aid in managing these many pressures and proposals for change, each individual administrator must for reasons of organizational survival and personal health find ways to balance personal commitment to the organization with a reasonable expectation of what can actually be accomplished. This balance will be at different levels for various individuals within the organization, but there is no question that organizational pressures can often place unreasonable expectations on employees, including administrators. School principals who have been rewarded for past organizational contributions are particularly vulnerable to this sometimes self-imposed pressure of unreasonable expectations.

In an article on managing stress, Gmelch observes: "Few principals know their own limitations, which is why so few people live long enough to happily reminisce about past accomplishments. Principals need to learn to accept the fact that administration has its limitations. Changes cannot be made over night, and some changes cannot be made at all" (Gmelch, p. 10). The need for personal commitment to the organization is very real and the education of future generations depends as much as anything on the genuine interest and concern of both administrators and teachers in our schools; yet, educators must learn how to deal with conflicting and sometimes impossible demands placed on them and to develop personal time-management skills for coping in a realistic fashion.

Before we move to a consideration of these important time- and stress-management skills, it is useful to clarify several concerns about the domain of time and stress management in the schools. These several concerns are essential to understanding the guidelines and skills presented and in determining the scope of their application to individual administrators working in a variety of school situations.

1. Time-management skills from an organizational perspective are needed only because of the need to marshal the resources of the organization in the accomplishment of its priority goals. There is really no time-management need for those administrators who refuse to admit that school goals exist or that they can be ranked. For the administrator without definable professional goals other than survival, there is no reasonable way to assess the organizational impact of any particular use of time on the job; hence, in these cases there is little point in talking about effective time management at all. A statement of concern about time management is itself rooted in the need to apply the resource of time more constructively in accomplishing goals. Those not sharing that interest may gain little from the reading of this chapter or from becoming involved in a self-improvement program of time management.

2. Because time- and stress-management skills are equally applicable to the personal and organizational domains, the mere act of implementing improved time-management techniques will not assure greater organizational effectiveness. If the commitment or thrust of the work is on low-priority concerns of the organization or on purely personal priorities, a given administrator can exhibit excellent time-management skills and yet be a very ineffective contributor to the organization. Recognizing this relationship, organizational impact is likely only when the time- and stress-management concerns of this chapter are linked in some useful way with the goal and action-program development work presented in Part I of the text.

3. Time and stress management as used here cover a range of techniques for making

the work load of the manager more realistic and for maximizing effectiveness of both the manager and those who work most closely with the manager. While some have made the claim that the very act of maximizing use of the time resource will be likely to increase vulnerability to undesirable stress (and, hence, lessen effectiveness as a manager), it is my opinion that time and stress management should not be viewed as conflicting phenomena. If, in our review of time utilization, we constantly look to overall effectiveness of the manager, it is absolutely essential to assess stress impact concurrently with that of time utilization. Time- and stress-management concepts viewed in this manner are seen as complementary.

4. The time-management skills presented here must be adapted to the style of each practicing or prospective administrator and there is no intent to suggest fundamental changes in the personality or personal managerial styles of the reader. Even if certain personal styles are more compatible with the time-management and stress-coping skills described herein, there is simply too much accumulated conditioning of personal style to make substantial style changes possible for most administrators. Some research suggests that major style changes, even when desired by the administrator in question, may be harmful to overall effectiveness on the job.[2]

5. Just as no particular personal or managerial style is required as a prerequisite for making effective use of time-management skills, neither should a particular style be used as an excuse for lack of interest in time management. Even the most outwardly laissez-faire administrator must at some point commit at least some of his or her limited time resources to organizational purposes. Administrators are often heard to say that all the ranking of tasks and goal-directed behavior represented in time management stifles creativity and freedom within the organization. More often than not this is a cover-up for lack of personal commitment to the organization and its goals. The reasons for this lack of commitment and suggested strategies for coping with it are very important to the school organization, but these are beyond the scope of this particular text.

ASSUMPTIONS ABOUT EFFECTIVE TIME USE

Many of the specific skills and suggestions covered in this chapter are justified in terms of certain assumptions about effective time management. These assumptions are basic to much of the current writing in the field of time and stress management.

Activities of school administrators should be meaningful and related to purposes.

There exists a considerable body of social science research showing that motivation for work increases when the work is seen to be meaningful by the worker. This is particularly true for persons like administrators who, for at least part of the time, operate at higher levels of need.[3] Workers lose a sense of meaning in their work and turn more and more attention to personal rather than organizational concerns when the work they are assigned to complete appears unrelated to the prime concerns of the organization. It is here that the importance of

[2]This notion of limitation in style flexibility is discussed in William J. Redding, *Managerial Effectiveness* (New York: McGraw-Hill, 1970), p. 52. Further evidence of rather unchangeable cognitive styles is reported in James L. McKenney and Peter G. W. Keen, "How Managers' Minds Work," *Harvard Business Review* 52 (May–June 1974): 79.

[3]The higher levels of need referred to here are the esteem and self-actualizing needs described in Abraham Maslow, *Motivation and Personality* (1970), pp. 45–47.

purpose becomes evident. Unless the administrator can reasonably see some relationship between his or her work and the purposes of the organization, it is a futile exercise to worry about good time-management skills, at least from the perspective of the organization.

The ease with which purpose and meaning can be communicated to managers is likely to vary across different forms of organization. Perhaps it is more easily communicated in managing a home than a school or business. The meaning of work for a person managing the home is immediately apparent to all concerned. With the frequent need to provide meals and to respond immediately to the hurt or sickness of children, the communication of meaning and purpose is constant. While the home manager may not always agree with the short-term purposes being communicated and may therefore lose interest at times, it is nonetheless true that the communication of this sense of purpose in a group so small as the home is frequent and generally consistent.

This is not nearly so true in a school organization. Here, the sense of collective purpose needs constant attention. In organizations with several administrative levels, there is a much greater need to employ certain of the action-program planning techniques presented in Chapters 1 and 2 of this text. Too frequently we find cases in school settings where an employee has been assigned some task to fill a time void rather than because the task addresses a particular need of the organization. As the person becomes increasingly aware of the meaninglessness of the work, loss of motivation and commitment is almost certain to follow. Administrators at all levels need to monitor this phenomenon, as it can quickly affect attitudes of employees throughout the organizaton.

This commitment to minimize meaningless work within the organization has led management experts like Carolyn Bird to propose that employees who complete their work early actually be rewarded by time off. She points out that the amount of time spent in the formal work environment may vary according to function, with decision makers requiring less formal work time than computer programmers.[4] Decision makers and administrative personnel in particular may need time away from the formal work setting in order to function at peak efficiency. To the extent that schools are genuinely interested in results rather than in time spent on the job, managers in the school setting should give serious consideration to these proposals for rewarding work completion with time off.

Activities of administrators should be challenging but not impossible.
Much of the research on motivation suggests that a challenging assignment for most people is likely to be more motivating than one lacking in challenge. Herzberg recommends motivating factors such as achievement, recognition, responsibility, and the task itself as ways of creating challenge and satisfaction for the employee; Likert similarly suggests the need for high performance goals by employees and proposes the System Four Management Model as a way of identifying and achieving these goals.[5]

Much of the rationale for the recent management by objectives (MBO) movement in education is founded on the assumption that organizational effectiveness is enhanced when employees are involved in the identification of challenging goals within the organization. It is also assumed that if the employee is involved in the goal-setting activity, there is less likelihood that the goals as selected will represent unreasonable or impossible expectations. Unreasonable and impossible goals are likely to reduce expectancy of success, which is an important requisite to goal attainment in most motivation theories. Furthermore, impossible

---

[4]This concept of functional schedules for workers is described in Caroline Bird and Thomas D. Vutzy, "The Tyranny of Time: Results Achieved vs. Hours Spent," *Management Review* 54 (August 1965): 34–43.
[5]For a discussion of Herzberg's motivating factors, the reader is referred to Frederick Herzberg, *Work and the Nature of Man* (1966), pp. 71–91. Characteristics of System Four (or participative group management system) are presented in Rensis Likert, *Human Organization* (1967), pp. 4–10.

goals will for most people introduce fear of failure into the situation and this is sure to reduce or eliminate any motivation to spend time in goal pursuit.[6]

Because school principals and other middle-management administrators in schools operate in at least part of their role at higher need levels, it is expected that they will initiate challenging tasks when given the opportunity by their immediate supervisors. As long as the accomplishment of these challenging tasks is viewed by the administrator as reasonable, given current conditions, there is every likelihood that the administrator will commit time to these tasks and that the time commitment will be effective in relation to goal attainment.

Administrator time should be focused on the most important things.

One of the most frequently used reasons for not starting on an important task is an inability to select that task from the several that could be done. When this uncertainty occurs, the administrator characteristically responds to the pressures of the moment and fails to begin any of the important tasks. On this tendency to pursue the immediate or urgent tasks, Charles Hummel observes: "The important task rarely must be done today, or even this week. The urgent task calls for instant action. Often we realize only too late that we have become slaves to the tyranny of the urgent" (quoted in MacKenzie, p. 43).

Because of their location close to the classroom, building administrators are particularly vulnerable to spending excessive time responding to urgent tasks, which seem always in abundance in the school setting. While responding to many of these is essential to overall school operation, there are ways to delegate the response in some cases to teachers and clerical personnel in the building or, in offices served by more than one administrator, to schedule a rotation of response time for these urgent tasks.

For middle-management personnel in schools, planning seems to be one of those important tasks that never quite gets done. How often does it happen that a new program starts without adequate equipment and textbooks simply because the advance planning was not started soon enough? Or can we remember when the installation of a new attendance or grading system had to be postponed because the committee recommending it had not carefully considered the interface for data processing? The frequency of occurrence of these sorts of implementation problems could be reduced if administrators were to insist on more careful advance planning.

R. Alec MacKenzie, well-known management consultant and author of *The Time Trap,* after observing a reluctance by managers to become involved in planning, compared the planning and execution times on a number of projects. He found that the extra time devoted to planning was more than saved in the execution phase. This observation certainly applies in schools, where careful advance planning can often prevent the expenditure of time in nonproductive directions. Furthermore, it is my observation that teachers are generally more satisfied working in a setting where they have confidence in the administrator's ability to plan carefully. The best administrators are those who plan carefully and are consequently able to work at a much less frantic pace during the implementation phase. This careful planning even encourages greater focus on important things during implementation, thus assuring better overall use of administrator time.

Administrator time should be wisely distributed between "availability" and "quiet" periods.

As part of the assurance that administrator time focus on the more important things, it is absolutely essential that each administrator schedule some "quiet" time for planning and reflection. The so-called open-door policy espoused by many building administrators has

[6]For a discussion of achievement motivation with specific focus on avoiding failure situations, the reader is referred to John W. Atkinson, *An Introduction to Motivation* (New York: D. Van Nostrand, 1964), pp. 240–268.

its limitations in terms of the overall school operation. While the open door does assure "availability" to a wide variety of student, staff, and parent concerns, it does little to assure the careful planning that should be central to the administrator role, unless of course the administrator is willing and able to schedule this needed quiet time outside the regular working day. Since for the typical building administrator, a significant portion of time outside the regular school day is already scheduled for availability-type activities such as Parent-Teacher Association (PTA) functions, athletic events, and district meetings, and because most administrators do need to reserve significant periods of time for their personal lives, it is essential that most of the quiet time be structured into the regular working schedule.

The building administrator who remarked to his secretary, "I am going to work on the proposal for the economics education grant. Don't interrupt me for the next two hours unless it's the superintendent or mother calling," may be on the right track, though there is even reason to question whether the exceptions for superintendent and mother should have been recognized. At any rate, this administrator at least realizes that careful and competent planning cannot be accomplished during availability time in the building. It has even been suggested that all school administrators make a practice of scheduling one-half day per week of planning time outside the school building. In these days of taxpayer concern about the use and misuse of public funds, this suggestion receives only minimal support from many administrators. Most say, "It sounds like a good idea but the public wouldn't buy it." While this anxiety on the part of administrators may be well-founded, it is unfortunate that members of the general public do not realize that such a plan would undoubtedly result in more rather than less effectiveness for the school program.

Perhaps, as a compromise, the building administrator could at least spend a half-day each week doing planning work in a quiet area in the building or in an extra office at the district headquarters. Some administrators may even find it possible to maintain sufficient quiet time in their own office by having the secretary hold all calls. If this latter approach is to be successful, it will require real determination by both administrator and secretary and understanding on the part of associates.

Alan Lakein, a time-management consultant who has written on this topic, cautions about possible backfire over long and frequent periods of quiet time. He tells of one executive who scheduled a daily quiet time from eight o'clock until noon. Unfortunately, his subordinates struggled during these periods; the executive eventually lost control of the department and was released. This problem of backlash underscores the needs to achieve balance between quiet and availability periods and to gain a clear understanding with associates about the need for the quiet periods. Without this understanding, there is a likelihood that subordinates will view these periods as a form of escape from the concerns and problems of the school. Such a view by associates can quickly spell problems for an administrator at any level.

Administrator priorities and activities should be known to associates.
In an organization like the school, which is subject to the constant pressures of a diverse set of public-interest groups and individuals, it is especially important that administrators from the superintendent to the building principal make priority concerns known to associates. Many of the techniques for establishing and implementing action programs (as discussed in Chapter 2) are really efforts at communicating this sense of long-range administrator priorities to others in the school organization.

Far too few administrators in today's schools see this communication of priorities as a real need or possibility within their buildings. Yet a common complaint from teachers is the lack of overall direction or commitment from their supervising administrators. Perhaps some of this resistance by administrators to action-program planning results from the erosion of administrator authority through various state and federal regulations, negotiated agreements, and the due-process arrangements emanating from recent court decisions. While these many outside forces do make the processes of change in schools a bit more difficult and time-consuming, they should not be used as an excuse for inaction by administrators. Schools even in this day of excessive rules and regulations still need a sense of forward motion and direction.

Even on a day-to-day basis, communicating short-term priorities and activities to associates has a positive impact on staff morale. This impact is perhaps best seen in looking at the administrator's relationship with his or her secretary. MacKenzie observes:

> The subject of communication is a sensitive one for most secretaries simply because most bosses do not keep them adequately informed. Consequently, they are unable to answer routine inquiries on such basic matters as where he is, when he will return, what he meant by a given memo, and so forth. These habits of course reflect on the secretary as much as on the boss. Keeping her informed makes her job much easier, resulting in a smoother running organization and puts her in a good light. (MacKenzie, p. 168)

This concern for administrator activity extends beyond the secretary. Immediate associates, whether teachers or fellow administrators, need to know about the administrator's priority concerns in order to properly anticipate needs for information and/or assistance. This does not mean that every detail of the administrator's schedule must be widely distributed; however, it does suggest that the smooth operation of the school and the maintenance of good staff morale are enhanced when subordinates have a general knowledge of administrator priorities and the confidence that the administrator is spending his or her own time in pursuit of those priorities.

At this point, we are touching on an extremely important component of administrator effectiveness, namely, authenticity in personal behavior. Teachers and the public in general can tolerate a variety of administrative styles. They are even willing to overlook some limitation in the ability necessary to successfully direct certain aspects of the school operation. They do not, however, look favorably on the administrator who demonstrates a lack of authenticity in relation to the job.[7] The authority of the administrator in a very significant way depends on the demonstrated ability to match verbal commitments with an appropriate investment of personal commitment and time. It is well for all administrators to give this matter serious consideration as they plan and carry out their time commitments.

Administrator time should reflect concentration of effort.

One characteristic of the competent administrator is the ability to concentrate on one thing at a time. Peter Drucker, a leading writer in the management field, underscored this by suggesting that concentration is the executive's only hope of becoming the master of time and events instead of their whipping boy. This ability to concentrate and to persevere in the task until it is completed often distinguishes the superior administrator from those who are operating at a minimum level. It can even go a long way in compensating for lack of mental genius.

The ability to concentrate is important for effective administration in every field, including education. The building administrator is not likely to make much progress on the

---

[7]For a discussion of authenticity as a key ingredient of a favorable school climate, the reader is referred to Andrew W. Halpin and Don B. Croft, *The Organizational Climate of Schools* (Washington, D.C. U.S. Office of Education, 1962), pp. 103–159.

master schedule or on detailing planning steps for the school carnival in the midst of answering phone calls or responding to student discipline referrals. Neither can the administrator expect to do a good job of completing the budget estimates for a grant proposal or even conduct a good personnel interview without shutting off the myriad interruptions occurring in the typical school office. Even isolating oneself in the office with instructions to avoid interruption is no assurance of the concentration needed for effective administrative work. The administrator must learn to shut off voices and bells ringing in the outer office and to exercise a certain discipline of mind to concentrate on the task at hand. Distractions should be eliminated whenever possible.

A common obstacle to concentration in the work setting is the mere awareness of other tasks requiring attention. Many administrators find the "To-Do List" helpful in achieving greater concentration in their work. It is simply a listing made at the beginning of each day of the things that need doing during the course of that day. Sometimes the list is in a priority order and some administrators actually schedule time for the specific items. The very act of commiting all these tasks to writing encourages greater concentration on the one task under consideration. The administrator using the To-Do List knows that other tasks will not be forgotten while concentrating on the single task at hand. One building principal known for his good time management skills indicated a preference for a weekly list on which items could be added and crossed out as the week progressed. This particular administrator felt that the task of creating a new list each day was itself too time-consuming and that the same advantages in concentration could be gained through a frequent updating of the weekly list.

Whether completed on a daily cycle or by daily update of a weekly listing, the To-Do List is almost universally supported by time-management specialists as a way of achieving greater concentration on priority tasks. Without this concentration on the most important tasks, the administrator can easily revert to being a mere fire fighter, dealing largely with the urgent but often unimportant items.

Application of Assumptions in the Real World of Administration

These six guidelines or assumptions closely parallel suggestions made in a time-management study completed in January 1974 by the Association of California School Administrators. In that study, the authors concluded that five key steps can help the busy administrator achieve more effective time utilization: define your goals, consider alternatives, work out a plan of action, set up a timetable, and concentrate on essentials (*Time Management,* p. 22). Each of these steps is in some way addressed in the preceding discussion on assumptions about good time management. Notice that the California administrative group concludes with the need to concentrate on essentials.

Many school administrators, because of problems in achieving concentration in their work, find that a relatively small amount of total available time is used to deal with the vital concerns of the organization. This phenomenon, appropriately referred to as a managerial application of the "80-20" rule, suggests that 80 percent of the results achieved are accounted for by approximately 20 percent of the total time spent. Other examples of this 80-20 phenomenon in schools include:

80 percent of the discipline problems are generated by 20 percent of the students
80 percent of the phone calls come from 20 percent of the parents
80 percent of the parental complaints about teachers are directed to 20 percent of the teachers
80 percent of the library books are checked out to 20 percent of the students
80 percent of the teacher absences are attributed to 20 percent of the teachers

80 percent of the late assignments are from 20 percent of the students
80 percent of the lost textbooks are associated with 20 percent of the students

Recognizing the application of this rule in administration should serve as a constant reminder to the administrator that time should not only be used in a concentrated manner, that is, with a focus on one thing at a time, but it should be concentrated on those tasks that will actually result in the highest value to the organization. This means that the goals, the selected plan of action, and particularly the To-Do List must constantly be reviewed to make certain that the tasks receiving the most time from the administrator are those with the biggest payoff in terms of overall organizational effectiveness.

BETTER TIME UTILIZATION FOR SCHOOL ADMINISTRATORS

The six assumptions discussed in the previous section can be applied with advantage to almost any administrative role in the school or school system. Some of these areas of application were identified as part of the explanation; some readers will already have gained from this explanation selected tips on improving time utilization. In this section, we attempt to focus on several key problems faced by building administrators as they work to increase job effectiveness. When possible, the suggestions are related to one or more of the six assumptions.

Before addressing these selected problem areas, it must be stressed again that no specific time allocation is going to be maximally effective for all administrative positions or for the same position in two different time periods. A variance in ideal time allocation is to be expected even on the basis of personal style. Hence, the reader is encouraged to adopt only those suggestions that clearly apply and to freely modify ideas to fit the circumstances of time, place, and personality. It is quite likely that those readers who have not yet experienced an administrative assignment will have difficulty identifying with certain of the problem areas discussed here. This is understandable, as most of us cannot seriously address our own problems with time management in an administrative position until we have had an opportunity to experience the administrative role in a school setting. It is hoped that even in these cases personal reflection on time utilization in other professional roles, most of which have some management functions, will increase the usefulness of the ideas presented.

Drop-in Visitors

One of the key time-wasters for school administrators is the drop-in visitor. Quite often, such visits are encouraged by the administrator who subscribes in excess to the open-door policy of administration. While scheduled open-door periods make sense in terms of creating and maintaining a receptiveness to staff and student concerns, the idea that this policy should always pertain just does not make good sense from a management standpoint. As mentioned earlier, each administrator should establish a reasonable balance between availability and quiet periods. During the quiet periods, visitors should be discouraged except in emergency situations.

Even during availability time, there is probably a need for some screening of nonscheduled visits of a strictly social nature, particularly when there are others waiting or when essential administrative work remains undone. Several options are available for this screening. Perhaps the best technique is to establish clearly at the beginning of the visit the time parameters available to the visitor, with an indication that if more time is required an appointment should be scheduled for another day. Few visitors will resent this advance declaration of time parameters and it almost always results in a more focused discussion of the important matters of concern to the visitor.

For visitors who are known to press for more than their due share of administrator time, it may make sense to visit with them in the outer office or even while walking through the hallway. Some administrators have tried simply standing up during the entire visit but that technique to be effective may have to be coupled with a statement of time limitations.

All visitors, and particularly those who have scheduled appointments, should be given considerate attention during the visitation period. Once the visit is begun, it is best that it not be interrupted by either making or taking phone calls. Other visitors should also be screened out while the conference is in session unless the matter is one that requires immediate attention.

Telephone Calls

The telephone is an obviously essential part of communication in any school or school system. Advances in the technology of telephone communication and the higher costs of transportation can only increase this dependence on telephone communication in the years ahead. This means that administrators must learn to utilize it to maximum advantage and to prevent telephone interruptions from interfering with important work of the school.

One of the more important concerns related to telephone usage is the way in which the secretary handles calls. Obviously, if the administrator is either in conference or in a quiet period of planning, it is best that he or she not be interrupted. Appropriate responses, following a cordial greeting, include an offer to have someone else answer the query, take a message, or promise a return call. It is best to avoid asking the caller's name prior to the time of indicating that the administrator is in conference and asked not to be interrupted. This prevents the caller from gaining the impression that only selected calls are being taken and this particular call does not happen to be one of them. Any selectivity used in channeling calls during a conference or planning time should be made based on prior identification by the administrator or by the secretary's judgment that the matter is truly one that cannot wait or cannot be handled by others in the office. With careful phrasing, this can be handled without the appearance of discrimination.

Administrators who ask secretaries to place telephone calls should always show the courtesy of being available when the contact is made. Too often, administrators give the secretary a list of telephone contacts to make and then either run down the hall for a quick errand or place a call on another line without informing the secretary. This lack of coordination does not reflect well on either the secretary or the administrator and it wastes time for both the secretary and the person being called.

Once a telephone contact is made by the administrator, it is well to assume that the other person is busy and to time the call accordingly. Except in rare circumstances, telephone contacts should be short and to the point, with the content planned prior to placing the call.

Any school administrator, and particularly those at the building level, must be prepared to handle the "angry parent or citizen" calls that come in to the school office. Whether such calls are taken by the secretary or the administrator, the best approach is almost always to be a good listener, at least until the caller's accusations are known for certain to be without foundation. Often, just listening for a few minutes to allow the caller to review the events can defuse the immediate anxiety and thereby permit some discussion of possible next steps. If the caller's problem is like most conflict situations, it is probably best not to try to settle the matter over the phone but to wait until all principle parties in the conflict have an opportunity to be involved.

Handling Paperwork

Each administrator must find an effective way to deal with paperwork. For those with secretarial assistance, it is generally expedient to have the secretary open and sort the mail. If instructed carefully, most secretaries can screen out certain mail before it gets to the administrator's desk. Sometimes it is helpful for the secretary to place the more urgent items on top of the pile.

In line with the principle of concentration discussed earlier and the obvious advantage of minimizing time spent on processing paperwork, it is generally best to handle each piece of paperwork only once and to do so at a time when concentration on the task is possible. Hence, following a quick sort into various levels of urgency/importance (if this has not already been done by the secretary), the administrator should deal with each piece of paper in sequence. Sometimes instructions for processing can be written directly on the paper, which is placed in the out-basket for the secretary. In other cases, a note recorded on a dictating machine may be the fastest way to dispose of the matter. In still other cases, the material should be immediately discarded or perhaps placed in a folder for leisure-time reading. The rationale for providing immediate response to each piece of paperwork is explained by Alan Lakein:

> Try not to put down an incoming piece of paper that requires a response until you have fired off that response. It is often easier to think of the right thing to say when you've just received the letter and your first reaction is fresh in your mind. In addition, you save the setup time required to familiarize yourself with it again later on. (Lakein, p. 80)

Obviously, not all paperwork merits an immediate response and sometimes the material will have to be filed for retrieval at a time when more information is available. This highlights the importance of a good filing system. The frequently used "piles around the room" system is not likely to result in the best use of time in the long run. It not only creates considerable time loss in retrieving materials, but the existence of materials scattered across the room often interferes with good concentration of effort by the administrator.

Postponing Decision Making

There is a feeling among many administrators that delaying a decision usually results in a better decision. This feeling is very likely based on literature suggesting that decisions should be made with a maximum of information about the probable consequences of available options. Unfortunately, some administrators, because of a great fear of failure and/or the desire to keep everyone happy, use this need for maximum information to rationalize delay in a decision or a confrontation that should be handled immediately. Sometimes to delay a decision provides a minimum of additional information and simply causes unneeded frustration for co-workers. Furthermore, it can often result in a lot of wasted worry time on the part of the administrator, who in most cases is avoiding the decision. Management consultant Charles Flory has concluded, on the basis of his many years of working with executives, that 15 percent of the problems facing the executive need to mature, 5 percent should not even be considered, and the remaining 80 percent should be decided right away.

Procrastination in decision making can be particularly costly in the personnel management area of school operations. Most states now have fairly rigid regulations and timetables relating to such important personnel actions as tenure, probation, dismissal, and suspension. Many of these timetables are written into contract agreements with teacher groups. The administrator who fails to have the case properly prepared according to the timetables as established in statute or contract agreement may effectively have lost the opportunity to initiate the needed action at all.

It is in the area of personnel management that we see the greatest tendency of administrators to avoid and/or postpone action. Some administrators avoid conflict with a passion. Being service-oriented people, they almost always try to smooth out conflict situations rather than to hit them head on. While a bit of thinking never hurts, it is usually best to deal with the conflict rather than to let it fester. Constructive change can often result from effective management of conflict situations; very little but lost time results from avoiding the confrontation.

Since decision making by the administrator often depends on the timely accumulation of relevant information by subordinates, the capacity to make early decisions is often dependent on a clear delegation of responsibility for information collection and analysis. Building principals working on budgets or master schedules should establish clear deadlines for obtaining essential information from the departments. Part of delegating the task is establishing the deadline for its completion. It is quite appropriate to involve the department chair or members of the department in establishing deadlines, but remember that projects are more likely to be completed in a timely manner if reasonable deadlines are set at the very beginning.

Meetings with a Purpose

One of the most common gripes of both administrators and teachers is having to attend meetings. In a recent study of time-wasters, a group of forty suburban school administrators considered "too many meetings" the single most important item.[8] It is not surprising that this negative feeling toward meetings is shared by teachers. Teachers as a group are especially critical of general faculty meetings, though the source of their concern is not always the same. If any one problem with meetings were to be identified, it would probably be the lack of clear purpose. Some building administrators feel compelled to call a meeting of the total faculty every other Tuesday afternoon, whether there are really any items needing attention or not. Meetings that begin in the state of "still looking for an agenda" are almost always a disaster, at least for those persons who are fairly structured and purposeful in their professional work. Not only is the meeting time itself wasted but there are usually follow-up informal meetings at which more time is wasted talking about the ineffective formal meeting.

Meeting time in schools is obviously needed as a way of assuring that important problems are addressed and that communication is achieved regarding essential operating procedures. Each administrator calling a meeting should realize, however, that despite their importance, meetings do cost money. From the figures in Table 5–1, we observe that a one-hour elementary school faculty meeting involving twenty faculty members with an average annual salary of $20,000 can be expected to cost $227.20. This is about the same price as a set of fifteen textbooks or a good tape recorder. Even a two-hour planning meeting involving just one administrator at a salary of $30,000 and two teachers at $25,000 each can be expected to cost over $90. The cost is even higher if a substitute teacher is required to cover the teachers' classes. Meetings must therefore be planned carefully if the district is to realize maximum benefit from money spent.

To guard against calling meetings without sufficient purpose, the administrator should

---

[8]This particular survey is reported in Gilbert R. Weldy, *Time: A Resource for the School Administrator* (Reston, Va.: National Association of Secondary School Principals, 1974), p. 3. Twenty-nine of the forty respondents complained that meetings are "too long, they don't begin on time, they are unnecessary, they are aimless and directionless, or they never reach closure."

Table 5–1 Hourly Cost of Meeting Time (in dollars)

	Number of Persons Involved						
Annual Salary of Persons Involved	*1*	*2*	*3*	*4*	*5*	*10*	*20*
35,000	19.89	39.78	59.67	79.56	97.45	198.90	397.80
30,000	17.05	34.10	51.15	68.20	85.25	170.50	341.00
25,000	14.20	28.40	42.60	56.80	71.00	142.00	284.00
20,000	11.36	22.72	34.08	45.44	56.80	113.60	227.20
15,000	8.52	17.04	25.56	34.08	42.06	85.20	170.40

Based on an assumed contract period of 220 days at 8 hours per day or a total of 1,760 hours per year.

never go into a meeting without some kind of written agenda. This agenda, even if not distributed to those in attendance, should clearly spell out persons who will be required to supply information on each agenda item. These persons should have been given plenty of time to prepare for their part in the meeting. Sometimes it helps if the administrator in charge of the meeting reviews at the very beginning the items to be covered and even specifies approximate time allocations for each of the items. This provides better concentration and focus and results in better utilization of time for all in attendance.

Because of the wide range of opinion existing among faculty members and the intense human problems experienced in life around a school, it is occasionally hard to keep the faculty meeting from degenerating into a shouting match. While it may serve a purpose at times to allow one or two volatile faculty members to let off steam in the group meeting, norms of human decency should be upheld. The administrator in charge of the meeting in such cases should attempt to bring the discussion around to a look at what can be done to bring about constructive change in the current situation.

Meetings are almost always a means to an end and follow-up is required if those ends have any chance of attainment. The administrator in particular is responsible for seeing that significant concerns and decisions are reviewed and that resolution of the problems is obtained according to a reasonable time schedule. This will require the delegation of some important tasks to other members of the staff and a willingness to conscientiously monitor the completion of these tasks.

Stress and Tension Relief

Someone recently mentioned that a sure way to make money was to follow a series of time-management workshops with the offer to provide assistance with stress management. While there is little question but that administrators with unrealistic goals or poor time-management skills can be expected to experience undue stress on the job, it is also true that time management as used in this text has as one of its major goals the reduction of unnecessarily high stress levels.

As an example of how time management might aid in reducing a stressful work situation, take the case of the junior or senior high assistant principal who spends a considerable part of his or her day interacting with students and parents regarding disciplinary actions. At times, emotions can run very high in work of this type, particularly when hearings and other quasi-judicial activities are involved. For this reason, it may be imperative for the assistant principal to schedule periodic relaxation time just to survive the intensity. Even switching to quiet work such as planning for a short period of time can often give the emotional relief needed to continue to the next disciplinary case. For some administrators, learning to take a mini-vacation of the mind right at the desk may be an appropriate stress reducer. There is some evidence that evoking pleasurable memories and dwelling on them briefly in times of duress will lower pulse rate, adrenalin flow, and blood pressure.[9] Unfortunately, those who see this sort of mini-vacation as a waste of time are usually the most in need of help.

One of the interesting findings of stress research is that change of any kind and not just these involving a negative impact can be stressful. Recognizing the most stressful life events as compiled by medical researchers can alert the administrator to be on guard for unusually high stress.[10] While many of these life events are of course beyond the administrator's control, just being aware of their potential impact can perhaps sensitize the administrator experiencing them to employ stress reduction techniques such as lowering expectations in relation to personal goals, scheduling mini-vacation or relaxation breaks more frequently, or developing a less idealistic view of what is actually possible.

Perhaps school personnel, because of their deep commitment to and belief in human growth, are more vulnerable to inflated expectations than most groups of employees. Many educators, due to their own successes in school, have developed very high standards of performance and some even have dysfunctional tendencies toward perfectionism. While high standards are obviously useful in modeling behavior for young people, they can be carried to extremes. Some administrators allow their perfectionism to get in the way of their ability to work effectively with co-workers. Their high standards may make it difficult to feel comfortable in delegating work to other persons. Administrators who have extreme perfectionist tendencies generally are not successful simply because they end up doing all the work themselves and often sacrifice home and family relationships in order to accomplish a desired level of perfection on the job.

Oncken and Wass, members of a Texas-based management consulting firm, make the point that many administrators invite their own stress by consistently "taking monkeys off the backs of their subordinates" (Oncken and Wass, p. 76). When asked a question by a subordinate, the manager too often says, "I'm sure glad you brought that to my attention. I don't have time to deal with it now but let me think about it and I'll let you know how I feel on it tomorrow." The subordinate in this instance just succeeded in transferring worry and thinking time from himself to the manager. An administrator who does this just a few times each day will take work home each evening and still not accomplish the really important things. The effective administrator in this situation will refuse to take on this extra burden until the subordinate has at least proposed several possible options for dealing with the problem. Employees at all levels of the organization are paid to make decisions and decisions are generally best made by those having the most knowledge about the problem and its possible solutions. School administrators who by their actions take on problems most appropriately dealt with at a lower level in the organization do the organization a disservice and probably manage in the process to increase the tension surrounding their own jobs.

ANALYZING TIME-MANAGEMENT PATTERNS

Few administrators are so effective in their time management that at least one or two of the suggestions in the previous section do not apply. For others, serious problems may be

[9]Results of a three-year longitudinal study of managing stress are reported in John H. Howard, Peter A. Rechnitzer, and D. A. Cunningham, "Coping with Job Tension—Effective and Ineffective Methods," *Public Personnel Management* 4 (September–October 1975): 317–326.

[10]One such listing, which includes items such as death of spouse, divorce, retirement, trouble with boss, and change in financial status, has been compiled in T. H. Holmes and R. H. Rahe, "The Social Readjustment Rating Scale," *Journal of Psychosomatic Research* 11 (August 1967): 213–218.

preventing success in a current administrative assignment. Whatever the level of concern, there will probably be very little change without the admission that a time-management problem does in fact exist. There is probably no better way to identify problems and to monitor their correction than to utilize a time log and to discuss the patterns shown in the time log with persons whose opinions are respected. Before discussing specific formats that might be used for purposes of this time log, several comments about time allocation for school administrators are in order.

First, there is clearly no one time-allocation pattern appropriate to all administrative positions or administrators. The application of assumptions and guidelines presented earlier in this chapter will lead to a host of possible patterns, depending on the nature of the position, the particular tasks facing the school or school system, and the individual administrator. Even the categories used to analyze time-allocation patterns will be different for each situation and each individual administrator.

Despite this claim that no universally preferred time-allocation pattern exists, it might be useful to look at the general categories employed in a recent nationwide survey of senior high school principals. These categories, along with actual and preferred rankings of time spent, are shown in Table 5–2. The greatest single rank-order discrepancy between actual and preferred time allocation occurs with respect to "program development," where principals indicated a preference to spend the most time and ranked it fifth with respect to actual time spent. As part of this same study, a select group of principals rated most effective by their employers ranked program development no higher than third in terms of time actually spent; this confirms that substantial role limitations force some investment of time away from this admittedly important area. Even the best high school principals are unable to overcome pressures for the presumably more urgent tasks of school management, personnel, and student activities and behavior.

One purpose in examining these time allocations of practicing school principals at this point is to review problems in arriving at a useful set of categories for a time log. The actual categories selected should be determined only after a careful analysis of the administrative tasks associated with the job and the particular concerns identified for study. For example, the set of categories used in Table 5–2 would hardly be appropriate for an administrator working full-time at the district office or one who is specifically interested in the amount of time spent on telephone calls and drop-in visitors.

Prior to establishing the categories to be used in the time log, it might be helpful to conduct a self-study of possible areas of need. Some administrators may find it helpful as part of this self-study activity to discuss the use of time with either colleagues or immediate supervisors. Still others may want to do an analysis of their own preferences in relation to

Table 5–2 Allocation of Time in a Typical Work Week

Areas of Responsibility	*Do Spend Time*	*Should Spend Time*
School Management	1	3
Personnel	2	2
Student Activities	3	4
Student Behavior	4	7
Program Development	5	1
District Office	6	9
Planning	7	5
Community	8	8
Professional Development	9	6

Source: Lloyd E. McCleary and Scott D. Thomson, *The Senior High School Principalship,* Vol. 3, p. 17.

Table 5–3 Examination of Time Utilization Patterns by School Administrators

Functional Areas of Administration	*Rank Order Across Functional Areas*				*Comment*
	Greatest Enjoyment	*Highest Proficiency*	*Most Time Spent*	*Greatest Contribution to Organization*	
1. Planning	3	2	3	1	Never seem to find time
2. Implementing	2	1	1	2	
3. Maintaining	1	3	2	4	
4. Evaluating	4	4	4	3	Minimal background in evaluation

Actions Suggested by Responses: Gain additional background in evaluation/protect more time for planning

time use and to contrast these with patterns that may be most beneficial to the organization. One format for this type of diagnostic activity is presented in Table 5–3. Note that in this particular case the administrator is rank ordering actual and ideal time allocations associated with an administrative position and is also looking at possible reasons for those allocations.

The four functions of planning, implementing, maintaining, and evaluating are used in this sample; however, other administrative functions may be more appropriate for a given situation. Questions of greatest importance should guide the specific functions selected. Does the administrator spend more time on certain activities because of greater enjoyment or high proficiency? How close does the actual time allocation reflect the ideal from the standpoint of the school as an organization? It is from the type of self–analysis recorded in Table 5–3 that the administrator can begin to formulate possible categories for a time log. If, for example, the building principal is not spending much time on planning, even though more time spent in this area would be likely to benefit the organization, the administrator may want to include planning as one of the categories on the time log. Similarly, if the administrator hypothesizes in the self–analysis that much of the time spent in maintaining is consumed by lengthy telephone conversations, the telephone time should be specifically identified as a category on the time log.

We are now ready to discuss the time log in more specific terms. One sample of a completed time log is shown in Appendix 4. The elementary school principal completing this particular time log used the categories of Table 5–4. The principal established a preferred allocation prior to completing the time log for a week's time period. While the preferred time allocation is obviously not necessary and the entire time log can be done simply as a diagnostic exercise, the act of establishing preferred allocations does force some advance attention to the major goals for the week and the specific days. It further encourages the administrator to commit to writing some semblance of a plan for the week

Table 5-4 Preferred and Actual Time Allocations for Building Principal

Category	*Preferred Allocation (in percent)*	*Actual Allocation (in percent)*
Group Meetings (3 or more persons)	6	11.0
Scheduled Conferences	14	4.2
Drop-in Conferences	8	19.6
Telephone Calls	7	17.9
Preparing Reports and Planning	15	4.3
Correspondence (reading mail, dictating, letter writing)	10	1.9
Classroom Observations (including follow-up conferences)	15	15.4
Tracking Information	5	2.9
Travel	5	.5
Professional Growth and Development	6	1.3
Reviewing Work Done by Others	4	3.9
Other	5	12.2

The actual time log on which this profile is based is included in Appendix 4.

and to think about the kinds of time allocations most likely to result in successful attainment of these plans.

The particular principal whose time allocation is summarized in Table 5–4 selected the categories as presented in an effort to follow up on a feeling that too much time was being spent on drop-in conferences and telephone calls. This clearly proved to be the case, as the percentage of time actually spent exceeded the preferred time allocation in each case by more than ten percentage points. This principal should also be concerned about the minimal amount of time committed to preparing reports and planning. At the very least, some questions should be raised about what organizational goals are not being addressed due to this very limited planning commitment. Based on a review of time-allocation patterns for a number of administrators, it is reasonable to conclude that this limited planning commitment is a problem for many. In a recent sampling of time patterns for elementary principals, only one of five showed an overall time allocation to planning of more than 10 percent. The average for the group was only 4.8 percent.[11]

In addition to this fairly standard use of the time log, many special problems can be examined using time-log analysis. One district asked all principals to classify items into three categories—those the administrator should be doing alone, those the administrator and someone else could do together, and those that could be delegated to someone else. In reviewing the results, administrators were able to identify certain types of tasks for possible delegation. One principal known to be concerned about the amount of negative communica-

[11]In the particular study of reference, each principal was asked to monitor time utilization for a single week using the categories of Table 5–4. The fourth category, "preparing reports and planning," at least when utilized along with other categories in this set, accounts for less than 5 percent of the working time for the selected principals. These results are generally consistent with other studies addressing ideal and real time allocations for school principals. For information on two such studies of fairly recent origin, the reader is referred to Larry W. Hughes and Gerald C. Ubben, *The Elementary Principal's Handbook: A Guide to Effective Action* (Boston: Allyn & Bacon, 1978), pp. 347–349 and Van Cleve Morris, Robert L. Crowson, Emanuel Hurwitz, Jr., and Cynthia Porter-Gehrie, *The Urban Principal: Discretionary Decision-Making in a Large Educational Organization* (Chicago: University of Illinois at Chicago Circle, 1981).

tion used the time log as a means of plotting positive and negative encounters during a single week. This helped in diagnosing the extent of the problem. An approach used by another principal was to identify specific items on the time log that represent even partially wasted effort. These items were then isolated and strategies for their elimination in future time logs were established.

Completion of the time log and related planning forms can be extremely useful as a way of both diagnosing and monitoring time utilization on the job. It does not take long to complete and analyze the time log as presented in Appendix 4, particularly if the entries are made based on the appointment calendar and memory at three or four checkpoints during the day. Even if such an analytic tool is used only once or twice a year, it can go a long way toward maintaining better time utilization habits. Only the will to improve on current time management practices is needed to get started. Most practicing administrators will find some form of continuing attention to time utilization a real key to their overall administrative effectiveness.

SUMMARY

This chapter began with a clarification of why good time management by administrators is essential in accomplishment of school goals. This was followed by a discussion of six guidelines or assumptions about time management for school administrators. Among these six is the need to focus attention on the most important tasks and to communicate the identification of most important tasks to fellow workers. This focus helps to avoid becoming overwhelmed by the always urgent but often unimportant demands facing today's school administrator. As a means of assuring that administrator time is focused on the more important things, it is recommended that each administrator schedule a balance of availability and quiet time into the regular school day and learn to concentrate on one task at a time.

In addition to these broad general guidelines, suggestions were given in relation to a number of specific time-management concerns such as drop-in visitors, telephone calls, excessive paperwork, and stress. The reader is encouraged to complete a self-assessment in relation to these potential time management concerns and sample forms for completing this self-assessment process are recommended. Self-assessment as used by one elementary principal was discussed in some detail in the final section of this chapter; building administrators are urged periodically to use this or a similar self-assessment process as a key to improving performance.

QUESTIONS AND PROBLEMS ON CHAPTER 5

1. The following statements have been made by school principals in recent years. Evaluate each statement in terms of your own reading and experience with time management in schools.
   a. The school administrator is imposed on by too many people; he no longer has control over the way he uses his time.
   b. Detailed planning is generally a waste of time, since most of the administrator's time is spent responding to other people's demands.
   c. There is probably no way to be successful as a school principal without committing a lot of long hours and hard work.
   d. With a little more determination by the principal, it may be possible to arrange time schedules to permit more attention to such important tasks as program development.

2. Each of the following tasks are at times completed by school principals:
   Task 1: Make up purchase orders for supplies.
   Task 2: Enroll new students and assign them to classes.
   Task 3: Organize and conduct school assembly.
   Task 4: Write newsletter to be distributed to parents.
   Task 5: Write job description for teacher position.
   Task 6: Supervise hallway during lunch period.
   Task 7: Draft a statement on discipline to be discussed at upcoming faculty meeting.
   a. For each of these seven tasks, rate the skill level required and the possibility of delegating the task.

TASK NUMBER	SKILL REQUIRED *H* (high) *M* (medium) *L* (low)	DELEGATE *N* (never) *S* (sometimes) *A* (always)
1		
2		
3		
4		
5		
6		
7		

   b. Why is it that school principals insist on completing even those tasks that require a medium or low skill level and can sometimes or always be delegated?
3. Using a blank sheet of paper and following the format of Table 5–3, analyze your own preferences for planning, implementing, maintaining, and evaluating activities. Based on this analysis, what actions might be appropriate in relation to your own time-utilization pattern and what steps might be taken to accomplish these actions?
4. In the text, there are a number of suggestions to help an administrator achieve greater concentration on essential tasks. These include tighter enforcement of quiet time, use of the To-Do List, and removal of possible distractions both within and outside the office. What strategies and specific actions by the administrator will aid in accomplishing these three suggestions and what other suggestions might be helpful?
5. Handling telephone calls is clearly troublesome for many school administrators. Suggest the most effective ways to handle each of the following, being careful to state any conditions you have assumed in making your suggestion. You may want to specify alternative dialogue for certain of the situations.
   a. An incoming call during a time when the administrator has specifically asked not to be interrupted?
   b. An incoming call from an obviously irate parent during an availability period?
   c. An incoming call during an availability period from someone known to be concerned about a decision that has not yet been made?
   d. Returning several calls that came in during a meeting?
   e. Placing long distance calls?
6. Several suggestions for handling drop-in visitors are mentioned in the text. Do you think that most of these will be effective without offending the person or persons involved? What alternatives might you suggest?

7. What are the biggest time-wasters for the school administrator and what steps will help in reducing the amount of time wasted on each?
8. Listed below are two sets of categories that might be used in a time log by a building administrator.

OPTION 1	OPTION 2
Communicate with students	Group meetings
Communicate with parents	Scheduled conferences
Communicate with building professional staff	Drop-in conferences
Communicate with general public	Telephone calls
Communicate with central office	Preparing reports and planning
Communicate with administrators in other buildings	Correspondence (reading mail, dictating, letter writing)
Communicate with secretaries, clerks, and aides	Classroom observation
Answer mail	Tracking information
Visit classrooms	Travel
Plan	Professional growth and development
Inspect buildings	Reviewing work done by others
Personal growth and development	Other
Other	

a. Which of the two options would you as a school administrator prefer to use as a basis for monitoring time and why?
b. For whichever option you selected, indicate the overall percentage of time you think the building administrator should allocate to each of the activities?
c. How do building administrators generally measure up to your preferred allocation in Part b and what reasons account for any major discrepancies?

9. Utilize one of the two sets of time categories listed in Question 8 (or a set of your own choosing) and keep a time log of your own activities for a period of at least three days. Analyze the results of your time log, being careful to comment on the extent to which your actual time allocation matches preferences specified prior to completing the log.
10. Critique the article "Management Time: Who's Got the Monkey?" by Oncken and Wass (*Harvard Business Review* 52 [November-December 1974]: 75–80). As part of the critique, address these two questions:
    a. Which of the techniques for transferring "monkeys" is most likely to be used on school administrators?
    b. Why are school administrators particularly vulnerable to so many subordinate-imposed time demands?
11. In the text, there is considerable discussion of the need to distribute time wisely between availability and quiet periods. Review this concept with at least two practicing school administrators and summarize their reactions to the concept. What do they see as major obstacles to achieving a reasonable distribution between these two activity modes?

CHAPTER 6
EVALUATION IN THE SCHOOLS

The term *evaluation* generally refers to a process used in establishing worth or merit. Evaluation in relation to school management, therefore, is more than making a judgment of worth and includes the several steps both leading up to and following the judgment act itself. It is clearly an essential part of completing Step IV of the overall management cycle presented earlier in Figure 1–4. Since judgments of merit are not generally limited to the assessment of program outcomes or accomplishments, it is also important that we understand that evaluation encompasses far more than the traditional product or outcome type of assessment. Evaluation includes the wide variety of data collection and analytic activities that relate to the process of making decisions in schools.

INCREASED EMPHASIS ON EVALUATION OF SCHOOL PROGRAMS

The recent emphasis on the product or outcome type of program evaluation is certainly to be encouraged, as it is consistent with the ultimate aim of increasing learning gains for students. Yet, from a management perspective, it must be admitted that many decisions are made in schools and school systems without substantial evidence of their impact on students. Sometimes valid and reliable information is simply unavailable when decisions must be made. Often, the impact on student learning is not intended to be among the important factors analyzed in relation to a particular decision or judgment. Sometimes the crucial concern is rather one of community acceptance of a given program, designing a program that satisfies certain federal or state guidelines, or making a judgment of the extent to which a staff member is carrying out prescribed processes in the classroom. Applying the term *evaluation* to these latter activities highlights the breadth and complexity of the evaluation and decision-making processes used in schools.

Before we review the several types of evaluation used in schools and the skill areas associated with them, it is useful to examine reasons for what appears to be an increasing public concern about evaluation in the school context. To some extent, these reasons vary according to the type of evaluation under consideration and the particular local school or school district circumstances. Beyond these local differences, however, it is possible to identify certain general societal pressures for evaluative information, including those discussed below.

Dissatisfaction with Student Performance and Behavior

In the mid-1970s, both educators and the lay public became increasingly concerned about substantial declines in test performance by students throughout the United States. These declines, which were most substantial in the upper grades, were apparent beginning in the mid-1960s on several of the national testing programs.[1] Perhaps more than any other single factor, this drop in test scores gave birth to a new emphasis on accountability and evaluation in schools. It led the College Entrance Examination Board to appoint a special panel to search out reasons for the decline and to suggest possible remedies. In its report published in August 1977, the relaxation of learning standards, both in schools and society, was cited as a dominant reason for the decline.[2]

The concern about low performance on tests has consistently been coupled with a general dissatisfaction regarding the discipline and behavior of young people.[3] For many, the only answer to these concerns about behavior and performance was to tighten up on evaluation of both students and teachers and to hold the schools more accountable for results. Many states responded by initiating systematic testing programs and some even established performance standards as part of the requirement for high school graduation. Popham, writing in the mid-1970s, described the overall dissatisfaction: "The honeymoon was over. It was no longer a widely held belief that the schools were functioning flawlessly. People began to wonder just how well those schools were doing their jobs. And when you wonder how well something is working, that sets the stage for evaluating it" (Popham, 1975, p. 3).

---

[1]For a detailed documentation of this decline in scores on the Scholastic Aptitude Test, the American College Testing Program, the Minnesota Scholastic Aptitude Test, and the Comprehensive Test of Basic Skills, see Annegret Harnishfeger and David E. Wiley, "Achievement Test Scores Drop. So What?," *Educational Researcher* 5 (March 1976): 5–12.

[2]Increased use of elective courses and the excessive time spent in watching television were cited as prime examples of these relaxed standards in Willard W. Wirtz, *On Further Examination: A Report of the Advisory Panel on Scholastic Aptitude Test Score Decline* (New York: College Entrance Examination Board, 1977), pp. 46–47.

[3]This concern is evidenced in the annual Gallup Poll on attitudes toward schools. Only once in the 1970–1980 period has discipline failed to be mentioned as "the biggest problem with which the public schools in this community must deal." For details, see George H. Gallup, "The Thirteenth Annual Gallup Poll of the Public's Attitudes Toward the Public Schools," *Phi Delta Kappan* 63 (September 1981): 33–47.

Shift in Funding to State and Federal Levels

In 1960, the revenue receipts for K–12 public schools generated at the federal level were approximately 4.4 percent of the total. By 1978, the portion generated at the federal level had more than doubled to 9.8 percent. Similar shifts occurred in the balance of funding between state and local sources, with the state share of the total K–12 funds increasing from 39.1 percent in 1960 to 45.7 percent in 1978. With the 9.8 and 45.7 percent, respectively, generated at the federal and state levels, we find that local funding sources today account for less than 50 percent of the total K–12 revenue. This contrasts with approximately 57 percent in 1960.

As more of the funding has been supplied from distant federal and state revenue sources, a greater separation has developed between the local program-delivery units and sources of financial support, thus encouraging greater demand for formal evaluation. It is only natural that federal and state legislators want to have written demonstration of the value of programs as a basis for the budget-allocation process. This interest in evaluation was seen when Congress originally passed the Elementary and Secondary Education Act (ESEA) in 1965. Both Title I and Title III of this act required formal evaluation procedures as a condition of receiving funds. School districts in some cases hired outside evaluators, but many have since moved to establish entire divisions responsible for program evaluation. At the national level, evaluation centers in universities and independent educational laboratories have committed resources to training evaluators and to the development and dissemination of evaluation models. With a probable continued emphasis on nonlocal funding sources for K–12 education programs, it is not likely that even the recent move toward block grants at the federal level will reverse this pressure for formal evaluation of school programs.

Distrust of Educators and Public Officials

Educators, with at least some level of support from the general public, encouraged large-scale innovations in the 1950s and early 1960s. Team teaching, differentiated staffing, modular scheduling, nongraded elementary schools, and individualized instruction were but a few of the ideas finding their way into the public schools during this period. Much of this innovation was sold to the public as a way to increase motivation for learning and to make school programs more relevant and enjoyable for students. While certain of these potential advantages were at least partially realized, the innovations in some settings proved either to involve serious implementation obstacles or to create problems not fully anticipated by the innovators. These obstacles and problems along with the previously mentioned decline in student achievement undoubtedly contributed to a lack of confidence in the educators themselves, which has resulted in increased demands for more careful evaluation of programs.

The apparent lack of confidence in educators and other public officials is reflected in public attitude surveys over the past fifteen years. One Roper Poll showed that those having a great deal of confidence in higher education boards and administrators declined from 61 percent in 1966 to 37 percent in 1977.[4] Comparable figures are not available for local public school boards and administrators; however, there is some indication that confidence ratings for local schools run parallel to, or even slightly below, those for higher education. We do know that the comparable number having a great deal of confidence in local government

[4]The reader interested in more detailed comparisons of attitude change over this time period is referred to "More Confidence in Leadership," *Current Opinion* 5 (Williamstown, Mass.: Roper Public Opinion Research Center, 1977), p. 37.

leaders in 1977 was only 18 percent. While these confidence ratings seem to be increasing slightly, there is no approximation to the much higher confidence ratings existing in the mid-1960s.

Proliferation of Alternatives in Education Programming

The 1950s and early 1960s, periods of change and innovation in education, produced a proliferation of alternative programs and schools. Often, these alternative schools had purposes different from those operating within the regular schools. Serious study was given to the development of voucher or clinic programs that would even further diversify the assortment of school programs supported by public monies.

In certain communities, both educators and members of the lay public developed uneasiness about these multiple options in school programming and questioned the efficiency of supporting so many special programs. Their questions in many situations focused on the purpose or mission of the school and whether public school systems can reasonably take on the additional cost of providing special programs and schools for the wide variety of special-interest groups existing in almost any community. As a condition for operating these many alternatives, school boards, either on their own or under pressure from school patrons and taxpayers, began asking for more systematic evaluation of these programs and schools.

Educators' Views on Evaluation Thrust

Recognizing these several reasons for increased attention to evaluation in no way suggests that evaluation has been eagerly accepted by educators. Educators often avoid evaluation, especially in situations where it might place under critical review programs in which they are directly involved. Many evaluation studies sit on shelves in school district, state, and federal offices and little or no action is taken as a result of the money spent on producing them. This inaction is often due to the fact that the evaluation reports relate to uninteresting or unimportant questions or they make suggestions that are totally unrealistic for political and/or financial reasons. Often, the evaluation studies are thrust on local personnel by state or federal government regulation. A limited impact under such circumstances is to be expected. This state of affairs caused one expert in the evaluation field to observe that "the federal requirements to conduct local evaluations quite naturally resulted in the production of tons of evaluation reports that would have, for the most part, better served a school's paper drive than a nation's need to know whether its education laws were working" (Popham, 1975, p. 4).

With this kind of reception given to many evaluation reports in schools, one can reasonably ask for some further delineation of problem areas faced by those involved in conducting evaluations in the schools. Several such problem areas were identified in 1971 by the Phi Delta Kappa National Study Committee on Evaluation.[5]

Of greatest importance in our discussion here is the failure of educational leaders to arrive at a common definition of the nature of evaluation in the education setting. At present, there simply is no clear definition as to the meaning and use of evaluation in the school context. For some, evaluation is synonymous with measurement and testing. For others, it is the act of making a judgment about some set of measurements. Still others view evaluation as expert review and judgment quite apart from any specific criteria or set of

[5]The detailed findings and recommendations of this Phi Delta Kappa National Study Committee on Evaluation are reported in *Educational Evaluation and Decision Making* (1971).

measurements. This latter view would parallel the common accreditation-site-visit procedure where experts review the data compiled at the local level and make rather immediate judgments about program value. These different conceptions of evaluation cause confusion between and among evaluators and the potential users of evaluation.

Perhaps no definitional problem causes as much difficulty as the distinction between evaluation and research. Popham and others have attempted to draw a distinction between the two concepts, suggesting that evaluation tends to be less interested in the generalizability of results or the search for ultimate truth. This distinction serves as a useful starting point, but the difference does seem to be a matter of degree, as evaluation studies can be structured for more or less generalizability. On occasion they can even be used to go beyond the limits of a specific situation, thereby adding to our fund of knowledge about some program or educational phenomenon.

TYPES OF EVALUATION USED IN SCHOOLS

Given the uncertainty of definition for the term evaluation, it is understandable that several different types of evaluation are used within the school context. Specialists within the field of evaluation have argued for some time the relative merits of different formats or models of evaluation. There is a wide variance of opinion as to the favored models; however, most would agree that the particular evaluation plan must be matched to the situation under investigation and the resources available for the evaluation task.

Within this diversity of evaluation models, it is possible to isolate four different clusters of evaluation activity and to suggest appropriate applications for each. Such a clustering of options should be helpful to the school principal who is often expected to either design or approve a plan for evaluating some aspect of the school program. Such an overview of evaluation types should also aid those who find themselves utilizing completed evaluation studies.

Assessment of Congruence Between Performance and Intentions

The congruence cluster of evaluation models is the one given greatest attention in the evaluation literature. It is also the type of evaluation that most closely matches the traditional research model, though the emphasis is on determining value of a specific set of program processes rather than making generalizations to all programs and student populations of a particular type. This category of evaluation is broad enough to include such specific models as discrepancy evaluation, behavioral objectives evaluation, and evaluation research.[6] The key feature of evaluation studies within this category is the preliminary identification of program intentions and some distinct effort to assess the extent to which performance actually matches intentions. Most proponents of this particular type of evaluation accept the distinction between the formative and summative purposes of evaluative activity.[7] This distinction describes the formative role as improving an ongoing process by providing feedback to the program administrator and the summative role as providing evidence relating to the attainment of final product goals or intentions. The formative

[6]Discrepancy evaluation is described in Malcom Provus, *Discrepancy Evaluation* (1971); an early development of behavioral objectives evaluation is found in Ralph W. Tyler, *Basic Principles of Curriculum and Instruction* (1950); and key components of evaluation research are outlined in Carol H. Weiss, *Evaluation Research* (1972).

[7]For a statement on the distinction between and uses of formative and summative evaluation, the reader is referred to W. James Popham, *Educational Evaluation* (1975), pp. 13–15.

evaluation role is of greatest help to program developers whereas the summative role is of assistance to others who may be thinking of adopting the program.

This congruence model of education evaluation often involves some type of experimental or quasi-experimental design, particularly if the level of congruence between product objectives and actual performance is to be interpreted in any meaningful way. These experimental or quasi-experimental models are detailed in other sources.[8] It should be mentioned here that the controls associated with such designs are often difficult to enforce when dealing with action programs in schools. Sometimes it is difficult to locate appropriate students for a control group. The random assignment condition on which statistical models are based is generally difficult to follow. It is usually unwise to ask interested parties and students to sign up for a program and then turn right around and assign part of the group to a nonprogram for purposes of control in the evaluation. The interest in making minimal change in the treatment condition or process during the period of evaluation has been viewed by some as another obstacle to the experimental approach in the school setting.

The first two concerns, namely, difficulties in locating control groups and problems in random assignment, will continue to present real obstacles to the research-oriented evaluator; however, there is some indication that the latter problem of instability in treatment condition does not need to present a major obstacle to evaluation in schools. Weiss observes: "The experimental method does not require a stable program. It can be used even when the program meanders. If there is interest in the effects of a program under developmental conditions or in its usual non-standardized form, randomized designs are perfectly suitable for studying outcomes" (Weiss, p. 65).

What Weiss seems to be saying here is that we need not give up on experimental approaches in congruence-type research just because the original program as designed does not remain intact. What is important is that the congruence analysis relate to both the outcome and process aspects of the program; hence, we must document carefully the differences between the planned processes and those that actually occur. Only then do we have some chance to explain relationships between such processes and our program outcomes.

Although the major focus of evaluations in this cluster tends to be on products or learning outcomes relative to students served by the program, there is for the reasons mentioned above at least some attention given to processes and their alteration as the program is installed and implemented. The intended results of this congruence-type evaluation are judgments of worth regarding the program and/or process based on interpreted comparisons between performance data and intentions. These intentions are usually stated in standards of performance or in comparative terms to some norm group. The judgments of worth can be made by both evaluators and administrators and should be based on the analysis of relevant evaluation data.

Professional and Expert Judgment

Often, in schools, we seek the judgment of specialists in deciding on the worth of some program or phenomenon. This is most often true when resources for other types of evaluation are limited, when time limitations prevent a more lengthy process for assessing worth, or when the issues involved are simply too complex to be addressed by current research and evaluation knowledge or methodology. Examples of this type of

---

[8]One of the earliest summary presentations on experimental and nonexperimental designs is found in Donald T. Campbell and Julian C. Stanley, "Experimental and Quasi-Experimental Designs for Research in Teaching," in *Handbook on Research on Teaching,* edited by N. L. Gage (Chicago: Rand McNally, 1963), pp. 171–246.

evaluation are numerous and include such common systems as accreditation, art or literary criticism, the Delphi technique, and legal adversary proceedings.

Perhaps the one evaluation type best known to educators is accreditation. Since the early 1900s, accreditation has served as a peer-review process for the evaluation of secondary schools and institutions of higher education. The accreditation process, as currently outlined for secondary schools, calls for a comprehensive self-study of program quality, complete with appropriate suggestions for improvement, followed by an external review by experts in the several fields.[9] Traditionally, the emphasis in the accreditation-review process has been on intrinsic criteria such as numbers of books in the school library, condition of physical plant, and staff selection procedures rather than such extrinsic or outcome factors as student academic growth or attitudes toward school. This emphasis on intrinsic criteria is no doubt a carry-over from the early 1900s when there was a definite need to upgrade certain of the essential provisions of the school systems across the United States.

Now that the general upgrading has been accomplished, many people think that the accreditation model has outlived its usefulness as an enforcer of quality. The detractors also point out that there exists little evidence of any specific set of intrinsic factors necessary for operating a viable school program. Conditions vary so much across school systems that it makes little sense to search for some standard set of conditions necessary for good education. These concerns have resulted in less rigid criteria for use in the accreditation process. There is even available now an alternative narrative form of accreditation self-study that makes no attempt to establish criteria for the evaluation process.[10]

Even with these adaptations, there appears to be reduced support for the formal accreditation process today. Few colleges require attendance at an accredited secondary school as a condition for admission and many states have adopted their own accreditation standards, sometimes under legislative mandate. Many administrators quite reasonably view the accreditation process today less as a means for proving worth of the current programs and more as a process for identifying needed areas of program improvement.

Like the accreditation procedures just described, the traditions of art and literary criticism fill a perceived gap in our process-product thinking about education evaluation. Not only do we not know the processes for achieving certain product outcomes among students, but in some cases we are unable even to specify these outcomes in any precise manner. This is particularly true in situations where desired outcomes are complex or unpredictable, as is often the case in the creative and fine arts. The traditional models of evaluation have not been particularly useful for such complex and unpredictable behaviors as critiquing an art work or utilizing a set of chords to create a new musical score. In situations like this, we have problems prespecifying the desired behaviors or measuring them with any degree of precision. Eisner has referred to these objectives as "expressive" and describes them as follows:

> The expressive objective is intended to serve as a theme around which skills and understandings learned earlier can be brought to bear, but through which those skills and understandings can be expanded, elaborated and made idiosyncratic. With an expressive objective what is desired is not homogeneity of response among students but diversity. In the

[9] The accreditation process and criteria are described in *Evaluation Criteria,* 5th ed. (Washington, D.C.: National Study of School Evaluation, 1978). An alternative narrative revision of the secondary school accreditation process was published in 1975. (see n. 10)

[10] The narrative form of secondary school accreditation is available in published form as National Study of School Evaluation, *Secondary School Evaluation Criteria: Narrative Edition* (Arlington, Va.: National Study of School Evaluation, 1975).

> expressive context the teacher hopes to provide a situation in which meanings become personalized and in which children produce products, both theoretical and qualitative, that are as diverse as themselves. Consequently the evaluative task in this situation is not one of applying a common standard to the products produced but one of reflecting upon what has been produced in order to reveal its uniqueness and significance. (Eisner, p. 16)

The type of reflective review referred to as appropriate for evaluation of expressive objectives will necessarily involve professional or expert judgment of some kind. Eisner has called for this critic or connoisseurship role to become an accepted format for educational evaluation. While it is lacking in scientific respectability, it may have potential for evaluation of the more complex and creative behaviors of students.

While not generally viewed as a distinct form of educational evaluation, the legal adversary process offers considerable promise for presenting the pros and cons of a particular program. In this regard, it seems reasonable to view such adversary reviews as being a legitimate part of the evaluation process, particularly when reasonable persons may differ on the merit of the program in question. This type of formal argumentation over program merit will conceivably take on even greater importance as more and more decisions are made through the quasi-legal process of professional negotiation and bargaining. The expert judgment in this type of evaluation is ideally drawn from a combination of educational and legal sources; the experts, if sensitive to the information needs of decision makers, can illuminate the critical issues surrounding program implementation in specific school situations.

Other evaluative approaches emphasizing professional and expert judgment are being used in schools today. The Delphi technique, whereby experts interact through a series of focused questionnaires, is one such example.[11] Peer-review panels used for the purpose of evaluating funding proposals or screening manuscripts also fall into this general cluster of evaluations. In all these situations, the individual or group performing the evaluation is involved both in assimilating the data and in making judgments about its meaning; the client is depending on the evaluator's competence both in the subject of investigation and in the general ability to synthesize data and make reasonble judgments based on that data.

Goal-Free and Transactional Approaches

The evaluation models discussed up to this point involve as a prime focus the examination and/or attainment of program and school goals as declared by program directors, teachers, or administrators. A minimum of attention has been given to discrepancies between professed goals and those that seem to dominate the actions of program participants. Neither has much effort been directed to studying what happens to the teachers and other school personnel involved in the delivery of programs. These apparent deficiencies in conventional evaluation approaches have led to a series of counterproposals or models within the evaluation domain. Among these are goal-free and transactional evaluations.[12] In a sense, one can view these counterproposals as a natural response to the product-

[11]A comprehensive review of applications of the Delphi technique can be found in Harold A. Linstone and Murray Turoff, eds., *The Delphi Method* (1975).

[12]The goal-free approach is described in Michael Scriven, "Pros and Cons About Goal-Free Evaluation," *Evaluation Comment* 3 (December 1972), pp. 1–4; the transactional approach to evaluation is explained in Robert M. Rippey, ed., *Studies in Transactional Evaluation* (Berkeley, Calif.: McCutchan, 1973). Some would also place the illuminative evaluation of Parlett and the responsive evaluation described by Stake in this category of counter proposals for evaluation. Both of these are discussed in David Hamilton et al., eds., *Beyond the Numbers Game: A Reader in Educational Evaluation* (1977), pp. 3–22, 163–164.

evaluation emphasis associated with the recent move toward greater accountability. There is no question but that certain evaluators have failed to properly qualify their goal-related findings. Perhaps there are even situations where this failure to qualify results has been done purposely to influence decision makers. There are certainly instances in which the maintenance of appropriate program procedures was not given adequate attention. It is these weaknesses in past evaluation studies that have given momentum to the goal-free and transactional movement in the evaluation field.

There is little point here in comparing the several specific evaluation strategies that fall into this goal-free and transactional category; however, it is useful to relate these approaches in a general way to the evaluation clusters already discussed. More than anything else, goal-free and transactional evaluation seems to be a reaction to the blind application of the congruency model of evaluation. Congruence evaluation seeks to identify the level of congruence between program performance and intentions, particularly as the congruence relates to summative goal attainment. Several advocates of the goal-free and transactional emphasis question whether certain worthy goals can or even should be defined. This concern is certainly apparent in Apple's critique of the usual process-product reasoning used in education:

> One can value, say, predetermined behavioral objectives for their supposed ability to lead to measurable outcomes; however, the very notion that such reductive and atomistic curricular formulations are worthwhile educationally in themselves is an arguable assertion to say the least. It can certainly be argued that they embody an ideology of control, that they place much too high a value on certainty above all else, that they are inaccurate representations of and trivialize the processes of inquiry, and that they are psychologically and philosophically naive. (Apple, p. 11)

Apple shares with some other evaluation critics a deep resentment against most attempts to match educational processes with certain stated product outcomes in the schools. There is a suggestion that this attempted match is impossible to accomplish and perhaps even anti-human. Bernstein, in elaborating on this theme, says:

> When we separate ends and means, when we think of means as mere means to some . . . goal, we are in danger of destroying the efficacy of our means and the potency of our ends. Means and ends, whether in educational, moral, or political life designate the same experience viewed from different perspectives. (Bernstein, p. 213)

Some recent critics of the more traditional evaluation models seem not so much to oppose the statement and pursuit of goals and objectives as to think that not enough attention is given to the goal selection on which evaluation information is based. Scriven's goal-free emphasis places him in this later group. Goal-free evaluation, according to Scriven, focuses on both intended and unanticipated outcomes of the program in question.[13] While goal-free evaluation is concerned with the statements of intent as formulated by program designers, it goes beyond these and attempts to look more broadly at all important results of the program. The techniques and strategies used in goal-free evaluation are still being developed but it is important to note that the process of selecting from among the multiple project outcomes those to be included is both complex and value laden. Naturalistic observation, where the evaluator observes program processes and outcomes in the natural classroom setting rather

[13]Scriven, "Pros and Cons," p. 1.

than in a laboratory, will undoubtedly prove useful, at least in the early stages of the goal-free evaluator's work.[14]

Within this group of evaluation critics are a number who would direct much greater attention to the activities and processes associated with the program being evaluated. Whether labeled descriptive, transactional, illuminative, or anthropological, this group of evaluators places particular emphasis on looking at the interaction between programs and organizational structure and the relationships among personnel working within the organization. Those advocating this kind of attention to system impact argue that such attention to organization and context concerns is absolutely necessary as a means of avoiding the frequent non-event phenomenon in educational evaluation.[15] *Non-event* as used here is simply the evaluation of a program that, due to system and/or personnel rejection, was never implemented. Acknowledgement of this phenomenon in social programs has understandably led to a demand for evaluation of the degree of implementation in a number of programs.

Decision-Related Evaluation Efforts

The fourth cluster of evaluation models can be viewed as an effort to achieve greater coordination between evaluation and decision making in schools. It draws on elements of the evaluation types already discussed and recognizes that even rational decisions can be made without limiting consideration to program and system processes and outputs. Examples of decision-related evaluation schemes are CIPP (context, input, process, product), developed by the Phi Delta Kappa National Study Committee on Evaluation; the Center for the Study of Evaluation (CSE) model, developed by researchers at the University of California at Los Angeles; the WICHE/NCHEMS Costing and Data Management System; and the Higher Education Planning System (HEPS), which is marketed by Education and Economic Systems, Inc. These latter two systems are built around a predetermined decision information need, whereas the specific information need in the first two is determined by the user.

The CIPP model is perhaps the best known of these decision-related evaluation models. Daniel Stufflebeam, a prime advocate of the comprehensive CIPP model, indicates that four basic assumptions underlie CIPP: (1) Evaluation is performed in the service of decision making; hence, it should provide information that is useful to decision makers; (2) evaluation is a cyclic, continuing process and, therefore, must be implemented through a systematic program; (3) the evaluation process includes three main steps—delineating, obtaining, and providing—which provide the basis for a methodology and evaluation; and (4) the delineating and providing steps in the evaluation process are interface activities requiring collaboration between evaluator and decision maker, while the obtaining step is largely a technical activity that is executed by the evaluator.[16]

In the implementation of these assumptions, the CIPP model of evaluation identifies four types of decisions made by organizations (represented by the letters of the acronym): context, input, process, and product. Each decision type can be expected to have different information needs and hence a different set of data collection procedures. Context evaluation is intended to aid decision makers in the determination of objectives and often concerns

[14]For a more detailed description of naturalistic observation, sometimes referenced as the ethnographic approach, see David Hamilton et. al., *Beyond the Numbers Game: A Reader in Educational Evaluation,* pp. 193–200.

[15]Concern for the non-event phenomenon in education evaluation and research is discussed in W. W. Charters, "On the Risk of Appraising Non-Events in Program Evaluation," (November 1973), p. 11.

[16]These four basic assumptions are presented and discussed in Blair R. Worthen and James R. Sanders, *Educational Evaluation: Theory and Practice* (1973), pp. 129–130.

itself with purposes of the organization and the factors influencing these purposes. Dominant methodologies employed in this type of evaluation are study visits to other systems, use of outside consultants, brainstorming, retreats, community attitude surveys, and system checks on the status of goal attainment.

Input evaluation is intended to aid in deciding how best to utilize resources to meet program goals. The result of this type of evaluation is an analysis of one or more procedural designs in terms of potential costs and benefits. The magnitude and complexity of the input evaluation will depend on the nature of the program setting and the level of detail desired by the program developers. Promising methodologies for input evaluation include the Delphi technique, Program Evaluation and Review Technique (PERT), cost-benefit analysis, and literature search. Consultants can also be helpful in structuring input at this design stage.

The third type is process evaluation, which has three main objectives—to detect or predict defects in the procedural design or its implementation; to provide information for programmed decisions; and to maintain a record of procedure as it occurs. Process evaluation generally requires less technical knowledge but it does require systematic documentation and hence time. The importance of process evaluation was mentioned earlier in the discussion of congruence evaluation models, but an illustration from the Pittsburgh Public Schools is worth noting. In reporting on the impact of a major team-teaching project in the Pittsburgh Public Schools, Provus states:

> The other phase (process) of the evaluation—a comparison of actual program activities with planned or anticipated program activity—went a long way toward explaining why student performance was so disappointing. In 39 schools, 131 teaching teams were found to be practicing 131 different varieties of team teaching. In fact, an adequate description of the actual team teaching program could not be found in the entire district. (Provus, p. 38)

Examples such as this make one wonder about the many evaluation studies where documented learning gains have been found. Is it not possible that some of these gains were made without knowing in any precise manner the probable cause of the documented learning?

The final type of evaluation under the CIPP decision-oriented model is product or outcome evaluation. Here, the emphasis is on measuring and interpreting program impact on the intended audience. Product evaluation reports that objectives were or were not achieved; process evaluation provides the basis for interpreting the reasons for these outcomes. Hence, the two work together in the interpretation and analysis of results.

The product evaluation can be of either the summative or formative type. Criteria for the product accomplishment may be either instrumental or consequential, a distinction made by Scriven.[17] Instrumental criteria are related to outcomes at an intermediate level and consequential criteria pertain to the more ultimate conditions being sought. For example, we might view consequential criteria as being related to an ultimate purpose such as developing in students more favorable attitudes toward school. Intermediate criteria could then relate to such accomplishments as less frequent class cutting, more classroom participation, or more assignments completed.

The process and product components of the CIPP decision-related approach involve the same assessment of congruence between performance and intentions that was outlined for the congruence evaluation; hence, the decision-related cluster of evaluations can be viewed

---

[17]This distinction between instrumental and consequential criteria parallels the differentiation between objectives and goals made in Chapter 1 of this text. For a description of the importance of these two types of criteria, see Michael S. Scriven, "The Methodology of Evaluation," (1967), pp. 39–83.

as an extension of congruence evaluation. From the perspective of the educational administrator, this extension appears to be an important one, primarily because it includes under the evaluation umbrella numerous additional activities that relate to educational decision making. No longer is evaluation limited to the traditional concern with matching intentions and performance in relation to school programs, but the term can now be applied to a number of planning and structuring activities that play an important role in school decision making.

IMPORTANCE OF PRODUCT EVALUATION IN THE SCHOOL SETTING

It is important now to consider which of the various models discussed above are most likely to assist the school principal and staff in fulfilling their respective decision-making roles. It is clear from the school management model outlined in Figure 1–4 and emphasized throughout this text that the product or learning outcome evaluation must continue as a key element of program evaluation. While advocates of the goal-free and transactional approaches have quite properly criticized the blind application of goal-oriented product evaluations and have raised useful cautions about looking only at these product outcomes, there is at this time no real substitute for a demonstrated evidence of learning gain by program completers. Critical as it is to study the degree of implementation of specific programs and the totality of system impacts, the bottom line for most school patrons is still what students learn. The building administrator must take a leadership role in seeing that this learning is assessed and that the assessment is communicated to the various client groups. Students may enjoy a particular elementary school mathematics program and teachers may gain new insights into the structure of the subject by teaching it; but, unless students are able to perform at least as well as before on standardized or program-related tests, it is likely that influential citizens and/or school board members will reasonably ask why. Because of this ultimate concern for product, it is advisable to have a carefully structured product evaluation for almost any major program change in the school setting.

Fortunately, a sound product evaluation does not necessarily require a sophisticated experimental or even quasi-experimental design. In situations where the program is still in a developmental stage or where controls in relation to school and/or student selection are unreasonable, one may have to settle for something with less precision and generalizability. Suchman has proposed a useful program-sequencing model that may help with this evaluation design problem.[18] Essentially, he differentiates between four phases of program development—pilot, model, prototype, and institutional. In the pilot phase, program development tends to be trial and error. The model phase calls for operating the program under controlled conditions. Not until the prototype phase is the program required to operate under realistic operating conditions. The institutional phase occurs only when the program becomes an ongoing part of the system operation.

Although program development in schools rarely follows exactly this four-stage model, most programs do go through some kind of developmental sequence prior to full-scale implementation. It is useful to observe that program stability and careful evaluation controls are not equally important at all stages of program development. Generally, only the model phase requires tight experimental controls; yet, evaluators have been known to attempt sophisticated research designs from the very beginning of the project. Such an imposition

[18]For more detail on the program-sequencing model, see Edward A. Suchman, "Action for What? A Critique of Evaluative Research," (1970).

should be assiduously avoided. Administrators should recognize the folly of attempting to apply controlled product evaluation to something that is just beyond the design stage.

EVALUATION SKILLS FOR THE BUILDING ADMINISTRATOR

Because evaluation and evaluation research are essential parts of measuring the worth or value of social programs of all kinds, the public will undoubtedly continue to demand that its leaders utilize the results of evaluation in the decision-making processes of the organization. This means that school administrators, including building principals, must develop an understanding of the evaluation options available and be capable of assisting in the design and analysis of a wide variety of evaluation studies. It is essential that building principals have at least a basic understanding of the various analytic tools required for evaluation studies. Above all, they need to be able to interpret the findings to interested client groups and to make recommendations for action that are consistent with results obtained.

Background material on evaluation skills is available in the literature.[19] The administrator should, during the time of initial training, gain firsthand experience with program evaluations conducted at the building or classroom level. Practice in the application and interpretation of basic tests of statistical significance should also be included in the initial training of all program managers in the schools.

As background to evaluation in schools, the administrator should be acquainted with the steps most often involved in the product or learning-outcome type of evaluation:

1. Examination of the context for program implementation
2. Identification of objectives for the program
3. Design of evaluation plan relating to program objectives
4. Collection of data required by the evaluation plan
5. Analysis of data
6. Reporting findings to relevant decision-making groups

The depth of understanding and the skill level required by the building administrator in each of the six areas will differ depending on the evaluation demands of the local situation and the amount of consultation assistance available. It seems important, however, that all building administrators have at least a minimum functioning capacity in relation to each of the six areas listed.

Practice in relation to certain of these evaluation skill areas was provided in earlier chapters of this book (e.g., the identification and clarification of objective statements in Chapter 2). Some further involvement with these skill areas is provided at the conclusion of this chapter. It seems appropriate at this point to comment on the final item on the list of skill areas, namely the reporting of findings to relevant decision-making groups. Most groups involved in making program decisions at the school level (including parent groups, central office administrators, and school boards) are not likely to have time to pore over individual test scores and other detailed evaluation data. It is important therefore that they be given reports that summarize data and address key issues in a clear and concise manner.

Evaluation reports will obviously take on a variety of formats and detail depending on

[19]Two general sources on program evaluation in schools are Carol H. Weiss, *Evaluation Research* (1972); and Thomas R. Owens and Warren D. Evans, *Program Evaluation Skills for Busy Administrators* (1977). A source that covers specific measurement and testing issues is Jum C. Nunnally, *Educational Measurement and Evaluation* (New York: McGraw-Hill, 1972).

their intended audience and purpose. They can be oral or written; they can be made on an interim basis or at a concluding point; they can be comprehensive in nature or focus on certain aspects of the program. Determinations as to report format will generally be based on the decisions to be made and must often be determined in relation to the timing required by those administering the programs. A rather limited oral report presented prior to making important program decisions is generally preferable to a summary written report presented a month after the major program decisions are already made.

The following possible format for a written evaluation report was suggested in a recent guide for school administrators:

- Executive Summary (a three- to ten-page overview of the report findings and recommendations)
- Introduction (identifies the purposes and audiences for the report, provides an overview of the contents, and describes disclaimers if needed)
- Program Description (includes a brief description of program activities and students to be served)
- Objectives/Questions Addressed in Evaluation
- Description of Evaluation Procedures, Designs, Instruments (usually includes only summary in text of report with appendices used for detail)
- Discussion of Findings (sometimes useful to organize findings first around instruments used and, second, around evaluation objectives or questions)
- Conclusions and/or Recommendations (including sufficient information for reader to see the rationale and data base for recommendations)
- Appendices (separate appendices containing locally developed instruments, technical data, and detailed tabulations can make the body of the report less technical)

Each of these components of a program-evaluation report is explained elsewhere[20] and persons involved in report preparation will make a decision on the inclusion and ordering of these components based on local circumstances.

It is important to stress, finally, the limitations associated with almost any program-evaluation activity. By its very nature, program evaluation represents a sampling of program activities and outcomes. To make it more than a sampling runs the risk of distorting the program in such a way that monitoring activities and testing results takes precedence over the program itself. The evaluator's prime responsibilities are to see that an adequate sampling of these program results is obtained without creating undue stress on the program activities and to assure that this sampling of results is made available to decision makers in an understandable and timely fashion.

SUMMARY

Several concerns have led to increased public interest in evaluation and accountability in education. These concerns include proliferation of alternative schools and programs, shifts in funding from local to state and federal sources, and an apparent distrust of public officials and educators. In responding to these many concerns, educators have devised numerous approaches to evaluation in the schools and have made at least some effort to consider

[20]For a brief discussion of this format and its component parts, see Owens and Evans, *Program Evaluation Skills for Busy Administrators,* pp. 55–59.

results of evaluation in making decisions at the district and school levels. The earlier emphasis on measuring attainment of product-type objectives and goals is still important but there is an increasing realization that evaluation of school programs must consider all results of a given program change and not just those intended by the original program developers. Schools are complex organizations and this means that if evaluation is to be of help in decision making, it must be viewed as a broad collection of analytic techniques for gaining a better match between community desires and school performance.

After examining several options or approaches available for evaluation of school programs, six skill areas most likely to be needed in conducting evaluations of product-type goals at the building level were identified. These six skill areas were (1) examination of the context for program implementation, (2) identification of objectives for the program, (3) design of the evaluation plan relating to objectives, (4) collection of data required by the evaluation plan, (5) analysis of the data, and (6) reporting findings to relevant decision-making groups. The depth of understanding and expertise required by the building administrator in each of these six skill areas will vary depending on the demands of the local school situation and the level of consultation help available. Each administrator should have an awareness of the requirements associated with each of the six steps and should develop at least minimal expertise in all of them.

QUESTIONS AND PROBLEMS ON CHAPTER 6

1. A number of schools and school districts have implemented minimum competency standards for high school graduation. Still others are requiring certain achievement standards for student promotion through the grades. In some cases, these standards are fixed in the sense that a diploma or promotion certificate is denied until the desired level of performance is actually attained. In others, the school prescribes certain remedial activities that must be accomplished before the diploma or certificate of advancement is awarded.
   a. List the major arguments supporting each of these approaches to the maintenance of competency standards.
   b. Present a written justification for one or the other of these approaches to the maintenance of minimum competencies.

2. The CIPP evaluation model discussed in the text outlines several types of evaluation in the schools. Identify the type appropriate to each of the following situations and briefly explain the reasons for your choice.
   a. Monitoring a set of instruction processes to make certain that time allocations given to these processes do not exceed predefined limits.
   b. Determining through a staff survey the classroom activities judged by teachers most likely to result in accomplishing improved performance on the statewide testing program.
   c. Examining the possible impact of the new advisory room system on student attitudes toward school.
   d. Summarizing the demographic characteristics of a given school community.
   e. Employing the Delphi technique to design the best way to teach energy conservation to junior high students.
   f. Conducting a community goals survey with the intent of establishing program priorities over the next five years.
   g. Establishing criteria for success of a new reading program.

3. Scriven, in *Perspectives of Curriculum Evaluation,* distinguishes between instrumental and consequential criteria of product accomplishment by students.

a. Explain the difference between these two types of criteria.
b. For each of the following consequential criteria, list three possible instrumental criteria that would have meaning within the school context.
    ◦ Adapting to new situations in life
    ◦ Successfully completing income tax forms
    ◦ Maintaining a positive self-image
    ◦ Making decisions consistent with value preferences
    ◦ Showing respect for the views of others

4. The goal-free or transactional approaches to evaluation have been criticized as representing a costly escape from accountability in our schools. Evaluate this criticism.

5. Suppose as a building principal you are asked to provide a brief explanation to a group of parents on the concepts of validity and reliability in testing. Present your ideas on the subject in written form, being careful to use examples that can be easily understood by parents.

6. A particular report comparing learning gains utilizing two different instructional processes—lecture versus discussion—seems to favor the lecture method. As a matter of fact, the report states that the difference in gains is significant at the .05 level of statistical significance.

a. What precisely is meant by this statement?
b. Would this statement of difference between the two instructional processes have been stronger or weaker if the significance level were .01 instead of .05? Explain.
c. As a school principal, how would you explain "significant difference" to members of the school faculty?

7. Context evaluation, as mentioned in connection with the CIPP model, often involves survey techniques. Assume that as a school principal you have been presented with the following sample items to be included in a parent survey. Identify instances of wording bias, lack of clarity, or inappropriate response format and, in each case, suggest an alternative wording or approach to obtaining the information requested.

a. The school faculty recently instituted a policy of sending notes home to parents whenever a student does not complete a routine assignment. Several parents have responded favorably to this notification procedure and we are now seeking views from all parents. How do you feel about the notification procedure? (Check one).

    ____Favor ____Oppose ____Undecided

b. The National Parent-Teacher Association (PTA) recommends that local units distribute ratings on television programs to their members at no charge. Do you think such a distribution might be an appropriate action for the Gooding School PTA; if it were done, who should pay for the postage? (Indicate your preference on each question by checking the appropriate spaces.

    Appropriate?_ _ _ _ _ _ _ _ _ ____ Yes
    ____ No
    Who Pays? _ _ _ _ _ _ _ _ _ ____ Parents
    ____ PTA
    ____ Other (please specify)________

c. Please indicate your level of agreement with each of the following statements by circling SA for strongly agree, A for agree, U for undecided, D for disagree, and SD for strongly disagree:

(1)	The staff in the library is both friendly and efficient.	SA	A	U	D	SD
(2)	My first-semester grades were above the average for the school.	SA	A	U	D	SD
(3)	Most students in this school eat a good breakfast.	SA	A	U	D	SD
(4)	Most faculty members in this school are over forty years of age.	SA	A	U	D	SD
(5)	Most students in this school have access to a power saw.	SA	A	U	D	SD
(6)	I read exactly three books each month during the school year.	SA	A	U	D	SD

8. Listed in Figure 6–1 are reading scores and percent of high school graduates for the five elementary schools in a particular school district:

Figure 6–1

School	*Number of Students*	*Average Reading Score*	*Percent of High School Graduates*
Fairwood	320	84	91.3
Gooding	450	75	85.4
Lake Youngs	240	59	78.4
Panther Lake	506	78	87.3
Springbrook	473	67	77.6

a. What is the average reading score for the school district? (In computing the average, you must recognize the different enrollment levels in each school.)

b. What correlation (positive or negative) seems to exist between the average reading score and the percent of high school graduates? Explain your reasoning.

c. Utilize the standard deviation formula used in the Statistical Package for the Social Sciences (SPSS), namely,

$$s = \sqrt{\frac{(\Sigma_{i=1}^{N} X_i^2) - N\bar{X}^2}{N - 1}}$$

where X_i is the ith observation, $\overline{X}$ is the average of all observations, and N the number of observations to compute the standard deviation for both reading scores and percent of high school graduates. (For this purpose, consider each school as having the same weight regardless of total enrollment.)

9. An evaluation from the research and testing office of the district has determined the regression line (or line of best fit) between reading score (R) and percent of high school graduages (H) in Question 8 above to be as follows:

$$R = 1.5629\ H - 58.6841$$

As principal of Springbrook School, you are interested in using this regression line to gain further insight into the scores obtained in the several schools.

a. Using this regression line, what are the predicted reading scores for the Fairwood and Springbrook schools and how do these predictions compare with actual scores?

b. How might these comparisons between predicted and actual scores be used to interpret the test scores and what cautions or conditions should be utilized in this explanation?

c. In which of the schools, if any, will the principal find the predicted reading score to be higher than the actual reading score?

10. Describe a needed curricular change in a school or school district setting and develop an evaluation plan for that curricular change. In presenting your plan, be certain to include a description of the context for the project, the identification and statement of objectives, a description of evaluation design (including data collection and analysis procedures and a reasonable time line), and the plans for reporting findings to relevant decision-making groups.

PART III

FINANCIAL MANAGEMENT OF SCHOOLS

OVERVIEW

Whatever the goals established for the school and the several action programs or activities associated with their accomplishment, the bottom line is the ability to acquire and monitor funds needed to carry out these activities. This means that school administrators and particularly those with direct budget responsibility must be familiar with funding sources and the programs to which those funding sources can legitimately be directed. In addition, the administrator must be skilled in budgeting on a program-by-program basis and in monitoring spending patterns in relation to the budget.

The material on financial management given here is not intended to be a comprehensive treatment of school finance. Little attention is given to the organization of financial services at the district level; neither is there any attempt to examine the political and community forces needed to acquire dollars for public education. The aim here is rather one of providing to the administrator an overview of current revenue and expenditure patterns in education with special attention as to how funds are distributed to local school districts and schools. Also included is an examination of the ways in which these monies are budgeted at the local school level and a discussion of alternate approaches for reporting financial status to various constituencies. Throughout, focus is on those concepts and skills that are likely to be most important to the building administrator.

These essentials of financial management have been organized into four chapters. Chapter 7 presents background material on the status of school finance and provides the administrator with an understanding of major revenue sources used in support of the public schools. Tax rates and assessment ratios as used in various revenue options are also covered. In Chapter 8, we examine various formulae for distributing monies to school districts and changes in these distribution patterns as necessitated by recent court action. Chapter 9 provides an overview of alternative approaches to budgeting, which should give the prospective administrator additional insight into appropriate means for involving parents, students, and staff in the budget-development process. The brief presentation on cost-benefit analysis should give the reader an understanding of the important tie between program evaluation and the budget-planning process. Problems included at the end of this chapter assess the reader's ability to make reasonable cost estimates and to present these estimates in a readable format. Chapter 10 describes basic principles of government or fund accounting and shows in some detail the necessary connection between development of the budget and the monitoring of that budget. Those with little or no accounting background may need to work with a school business official and/or to review supplementary materials in order to fully understand the derivation of certain of the financial reports presented in Chapter 10. Special attention in this final chapter is given to alternative means for reporting revenue and spending patterns to the general public.

This latter concern with reporting results to the public is justified by noting that this is the one aspect of school finance that is and always will be crucial to the building-administrator role. Often, at PTA meetings or school athletic events, administrators are confronted with questions about the cost of a given program or school activity. Even people who have no particular interest in the program goals or the school's success in attaining these goals (and there are many such people in our school communities) seem to develop a sudden interest when they recognize that these programs do affect their lives, if in no other way than through the payment of taxes.

Because of dissatisfaction with results being achieved in the schools today, rapidly increasing costs of running the schools, and general distrust of public servants, some people have questioned whether school administrators are capable of managing public funds wisely. Since most school administrators are former teachers and have had a minimum of background and experience in financial management, it is all the more important that prospective candidates for administrative positions commit time to mastering the concepts and skills included in this part of the text. To do otherwise is to threaten the credibility of school administrators and to provide opponents of schools with just that much more reason to question the whole education enterprise.

CHAPTER 7
FINANCIAL SUPPORT IN THE SCHOOLS

From the earliest years of our nation, education was thought to make an important contribution to the national welfare. This contribution occurs in a number of ways, including the support of general economic growth, the maintenance of cultural values among future generations, and the extension of knowledge essential to our technological advance. Numerous attempts to demonstrate these positive impacts of education have been made, and additional efforts will no doubt be initiated. One writer, summarizing research efforts over the past 50 years, stated: "That expending adequate funds for education will provide economic dividends to society is now established as a fact that is seldom disputed by students of economics. Quality education is expensive but it brings commensurate benefits to individuals, to families, to business and professional people, and to social agencies and institutions" (Burrup, p. 10).

Table 7–1 Comparative Enrollments and Expenditures for K–12 and Higher Education in Selected Years

	Enrollment (in thousands)		*Total Expenditures (in billions of 1978-79 dollars)*	
School Year	*K–12*	*Higher Education*	*K–12*	*Higher Education*
1977–1978	48,671	11,284	98.2	54.2
1983–1984	43,768	11,613	99.5	56.6
Percent Change	−10.1	+2.9	+1.3	+4.4

Figures for the 1977–1978 school year are actual and for 1983–1984 are projections. Enrollment and expenditure figures include both public and private schools.

Source: National Center for Education Statistics, U.S. Department of Education, *Projections of Education Statistics to 1988–89*, 1980, Tables 2 and 37.

As continuing recognition of our belief in education as an investment in the nation's future, it is useful to note that education's share of the gross national product (GNP) increased from 3.1 percent in 1930 to 5.1 percent in 1960 and to an estimated 6.9 percent in 1980. There is some indication that this rate of growth in education's share of the GNP is on the decline and few are predicting that it will exceed 8 percent at any time in the foreseeable future. Short-term enrollment losses, federal government efforts to reduce inflation, and mounting energy costs can all be expected to place a lid on education expenditures in the years ahead. The effect will be particularly great in the K–12 systems, which, according to the trends illustrated in Table 7–1, are likely to experience substantial enrollment losses in the near term.

Notice in Table 7–1 that expenditures, even in constant 1978–1979 dollars, are increasing at a more rapid rate than enrollments in the K–12 sector. In higher education, the rates of increase in enrollment and expenditures are more nearly equal. Energy-cost increases are of course a contributing factor in these increased overall costs; however, the recent expansion of programs provided for special populations such as the handicapped and bilingual are also a factor.

We observe in Table 7–2 that nonpublic school enrollments have been quite stable during the past five years while public school enrollments have declined just over 4 million students. This pattern of decline is projected to continue, but at a lesser rate, through the 1985–1986 school year. Adoption of any of the recent proposals for increased financial support of nonpublic schools could serve to accelerate the projected enrollment declines in the public schools.[1]

Table 7–2 Projected K–12 Enrollments for Selected Years

	Public		*Nonpublic*		
School Year	*Number (in 000)*	*Percent*	*Number (in 000)*	*Percent*	*Total Enrollment (in 000)*
1975–1976	44,791	89.8	5,087	10.2	49,878
1980–1981	40,696	88.9	5,075	11.1	45,771
1985–1986	38,548	88.1	5,205	11.9	43,753

Source: National Center for Education Statistics, U.S. Department of Education, *Projections of Educational Statistics to 1988–89*, 1980, Table 2.

[1]Several proposals for increasing financial aid to nonpublic schools are being considered by the federal and state governments. The tuition reimbursement and tax-credit plans have considerable support in Congress and the voucher plan has been considered in a number of states, including New Hampshire and California.

Our focus in this text is on the financing of public education, though many of the concepts and ideas apply equally in the private or nonpublic sector. In looking at the status of public education finance over the past decade, we see considerable change and turmoil, brought on primarily by taxpayer resistance to rising school costs and a series of court challenges to existing systems of school finance. These court challenges have been based on certain defects in many of the state distribution schemes, regarding which one recent National Institute of Education publication observed:

> Existing school finance systems did not go very far toward equalizing tax burdens and educational spending among different school districts. Support per pupil ranged widely; some districts were found to spend two, three, and four times as much per pupil as others within a single state. Local tax rates also varied markedly. But what was particularly disturbing was the demonstration that communities with high tax rates frequently achieved only average or even lower than average school spending levels. (Goertz, Moskowitz, and Sinkin, p. 1)

Since court challenges to funding schemes have in some cases necessitated changes in the revenue sources used to support school systems, it seems appropriate to examine arguments raised by certain of these cases before looking at either revenue sources or the ways in which these revenues might be distributed to local schools and school systems.

RECENT REFORM IN SCHOOL FINANCE

School finance reform has never been a simple matter. Any proposal for reform is likely to be viewed differently by the several interest groups existing within the state. Funding proposals almost always contain varying tax and service-level impacts on citizens from different income groups and school communities. To many citizens, the stability of the present inequity is clearly preferable to the uncertainty of some proposed and untested remedy. Furthermore, any proposal for changing revenue sources or the system for distributing these revenues is likely to awaken that portion of the population which is convinced that change of any kind is likely to cost more and must therefore be opposed.

Understanding this state of affairs gives us some insight into the lack of self-initiated legislative action in reforming state school finance plans, even when these existing plans have been known to incorporate inequitable treatment for selected students and taxpayers. It also explains why citizens across the United States found it necessary in the early 1970s to take their concerns about school finance into the courts. Most of the state legislatures, anticipating the overall cost of school finance reform and the desires of powerful interest groups in the state, were simply unable to come to agreement on needed changes without some kind of pressure from the court system. Most often, this pressure from the court came in response to a complaint that the existing system of school finance treated students in districts with lower education costs unfairly, discriminated against taxpayers in poorer communities, failed to meet constitutionally mandated levels of schooling, or neglected the special needs of certain classes of students such as handicapped or bilingual children. Often, two or more of these concerns were part of a single court challenge.

The legal basis for these several court challenges of school finance systems is found in the federal constitution and the constitutions of the several states. Since education is not explicitly cited as a responsibility of the federal government in the U.S. Constitution, most of the legal challenges to school finance plans have occurred at the state level. This has been especially true since the U.S. Supreme Court turned down, without a formal hearing, a plaintiff challenge to the school-funding plan in Illinois in 1969 and ruled against plaintiffs in the San Antonio (Texas) Independent District in 1973.[2] The few recent challenges that have been made on federal grounds have generally been based on the equal protection clause of the Fourteenth Amendment to the Constitution. This challenge often focuses on discrimination against a particular group of students that is being deprived of equal or at least protected services. The plaintiffs in these cases sometimes have combined this "special group" concern with the more traditional concern that the state support program encourages large differences in either taxpayer effort or educational quality across the several districts of the state.

Federal government reluctance to get involved in challenges of state school finance programs has some historical precedent. Not only is support for education omitted as an explicit requirement in the federal Constitution but the language of the Tenth Amendment essentially delegates powers over public schools to the states. While the general welfare clause (Article I, Section 8) of the federal Constitution has frequently been used as justification of some federal support of public education (e.g., in vocational education, compensatory instruction, and science and mathematics training), the possibility of using this same clause as a basis for altering state finance schemes has, up to this point, not been justified in the eyes of the federal courts.

It was this generally weak constitutional role for education that required plaintiffs in the cases mentioned earlier to build arguments around possible violation of the equal protection clause of the Fourteenth Amendment rather than some direct federal guarantee of education service. Here again, however, the absence of any specific language suggesting that education is a protected right under the federal Constitution has up to this point made the U.S. Supreme Court reluctant to declare relative differences in educational opportunities among school districts a violation of the equal protection clause of the Fourteenth Amendment.

Failing to gain relief through the federal courts, plaintiffs have in recent years concentrated on the equal protection clauses of the several state constitutions and/or other specific language of those constitutions requiring the state to provide a particular standard of education. *Robinson* v. *Cahill* in New Jersey and the Seattle School District challenge in Washington represent this latter type wherein state constitutional language requires maintenance of an education standard not currently being met by the state.[3] *Serrano* v. *Priest* in California focused on the equal protection clause of the state constitution.[4] In this case, plaintiffs were able to show that education is a fundamental state right and should therefore not be dependent on the wealth of the district in which the student happens to reside. This principle, often referenced as "fiscal neutrality," suggests that a given child's education should be dependent on the wealth of the state as a whole rather than wealth in the specific locality of residence.

---

[2]The Illinois plaintiffs (in *McInnis* v. *Ogilvie,* [394 U.S. 322, 1969]) challenged the wide disparity in spending among local school districts and the fact that this disparity was related to property wealth. They sought a distribution scheme based more on student need. The San Antonio challenge (*Rodriguiz* v. *San Antonio Independent District* [441 U.S. 1, 1973]) came from a group of parents and students living in a low-wealth district. The group felt that its Fourteenth-Amendment right to equal protection of the law was violated by a financial support system that depended heavily on local property wealth.

[3]In *Robinson* v. *Cahill* (62 N.J. 473, 1973), the court was concerned, at least in part, with the interpretation of a state constitutional requirement to provide a "thorough and efficient system of free public schools." The Seattle School District challenge in Washington (585 P 2d 71, 1978) was based on a state obligation "to make ample provision for the education of all children residing within its borders." In both cases, the state courts determined that current plans of financial support did not meet the stated constitutional requirement.

[4]*Serrano* v. *Priest* (135 Cal. Rep. 345, 1976) was decided in favor of the original plaintiff, who maintained that the California system of distributing state monies made the education of students dependent on the property wealth of the community of residence. Such a situation was judged to violate the equal-protection provisions of the California constitution.

Despite these successes in challenging state finance plans on the basis of language in the state constitution, the absence of any compelling pressure for change through the federal courts has clearly slowed the rate of change in school finance plans since the late 1970s. Also, there has been a distinct shift toward concern for groups of students with special needs—handicapped, bilingual, or educationally disadvantaged. This shift is seen in the *Board of Education of Levittown* v. *Nyquist* case being heard in New York and the *Lau* v. *Nichols* case decided by the U.S. Supreme Court.[5]

In the first of these cases, four cities in New York State (New York City, Rochester, Buffalo, and Syracuse) have successfully argued in the Supreme Court of the State of New York that strict application of the "fiscal neutrality" concept as a remedy would harm educational opportunities for minority populations in the urban centers of the state. This latter claim is based on the recognition that simply placing generation of revenue on an equal basis throughout the state does nothing to recognize the special remedial needs of urban students. In *Lau* v. *Nichols,* the court determined that teaching non-English-speaking students exclusively in English deprives them of any meaningful education, thus removing from these students rights guaranteed under the Civil Rights Act of 1964. The Lau decision demonstrates this increasing concern in school finance litigation for students having special educational needs or handicaps. Despite the frequent reluctance of both federal and state governments to provide funds for certain of these special groups, there is little question that their right to some level of supplementary educational service has been demonstrated.

REVENUE SOURCES IN PUBLIC SCHOOLS

Most revenues for operating public schools come from some form of taxation. Economists generally have identified four specific forms of taxation—income, consumption, wealth, and privilege. The privilege tax is essentially a fee for engaging in an activity regulated by the government, and, because these fees represent a relatively small portion of total revenue for schools, the focus here is on the first three tax types. The income tax, a major form of taxation at the federal government level, includes both individual and corporate forms. Of the 431 billion in federal government revenues for 1978, the individual income tax accounted for 42 percent, the corporate income tax for another 14 percent.[6] Hence, together these two income taxes account for over 50 percent of all federal government revenues. Another 30 percent of federal government revenues comes from the payroll taxes that are earmarked for financing the social security and unemployment programs of the federal government.

Consumption taxes are a major source of revenue at the state level. Examination of Table 7–3 shows that consumption taxes in the form of general sales and excise on motor fuels, alcohol, and tobacco accounted for 44.4 percent of all state tax collections in 1979. There is a definite trend toward increased use of the income tax at the state level, with the collective individual and corporate income forms as a percentage of total state taxes increasing from 26.9 percent in 1970 to 35.8 percent in 1979. This shift is based in part on the fact that

---

[5]Among the many challenges raised by the board of education in *Levittown* v. *Nyquist* (NY Supp., 408 NYS 2d 606, 1978) is the possible requirement that the state of New York recognize special needs of urban disadvantaged students in satisfyng both the state and federal equal-protection requirements. Similarly, *Lau* v. *Nichols* (414 U.S. 563, 1974), though decided on the basis of Section 601 of the Civil Rights Act of 1964 rather than the equal-protection clause of the Fourteenth Amendment, suggests a definite need for special compensatory assistance in language development for non-English-speaking children.

[6]For a complete breakdown of federal government tax sources, see Bureau of the Census, U.S. Department of Commerce, *Statistical Abstract of the United States* (Washington, D.C.: U.S. Government Printing Office, 1980), p. 290.

Table 7–3 State Government Tax Collections 1970 and 1979

	1970		1979	
Type of Tax	*Amount (in millions)*	*Percent*	*Amount (in millions)*	*Percent*
General Sales	$14,177	29.6	$ 39,505	31.6
Excise on Motor Fuels	6,283	13,1	9,980	8.0
Excise on Alcohol and Tobacco	3,728	7.8	6,040	4.8
Individual Income	9,183	19.1	32,622	26.1
Corporate Income	3,738	7.8	12,128	9.7
Motor Vehicle Licenses	2,728	5.7	4,779	3.9
Other Taxes and Licenses	8,124	16.9	19,854	15.9
TOTAL	$47,961	100.0	$124,908	100.0

Source: U.S. Bureau of the Census, Department of Commerce, *Statistical Abstract of the United States* (Washington, D.C.: U.S. Government Printing Office, 1980), p. 304.

several states have either added an income tax or increased the rate on existing income tax to meet the needs of school finance reform. New Jersey, as a case in point, added an income tax in 1976 as a direct response to the *Robinson* v. *Cahill* mandate that the state assume a larger role in the funding of public schools.

The property tax, a form of assessment against the wealth of the individual or business, is clearly the major tax source for local governments. In Table 7–4, we note that in 1978 the property tax accounted for 79.7 percent of all tax collections at the local level. This dependence on property tax is especially true for local school districts, most of which are prohibited from collecting either sales or income taxes. It should be noted that Tables 7–3 and 7–4 include tax collections only. The state governments secure revenue from federal grants and local governments from both federal and state sources, none of which is considered tax revenue. As an illustration of the importance of these intergovernmental transfers, local governments in 1978 received $84,053 million from federal and state sources, an amount that more than matches the total tax revenues of these same local governments.[7]

In analyzing revenue patterns of public elementary and secondary schools, we observe in Table 7–5 that the federal government in 1978–1979 accounted for 9.8 percent of all school revenues. On a state-by-state basis, this ranged from a high of 24.8 percent in Mississippi to

Table 7–4 Local Government Tax Collections 1970 and 1978

	1970		1978	
Type of Tax	*Amount (in millions)*	*Percent*	*Amount (in millions)*	*Percent*
Property	$32,963	84.9	$64,058	79.7
Sales and Gross Receipts	3,068	7.9	9,326	11.6
Individual and Corporate Income	1,630	4.2	4,071	5.1
Other	1,173	3.0	2,926	3.6
TOTAL	$38,834	100.0	$80,381	100.0

Source: U.S. Bureau of the Census, Department of the Commerce, *Statistical Abstract of the United States* (Washington, D.C.: U.S. Government Printing Office, 1980), p. 292.

[7]Both state and local intergovernmental revenues are presented for 1978 in ibid., p. 291.

Table 7–5 Revenue Support in K–12 Public Schools by Level of Government (in thousand dollars)

Year	*Federal*		*State*		*Local*		*Total*	
	Amount	*Percent*	*Amount*	*Percent*	*Amount*	*Percent*	*Amount*	*Percent*
1973–74	4,930,351	8.5	24,113,409	41.4	29,187,132	50.1	58,230,892	100.0
1978–79	8,642,978	9.8	40,245,891	45.7	39,168,128	44.5	88,056,997	100.0

Source: National Center for Education Statistics, U.S. Department of Education, *Digest of Education Statistics* (Washington, D.C.: U.S. Government Printing Office, 1981), p. 74.

a low of only 5.4 percent in Wisconsin. Most of these federal revenues are categorical in the sense that they must be used for a specific purpose. The largest single federal revenue source is Title I of the Elementary and Secondary Education Act (ESEA) of 1965. While the dollars received in a given district under Title I have traditionally been based on the numbers of students from poverty-level families, the money is applied to students with compensatory education needs and is to be in addition to the regular program provided for these students. In other words, the funds for Title I are intended to supplement rather than to supplant the regular school program. Other specific school programs receiving federal revenues either separately or in block grants are vocational and bilingual programs and those for the handicapped. General federal aid for maintenance and operation of elementary and secondary schools is limited largely to P.L. 874 monies. Sometimes referred to as "impact aid," these monies come to a district as a result of students whose parents live and/or work on federal lands. This aid is intended to offset the loss in property tax revenue associated with land used by the federal government.

The state share of public school revenues has been increasing steadily over the past ten years. Table 7–5 indicates that the percentage of all revenues generated at the state level in 1978–1979 was 45.7 percent. Most finance experts expect this percentage to exceed 50 percent by the mid-1980s. A prime factor in the increasing state role in education financing has been the many court challenges of generally inadequate funding systems and recognition that state government has the capacity for raising the tax funds required to correct these inadequacies. Although the frequency of court challenges has been reduced since the U.S. Supreme Court ruling in *San Antonio Independent School District* v. *Rodriguiz* in 1973, fifty-two court actions were cited in some thirty-one different states in the two years just prior to this particular ruling.[8]

With respect to overall taxing capacity, education finance specialists have for a number of years observed that the public schools are at some disadvantage because of their heavy dependence on state and local funding sources. The federal government has by far the greatest taxing capacity and yet supplies less than 10 percent of the revenues in our public schools. School finance experts point out that this skewing of taxing power in favor of the federal government represents a potential exclusion of funds available to the public schools. With the generally tight limitations placed on local school district taxing authority, future increases in the funding of local schools are largely dependent on distributions made from the state and federal levels of government.

[8]A summary listing of the early court challenges to state finance systems is found in Betsy Levin, "Recent Developments in the Law of Equal Educational Opportunity," *Journal of Law and Education* 4 (July 1975): 429–430. Details on more recent cases can be found in various issues of *Finance Facts*, a publication available through the Education Finance Center of the Education Commission of the States, located in Denver, Colorado.

CRITERIA FOR EVALUATING TAX ALTERNATIVES

Because local and state governments account for over 90 percent of all revenues in the public schools and because major tax sources at these two levels of government are property, general sales, and individual income it is important that each of these taxes be examined in greater detail. However, prior to examining these tax forms, a review of criteria used in determining the merits of various tax alternatives is needed. Economists have developed a number of important areas for consideration. For our purposes, the principles of equity, yield, complexity of administration, and neutrality seem sufficient. The discussion of these four criteria draws attention to the advantages and disadvantages of the above-mentioned major sources of school taxation.

Equity in Taxation

Few would argue against equity whether talking about taxes, human rights, or educational opportunity. The only problem is that different people have different conceptions of equitable treatment and equity is sometimes achieved only at a considerable cost to some particular group or individual. In taxation, two versions of equity are most often discussed by economists. The first is the "benefit" principle, which suggests that people should pay the tax in accordance with the benefits received. Hence, those persons driving on the highways should pay more for highway maintenance than those who do not drive. This is the reasoning used in earmarking gasoline taxes for highway maintenance and construction. Unfortunately, it is not always easy to determine the benefit received by individual taxpayers or even groups of taxpayers. Should the cost of a child's education be borne entirely by the child (or the immediate family of the child) or are there benefits from the child's education that are realized generally by the population? The same question can be raised regarding police and fire protection. Should those people needing considerable direct services of the police and fire departments bear the financial burden of their support to a greater extent than those who rarely need special assistance from these departments of government?

Right or wrong, our society has determined that services that provide a general benefit to all citizens are to be financed by the general population and that this financing will be accomplished with at least some attention to a second concept of equity, known as "ability to pay." In other words, those people most able to pay for these general social benefits will bear a greater share of the total cost than those with lesser ability to pay. This concept is perhaps best illustrated by the federal income tax, where persons with higher incomes not only pay more in total dollars but also, at least in theory, pay a higher percentage of their total income.

Any tax in which the rates of taxation are higher for persons of higher incomes is classified as a progressive form of taxation. Forms of taxation in which the rate is similar over the entire range of incomes are known as proportional; those in which the rate of tax declines as the income increases are called regressive. As an illustration, let us assume that, for a given form of education, the person with a $20,000 income pays $200 (or 1 percent) in taxes. If this tax is to be proportional, we would expect that the person with a $40,000 income would pay exactly $400 (or 1 percent). If the person with the $40,000 income pays any amount over $400, the tax takes on a progressive character; likewise, if this same individual pays an amount less than $400, the tax would be classified as regressive.

The mere act of classifying taxes as progressive, proportional, or regressive does not assure a desired level of equity according to the ability-to-pay criterion. This judgment of desired level of equity must be made separately and depends largely on values held by the individual making the judgment. Returning to the comparison of persons with $20,000 and $40,000 incomes, note that a person with a $40,000 income who pays a $320 (or .8 percent) tax is paying more of the total tax bill than a person with a $20,000 income paying a $200 (or 1 percent) tax. In this instance, the person with the greater income or ability to pay is indeed paying $120 more in taxes; however, the fact that this higher-income person is paying a lesser portion of income in taxes (.8 as contrasted to 1 percent) means that the tax form itself is regressive and therefore not supportive of the ability-to-pay concept of tax equity.

This of course highlights the idea that the amount of equity in a given form of taxation is largely in the eyes of the person making the judgment. We can gain general agreement that a regressive or even proportional tax is probably unfair to poor people in that it deprives them of life's necessities and an extremely progressive tax is probably unfair to rich people; however, between these two extremes the normal political processes will have to be used to determine what is fair and equitable. Established standards of tax equity, whether using the benefit or the ability-to-pay principle, are simply not available to us and our decisions in this area must balance the traditional values of providing an acceptable living for all and offering each individual the motivation for personal accomplishment.

Yield of Tax

An obvious concern about any tax is its capacity to generate revenue. It is particularly important to assess the extent to which the tax responds to general changes in the national or regional economy. Taxes that yield greater or lesser amounts depending on the status of economic growth are generally considered superior to those with a yield unresponsive to such growth.

In general, the broader-based the tax in terms of items covered, the greater the yield potential. This can be seen by contrasting an excise tax on faucet washers with a special tax on all home appliances such as refrigerators, stoves, freezers, microwave ovens, and washing machines. The tax on faucet washers is not likely to generate much income; because it covers many more items and items of considerably greater value, the tax on home appliances can be expected to yield much more in total income.

While the cost and problems of administration in either case may raise questions about such forms of excise tax, there is little question that the tax on home appliances not only has greater yield potential but it is probably also more responsive to economic change. The demand for certain home appliances, and particularly those not considered to be absolute necessities, will probably respond much more to economic conditions, thus yielding greater amounts in periods of economic growth.

Economists have derived a fairly standard measurement of this elasticity of tax source, called the "income elasticity of yield." The formula is as follows:

$$E = \frac{\text{percentage change in tax yield}}{\text{percentage change in national (or regional) income}}$$

Obviously the higher the E value for a given tax, the more responsive it will be to changes in the economy. In the case of the faucet-washer excise tax mentioned earlier, we would expect an E value less than the 1.0 level. This can be seen by applying a tax of 1 cent on each individual faucet washer. If incomes increase an average of 20 percent, is the yield of the faucet washer tax likely to show a similar 20 percent gain? The answer is undoubtedly no, as very little of the increase in income is likely to be directed to additional purchase of faucet washers, the demand for which is generally fixed. This causes us to conclude that the proposed excise tax on faucet washers is likely to be inelastic, with an E value less than 1.0.

The federal income tax, with an E value of 1.5, is probably the most elastic of the taxes in general use today. Extensive use of exclusions and deductions and the progressive rate structure are major reasons for this high elasticity of yield. Most of the taxes collected by state and local governments average a 1.0 elasticity of yield. Certain of the tax-limitation initiatives and legislation approved in the past few years will effectively reduce the overall elasticity of yield for state and local taxes. As a case in point, the "Jarvis-Gann" limitation passed by California voters in June 1978 places a lid on property tax rates at 1 percent of market value and further limits reevaluation of taxable value to 2 percent a year unless the property is transferred or has a major improvement. In light of the continued economic growth in the state, these two provisions have clearly reduced the elasticity of property tax for both state and local government units in California.

Since local governmental units, including school districts, depend heavily on tax sources with relatively low E values, they are placed in a position of disadvantage relative to the federal government. In discussing this matter, Benson states:

> We now see why money is available for defense and space exploration in good times and bad and why money is not available, not in the 1970s at least, for improving the quality of life in the large central cities. At given tax rates, federal revenues over the long run will expand much more rapidly than national economic growth, while state and local revenues will approximately keep pace. (Benson, p. 280)

This favored status of the federal government in relation to income elasticity of tax yield is partially offset by its sharing revenues with state and local governments. The distribution of federal revenues may have to be increased as more and more restrictions are placed on the taxing capacity of states and localities.

Complexity of Administration

As used here, complexity of administration refers to the difficulties encountered by the government in levying and collecting the tax and the cost in time and money to the taxpayer in complying with the requirements of the taxing authority. If we again look at the tax proposed on home appliances, it would be much simpler for both the government and the home appliance owner to levy this tax at the point of manufacture than to attempt a special excise or sales tax at the point of sale or to inventory each home on an annual basis and levy the tax based on depreciated value of the appliances. This latter option would be especially difficult, as some home occupants would attempt to remove certain appliances at the time of the home inventory. Difficulty in policing this kind of activity is no doubt the reason many states and localities have limited their property taxes to land and dwellings and make no effort to include tangible personal property as part of the tax program.

The difficulties involved in levying and collecting taxes seem to vary depending on the size of the population to be taxed and the amount of inequity tolerated within the tax system. If we use cost of administration as an overall indication of this difficulty level, difficulties are probably least with respect to the income tax. The income tax typically costs just over 1 percent of receipts to administer; both the sales and property taxes seem to run slightly higher in terms of overall administrative cost per unit of revenue and there are those who would argue that property tax administration would be even higher if an adequate and fair job of assessing properties were to be achieved. When it comes to cost in time and money to the individual taxpayer, the federal income tax does not fare so well. Complying with federal tax regulations can be a very costly exercise and often involves paying for special assistance in the preparation of the tax statement.

Overall complexity of administration may vary for the different forms of taxation and in accordance with the level of government attempting to utilize the tax. For example, the general sales tax presents much greater difficulty in administration to the local government unit than to the state. In the first place, the number of merchants collecting the sales tax in some communities would be too small to justify hiring government staff for maintaining the records and assuring compliance. Overlapping boundaries for many local government units could also add confusion for the local government and extra compliance costs for local merchants. Perhaps more important, no local government unit can afford to have greatly different sales tax rates from those existing in nearby communities. If such were to occur, shoppers would quickly learn to concentrate their purchases in the low-tax communities. This situation would soon prove intolerable to merchants in the high-tax communities. Since this pressure to keep local sales taxes at a standard rate would probably succeed, it makes much more sense to have a central agent like the state collect the tax in the first place. State collection simplifies the process for the merchant and is likely to be a more efficient form of taxation for all concerned.

Neutrality of Economic Choice

The neutrality principle of taxation simply suggests that given the choice between two forms of taxation, the government should logically select that form which has a minimum effect on the economic decisions made by individuals or on their social well-being. Generally, taxes on price-elastic goods such as household appliances, automobiles, and pleasure boats are most likely to violate the principle of neutrality. This is particularly true when the excise or selected sales taxes on these items are set at a high rate. Examples of some neutral tax forms include excise taxes on such inelastic commodities as salt, light bulbs, and bread. The purchase of these commodities is not likely to be greatly affected by the rate of taxation and hence they have a minimal effect on the economic choices of individual persons. The most neutral tax of all is a head tax. Since this tax is applied equally to all individuals, regardless of income level or spending pattern, imposition of the tax cannot alter the investment or consumption patterns of the individual. Unfortunately, most truly neutral taxes are likely to be regressive in impact and may therefore have to be dropped due to direct conflict with the ability-to-pay equity principle.

Sometimes governments purposely tax selected items to reduce consumption of those items. Examples here include the excise taxes on alcohol and tobacco. Taxes levied against gains accumulated in various forms of betting and gambling are other examples of purposeful nonneutrality in taxation. While these forms of taxation are not likely to yield large amounts of revenue, they do serve a useful social purpose and reduce the rates needed for other forms of taxation.

A slight extension of the principle of neutrality in taxation can be used in support of general sales taxes in contrast to selected sales taxes. The general sales tax, because it can be applied equally to the purchase of all goods and services, is less likely to alter economic choices in the marketplace. The neutrality principle can also be used to support a varied set of tax instruments. Since most tax instruments are known to have some negative effects (such as distorting consumption patterns, reducing incentive for work, or reducing willingness to invest capital), the existence of many different forms of taxation can serve to balance these negative effects, assuring a more neutral tax system overall.

EXAMINATION OF PRIMARY TAX SOURCES FOR SCHOOLS

Now that we have examined the criteria most often used by economists to assess the merits of various forms of taxation, we are prepared to look in more detail at the three forms of taxation on which public schools are most dependent. As mentioned earlier, these are the property, general sales, and personal income forms of taxation. While it is impossible in this context to look at the specific tax programs of individual states, the reader should be able to draw some inferences about the tax structure of a specific state from the explanatory material provided. More important, the specific illustrations of tax-rate computation should apply equally to all states having the indicated form of taxation.

Property Tax

Property tax is clearly the most important tax used to support the public schools. Property taxes today account for approximately 45 percent of all public school revenues and over 90 percent of the school revenues collected at the local level. The property taxes used to support schools are generally limited to real property, including land and improvements firmly attached to that land.[9]

A key prerequisite of the collection of property tax is fair assessment of properties within the specific taxing district. This procedure, for single-family homes, usually involves a compilation of recent sales data by the tax assessor's staff and the assignment of an assessed value to each home based on the sale price of comparable properties in the community. For multifamily dwellings and commercial properties, the procedures are more complex.

Whatever method is used, the resulting assessed values on all properties are accumulated to determine a total assessed property value for the taxing jurisdiction. The ratio of the amount of money to be raised to this total assessed value is essentially the property tax rate for the ensuing time period. An illustration should aid in understanding this process.

Let us suppose that a given school district has a total assessed property valuation of $300 million and needs to raise exactly $450 for each of its 10,000 students. As indicated above, the tax rate required to raise this amount of revenue is the ratio of the amount of money to be raised to the total assessed value of property. In this case, we divide the total amount to be raised, $4,500,000 (450 × 10,000), by the assessed value of $300,000,000, thus giving a tax rate of .015 or $15 for each thousand dollars of assessed value.[10] Alternatively, and as a way of keeping the numbers used in the calculation smaller, we could first divide the total assessed valuation of $300 million by the 10,000 students, giving an assessed value per student of $30,000. Dividing the $450 to be raised for each student by this $30,000 figure yields the same tax rate of $15 per thousand or 1.5 percent of assessed value.

Applying this computed tax rate to an individual piece of property assessed at $40,000 yields a tax payment of $600. Two equivalent approaches to this computation are as follows:

$.015 \times 40{,}000 = 600$	(applying the tax ratio as computed directly to the assessed value of the specific property)
$15 \times 40 = 600$	(using the tax rate of $15 per thousand or 15 mills and multiplying by the number of thousands in the value of the specific property)

Most administrators find it easier to utilize the second of the two approaches, as it avoids decimal notation and seems easier to explain to homeowners, who usually think of their property as being valued at a certain number of thousand dollars.

---

[9]In previous times, tangible personal property such as automobiles, furniture, and appliances was often included as part of the regular property tax base. Due to the high cost of fairly administering the tax when these less permanent items are included, most states have eliminated tangible personal property from the regular tax program.

[10]Alternatively, one can view this tax rate as $1.50 per hundred dollars of assessed value or 1.5 percent; however, the $15 per thousand of assessed value is more frequently used in discussing property taxes.

One common characteristic of property assessments is that they are rarely maintained at a full 100 percent of market value. Although the assessment practices in the several states vary widely, few assess at more than 60 percent of market value. From the standpoint of property tax administration, this does not necessarily mean that the system is unfair; the unfairness of assessment practice comes only when two properties in the same taxing district and of the same value receive different assessments.

This concept of assessing at less than full market value is best explained by returning to our earlier example of a community with $300 million in assessed value and the need to raise $4.5 million in school revenue. Let us suppose that property was actually assessed in this community at only 25 percent of market value and we desired to express the tax rate in relation to the full value of property. In this instance, one can quickly derive the full market value of property as $1.2 billion or $120,000 per student. Computing the tax rate in relation to the full value gives us a tax rate in this case of .00375 (450/120,000) or $3.75 per thousand. Notice that increasing the value of the property by a multiple of 4 results in dividing the tax rate by exactly the same amount, that is, increasing the property value from $30,000 to $120,000 per student results in reducing the tax rate from $15 per thousand to the $3.75 per thousand as computed. If in fact a property assessed at $40,000 is actually worth $160,000 (or four times the assessed value), we arrive at the same tax bills applying the $15 per thousand to the assessed value and the $3.75 per thousand to the market value:

$15 × 40 = $600 (tax bill using assessed value)
$3.75 × 160 = $600 (tax bill using market value)

The possible inequity in this particular case stems not from the use of the 25 percent assessment rate but from the possibility that some individual properties will be assessed at something substantially different from that rate. For example, let us take two properties, each having a market value of $160,000, in the community setting identified earlier. We will assume that Property A is assessed at $40,000 (according to the appropriate assessment rate of 25 percent) and Property B is assessed at $16,000 (only 10 percent of market value). In this case, the owner of Property A pays a considerably higher tax bill and is thus treated unfairly, at least in relation to the owner of Property B:

$15 × 40 = $600 (tax bill for Property A)
$15 × 16 = $240 (tax bill for Property B)

This problem of variable assessment practices must be continually watched by local officials. It is also a problem for state officials, who are concerned with the overall equity of property tax administration. Where property taxes are collected at the local level but for support of state government, it is almost always necessary to adjust tax rates in the several local districts in order to account for varying assessment rates used in these several local government units.

It is also important to at least comment on the ability-to-pay principle of equity as previously discussed. Most economists agree that the property tax on single-family owner-occupied dwellings is regressive in nature, that is, those persons with lower incomes tend to spend a greater part of their income on housing and the fixed-rate property tax therefore has a greater impact on their incomes. With respect to rental housing, there is no real agreement among those who have studied the issue. Even if the property tax is regressive overall, it is clear that some of this burden on low-income families can be removed by the "circuit-breaker" concept, which essentially excuses all or a portion of the property taxes that exceed a specified percentage of income. Since its first appearance in Wisconsin in 1964, the circuit breaker has been adopted in one form or another in twenty-seven of the fifty states.[11]

With respect to yield, the property tax can be judged as at least adequate. Its stability is generally good, because even in times of economic recession property values have increased. Most recent problems with yield on the property tax have been the result of voter refusal to approve maintenance of current spending levels and voter approval of property tax limitations. While these cannot be used as criticisms of the property tax itself, they do point to the fact that the property tax is probably more vulnerable to direct voter influence than any of the other major taxes. The property tax is neutral with respect to altering economic choices; however, there is a growing concern in urban areas that the high property taxes have forced owners of low-rent housing to convert units to condominiums or to other uses. The claim here is that the property taxes along with other expenses exceed the low-income renter's available resources. Whether true or not, there is little question but that rentals for low-income persons have become scarce in some areas and more extensive use of the circuit-breaker concept may be at least a part of the solution.

Because of the problems in maintaining equitable assessments of property, the property tax is fairly complex to administer. From the standpoint of cost, however, it is one of the lowest when expressed as percent of yield. The cost would probably be greater if more of the states and local government units did a better job of maintaining equitable assessments. Because the property tax is paid annually (in just one or two installments) and the payment is often coupled with the home loan payment process, it is clearly one of the easiest for the taxpayer. Its many advantages, particularly as a source of local government revenue, will assure its continued position as a major revenue source for schools.

General Sales Tax

Forty-five states utilize a state general sales tax. Over half of these same states have some provision for the collection of local sales taxes. State and local general sales taxes account for approximately 20 percent of all taxes collected below the federal government level. Thirty of the states exempt purchases of medicine and drugs from the general sales tax and most of these thirty also have some exemption on food used for off-premises consumption. These exemptions make the sales tax less regressive as a tax instrument and, hence, more equitable in relation to the ability-to-pay principle.

When the sales tax is applied to all purchases except food and prescription drugs, it is considered a fairly neutral tax instrument. There is, however, some problem with mobility in relation to the general sales tax. This can be illustrated in relation to New York City, which has a 3 percent sales tax added to the 5 percent sales tax of New York State. Residents, particularly when purchasing larger items, will sometimes travel to locations outside the city to avoid the high sales tax rate. A similar problem occurs between the states of Washington and Oregon. Washington, with a combined state and local sales tax of 6 percent, often finds its residents crossing the Columbia River to Oregon, which has no sales tax. Part of the cost of the sales tax in this instance is assumed by Washington merchants, who find themselves in a position of disadvantage in the marketplace. Washington State has developed a separate taxing system for the sale of automobiles just to prevent an escape from the sales tax on this particular item.

---

[11]The circuit breaker is less costly to the state than other common types of exemptions, as the prime beneficiaries are low-income families that would otherwise pay small amounts of the total property tax. There is little question but that the circuit breaker makes the property tax less regressive; however, some have observed that in certain situations it indirectly rewards those who choose to invest in extravagant homes. This is so because the circuit breaker excuses all or part of the property taxes beyond a certain percentage of income.

The elasticity of most sales taxes is estimated to be approximately 1.0, which means that the tax yield rises at approximately the same rate as the growth in income for the state. States that find this rate of growth in sales tax revenue inadequate to meet the growing demand for government services have in many cases made small increases in the state sales tax rate in order to generate additional revenue.

In some respects the sales tax is one of the least costly to administer. The state needs to interact only with a small group of retailers in collecting the tax and the retailers themselves have only limited additional costs in accomplishing the collection process. The sales tax is probably the least visible of all the taxes, as it is collected in fairly small increments at the time of purchase. Hence, in relation to complexity of administration, it is a good tax instrument.

School districts have typically been prohibited from assessing a sales tax. Local governments allowed to utilize the sales tax are given fairly rigid rules as to rate structure and collection procedure. These rules are needed to avoid mobility problems as discussed earlier and to prevent chaos for the retailers, who serve as agents of the government in collecting the tax. If each unit of local government were allowed to collect its own sales tax and at the rate of its choosing, each retailer would be expected to collect a different amount of tax depending on the particular set of taxing districts in which the business is located. Such confusion would not only add to the mobility problem but it would be totally unacceptable to the retailers and the purchasing public.

Income Tax

The personal income tax is the largest single tax source in the United States. In recent years, personal income tax has accounted for almost 50 percent of the taxes collected by all levels of government. The combination of personal and corporate income taxes represents approximately 60 percent of the total taxes collected. Because almost all taxes are ultimately paid from income sources, it is perhaps no surprise that the income tax is the largest of the several taxes. Due to the progressive rate structure of income taxes at both the federal and state levels, these taxes are also the most equitable in relation to the ability-to-pay principle.

From the standpoint of financing public education, the state income taxes are probably more important in terms of total dollars than the federal income tax. At present, forty-four states have some form of personal income tax. Most of these states base the income tax liability on either the adjusted gross income or the taxable income as reported to the federal government. In many cases, the states maintain a progressive rate structure similar to that used with the federal income tax.

Not only does the income tax yield large amounts in tax revenue, but, in most states and the federal government, it also has an elasticity approximating 1.5. This means that an overall income increase of 10 percent (whether through inflation of dollars or a real-dollar increase) will result in a revenue increase of 15 percent. Additional revenues are raised through the income tax even without raising the rate structure. Garms and his co-authors point out that this elasticity of the income tax has been a politician's dream over the years:

> Not since World War II has there been a significant increase in income tax rates. However, the percentage of income that the average person pays in income tax has increased substantially in that period of time because inflation has put everyone in a higher tax bracket. But because it has not been necessary to increase the rates there has been very little public outcry. (Garms, Guthrie, and Pierce, p. 131)

While the progressive rate structure does support the ability-to-pay concept of equity, income taxes have been criticized for this graduated tax structure; steps are now being taken by both federal and state governments to reduce the impact of rate increases associated with inflationary wage adjustments.

The income tax is also criticized for not always treating taxpayers with the same income status equally. The income taxes do have various exemptions and deductions as well as varied rates of tax on different income sources. Depending on the individual perspective, these differences can be viewed as loopholes in the taxing system or as adjustments needed to support worthy social and economic aims.

No matter what a person's view of the merit of various special features of the income tax system, there is little question but that these special features add greatly to the complexity of administration. Although the cost to government for administering the income tax is quite high, it is among the lowest when computed as a percentage of yield. A considerable part of the total cost involved in income tax administration is assumed by the taxpayer in attempting to comply with the many requirements of the Internal Revenue Service. Often it is necessary to employ someone else to maintain the necessary records and to prepare the tax return.

The income tax is theoretically neutral with respect to allocation of resources in the economy. It does, however, have the effect of encouraging certain types of investment income, which either are not taxed or are taxed at lower rates than ordinary income. As examples, some income in the form of long-term capital gains is exempt from taxation and no tax whatsoever is paid on income from municipal bonds.

The income tax is clearly a needed form of taxation. Its progressive structure makes it the most equitable of all taxes, and, without state and federal income taxes, the overall tax structure in the United States would be extremely regressive. The high elasticity of the income tax has and will continue to provide for growth in government services without noticeable increases in the rate structure itself. It is likely that the income tax will become an increasingly important tax instrument at the state and federal government levels. As a greater share of education funding is provided through taxation at these higher levels of government, public education will itself become more dependent on income tax revenues.

SUMMARY

This chapter provided an overview of financial support for schools in the United States. Recent changes in school finance were discussed, as well as the impact of court decisions on some of these changes. In general, these court challenges have encouraged a move toward increased state financing and control of schools. At present, almost 50 percent of all public school revenues are generated at the state level. This contrasts with 17 percent in 1930 and 39 percent in 1960.

Following the brief review of court dictates in the area of school finance, various types of taxation used to support public schools were examined. Several criteria for assessing forms of taxation were discussed in some detail. These criteria, including equity, yield, complexity of administration, and level of neutrality, were then applied to property, sales, and income taxes. These tax forms provide the bulk of public support for schools in the United States. The income tax is likely to increase as a means for educational support as school systems increase their financial dependence on state and federal governments.

Since the continuing debates on school finance often hinge on the availability of funds, it is important that school administrators understand the way in which these several tax instruments operate and the level of support provided by each. It is equally important that the administrator have at least a basic understanding of how tax rates for the major tax sources are computed and explained. Practice of this type, particularly as it relates to the property tax and related assessment practices, is provided in problems at the end of this chapter. A working knowledge of tax structure used to support education and other public services will aid the administrator in carrying out the planning and financial management tasks involved in operating our schools.

QUESTIONS AND PROBLEMS ON CHAPTER 7

1. Table 7–5 presents information about school revenues and shows trends by governmental level.
   a. What major programs have historically been supported by the federal monies?
   b. The state portion of total revenues has increased in recent years. What factors or pressures have contributed to this increase and are these pressures likely to continue at the same level in the future?
   c. The state tax collections presented in Table 7–3 show that the general sales tax accounts for approximately 30 percent of state tax revenues. It is likely that general sales taxes account for an even higher portion of the state revenues for education, as shown in Table 7–5. Explain this difference.
2. Most property tax rates presented in this text are expressed in terms of "dollars per thousand of assessed value." On occasion a simple tax rate has been used. (For example, $35 per thousand of assessed value is also expressed as .035.) Some states express their sales tax rate in mills; others use the term "dollars per hundred of assessed value." For each of the following, express the indicated tax rate in the requested form.
   a. $54.20 per thousand as a simple tax rate
   b. 5.42 mills in dollars per hundred of assessed value
   c. $3.80 per hundred of assessed value in dollars per thousand of assessed value
   d. 380 mills in dollars per hundred of assessed value
   e. 38 mills as a simple tax rate
3. Given a school district with 5,000 students, an assessed value of $175 million, and market value on property of $218.75 million, compute each of the following:
   a. Assessed valuation per student
   b. Market valuation per student
   c. Tax rate in dollars per thousand (on assessed value) required to raise $175 per student
   d. Tax rate in dollars per hundred (on market value) required to raise $175 per student
4. Mr. Jones has a house assessed at $42,000 (in a district where properties are assessed at 60 percent of market value) and his tax is $7.50 per thousand of assessed value. Ms. Smith has a house assessed at $37,800 (in a district where properties are assessed at 45 percent of market value) and her tax is $9 per thousand of assessed value.
   a. Which house has the higher market value?
   b. Who makes the greater tax payment?
   c. Using the tax rate and assessment practices of Mr. Jones's district, how much tax would Ms. Smith pay?
5. Examine the current tax structure supporting schools in a single state and discuss the equity, yield, complexity of administration, and level of neutrality associated with the tax structure. Based on this examination, what recommendations might

be made for improving the current tax structure? (Be careful to identify the assumptions or goals inherent in the recommendations for change.)

6. Explain the meaning of each of the following terms and indicate the importance of each to school finance programs at the federal and state levels.
   a. Gross national product
   b. Regressive taxation
   c. Fiscal neutrality
   d. Fundamental right or interest
   e. Circuit breaker
7. In the *McInnis v. Ogilvie* case from Illinois (394 U.S. 322, 1969), the U.S. Supreme Court resisted strongly the suggestion of determining state aid based on student educational needs. What problems might be associated with such a procedure and in what ways, if any, have state and federal courts softened their resistance to the use of "student need" as a basis for financial aid?
8. It has been argued that the sales tax is one of the more regressive taxes used by state and local governments. Does this seem to be true and what changes in the sales tax might make it a less regressive tax instrument? (It might be helpful in responding to this question to utilize the sales tax of a particular state or municipality.)
9. In several states, public monies are used to support transportation and textbook costs in the nonpublic (and even religious) schools. What rationale have the courts used in approving these cost categories and yet resisting the use of public monies to support teacher salaries in the same schools?

CHAPTER 8
DISTRIBUTING EDUCATION FUNDS TO SCHOOL DISTRICTS AND SCHOOLS

The largest share of funding for public schools in the United States comes from nonlocal tax sources. As seen in Table 7–5, 45.7 percent of all public school revenues in 1978–1979 came from the states and another 9.8 percent originated with the federal government. Continuing reform in state school finance programs is likely to increase the state portion alone to over 50 percent in the next few years. Since the major part of these federal and state revenues is eventually used to cover costs incurred in local school districts and schools, it is useful to examine alternative means by which this transfer of tax revenues is accomplished.

ALTERNATIVE TYPES OF REVENUE DISTRIBUTION

As a background to various distribution plans, it is useful to examine several types or classifications of distributions. First, as we have already seen, both federal and state monies are sometimes distributed for specific categories or programs; alternatively, monies can be provided for general school purposes, with each local school district or school determining the precise application of the funds. Examples of federal monies that have traditionally been distributed for specific or categorical purposes are those intended for disadvantaged, handicapped, and bilingual students and for vocational training. Recent efforts at the federal level to place certain of these monies into block grants to states and local districts have met with considerable resistance; however, proponents of the block or general-purpose approach have made strong arguments for the increased efficiency associated with block funding. At the state level, most grants have traditionally been made on a general-purpose basis with the local district determining the precise allocation to programs.

A second classification that is sometimes used in describing distribution schemes relates to the way in which need is defined. The concern here has to do with whether the aid is distributed in a fixed amount on a total or per-student basis or whether the amount of aid (either per-student or total) varies according to district preference. The term *fixed* as used here means that a fixed rate of educational need is determined at the state or federal level and it does not mean that two districts with the same number of students will necessarily receive the same dollar allocation. The actual amount of aid can vary even with a fixed-distribution plan depending on the number of students requiring the aid and the degree to which the distribution plan is equalized. As an example, a given categorical aid program that is fixed at a rate of $100 for each student with a particular remedial need may call for different amounts of aid in two districts of the same overall size. One of the districts may simply have more students with the remedial need. Even if the number of students requiring remediation is the same in the two districts, the wealthier of the two may receive less state aid based on the assumption that it has local resources for dealing with the need. In any case, the distribution plan is still of the fixed type even though the districts receive variable amounts of financing from the state. The label *variable* in this context is reserved for those plans where the district itself determines the level of spending desired or needed in its schools. This is most often found in the percentage- or power-equalizing plans discussed later.

The distinction between equalized and nonequalized is a third important classification of funding distributions. This is actually one of degree, as there is no such thing as a totally equalized or totally nonequalized grant. As we shall learn later, even flat-grant distributions generally have minor equalization effects in the sense that they redistribute some tax monies from the rich districts to the poor districts. Hence, in the case of state distribution plans this equalized/nonequalized distinction simply refers to the extent that money received from the state is inversely proportional to some measure of local wealth. In the case of equalized plans, the rich districts are expected to contribute more to the tax support and/or receive lesser amounts of money from the state than are the poor districts. The traditional foundation program of state support certainly follows this equalization principle, at least with respect to property wealth. Occasionally, the equalizing factor is based on cost differentials rather than differences in local wealth. In the latter case, the greater amount of aid would go to those districts where the cost of services is known to be greater.

Certain of the distribution types suggested in this three-part classification system are rarely if ever encountered in the real world of school finance. For example, categorical funds are almost always allocated at a fixed rate based on the numbers of students having certain characteristics. Rarely does the local district have a say in the support level for categorical funding. There may on occasion be a cost differential for high- and low-cost districts but the amount of need is basically determined by the government unit distributing the monies and not by local district desires. If such a choice were given, the aid format would undoubtedly consider local wealth as an equalizer in determining the amount of state aid. Hence, we conclude that categorical grants of a variable nature are extremely rare; furthermore, such grants when they do exist are virtually assured of being of an equalized nature.

Before we examine specific distribution plans, it will be helpful to understand three key concepts often used in determining fund allocations to states or local school districts. These concepts have been referred to in previous discussions but require more precise definition at this point.

Need

To determine the amount distributed through a federal or state revenue source to a school district, some measure of need is usually required. The measure of need most often used is the number of students to be served. Sometimes the distribution formula uses the membership or registration figure for the student count and sometimes it is based on actual attendance.

In some distributions, there is an attempt to weight students according to level of need. For example, kindergarten students are almost always weighted .5 due to their attendance on a half-time basis. Sometimes vocational students or students with special handicaps will be given extra weight, thereby assuring additional dollars to coincide with the greater level of need.

A few states utilize a classroom or professional staff unit rather than number of students as the need measure for purposes of distributing state aid. This is generally done as a way of establishing control over variable teacher costs in the different districts. In any event, since the staff units are themselves generally composed of a certain number of students, this can be viewed as simply another way of expressing the need level in relation to student load.

Wealth

When distributing funds with an intent to achieve greater equity for taxpayers, it is often necessary to control for the variance in wealth in the several school districts of the state or, in the instance of federal aid, among the various states. This is true at least in connection with the equalizing types of distribution plans discussed earlier. The logic behind this control for wealth is that districts with greater local wealth should receive a lesser amount of state aid than those districts having less local wealth. In theory, if such an adjustment is made for local wealth, all districts in the state can have the same level of services with approximately equal tax sacrifice or effort.

The measure of wealth most often used in the distribution of school funds is the property value backing each student. Most often this is an equalized property value measure as there is need to eliminate the variance in local assessment practices used in different areas of the state. Some states, including Connecticut, Kansas, Maryland, Pennsylvania, and Virginia, have incorporated an income measure into their equalization scheme and feel that this provides a more reasonable measure of the true wealth of a school district. If taxes are to be paid from income, it seems clear that the amount of income should at least be considered in assessing wealth or ability to pay.

Effort

As used in the distribution of state funds, effort usually refers to the amount of tax effort made by the local community. This tax effort or tax rate is most often measured in dollars per thousand of assessed property valuation; however, it could just as well be the ratio of locally raised revenues to some other measure of local wealth such as income or residential land values.

SYSTEMS FOR DISTRIBUTING FUNDS TO LOCAL SCHOOL DISTRICTS

With an understanding of these three concepts of need, wealth, and effort, we now turn to an examination of several alternate distribution plans. Since the majority of revenues to be distributed are generated at the state level and then sent to local districts, it seems most helpful to focus on state distribution schemes, always remembering that similar distribution schemes can be applied at the federal-state and district-school transfer points. This presentation is limited to the four models most often used today as part of the various state systems for funding public education. These include the flat-grant, foundation, district-power-equalizing, and full-state-assumption models.

Flat Grants

At the beginning of this century, almost all states were using some form of the flat grant as the basic support structure for schools. Most of these flat grants were general-purpose in nature and used the school census as the base for distribution. Because of the greater need for transportation and small class sizes in the rural areas, the flat grants of this early period generally favored the cities.

The major problem associated with flat-grant aid systems, even from the beginning, was the failure of the state political system to maintain a flat grant of sufficient size to cover the intended costs of education. Not only did the state typically have problems deciding on what that appropriate cost should be, but it also found it difficult to consistently fund what most people might agree to be a reasonable level of education. This meant that most communities ended up supplementing the basic flat grant with whatever was necessary to meet their own expectations of quality education.

These problems are illustrated in Figure 8–1. Notice here that the state employs a $500 per student flat grant in two districts, A and B, which are each attempting to maintain an educational spending level of $1,700 per student. The entire cost of education above the $500-per-student level must be raised through local taxes; hence, a serious taxpayer inequity is introduced into the system. Notice in this particular case that District A, because of its lesser wealth, is required to employ a tax rate of $16 per thousand whereas District B can accommodate the same educational services with a tax rate of only $8 per thousand of assessed valuation.

If both districts in this case were to employ the same local tax rate of $8 per thousand (i.e., achieve taxpayer equity), there would result a severe case of inequality for students. Notice in Figure 8–2 that the students in District A receive much less in total educational services than those in District B. Specifically, District B spends $1,700 per student compared with only $1,100 per student in District A. Students in District A are receiving just slightly more than half of what is received by students in District B. Had it not been for the $500 per-student flat grant from the state, District A students would have received exactly one-half the amount received in District B.

From this example, we can see clearly that unless the flat grant is at such a level that it covers the total amount of education required by all students in the state, there is great likelihood that some form of taxpayer and/or student inequity will creep into the system. As mentioned earlier, this maintenance of a flat-grant amount equal to that judged necessary to educate all students is difficult, given heterogeneity of opinion regarding necessary or adequate education and the political systems existing in our several states. Furthermore, if the state were to maintain a flat grant of adequate size to cover all educational costs, the

Figure 8–1 Flat Grant Program of $500 per Student (with total cost of $1,700 per student)

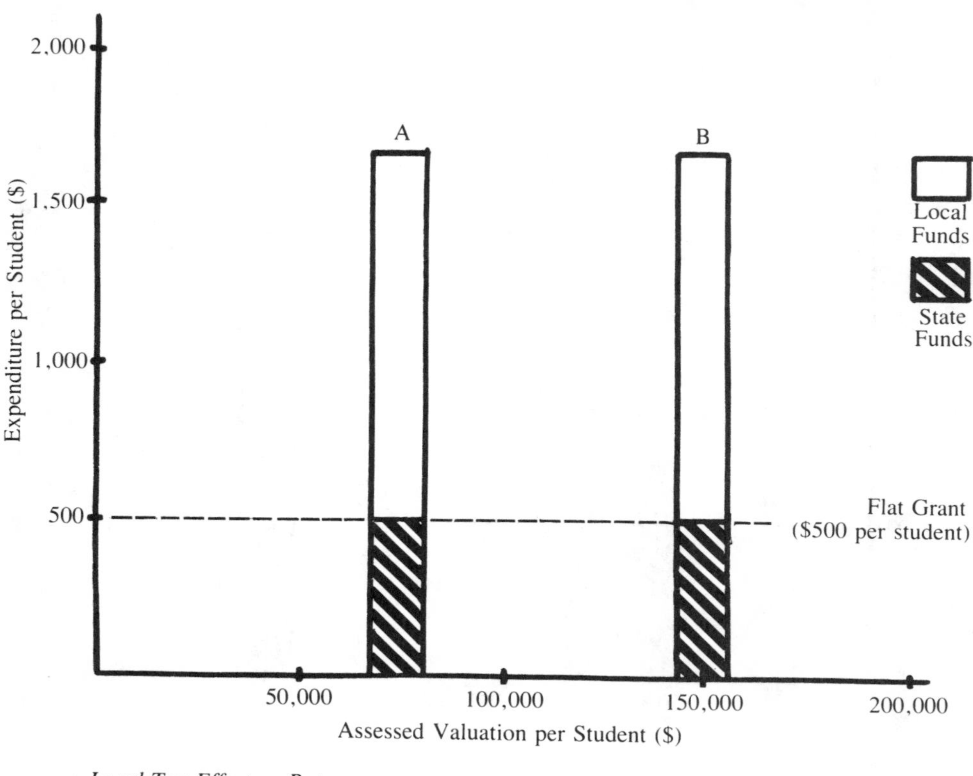

Local Tax Effort or Rate:

District A —— 1,200/75,000 = .016 or $16 per thousand
District B —— 1,200/150,000 = .008 or $8 per thousand

collection of local taxes for schools must be shifted almost entirely to the state level. Such a move meets resistance from those who value local control over taxes; but if this shift were to occur, we would have something close to the full-state assumption model discussed later.

Because of these problems in maintaining flat grants of adequate size, most states early in this century converted the major portion of school funding to some type of foundation plan, in which the state support level was established with an inverse relationship to a measure of local wealth. Those flat grants in effect today are generally of a categorical nature and tend to represent a small part of the total cost of education.

Foundation Program

The flat-grant program, because of problems discussed above, proved inadequate as a basis for the general state funding system. As operated in most states, it failed to take into consideration the large variance in wealth existing in local school districts. Consequently, inequities for taxpayers and/or students became intolerable. George D. Strayer and Robert M. Haig proposed a solution to these problems as early as 1923. Their solution became

Figure 8–2 Flat Grant Program of $500 per Student (with common tax effort of $8 per thousand)

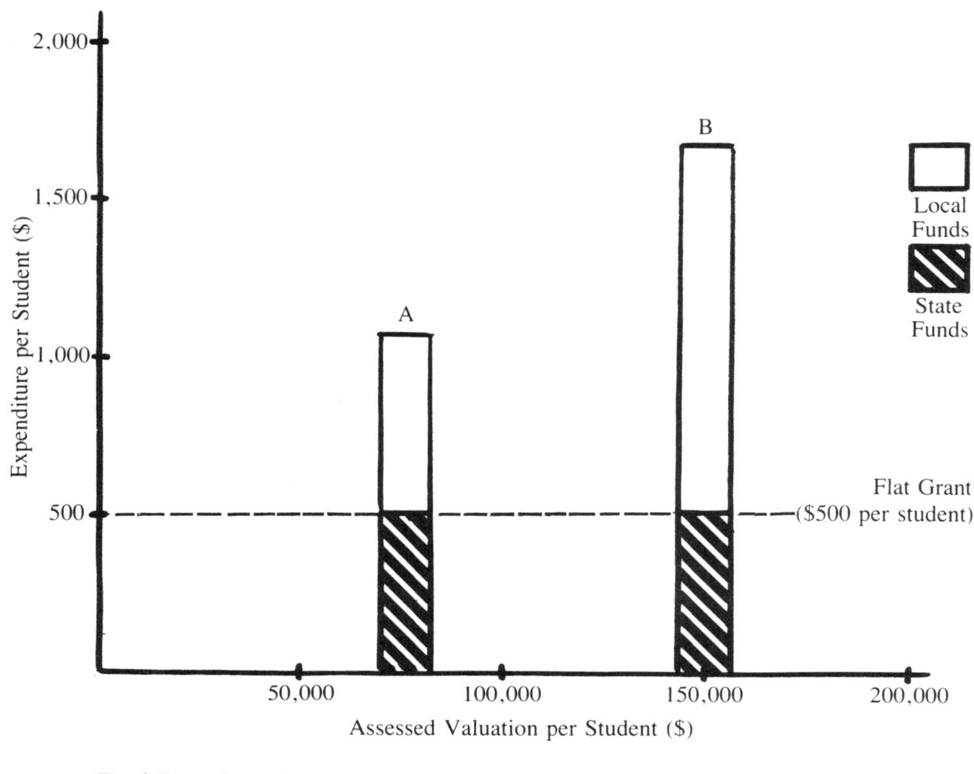

Total Expenditure Level:

District A —— (.008 x 75,000) + 500 = $1,100 per student
District B —— (.008 x 150,000) + 500 = $1,700 per student

known as the "foundation program" or "Strayer-Haig plan" and is still used as a basis for general state aid in thirty-five of the fifty states.[1]

Under the foundation program, the state establishes a dollar amount per student (usually weighted for special classes of students such as kindergarten, vocational, and educationally deprived) that is required to maintain a minimally adequate education. Each local district is assured the maintenance of this level of education with the same local tax effort. This concept is illustrated using the same two districts considered before. Notice in Figure 8–3 that both districts, A and B, are able to maintain a foundation level of $1,700 per student with exactly the same tax effort of $8 per thousand of assessed valuation. In each district, the state picks up the difference between the foundation level and the amount raised by the local foundation tax. In the case of the two districts in Figure 8–3, the state aid is $1,100 per

[1]This estimate of thirty-five states still using some form of the foundation program for general school aid is based on a listing in Margaret E. Goertz, Jay H. Moskowitz, and Judy G. Sinkin, *Plain Talk About School Finance* (1978), p. 29. A more recent reference, namely, Orlando F. Furno and Dexter A. Magers, "An Analysis of State School Support Programs," (1981), p. 181, indicates 29 states are currently operating some form of the foundation program. It is reasonable to conclude from this that at least 60 percent of the states utilize a foundation concept in distributing state aid. Most states not using the foundation program are utilizing some form of district power equalizing for at least a part of their general-purpose aid to school districts.

Figure 8–3 Foundation Program of $1,700 per Student (with local foundation tax of $8 per thousand)

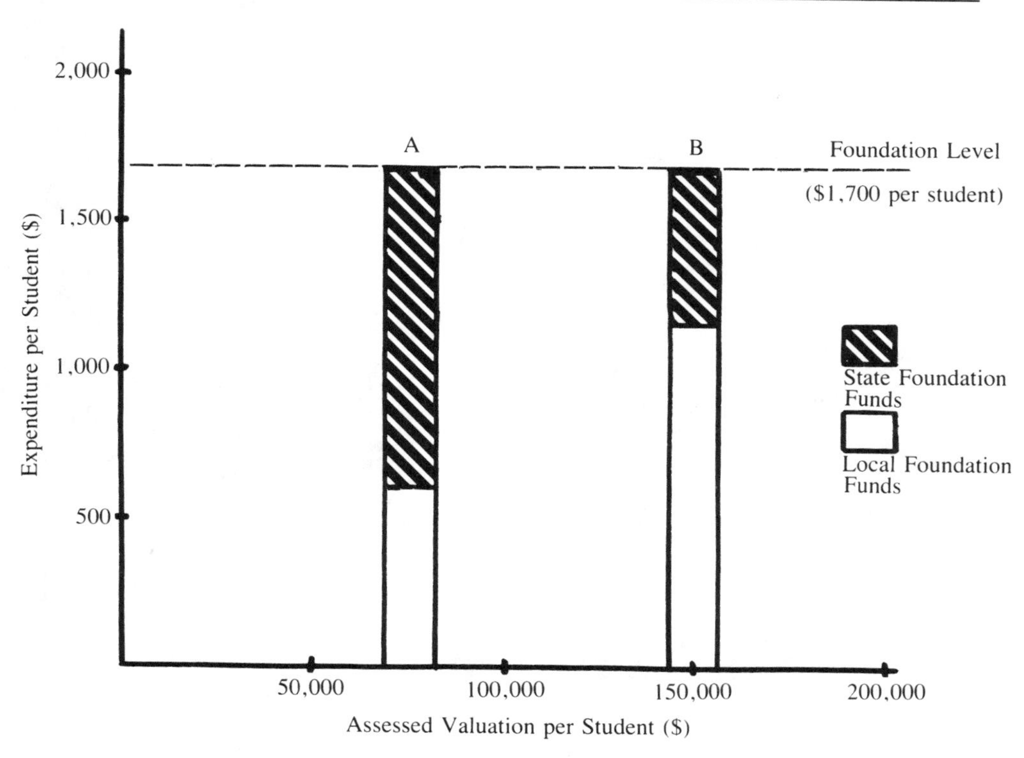

Local Foundation Funds:

District A —— (.008 x 75,000) = $600 per student
District B —— (.008 x 150,000) = $1,200 per student

student (1,700 – 600) in District A and $500 per student (1,700 – 1,200) in District B. As expected, the state aid is greater in the school district with the lesser amount of wealth. This of course makes the foundation program much more equitable to both taxpayers and students than the flat-grant program. In the case of the foundation program (Figure 8–3), both districts obtain the $1,700 per-student expenditure level with a local tax rate of $8 per thousand; with the flat-grant program (Figure 8–1), District A was required to levy twice that rate of taxation to reach the $1,700 per-student expenditure level.

While it is impossible to compare the level of taxpayer equity realized in the foundation and flat-grant plans without knowing something more about the sources of taxation used to supply the state funds, it is clear that the foundation program considers local community wealth in determining the amount of state aid. For this reason, it is generally speaking a more equalized form of aid than the flat grant. Most foundation programs used today can be classified as general-purpose aid distributed on a fixed-unit indicator (usually per weighted student) of need. Unfortunately, most do not cover the totality of education costs deemed necessary by the population at large and hence lose some of their potential for equalization.

It is this problem of maintaining an adequate foundation level that causes some critics to question the viability of the foundation program for school funding in the future. When the foundation level is set considerably below that required for acceptable education, the

Figure 8–4 Foundation Program of $1,700 per student (with local foundation tax of $8 per thousand, no recapture, and $4 per thousand in local leeway)

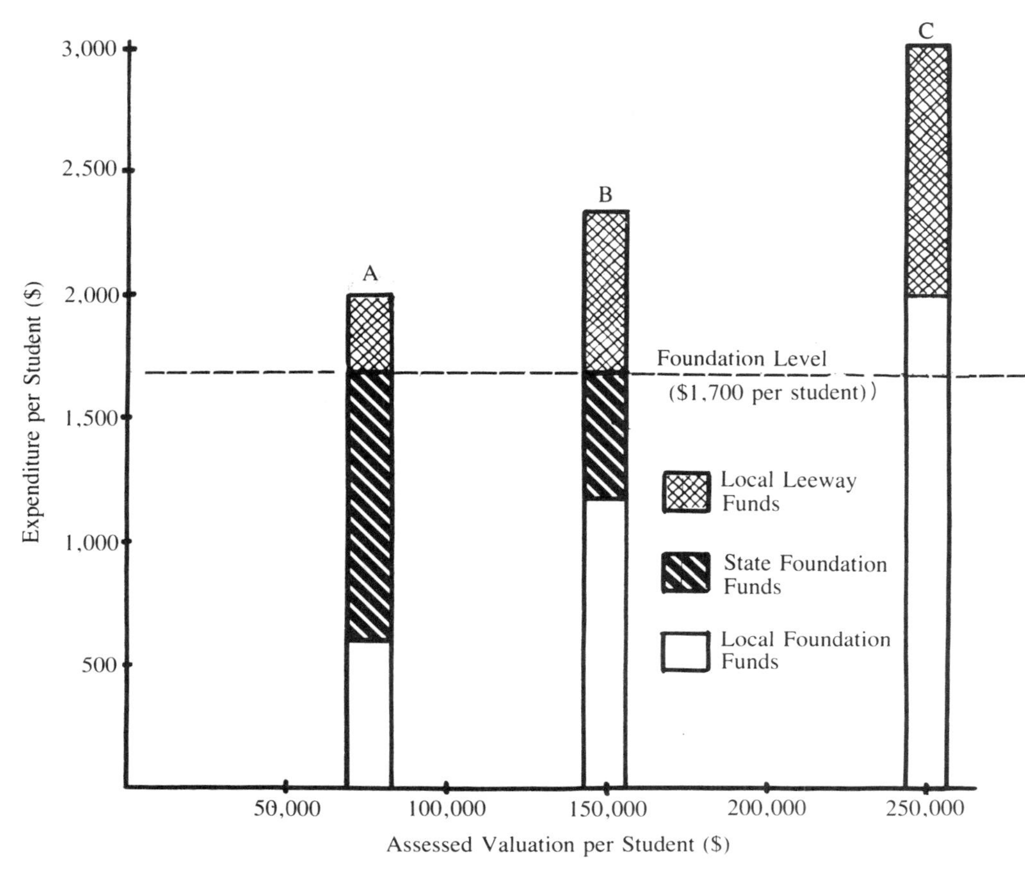

Local Foundation Funds:

District A —— .008 x 75,000 = $600 per student
District B —— .008 x 150,000 = $1,200 per student
District C —— .008 x 250,000 = $2,000 per student

Total Expenditure Level:

District A —— 1,700 + (.004 x 75,000) = $2,000 per student
District B —— 1,700 + (.004 x 150,000) = $2,300 per student
District C —— 2,000 + (.004 x 250,000) = $3,000 per student

inequities of strictly local funding become involved in efforts to make up the difference. Hence, we run into exactly the same problem as was experienced with the flat grant, namely, if the level of support is below the recognized need, local inequities become involved in filling in for the difference. Also, without a recapture provision applied to the very wealthy districts, there is concern in the foundation program that even more serious inequities will be involved. Both of these problems can be examined by referring to Figure 8–4. In this case, we still have the two districts, A and B, involved in a $1,700-per-student foundation program. The plan is clearly equalized up to the foundation level; however, beyond that point, District A is able to raise only $300 per student with its local leeway of $4 per thousand as compared to District B's $600 per student.[2] This is a clear case of equal effort not achieving the same results. Such a plan would be suspect under the fiscal-neutrality principle, particularly if it can be shown in practice that a student's education is dependent to a considerable degree on the wealth of his or her neighbors. It may also fall victim to a challenge that inequities in expenditure level in the different districts violate a given state constitutional requirement for a "uniform" or "thorough and efficient" system of education.

A second and perhaps more serious inequity surfaces in relation to the very wealthy districts, which are able to raise more than the foundation level with the mandated local tax rate. District C is one such district. Notice in this case that District C raises $2,000 per student with the foundation tax of $8 per student. If this district is allowed to keep the $300 per student excess over the foundation level of $1,700 per student, it enjoys a distinctly better education provision than the other two districts just within the foundation support portion of the program. This problem, coupled with the usual inequity of the local leeway portion of the program, simply compounds the unfair treatment of taxpayers and encourages less equality in school programs across the state. While much of this problem can be corrected by either a recapture of the excess foundation taxes or state assumption of all or part of the property tax, these steps are often not politically possible. Citizens think of property taxes as local taxes and are very reluctant to give them up to the state. Recapture has been tried in only a few states and in at least one case the attempt to recapture these local taxes was challenged in the courts.[3]

Thus the foundation program, despite its early acceptance, has fallen into disfavor for a number of reasons. The most telling criticism is the failure of the state legislators to maintain the foundation amount at a minimally adequate level and to gain general agreement on what that level should be. While this problem is not at all unique to the foundation program of financing education, it is a key element of the total funding program and one that must be resolved. In actuality, the foundation program for distributing state support for schools could have satisfied virtually all the court challenges experienced over these past ten years if only the foundation level of support had been set high enough and tighter limits had been placed on the capacity of local districts to exceed that foundation level. There is nothing fundamentally wrong with the foundation program itself but only problems associated with the way in which it has been formulated and administered in the several states using it.

District Power Equalizing (DPE)

Both the flat-grant and foundation plans, as originally designed for general school aid, began with the assumption that the state should define a minimally accepted level of education program and see that all districts in the state were able to achieve this level with equal tax effort. The district-power-equalizing (DPE) plan begins with a different perspective, namely, that districts should have some flexibility in deciding their own acceptable expenditure level. Once a district decides on a particular expenditure level, however, the

[2]Local leeway is used here to indicate that local districts are allowed to impose a given tax rate or dollar amount above and beyond that authorized at the federal and state levels. Most states impose some limits on district local leeway and often such leeway is subject to voter approval.

[3]Among the states attempting to recapture funds from local taxing districts are Utah, Maine, Montana, and Wisconsin. In 1976, the Wisconsin Supreme Court decided that the state's attempt to recapture locally collected taxes in connection with the DPE program of school finance was a violation of the uniformity-of-taxation rule in the state constitution.

DPE plan is similar to the foundation program in that it calls for all districts selecting that particular level of expenditure to make roughly the same tax effort. In a sense, DPE is a variable or floating foundation program and it necessarily equalizes to some measure of local district wealth. In short, DPE can be viewed as a general-purpose, equalized form of state aid where the need is determined, at least in part, by the recipient district. According to one recent count, twelve states utilize some form of DPE in their state school funding program.[4] Several states have recently adopted DPE in response to legal challenges of flat-grant and/or foundation programs.

The DPE plan is often explained in ways that seem more complicated than necessary. Since it is basically a way to guarantee a certain expenditure level (or power to raise money) for a given tax effort, it is probably best to begin our explanation by reviewing a set of tax-rate guarantees. Tax rates generally corresponding to those used in the earlier explanation of the foundation program are provided in Table 8–1.

This DPE program of Table 8–1 guarantees $212.50 for each $1 per thousand in local tax effort. Hence, any district choosing a tax rate of $8 per thousand can expect to spend a total of $1,700 per student. Likewise, any district choosing to levy a $10 per thousand tax is assured a spending level of $2,125 per student. These relationships are illustrated graphically in Figure 8–5. Notice that once the tax rate and related expenditure guarantee are selected, the state aid is simply the difference between the guaranteed expenditure level and the amount raised locally by the indicated tax.

Comparing Figures 8–4 and 8–5, we see the close relationship between the foundation and DPE programs of state funding. District A, because it selected the $8-per-thousand tax rate and $1,700-per-student expenditure guarantee, receives exactly the same state aid under the foundation and DPE programs. As a matter of fact, any districts selecting this particular tax rate and funding level will be treated the same under both the DPE and foundation plans. The important difference with DPE is the provision that any district deciding to increase its expenditure level beyond the $1,700-per-student level can do so with the same tax rate as all other districts making a similar choice. In the illustration of

Table 8–1 Tax Effort and Expenditure Guarantee for Sample District Power Equalizing (DPE) Program

Tax Effort in $ per Thousand	*Guaranteed Level of Expenditure*
1	212.50
2	425.00
3	637.50
4	850.00
5	1,062.50
6	1,275.00
7	1,487.50
8	1,700.00
9	1,912.50
10	2,125.00
11	2,337.50
12	2,550.00

[4]All twelve states using DPE are identified in Goertz, *Plain Talk*, p. 29. Of the twelve states, only Wisconsin and Rhode Island were operating versions of DPE as early as 1960. A DPE-type plan was proposed under the name "Ability and Effort Plan" as early as 1922 in Harlan Updegraff and Leroy A. King, *Survey of the Fiscal Policies of the State of Pennsylvania in the Field of Education* (Philadelphia: University of Pennsylvania, 1922), pp. 56–92.

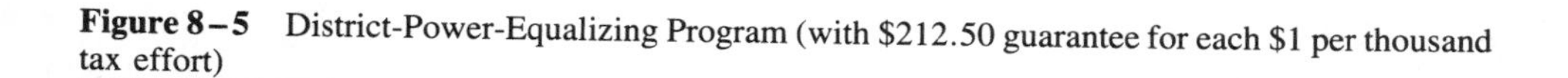

Figure 8–5 District-Power-Equalizing Program (with $212.50 guarantee for each $1 per thousand tax effort)

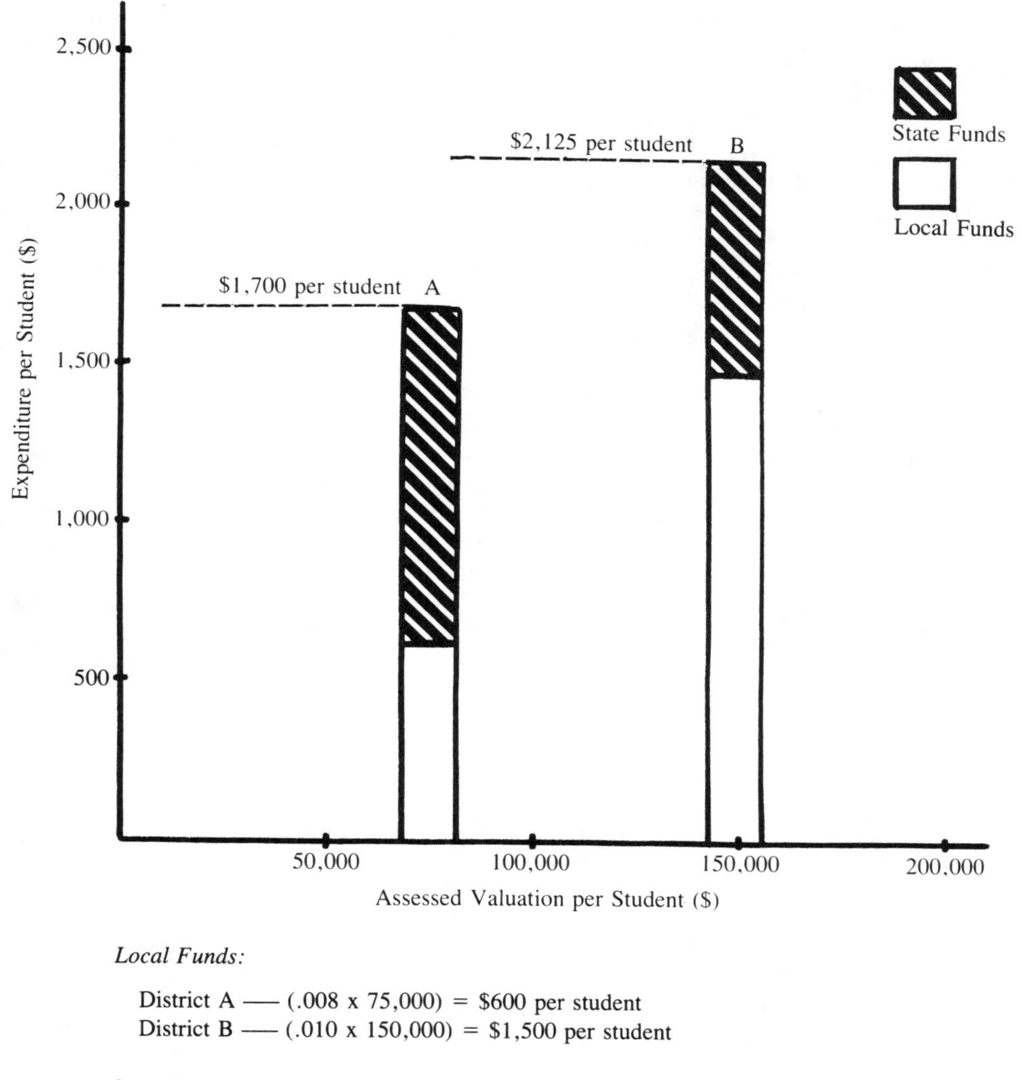

Local Funds:

District A —— (.008 x 75,000) = $600 per student
District B —— (.010 x 150,000) = $1,500 per student

State Funds:

District A —— 1,700 – 600 = $1,100 per student
District B —— 2,125 – 1,500 = $625 per student

Figure 8–5, District A can increase its expenditure level to $2,125 per student with the same $10-per-thousand tax rate currently required of District B. It is this equalizing effect at all expenditure levels that makes DPE different from the foundation program.

If it were decided that all districts should provide at least $1,700 per student in educational services, there is nothing to prevent the state under the DPE plan from establishing the $8-per-thousand tax effort as the minimum level of support. This effectively removes the earlier steps in the tax table from consideration by local school districts. In other words, no district is allowed to consider any expenditure level below the \$1,700-per-student level. Similarly, the state may decide to place certain upper limits on the amount to be funded on a shared basis with the state, thus making the state less vulnerable to the extremely high educational aspirations of selected districts. When these upper limits are placed on the DPE program, districts are required to fund any amounts above the limit out of local sources, thus introducing some student or taxpayer inequity into the system.

Most DPE programs allow for expenditure levels that are not even multiples of the amount guaranteed by \$1 per thousand of local tax. In the DPE plan illustrated in Figure 8–5, this means that expenditure levels that are not even multiples of \$212.50 are permitted. The tax rates associated with any desired expenditure level can be computed simply by dividing the expenditure level by \$212.50, the guarantee associated with each dollar of tax effort. The following tax rate computation would be used for any district desiring a \$2,000-per-student expenditure level in the particular DPE plan of Figure 8–5:

$$2{,}000/212.50 = \$9.4118 \text{ per thousand}$$

The state aid per student in this instance would equal the difference between the \$2,000 and the per-student amount raised by a local tax rate of \$9.4118 per thousand of assessed value.

The design of the DPE program for a specific situation can become rather complicated, particularly if nonlinear models are to be considered. Such formats are beyond the scope of this text; however, it should be mentioned that the DPE program is often referred to by other names, such as "percent-equalizing" or "guaranteed-tax-base" plans. It is important here to at least demonstrate the relationship between the DPE program and Figure 8–5 and the often-used formula for the percent-equalizing plan of school finance. This percent-equalizing formula for the state share of school costs on a per student basis is as follows:

$$S_i = C_i\left[1 - k\left(\frac{y_i}{y}\right)\right]$$

where S_i is state aid per student in District i
C_i is total expenditure per student in District i
y_i is the assessed value per student in District i
y is the average assessed value for the state
k is a scaling factor representing the local share of total expenditure support for a school district of average wealth

If, in the state of reference in Figure 8–5, we know that the average assessed value is \$95,625 per student (y) and we establish the local share in a district of average wealth to be .45 (k), the formula for state support under the percentage-equalizing program can be restated as follows:

$$S_i = C_i\left[1 - .45\left(\frac{y_i}{95625}\right)\right]$$

Using Districts A and B of Figure 8–5, we apply this computational formula to derive state aid and note that the results exactly match those computed earlier using the DPE table:

$$\text{District } A \text{ ---- } S_A = 1700\left[1 - .45\left(\frac{75000}{95625}\right)\right] = \$1{,}100 \text{ per student}$$

$$\text{District } B \text{ ---- } S_B = 2125\left[1 - .45\left(\frac{150000}{95625}\right)\right] = \$625 \text{ per student}$$

A more generalized proof of the equivalency of these two support programs is presented in Appendix 5. Practice exercises at the end of the chapter also build on the equivalency of these two support systems.

Despite its advantages, particularly as a protection for taxpayer equity, DPE has never received widespread use as a basis of state aid. This is largely due to the open-ended nature of spending under the plan. The guarantee that the state will share in any budget selected by the local school district makes many state legislators nervous. Consequently, the legislature is inclined to place upper limits on the total amount of expenditure eligible for DPE sharing. These limits allow taxpayer inequity back into the system, particularly if local leeway is allowed in those districts desiring to go beyond the limit.

Other problems associated with DPE include the potential for wide variance in spending patterns, the strong probability that some districts will get no support from the state, and the potential for distorting public spending in the direction of education. The problem with wide variance in spending patterns has already brought legal challenges in some states. In Ohio, for example, a lower court declared the DPE program unconstitutional because of its failure to encourage a "thorough and efficient" system of financing education. While the Ohio Supreme Court eventually upheld the constitutionality of the DPE program for funding Ohio schools, the challenge nonetheless does draw attention to the fact that DPE encourages sizable differences in local school expenditures. The problem created by some districts' getting no support through the DPE plan is exactly the same as the recapture problem with the foundation program. Very wealthy districts end up raising more than the guaranteed expenditure level with the required tax effort and the state in these cases must decide whether to recapture the excess funds or to allow the related inequity to exist. Recapture is never an attractive alternative within the state legislature and few DPE plans have employed the recapture provision. The concern about distorting expenditure patterns is essentially a claim that districts, knowing that the state will share at a certain percentage rate in all education costs, will be tempted to spend on education rather than other needed public services. This concern is probably a valid one; however, the DPE plans in effect today are so limited in either total allowable expenditure or in local percentage contribution that substantial concern with skewed expenditure choices is hard to document.

In summary, it has been shown that DPE is an extension of the foundation program for school support. In its pure form, DPE provides an equalizer for local wealth at all possible expenditure levels rather than being limited to a single level as in the case of the foundation program. In practice, DPE equalization is almost always limited to a certain range of expenditure levels. This prevents districts with low educational aspirations from falling below a minimum level of education as established by the state and it places a limitation on the amount of state money required to support the program in districts with extremely high educational aspirations. The DPE support plan is almost certain to pass the test of fiscal neutrality but it may fall down with respect to equalizing educational opportunity for students across the several districts of the state. In states where equality of schooling is a high priority, the DPE expenditure range will need to be restricted. When this restriction becomes excessive, the major advantage of DPE is, of course, lost.

Full State Assumption (FSA)

Under full state assumption (FSA), the state supplies all of the resources for education and local leeway for going beyond the basic level of education as defined by the state is either severely limited or nonexistent. This system of funding education was promoted as early as 1930 and is based on the philosophical position that education is indeed a state responsibility; it must therefore be available to all students in the state on an equal basis.[5] This being so, there is really no reason not to control expenditures (and to some extent programs) at the state level.

In actuality, the FSA model is nothing more than a general-purpose flat grant that is set at a level designed to cover the cost of an acceptable education for each student in the state. This flat grant is then coupled with a tight restriction on the amount of money that can be raised and spent locally to increase educational offerings beyond the acceptable level as defined by the state. The FSA model can also be approximated by a foundation program in which all local taxes are assumed by the state and limits on local leeway are clearly established. The FSA plan is perhaps best described as an equalized and general-purpose form of state aid that utilizes a fixed-unit definition of need.

Full state assumption of education does not require that equal amounts of money be spent on each student. Quite the contrary; the weighted student concept is still available to FSA designers and the state is often encouraged to make needed adjustments for cost differentials existing in the several local school districts. This consideration of differences among students is clearly supported by Benson:

> Nothing in the idea of full-state funding implies that equal dollars be spent on each student. To adopt full-state funding means that wealth-related disparities must first be removed, and this implies making basic educational expenditures equal in the first instance. From then on, resource allocation would be directed in accordance with the learning requirements of children. (Benson, p. 347)

Proponents of FSA are not particularly concerned about the potential for increased control at the state level. Some would even argue that education will be much better off if certain of the major economic considerations such as teacher salary negotiations and the passing of financial levies are moved from the local district level to the state legislature. Much time is currently involved in these activities and advocates of FSA would say that most of this time is of little benefit to the education of students. The time made available by moving many of the revenue and negotiating tasks to the state level could be applied to doing a much better job in utilizing parent and student involvement to create better programs at the local school level.

Only a very few states approach FSA at the present time. Hawaii, New Mexico, Florida, Minnesota, and Washington have made definite moves in this direction; however, in every case except Hawaii, which actually operates its schools at the state level, some dependence on local leeway still exists. This is so in part because of the difficulties in controlling for all possible differences in student need and price levels across the many local school districts of the state.

While FSA would appear to solve many of the problems mentioned in relation to other school finance plans, the real test is whether the legislatures can establish a level of funding that is acceptable to the wide variety of local school districts. Even more important is the state's diligence in seeing that this level of funding is maintained and that sufficient state tax revenues are raised to assure this maintenance. In periods of economic recession, it is

[5]An extensive rationale for full-state funding was developed in Henry C. Morrison, *School Revenue* (Chicago: University of Chicago Press, 1930). In this book, Morrison suggests that there is in process a long evolution toward a state school system and he concludes this is a reasonable direction given the inequalities in wealth among districts and the traditional state responsibility for education.

always easy to transfer some of the school support requirements to the local level. With FSA, this is simply not permissible as such a transfer introduces the same inequities associated with the other distribution plans.

Another challenge in FSA is to guard against excessive control at the state level. It is inevitable that some additional state control will be associated with the move to FSA. In Washington State, for example, the state imposed additional accountability on "time in classroom" for both teachers and students in the same year (1978–1979) that it took over almost total responsibility for basic education funding. At this same time, the legislature attempted to restrict salary increases for teachers, with particular attention given to those districts where average pay exceeded the state average. Such controlling steps must be accepted as an integral part of the FSA plan for school finance; it remains to be seen how many states will feel comfortable in accepting these inevitable controls and whether local interest in and concern for other aspects of the school operation can be maintained under such a plan.

DISTRIBUTING FUNDS TO THE BUILDING LEVEL

State and federal monies are combined with local funding sources in preparing a total spending plan or budget for the local school district. Procedures and categories used in preparing the school district and individual building budgets will be covered in Chapter 9, but it is appropriate here to comment on procedures used in allocating monies to individual school buildings. In most school districts, this procedure involves two separate allocations, one for staff salaries and the other for instructional supplies and equipment. Applying monies designated for staff salaries to the instructional supplies and equipment budget or visa versa is usually not permitted; however, experimentation with this type of transfer option has occurred in some districts.

The staff salary budget is generally subdivided according to types of personnel (e.g., teachers, counselors, librarians, and custodians) and it usually includes a set number of full-time-equivalent persons in each of the staff categories used by the district. Often, the building principal and staff are permitted to deviate from the allocated amount in the several categories but must stay within the cost parameters of the total staff allocation. In districts experiencing declining enrollment, this provision for flexibility is often restricted due to the need to maintain all persons on continuing contract provisions.

The staff allocations to a given building most generally are based on total enrollment and include special allocations for unique needs represented by these enrollments. Unique needs recognized in the building staff allocation might include the presence of handicapped or vocational students, requirements for operating special classes for gifted or bilingual students, or special curriculum-development tasks required of staff members assigned to the school. The factors recognized in developing the staffing budget as well as the subcategories on which it is based vary considerably across districts. A few districts have developed fairly complex weighting formulas for allocating staffing monies to the building level. These weighting formulas parallel those used at the state level for determining district need.

The increased practice of mainstreaming special-need students into regular classes has brought even greater pressure for weighting formulas for staffing individual buildings. As one example, the Denver Public Schools in 1977 used a weighted point system for allocating $268,039 in supplemental staffing funds. This point system was part of the negotiated agreement with the Denver Classroom Teachers Association.[6] Systems of the type used in the Denver schools have considerable potential for responding to special needs at the building level. Enrollment alone is not generally a good indicator of teaching load, and weighting formulas, if managed with some degree of flexibility, can be used to respond more equitably to special student needs at the building level. Allocating a set number of staffing dollars to the most critical need areas is likely to be less costly than reducing class size a set amount throughout the district.

The instructional supply and equipment budget is usually allocated in a dollar amount with considerable flexibility to determine the object of expenditures at the local building level. The basis of the allocation is usually total enrollment; however, where special equipment needs are associated with particular programs, enrollment in these programs is almost always reflected in the instructional budget-allocation system. The secondary school vocational program is one example of a program having these special equipment needs. It is often desirable to plan major equipment purchasing and maintenance on a district basis as these needs can fluctuate widely in a single building, or even district, from year to year.[7]

The move to greater decentralization in budgeting and in budget control has been facilitated by modern data processing and business procedures. It is now possible to maintain records on individual building budgets and to compile the periodic status reports needed to monitor these budgets. At earlier times, such monitoring was quite cumbersome and many superintendents and school boards were reluctant to give up control to the building staff. One superintendent, in commenting on this move to decentralized budgeting, said:

> If we expect the principals to be building leaders, then we should give them the resources with which to accommodate the education climate they desire. Another benefit is that the superintendent-principal relationship has been strengthened. The principals have the responsibility and authority, and their staffs realize this. As a result their performance has improved. Yet another benefit of individual building budgets is that the superintendent doesn't spend a major part of the day approving individual teacher requests, rather more time is spent for other educational decision making. (Deal, p. 1)

No matter what level of decentralization is utilized in budgeting, there is always need to explain carefully the parameters used in determining building staffing and instructional budget allocations. Principals, teachers, and even community leaders need to have a good understanding of the formulas used and should periodically be given an opportunity to review these formulas. Because the formulas used in developing staff and instructional budget allocations to the several buildings of a district do not generally involve an equalization factor (as is the case with some of the state and federal distribution formulas), they are usually relatively easy to explain to a lay audience. Administrators are nonetheless cautioned to work carefully with the staff and community in assuring better overall understanding of the budget-allocation process.

---

[6]This particular point system was a modification of one used earlier by the Lodi Unified School District of California. The following weightings were used: 1.0 (normal achieving), 1.5 (gifted, slow learners, bilingual, mobility, chronic absenteeism), 2.0 (reading disability, discipline problems, significantly limited intellectual capacity), 2.5 (emotionally disturbed, perceptual and communicative disorder, hyperactive, monolingual). For further detail, the reader is referred to *Class Load Relief: Denver's Program to Solve the Class Size Problem* (Denver: Denver Classroom Teachers Association, 1535 High Street, Denver, Colorado 80218, 1978).

[7]Such planning of major equipment purchases and maintenance may be required in order to conform to "bid" laws.

PRESENT AND FUTURE OF SCHOOL FINANCE

In the previous sections, a number of plans for distributing school funds to local districts and individual buildings were discussed. The funding distribution system existing in any single state or district will consist of some combination of these various plans. Looking primarily at state plans for distributing educational dollars, it is important to note that the actual plan in operation is rarely recognizable as one of the four basic plans discussed in this chapter. The various parts of each state plan incorporate so many upper and lower limits, save-harmless provisions, deductible local taxes, student-weighting mechanisms, and excess-cost formats that their classification as one of the four basic programs is often obscured. The general state aid plan in most states today is probably best described as the foundation program; however, a number of states have taken definite steps toward the district-power-equalizing and full-state-assumption models. These steps have often been in response to court challenge and have almost always been made with the intent to increase equity for students and/or taxpayers. While this concern for equity is not a new one, it certainly took on renewed importance in the late 1970s. Many education finance experts are directing increased attention to the equity concept. They seem most concerned about measuring the extent to which various types of student and taxpayer equity have been enhanced by recent reforms in state education finance systems. As might be expected, their work to date has uncovered the need for more reliable data sources relating to possible measures for equity. In response to this need, the National Center for Education Statistics, beginning in 1979, is compiling biennial profiles of school finance systems both within and among the states.

Despite the paucity of data sources, there is some early indication that only very modest gains have been made in either the reduction of variance in spending level across districts within the states (student-equity measure) or the reduction of positive relationship between property wealth and school revenues in those same districts (taxpayer-equity measure). Some encouragement can be found in the observation that reductions in these two measures seem to be greater for those states in which definite school finance reform has been accomplished.[8] It remains to be seen whether these indications of increasing equity in school finance will hold up in additional studies now underway. It will also be interesting to learn more about which specific school finance reform models result in desired changes in the several and sometimes competing measures of equity.

As one looks to the future of education finance, it appears likely that the concerns for equity demonstrated in the court challenges of the 1970s may very well conflict with growing concerns about accountability and choice in the operation of schools. The demand for competency rather than hours spent in school as the basis for granting a high school diploma is but one manifestation of this growing concern with accountability. The statewide testing programs installed in many states during the 1970s is another indication that, for the general public, accountability for learning and academic excellence is at least as important as equity in spending.

Certain critics of the recent emphasis on attempting to achieve more equal schooling opportunities for all students contend that, in so doing, the public schools are in danger of losing support from the large middle-class population. In the quest to achieve greater equality for students and taxpayers, several states have had to place limitations on the ambitious spending patterns of certain districts (usually in the upper-middle-class category) that have higher-than-average expectations for their educational system. These expenditure

[8]The rationale supporting this conclusion is developed in Allen Odden, Robert Berne, and Leanna Stiefel, *Equity in School Finance* (1979), pp. 32–45.

limitations have generally been softened by the use of a save-harmless provision (an assurance that past funding levels will be maintained); but, with the increased frequency of taxpayer referenda calling for tax and expenditure ceilings, prior levels of financial support in such districts are extremely difficult to maintain. Some of those who have the financial means have already opted for what they consider to be better opportunities in the nonpublic schools. Others who are disenchanted with the regimentation and control of public schools are looking seriously at options such as the voucher plan that, at least in theory, increase family choice in the provision of schooling. Several states have already been involved in studying or even voting on options of this sort.

SUMMARY

A number of possible systems for distributing state and federal monies to local school districts were presented in this chapter. These systems were classified as general-purpose or categorical and fixed or variable. Each system can also be classified according to its level of intended equalization. Included as basic distribution options were the flat-grant, foundation, district-power-equalizing, and full-state-assumption models. Most existing systems of state support represent some combination of these four distribution models.

The programs of state financial support for education are under continuing review in the respective state legislatures and more court challenges can be expected in the years ahead. Education finance experts continue to assess the impact of the school finance reform measures of the 1970s and this review process will no doubt result in further recommendations for change.

As a supplement to this review of state and federal distribution plans, some attention was directed to the allocation of funds to the building level. A possible trend toward greater decentralization of budget planning was noted, as was the administrator's responsibility to seek ways of making financial allocation systems more intelligible to staff members and to the community.

As school finance plans are modified in the years ahead, it is clear that a multitude of conflicting forces and ideas will continue to surface. Better solutions are likely to evolve only if the general public and school professionals become better informed as to the options available. Only with this increased understanding of the options available can we hope to develop school finance support systems that maximize the values and ideals deemed most important by the citizenry.

QUESTIONS AND PROBLEMS ON CHAPTER 8

1. The flat grant combined with a local leeway tax of $8 per thousand is illustrated in Figure 8–2. How would the total expenditure per student differ in the two districts if the flat-grant amount is increased to $700 per student and the local tax is decreased to $6 per thousand of assessed property value?
2. Given a school district with 5,000 students, a market value on property of $218.75 million, an 80 percent assessment ratio, and a foundation program of $1,000 per student with a $6 per thousand local tax rate, compute each of the following:
   a. Assessed property value per student.
   b. Total state aid received assuming the foundation tax rate is applied to the market value of property.

c. State aid per student assuming the foundation tax is applied to the assessed value of property.

3. Mr. Baker and Ms. Brown live in the same school district. This district operates the foundation school support program as described in Question 2 above, with the $6-per-thousand local foundation tax applied to assessed value of property, which is currently $40,000 per student. Mr. Baker owns a house assessed at $65,000 and Ms. Brown owns a house assessed at $50,000.
   a. If the school district decides to raise from local property tax $300 per student beyond the $1,000 foundation program, what additional tax payment will be required on each house?
   b. What tax payment is required on each house to support the foundation program?
   c. If Mr. Baker's house is known to be assessed at 80 percent of market value and Ms. Brown's at only 50 percent, which is actually bearing the greater support for the foundation program and how might this inequity be eliminated?

4. Consider a foundation program as presented in Figure 8–3. Assume a $4-per-thousand local foundation tax rate rather than the $8 per thousand presented.
   a. What level of state aid is obtained in Districts A and B?
   b. What level of state aid would be obtained in a district of $425,000 per student in assessed valuation?
   c. Which of the two foundation plans—the original with an $8-per-thousand local foundation tax rate or the alternate with a $4-per-thousand local foundation tax rate—is likely to achieve greater equity and why?

5. District A has 5,000 students and an assessed valuation of $35,000 per student and District B has 6,000 students and an assessed valuation of $110,000 per student.
   a. Assuming a $12-per-thousand tax rate (applied to assessed value) required to support a $1,400-per-student foundation program in the two districts, how much state aid would each receive?
   b. Each district decides to spend an additional $300 per student, raising the additional money with a special local property tax levy. What total property tax rate (including foundation and special levy components) would be required in the two communities?
   c. Suppose, instead of the foundation program, each district is simply guaranteed $350 in expenditures for each $3 per thousand or fraction thereof. How much would each district receive from the state if each was spending $1,050?
   d. The program described in Part c is of the DPE type. What is the k value in the percent-equalizing formula for this particular support plan, assuming a state average property value of $70,000?
   e. Using the formula referenced in Part d, at what valuation per student would a district be subject to possible state recapture of local funds? (Hint: This is the valuation at which the entire guarantee is raised with the local contribution.)

6. A given state has an average local assessed property valuation of $58,000 per weighted student and a total of 600,000 weighted students. Data for two school districts within the state are as follows:

DISTRICT	WEIGHTED STUDENTS	ASSESSED VALUATION PER WEIGHTED STUDENT
A	700	46,000
B	400	85,000

Unless indicated otherwise, assume the state operates a combination of a flat grant of $100 per weighted student along with an $800-per-weighted student foundation program. The local foundation tax rate is $5 per thousand of assessed valuation and all state funds used to support both the flat-grant and foundation programs come from general sales and income tax sources.

a. What is the total assessed valuation in the state and what percent of this total valuation is accounted for collectively by Districts A and B?
b. How much in total dollars (including both flat-grant and foundation programs) does District A receive from the state? (Assume no funding other than the flat-grant and foundation programs.)
c. Districts A and B decide to support an expenditure level of $1,360 per weighted student, that is, an expenditure of $460 per weighted student above and beyond the flat grant and foundation guarantees. What local tax rate will be required in each district to support this level of spending and how much tax will be paid on a home assessed at $65,000 in each of the districts?
d. How would this tax payment on a $65,000 home in District B change if the foundation tax rate of $5 per thousand were applied to the market value rather than assessed value of property? (Assume here the homes are assessed at 92 percent of market value.)

7. Explain through the use of a particular example how the absence of a recapture provision in either a foundation or DPE funding formula can reduce the amount of equalization actually accomplished.

8. Several states have considered the FSA model of distributing monies to local school districts:

a. The suggestion has been made that, with the FSA model, states should consider adjustments for cost differentials in the several regions of the state. Why is this a special concern with FSA and what problems are likely to be encountered in establishing such adjustments?
b. Some have proposed that the determination of salaries and other expenditure allocations must necessarily be moved to the state level under FSA. To what extent is this true and what problems are likely to be created for collective bargaining under such a plan?

CHAPTER 9
BUDGETING PRACTICES IN SCHOOLS

Several chapters of this text deal with aspects of organizational planning. The goal-development and action-program planning of Chapters 1 and 2 are essential first steps to program planning within the school; the network planning and scheduling techniques of Chapters 3 and 4 provide the administrator with needed tools for making these plans work. In many respects, the budget can be viewed as the master plan that pulls all these other aims, purposes, activities, and schedules together to make certain that financial support will be available. As Buck states in his book *Public Budgeting:* "The financial plan is, strictly speaking, the budget. It sets forth the complete monetary requirements of a government for a definite period in advance and, in so doing, balances the expenditure needs with the anticipated income" (Buck, p. 3).

According to this definition, the financial plan or budget is made in advance; hence, we see that budgeting is intended as a way of substituting planning for chance in the financing of schools and other public agencies. It involves an advance review of total organizational needs and priorities. In recognition of this requirement, it is important to view the budgeting process as cyclical in nature and involving three steps: (1) preparation of budget or spending plan, (2) adoption and administration of budget, and (3) evaluation of budget results. Each step is performed in relation to a preestablished fiscal period. Collectively, the steps are called the planning-control-evaluation cycle of budgeting. The specified fiscal period for budgeting the regular operation of schools is usually the school year; however, the designated time period for much of the project budgeting discussed later in this chapter can vary from 2–3 months to several years. Whatever the fiscal period used for a given budget, the preparation or planning activity must be initiated well in advance of the budget adoption and must in some way incorporate evaluation of results from previous budget periods. The technical skills associated with this planning activity are our major focus in this treatment of the budget process.

DEVELOPMENT OF BUDGETING IN THE PUBLIC SECTOR

The story is told about the editor of a New York City newspaper who, when asked in the early 1900s to use the newspaper as a vehicle for telling people about the city's finances, replied: "It can't be done. We don't make news; we print news. . . . Most of the people never heard of a budget; and the rest of them don't care to hear about fiscal management or budget methods" (quoted in Buck, p. 10). This statement not only says something about the general public interest in budgeting prior to 1900 but also reflects on the general financial practices tolerated during the first one hundred or so years of our nation's existence.

Even the national government at the turn of the century had nothing that could really be called a budget, only the "Book of Estimates" kept by the secretary of the treasury. This "Book of Estimates" was presented to Congress but served merely as a starting point for the several congressional committees dealing with appropriations. Congress in these years found it hard to avoid the "pork barrel" approach to legislation. This approach involved almost no serious public review, nor was it a controlled and systematic approach to the management of public funds. Comprehensive planning and budgeting at the local level was also virtually nonexistent at this time.

With the development of public interest bureaus of municipal research in the early 1900s, there came an interest in studying and improving the budgeting processes of governmental agencies. The New York Bureau of Municipal Research, established in 1906, is perhaps the first such group to direct attention to the budgeting processes at the local government level. Its 1907 report "Making a Municipal Budget" contained a rather convincing statement on the need to adopt an overall budgeting system.[1] President Taft's Commission on Economy and Efficiency, organized in 1910, also gave support to state governments concerned with improving their budgeting processes both for their own affairs and for those of various local government units.

A great deal of confusion in this developmental period arose over the proper budgeting roles of the executive and legislative branches of government. The English model, from which many of the early budget practices in this country evolved, was simply not applicable to government budgeting. Traditional practice in England saw the executive and the executive's immediate staff as controlling the budgetary process. This works reasonably

[1]This statement dealt with expenditures in New York City's Department of Health but was used to bring pressure for more systematic budgeting throughout city government. For further detail, see *Efficiency in City Government* (Philadelphia: American Academy of Political and Social Science, 1912).

well in their system of government, where the prime minister is already part of the legislative branch, but it has always been viewed with caution in the United States. In this country, legislative bodies, including local school boards, have demanded a greater role in the budgeting process. This demand for broader legislative and public involvement in budget matters is evidenced today in the numerous legislative budget review committees in the several states and the many local fiscal committees that serve in advisory roles to local town councils and school boards.

The reasons for development of improved budget practices in schools are many. Perhaps the most important is the increased interest by legislatures and education departments at the state level. Recognizing the need for expanded educational offerings, states increased their financial support of and involvement in the schools. In the process of increasing the portion of school funds coming from state revenue sources, it is only natural that the states would insist on better planning and accounting in relation to those funds. Gradually, all the states enacted laws establishing guidelines for local school districts in the receipt and disbursement of school funds. The extent of these requirements and the degree of detail in accounting have increased to the point that most states now have accounting manuals with standardized budgeting and accounting procedures for all districts within the state.

Another significant factor in the drive for improved budgeting procedures in local school districts is the public demand for greater efficiency and accountability in school operation. Institutions have always managed to tighten up on budgetary practices when serious financial problems are encountered. So long as revenues are ample, government agencies are not likely to plan their priority needs and related expenditure requirements carefully. On the other hand, when expenditures are increasing much faster than available income, immediate attention is almost always directed to the planning and sequencing of programs. Such a condition may also force involvement in the processes of acquiring needed revenues. Since both require more deliberate planning of and control over programs, there is every likelihood that improved budgeting will result. Closely related to this public demand for efficiency and accountability is the public's desire to monitor the school operation itself more closely. It is fair to say that both the public and various teacher bargaining groups have discovered the importance of the budget as a plan for the future; and, having discovered its importance, they are not likely to be satisfied with anything less than a complete review of programs and their costs.

A final factor of note in this development of improved budgeting and reporting is the advent of high-speed data processing capability. Business officials in school districts today are able to examine the school operation in a much more sophisticated manner than ever before. Each expenditure can be classified according to different programs or functions; and, with computer assistance, budget summaries can be prepared with considerable precision and detail. Budget-status reports and statements of financial condition are similarly much more likely to provide information needed by both administrators and the public in their efforts to maximize benefits from dollars allocated to education.

BUDGETING IN SCHOOL SYSTEMS

Because local schools and school systems are most generally part of a larger state system of education, it is reasonable to expect that a considerable portion of revenues is generated at other levels of government. This means that the school district must maintain close liaison with state and federal budget personnel to ensure accurate estimates of future revenues. In many cases, ties with legislators and legislative budget specialists are also advantageous. Since Chapter 8 dealt in some detail with the revenue sources used to support school operations, the focus here is on the expenditure or need-estimation process of budget preparation. This planning process, if done properly, is an ongoing activity of the school system and can involve many of the procedures discussed earlier in this text, for example, goal setting, action-program planning, and network scheduling.

Since primary interest in this text is with the building administrator and/or program manager, particular attention is directed to budgeting skills most frequently required in planning and controlling program costs at the building level. With this as our focus, it is useful to first comment on the fund as a budget entity in schools, and to follow this with explanations of the distinction between traditional line-item and program budgeting and of the interrelationships between school district and school building budgets.

Fund Accounting and School District Budgeting

Schools, like other governmental units and agencies, utilize what is known as fund accounting. Specifically, a fund is a self-balancing set of accounts that includes resources and related liabilities, reserves, and equities associated with some definable portion of the school district operation. The need for separated funds stems from the desire to monitor use of selected revenue sources. Most school districts have separate funds for school operation and for building and capital improvements. Likewise, school districts often operate special insurance funds or funds to be used solely for support of student activities. Where such multiple funds are in operation, the budgeting process must be designed to specify which parts of each program or activity are to be financed from each separate fund, as there is need to establish separate revenue and expenditure budgeting for each fund at the beginning of the fiscal period.

A brief description of some of the most common types of funds used in school districts follows.

General Fund

This fund is used to account for all financial transactions not properly accounted for in another fund. It is financed primarily from local tax collections and state and federal grants. For the most part, revenues coming into this fund are used specifically for financing the ordinary and legally authorized operations of a school district from kindergarten through grade twelve.

Capital Projects Fund

Usually financed from proceeds of the sale of bonds, state matching money, and special levies, this fund is used for the acquisition of fixed assets such as land and buildings and for additions of existing fixed assets.

Debt-Service Fund

This fund is used for the payment of interest and principal on long-term debt other than special assessment and revenue bonds. Revenues are generally gained through local taxation, which is authorized at the time voters approve the debt, generally in the form of a bond issue.

Student Activity Fund

Often referred to as a student-body program fund, this fund is used to account for revenues and expenditures associated with school-sponsored pupil and interscholastic activities in the several schools of the district. It is financed primarily through fees collected from both students and nonstudents attending the events. In some situations, the student activity fund is operated as a trust or agency fund with the school board simply acting as custodian for the students.

These various funds are given different names in the several state and local district accounting systems and are often supplemented with other funds. In some situations, certain of the above-listed funds may even be combined. The important point here is that budgeting in the public schools almost never involves a single general fund but is rather built around several different funds. Because the general and student-body program funds are of greatest concern to building-level and program administrators, attention in this text will be limited largely to these two funds.

Traditional and Program Budgeting Approaches

The traditional "object-of-expenditure" approach to budgeting has an expenditure-control orientation. It has historically served as an effective legislative control over the operational branch of government and continues to be used in many school settings. Simply described, this approach involves (1) developing budget requests around expenditure categories or objects such as salaries, employee benefits, supplies, textbooks, equipment, and purchased or contracted services; (2) compiling and modifying the budget requests according to these same object categories; and (3) submitting the line-item budget request to the school board for review and approval. Performance or program data may be included within the budget document, but these are generally used only to supplement or support the object-of-expenditure requests.

The degree of detailed breakdown within the broad object categories is always a concern in the budgeting process. For example, a school board member concerned about the budget request for the broad category of salaries may very well want to know the component part of this salary request that is allocated to positions of principal, teacher, and custodian. On occasion, the board member may even want to know the amount allocated to a particular principal or teacher. Unless this information is provided as an addendum to the salary budget, very little analysis of the salary item can occur. Often, this salary figure in the proposed budget is gained through an inflationary increase in the figure for the prior year and little attention is given to the impact on the program of those persons whose salaries are included in the budget request. This latter point is often cited as a criticism of the traditional approach to budgeting. Critics point to the fact that the budget is almost always based on past levels of spending and reflects no particular effort to examine organizational goals or the relationship of various programs in achieving those goals. This problem has led one budget analyst to conclude that the traditional line-item approach is really a "budgeting by default" system that forces the school board to become more concerned with the number of telephones or the salary of a particular individual than with the broad programs and policies of the organization.[2]

A related criticism of the traditional approach is its focus on spending. Critics claim that too many managers in public agencies feel pressure to spend the entire appropriation, whether needed or not. Such behavior can certainly occur with any budgeting system; however, since the prime focus in line-item budgeting involves the comparison of costs by object category in succeeding fiscal periods, there is often no effort made to examine program merits of specific financial allocations. Furthermore, the central administration and school board may interpret failure to spend a particular line-item appropriation as an

[2]A review of this and other criticisms of the line-item budget approach is found in Edward S. Lynn and Robert J. Freeman, *Fund Accounting* (1974), pp. 66–69.

indication that the money is not needed; since budgets are often based on the prior year's operation, the building administrator can hardly be blamed for spending the full measure of each budget allocation.

Defenders of the traditional approach note its simplicity and ease of preparation. They also indicate that this particular method of budgeting facilitates accounting control in the administration of the budget. Most programs are ongoing in nature and decisions in the real world must be based on changes in these programs rather than wholesale review. The failure of administrators and school boards to review programs and organizational purposes as part of the budgeting process is less a problem with the budgeting system and more a matter of attitude on the part of those involved. Even with traditional line-item budgeting, programs can be reviewed if management is willing to collect the necessary data and ask the tough questions.

This defense of the traditional budgeting practice has not persuaded some of the advocates of performance or program budgeting. One such advocate is Hartley, who in 1968 expressed this hopeful view on the potential of program budgeting:

> Planning has two major components: Instructional programs and the resources needed to support them. The budgeting system (PPBS), provides a carefully conceived framework for systematically relating the expenditure of funds to the accomplishment of planned goals and programs. Demands for more and better educational services have placed tremendous burdens upon the schools, and the program budget may serve as the vehicle for transforming public demands into school programs. (Hartley, p. 20)

There is little doubt but that the program budgeting approach has had an impact on the planning procedures of the public schools. Many districts have attempted in recent years to build budgets, or at least parts of budgets, around operating curricular programs rather than simply presenting the conventional line-item, object-of-expenditure formats. These efforts, for reasons to be discussed later, have rarely been completely successful; nonetheless, efforts to establish program cost information in the schools has led to more extensive dialogue between the educational planners and those charged with the responsibility of building and administering budgets.

The performance or program approach to budgeting is not new in the governmental sector. It was encouraged in the early part of this century, but got a real boost in 1949 when a Hoover Commission report recommended that "the whole budgetary concept of the federal government should be refashioned by the adoption of a budget based on functions, activities, and projects."[3] This approach embodies a shift of emphasis from objects of expenditure to the measureable performance of programs. Perhaps the most elaborate version of program budgeting, of rather recent origin, has come to be known as the Planning-Programming-Budgeting system (PPB or PPBS). This version originated with the Defense Department and was required in all federal departments and agencies beginning in 1965 as a result of President Johnson's Bulletin No. 66–3.

Within the public school domain, program budgeting of some form has been investigated in a number of national and state projects. As early as 1968, a joint PPBES (Planning-Programming-Budgeting-Evaluating System) project sponsored by the Association of School Business Officials and the Dade County, Florida, schools attempted to apply principles of PPBS budgeting in the school setting. The School Planning, Evaluation, and Communication System (SPECS) developed under a federal government grant at the

[3]Commission on Organization of the Executive Branch of the Government, *Budgeting and Accounting* (Washington, D.C.: U.S. Government Printing Office, 1949), p. 8.

University of Oregon also included an important program budgeting component. This budgeting approach was tried out in a number of districts across the United States in the 1970s.[4]

Despite these tests of the PPBS in school districts and the actual adoption of modified versions of program budgeting in a number of states and school districts, it is doubtful that the early promise of the program budgeting movement has been or will be realized in our public schools. Early in the 1970s, Knezevich expressed some of this pessimism:

> Perhaps by the end of the decade more promising results in the use of PPBS in universities and K–12 school systems will be evident. For the present, however, more rhetoric than reality exists. . . . All too often on-site visits to publicized institutions end in disappointment as incompletely conceptualized PPBS and oversimplified budget documents are noted. The haste to gain recognition as a PPBS innovator may end in discontinuation in a relatively short period of time. (Knezevich, p. 249)

There is little indication that the status of program budgeting implementation has changed much since Knezevich made his observation. Difficulties experienced in the pioneering efforts have been a source of frustration to the PPBS advocate group. Reasons for this, in addition to the usual resistance to change, include difficulties in maintaining records on programs cutting across school and departmental lines, inability to isolate the specific programs leading to particular student performance gains, and the sheer volume of record keeping required in a full application of PPBS procedures.

These several difficulties may very well prevent full application of program budgeting in the public schools; yet, it is likely that many school systems will follow the lead of program budgeting in assuring more definitive breakdowns of school expenditures, at least to the building level. It is also true that more school systems as a result of the program budgeting movement in education can at least begin to answer questions regarding the historical cost of certain program offerings, such as music or elementary school reading. Even if the measurement of program outcome in these several areas is a rather uncertain exercise, it does permit at least some improvement over the traditional line-item approach where the input objects of expenditure typically bear no discernible relationship to specific programs and activities of the school system.

Relationship Between School District and School Building Budgeting

The school district in most states serves as the legal budget entity.[5] Monies to be spent in the individual schools are therefore allocated by the local school board and thus become part of the school district budget. Viewed in this way, the individual school building budgets are actually a subpart of the total school district budget. In most districts, regardless of the level of fiscal dependence on the city or town government, a large portion of the budgetary control is maintained at the school district level. This centralized approach to school budgeting is often justified on the basis of state regulations. With the numerous federal, state, and foundation revenues, it is often easier to manage the entire budget formulation in

---

[4]A description of SPECS is found in Terry L. Eidell and John M. Nagle, "SPECS: School Planning, Evaluation, and Communication System," *CASEA Progress Report* (Eugene, Ore.: Center for the Advanced Study of Educational Administration, August 1972).

[5]While the school district is the legal budget entity in most states, this is not always so. In certain New England states, including Massachusetts, the city government (usually the city council or town meeting) must appropriate the school district budget. In Hawaii, the state appropriates funds and local school boards have no legal authority for budget appropriations.

a single office. Furthermore, the state forms required in revenue calculations are often complex and time-consuming, as are many of the approval forms requiring financial information. It may just be easier and less costly to handle these many informational requirements on a centralized basis.

Despite these strong arguments for centralized budgeting, there has been some movement in recent years toward decentralizing at least some aspects of budget planning and control. Most important in this decentralization process is to give building principals and program managers more control over selected nonsalary expenditures such as equipment and supplies. Rather than allocating line-item amounts on a per-student basis for each of these nonsalary expenditure categories, the principal is often given a lump sum and is expected to work with the community and staff in determining the best distribution of spending across the several categories.[6] Even in the staffing area, some districts have increased local building flexibility in terms of staffing distributions. In these situations, each school is no longer required to accept the district staffing formula for numbers of teachers, counselors, teacher aides, and so forth, but has some degree of flexibility in trading a staff allocation in one area for that in an area of greater need.

Several reasons have been suggested for this more decentralized control of the budgeting process. High on the list is an increasing skepticism as to whether any single approach to education can satisfy our many and diverse public interests. With such diversity of opinion, it seems pointless to try to make all schools conform to a particular format of instruction. District administrators in some cases have simply given up on that battle and would much rather have the building principal take responsibility for the building program and its development.

Another factor pushing some to advocate a more decentralized budgeting process is the intent to strengthen parent and community involvement at the local school level. Traditionally, parents have been most interested in working at the school or schools their own youngsters attend. Even in this period of enrollment decline, when budget decisions often involve a redistribution of existing resources rather than expansion into new programs, parent involvement is probably easier to maintain when this involvement is direct. Parent involvement is likely to be most satisfying when there is a possibility of influencing decisions on staffing patterns and spending at the building level. Hence, it makes considerable sense that the least possible budget control be exercised at the central office level, thus allowing school principals the latitude of working with parents and staff in developing the spending and staffing priorities most likely to meet the needs of students attending the school.

Running strongly against this move toward decentralized budgeting are the pressures toward accountability at the federal and state levels. Whether through legislative mandate or court decision, there is little question but that required services for handicapped, bilingual, and other special student groups have had the effect of reducing budgetary flexibility at the local school level. Statewide testing programs have similarly encouraged a standardization in programs and budgetary planning. These various elements of accountability are a natural outgrowth of increased external financial support, especially from state revenue sources. Collective bargaining can also be viewed as a centralizing influence on the budgeting process. Building principals have for some time sensed that decisions that used to be made at the building level have been moved to the negotiations table or have been tied up in lengthly grievance hearings. The tendency to bargain away the authority of the principal cannot be denied; yet, it seems likely that creative attempts to restore maximum building-level autonomy in the budgeting process will continue.

[6]Because of differences among buildings in terms of maintenance and energy demand, such nonsalary items as heat, light, and water would rarely be included in this lump-sum budget allocation. If they were included, a corrective factor for building construction would probably have to be included in the formula allocation.

One argument frequently used in favor of greater decentralization in school district budgeting is that it does result in different spending and staffing patterns in schools. Diana Thomason points to a considerable difference in expenditure allocations in the Newport-Mesa Unified School District in California when elementary school buildings were given budgetary autonomy. For example, allocations for instructional supplies in 1972–1973 ranged from $8.25 to $33.68 per student compared with the previous districtwide norm of approximately $13 per student. The corresponding range for new equipment was $.07 to $11.07 per student. Similar variations were reported in the staffing areas. When permitted, building administrators did select a wide mixture of teachers, aides, and special-service personnel.[7]

Obviously, the mere existence of a difference in spending patterns does not prove an improved educational program for students. However, it does indicate at least indirectly that school communities do vary in their definition of what is needed to achieve quality education. Since we have few absolutes in the technology of education and there is no single best way to teach mathematics or to group students for social studies, it is doubtful that some decentralization in budgeting can suddenly spell the end of good education practice. There are admittedly certain advantages in program commonality, not the least of which are greater efficiency in purchasing and elimination of the need to explain differences to an always suspect public; but to defend this requirement for commonality on the basis of educational quality seems largely unjustified given the present state of education technology.

In view of these different positions on decentralized budgeting, it is expected that some limited form of decentralization will continue to be the norm. Few schools today are given total budget flexibility within a single dollar figure and few are expected to gain approval during the budgeting process for each and every anticipated expenditure. The normal practice is between these two extremes with some increased interest in recent years toward maximizing budget flexibility at the building level. This flexibility must, of course, be accomplished within the usual contraints of state regulation, negotiated agreements, and local board preferences.

REVENUE AND EXPENDITURE CLASSIFICATIONS

Whatever the level of centralization in budgeting procedures, there is almost always some effort to utilize a set of categories for developing revenue and expenditure projections. Revenues often come from local property or sales taxes and from federal and state government sources. A partial listing of revenue accounts typically used in public school systems is found in Table 9–1. The revenue classifications utilized in any given school district are established by the state department of education and generally reflect state and local tax structures. Since school revenue projections are generally handled by the business office of the school district, these matters are of minimal concern to the building administrator. It is important, however, to note that local nontax revenues such as fees and gifts may become more important in the years ahead, as tighter restrictions are placed on the use of traditional tax sources. These increased restrictions on public spending have been brought about by state efforts to equalize expenditure levels across districts and by voter referenda restricting either tax increases or expenditure levels, or both. Continuation of needed services has therefore become dependent in some districts on local parent group assistance or even the formation of local education-related foundations. Administrators at all levels must learn to work creatively with local citizens' groups in identifying new and better sources of revenue, but must of course do so within the parameters of existing state statutes

[7]The comparative figures for the Newport-Mesa Unified School District are reported in Walter I. Garms, James W. Guthrie, and Lawrence C. Pierce, *School Finance* (1978), pp. 287–289.

Table 9–1 Suggested Revenue Accounts for School Districts

Account Code	*Revenues*
100	*Revenue from Local Sources*
110	Taxes
111	Ad Valorem Taxes Levied by School System
112	Ad Valorem Taxes Levied by Another Government Unit
113	Sales and Use Taxes
•	•
•	•
•	•
120	Revenue Received from Local Governmental Units Other Than School Systems
130	Tuition
140	Transportation Fees
150	Earnings on Investments
160	Food Service
170	Pupil Activities
190	Other Revenue from Local Sources
200	*Revenue from Intermediate Sources*
210	Grants-in-Aid
220	Payments Received in Lieu of Taxes
230	Direct Expenditures for/on Behalf of LEA
300	*Revenue from State Sources*
310	Grants-in-Aid
311	Unrestricted Grants-in-Aid
312	Restricted Grants-in-Aid
320	Payments Received in Lieu of Taxes
330	Direct Expenditures for/on Behalf of LEA
400	*Revenue from Federal Sources*
410	Grants-in-Aid
411	Unrestricted Grants-in-Aid Received Directly from Federal Government
•	•
•	•
•	•
420	Payments Received in Lieu of Taxes

Source: U.S. Office of Education, *Financial Accounting,* Handbook II, rev. (Washington, D.C.: U.S. Government Printing Office, 1973), pp. 14–15.

on finance. On this latter point, building administrators must be particularly cautious about establishing special cash funds outside the regular financial accounting system. Even if such funds are not illegal, they generally do not represent good accounting practice. There is always a danger that such funds will be used for private interests rather than an agreed-upon public purpose.

Building administrators and program managers are much more likely in their budgeting activities to become involved with expenditure classification systems. These classifications vary considerably from state to state and even district to district within the state. Expenditure classifications are generally different for the various fund types as well. For the general fund most states are required to maintain expenditures according to traditional object-of-expenditure classifications. This classification scheme requires that each expenditure be identified on the basis of articles or services purchased. The broad objects as suggested in the 1973 U.S. Office of Education study and published in *Financial Accounting,* Handbook II (revised), are:

Salaries

Includes over 70 percent of all expenditures for the school district and is almost always separated into certificated and noncertificated classes. Regular and temporary salaries are also usually separated, thus making it possible to differentiate even further the component parts of the salary figure.

Employee Benefits

Includes a wide range of employee benefits such as social security, health and dental, and insurance plans.

Purchased Services

Involves professional services such as legal counsel and curriculum consulting assistance not included as part of the regular district staff. Also included are transportation and utility services purchased by the district.

Supplies and Materials

Includes textbooks, library books and materials, and instructional supplies and materials required as part of the program. Also included are a wide variety of noninstructional supplies needed to operate transportation and food services departments in the district.

Capital Outlay

Expenditures that are of a capital nature. Includes improvements to grounds, improvements to buildings, replacement of equipment, and additional equipment.

Other Objects

Includes principal and interest payments on loans made to the school district or other miscellaneous objects not placed in separate classifications.

Transfers

Includes fund modifications, transits, and other transfers. These transfer objects permit costs to be transferred from a cost center that creates the product or service to the cost center that actually uses the product or service. An example is the transfer of the cost of a field trip from the transportation division to the school location that actually uses the field trip as part of its program.

A second expenditure classification system often used in school districts is based on functional areas. Five functional classifications were identified in the 1973 study by the U.S. Office of Education: instruction, support services, community services, nonprogrammed charges, and debt services. The instruction category includes the vast majority of expenditures and is therefore separated further into subfunctions such as regular and special programs and adult education. Similarly, the support-services function is subdivided into attendance and social work services, guidance services, health services, and instructional support.

The program is a third classification sometimes applied to expenditures in school districts; however, there is probably less agreement on what programs should be. Some districts utilize the program classification as little more than a location or building code; others utilize program codes for such things as reading, music, or vocational education cost centers. Some utilize these latter categories as subprograms within the location or building programs.

Whatever the choice of classification systems in a given school system, each expenditure item at the time of issuing the purchase order is coded to reflect the proper classification. For example, take sample expenditure items in a district using the three classification systems—objects, functions, and programs. Assume further that this particular district has a single-digit code for the object of expenditure, two digits for the function, and two digits for the program. Hence, each expenditure will be classified according to a five-digit code, the first digit for object, the second and third digits for function, and the final two digits for program.

Table 9–2 Sample Object, Function, and Program Classifications

Object	*Function*	*Programs**
1 Salaries	11 Regular Instruction	11 Gooding Elementary
2 Employee Benefits	12 Special Programs	12 Medina Elementary
3 Purchased Services	13 Adult/Continuing Education	13 Horizon View Elementary
4 Supplies and Materials	21 Attendance Services	21 Meeker Junior High
5 Capital Outlay	22 Guidance Services	22 Columbus Junior High
6 Other Objects	23 Health Services	31 Interlake High
7 Transfers	24 Food Services	32 Franklin High
	31 Direction of Community Services	41 Special Education Center
	32 Community Recreation	42 Vocational Skills Center
	41 Payment of Other Government Units	51 Central Office
	50 Debt Service	

*The programs as defined in this sample classification scheme are essentially location codes. In a more detailed program budget application, these programs could be further divided into programs such as reading, mathematics, physical education, etc. in each location. For further samples, see U.S. Office of Education, *Financial Accounting,* Handbook II, rev. 1973, pp. 28–29.

Sample categories of these classification schemes are presented in Table 9–2. Using these categories, the coding of four sample purchases is as follows:

Salary for Fourth-Grade Teacher at Medina Elementary	1–11–12
Pencils for Classroom at Special Education Center	4–12–41
Can Opener for Kitchen at Franklin High	5–24–32
Consultant to Staff Workshop at Vocational Skill Center	3–12–42

This coding process seems relatively straightforward. In the first case, the code is 1–11–12, with the 1 representing the "salary" object, the 11 the "regular instruction" function, and 12 the "Medina Elementary" program.

As with any classification system, there are always items that appear to overlap several categories. This potential for overlap is evident with an expenditure such as "Principal's Salary at Interlake High." Note that one reasonable expenditure coding using the five-digit system might be 1–11–31. In this particular coding, we have made the salary figure part of the "regular instruction" function. If, however, there are several special programs operating within the Interlake facility, another possible coding for this salary item might be 1–12–31. This district could even decide to prorate the salary across both function categories, thereby providing a more accurate functional allocation of the salary expenditure. Decisions of this type are made frequently by business managers and state guidelines often provide assistance in the standardization of coding across schools and school districts. Whatever the coding system involved in expenditure budgeting, it is important to remember that the budget should be built using the coding classification system that will be used later in the coding of actual expenditures. Without compatibility between the budgeting and purchase-order coding, accounting and control systems bear almost no useful relationship to the budget-planning activities of the school or district.

Overlapping expenditure classifications have presented serious problems to the application of detailed program budgeting in the schools. One of the prime benefits initially attributed to PPBS was the ability to identify costs for such programs as "reading," "foreign language," or "music" and to compare these costs to the outcomes generated by these same programs. Only through this comparison can we begin to make cost-benefit judgments about program worth. Earlier in the text, problems involved in measuring program outcomes were discussed; the problems of accurately accounting for program cost, even with sophisticated computer capability, are equally problematical to PPBS advocates. These accounting problems stem from difficulties involved in coding each and every expenditure to an appropriate program designation. This can be explained by first observing that purchases made by an individual building or cost center are often shared by several programs. For example, the fourth-grade teacher's salary may be applied to several instructional programs, such as reading, mathematics, social studies, and physical education. So also will the ditto paper ordered at the senior high school be allocated to several different departments or programs in the school. It is clear that either an extremely burdensome record-keeping system will be required in allocating teacher time and ditto paper to all applicable programs or some gross estimating will be needed to accomplish this allocation process. In either case, the meaningful comparison of program-cost data is further complicated by teacher salary differences (usually based on seniority rather than performance) between programs and the assignment of district overhead costs. Unfortunately, by the time one has made the necessary decisions regarding program coding for each and every expenditure item, it is almost easier, and probably more accurate, to create the desired program-cost figures using estimates based on school district averages. These difficulties in expenditure tracking by program and/or location are even more serious when the programs involve areas like "citizenship education" or "career and vocational education," which are not only hard to define but also cut across the traditional course and departmental lines of the school.

These several problems in expenditure coding have discouraged most districts from tracking program costs much beyond the building level. Frequently, there are efforts to track certain types of expenditures, for example, supplies, textbooks, and equipment, to the departmental or course level, but this will rarely involve the allocation of overhead costs or teacher's salaries. In light of the difficulties mentioned above, this limitation of tracking costs only to the building level seems reasonable. The building is definitely an appropriate cost center for overall management responsibility and districts will continue to track costs beyond that level only as such costs can be obtained in a useful and reasonably efficient manner.

DEVELOPING BUDGETS AT THE BUILDING LEVEL

Revenue and expenditure requirements must be identified in the preparation of a budget for any program (or set of programs). If the program designation is the general school operation, revenues are likely to be established at the district level and are based on per-pupil allocations for selected expenditure categories such as certificated and classified staff, supplies and materials, equipment and transportation. Often the staffing budget is established through staffing ratios (e.g., one certificated teacher per 20.7 students, or one counselor per 320 students) and a fixed per-student dollar amount is allocated for all nonsalary items.

Whatever the specific staffing ratios or the level of differentiation made in nonsalary items, an important preliminary task is that of projecting student enrollment for the next budget period. Since enrollment estimates are generally provided by central office staff, the various projection methods will not be reviewed here. Suffice it to say that the most frequently used projection techniques, namely, the cohort-survival and regression-line models, are explained in more advanced books on school finance.[8] It should also be

[8]Several alternate projection techniques are presented in Guilbert C. Hentschke, *Management Operations in Education* (1975), pp. 361–381.

mentioned that the student enrollments for budgeting purposes can be based on either student registration or attendance figures. The registration figures generally provide greater stability; however, some states still allocate monies on a daily or aggregate attendance basis and local districts in such states may choose to structure individual school budgets in a similar manner.

Once a reasonable set of enrollment and revenue parameters is available for the next budget cycle, the more complex task of allocating amounts to the several expenditure categories can begin. The principal's responsibility at this point is to decide on the preferred approach to the allocation process. Several key questions must be addressed in making this decision.

What level and type of involvement of staff, students, and parents is desirable in budgeting of expenditures at the building level?

The answer to this question will depend in part on the level of decentralization involved in the budgeting process. If the process is heavily centralized, with each building receiving a set allocation for each course area depending on the anticipated enrollment, there is little point in involving more than the department chairpersons in the process. If, on the other hand, there is a lump-sum district allocation to the several programs and courses offered within the school, the principal might take advantage of the opportunity to gain significant participation by all three of the groups—staff, students, and parents. There should definitely be both a review of past spending patterns in the several departments or grade levels and an examination of new priorities and new ways to deliver existing services.

If time permits, it may be useful to brainstorm possible action programs designed to meet the goal priorities of the school. The activities developed out of this brainstorming effort can then be planned at least to a point that costs can be attached to each. Various student, staff, and parent representatives can then be given an opportunity to indicate preferences for the several possible activities. One sample preference inventory form for this type of priority-setting effort was presented in Figure 2–5. Certain aspects of the zero-based budgeting process (to be discussed later in this chapter) can also aid in this review of expenditure priorities.

Should fixed parameters be established in advance of budget preparation or should participants simply outline all possible requests?

The answer to this question again depends on the specific circumstances. It is generally best to share with those involved in the budgeting process any overall parameters that must be maintained throughout the budgeting process. For example, if it is known that the total budget request cannot exceed $150 per student, it seems reasonable that this information be shared with the budget advisory group at the very beginning. If such information is not shared, there is a tendency for people to adopt the "shopping wish list" mode of behavior and then become upset when funds prove inadequate or when suggested changes are found to violate contractual agreements.

Obviously, the task in budgeting is one of getting people to think creatively about options but, at the same time, to do so within the limitations that reality almost always places on the school operation. Often it makes sense to phase the budget requests into levels of priority. Using this phasing model, a budget matching the most-likely allocation of revenues can form the basis of the request. One or more supplementary budgets can then be formulated to handle any revenues that might be received beyond this most-likely budget level. These supplementary budgets, if not used in the current budget cycle, can be helpful in beginning the budget-review process in the next fiscal period.

It is often helpful as budgets for a school organization are planned to look beyond a single year. Certain purchases, especially in the equipment area, may need to be planned several years in advance. By cutting the instructional materials or supplies requests in one year, it may be possible to protect funds for a needed equipment purchase in the next budget period. In situations where both salary and nonsalary expenditures are to be budgeted out of a single revenue amount, there may even be ways to alter the staffing configuration to accommodate a large equipment need of the school. For example, one secondary school staff involved in decentralized budgeting opted to trade slightly larger class sizes in several of the basic courses in order to acquire a copy machine. After reviewing the options, they simply felt that the copy machine could more than offset the disadvantage of having one more student in each of the basic courses.

What mechanisms can be used to settle differences of opinion on budget priorities and to bring greater rationality to the decision-making process?

Differences of opinion are inevitable both within and across the student, staff, and parent groups that may become involved in various aspects of the budgeting process. When the groups are small, these differences can usually be resolved through discussion. As the groups become larger, certain of the survey procedures discussed in Chapters 1, 2, and 6 may prove helpful in reaching a decision.

Cost-effectiveness techniques can sometimes aid in making decisions regarding specific program alternatives.[9] The most common situation at the building level is the comparison of alternative procedures (with varying staff and material requirements) to accomplish a particular goal. The alternative procedures referred to here are essentially the competing action programs discussed in Chapters 1 and 2. The decision maker in this situation must rely on existing research information and/or informal opinion in estimating the likelihood that each alternative procedure will indeed accomplish the goal or goals involved. Once this determination is made, it remains only to compare the costs of the alternatives under consideration and to select the least expensive. Only costs are expressed in dollar terms; the benefits side consists of some quantifiable measure of goal attainment or effectiveness. A contrasting cost-effectiveness approach calls for assessing the probable goal or action-program level achieved through several alternative procedures known to be of approximately equal cost. Again, in this situation decision makers must rely on research and/or informed opinion to assess probable levels of goal attainment. With either approach, the aim is one of bringing greater rationality to the budget-planning process and the decision rule is also the same in both approaches: Select the alternative that is maximally effective.

Even with the most careful evaluation of alternatives for possible inclusion in the budget, there is a strong possibility of disagreement and conflict among those involved in the budgeting process. As pointed out earlier, the technology of education does not always provide clear relationships between learner outcomes and particular organization or teaching approaches. The conflicts that are sure to arise in such an uncertain situation, especially when participants come from widely varying value positions, can often be reduced if the administrators charged with budgetary responsibility encourage those involved to take a total program perspective. This concern was emphasized by Duncan following his recent study of decentralized budgeting in the schools of Canada:

---

[9]Cost-effectiveness is actually a truncated version of the more sophisticated cost-benefit analysis and is a logical extension of the program-evaluation process. For a detailed treatment, see Edith Stokey and Richard Zeckhauser, *A Primer for Policy Analysis* (1978), pp. 153–158; or Mark S. Thompson, *Benefit-Cost Analysis for Program Evaluation* (1980), pp. 221–248.

> Taken overall, the single organizational change of transferring discretionary budget control to the school has many far-reaching implications for the principal. In addition to changes in decision-making processes and communication patterns, the school may be thrust more into public view. Along with the professional educators, the community may more readily realize the cost of equipping and supplying the school. Consequently, along with the need for more thoughtful and precise planning, careful evaluation of all activities becomes mandatory. The principal, then, must take the initiative to broaden the perspective of all staff members so that all programs can be carefully analyzed and assessed. (Duncan and Peach, p. 41)

Maintenance of this broad perspective of the school is crucial if the budgeting process is to result in better programs for students. The principal has a key role to play in keeping the total school needs always before those involved in the budgeting process. Only through this concern for the total program can one expect to minimize the type of self-serving behavior so often observed in discussions of school budgets.

ESTIMATING COSTS AND PRESENTING BUDGETED EXPENDITURES

In addition to deciding how and when to involve other persons in the budgeting process, the budget administrator at the building or program level must be skilled in estimating the staffing, supply, and equipment needs associated with school programs. If these programs have operated in a similar format in previous budget cycles, the projection process can be accomplished with reasonable accuracy by translating existing costs into the future with appropriate inflation and enrollment adjustments. The expenditure projection process is not so easily accomplished where either new programs or major changes in existing programs are involved. In these latter cases, the allocation of projected revenues to the several expenditure classifications is accomplished by carefully planning both the item and the timing of purchases on a program-by-program basis. Equipment and supply catalogs of various vendors can be helpful in providing needed nonsalary cost estimates and salary figures can usually be obtained through the school district personnel office or through regional or state personnel service bureaus and employee organizations.[10]

In the process of budgeting nonsalary costs, the administrator will often need to seek cost estimates from business representatives in the private sector. This interaction with the business community must be conducted in concert with existing state and local district purchasing policies. Many states have enacted regulations requiring bidding of supply and equipment orders exceeding certain limits and vendor lists are often required to assure fair treatment of the business community. As part of this fair treatment, principals, as they proceed with the collection of budget estimates, must avoid making promises to selected vendors. They should have a general familiarity with contract law relating to the purchasing field and should consult with the district business office before entering into purchasing agreements.[11]

---

[10]Often, regional or statewide purchasing cooperatives can provide current costs on the more common furniture and equipment items. The Thomas Register of American Manufacturers (New York: Thomas, 1981) is an excellent source of vendor addresses and telephone numbers. Periodicals such as *School Product News* and *Athletic Purchasing and Facilities* can also aid the school principal in evaluating various equipment options and in more accurately forecasting costs of nonsalary items. Also, Kingsley Publications, Inc., of Florham Park, New Jersey, publishes purchasing guides in selected states. These guides are essentially lists of business firms desiring to provide products and/or services to schools.

[11]A comprehensive treatment of legal guideliness associated with commercial transactions of all types is found in Ronald A. Anderson, *Uniform Commercial Code* (San Francisco: Bancroft-Whiting, 1970).

Because the program designations and to a lesser extent the object categories vary considerably across different districts, there is little point in attempting to present a single best model for this cost-projection process. However, it may be useful to illustrate the process and skills involved in expenditure planning with a sample budget for a specific project. This project, titled the Montclair District Pilot Economics Project, should be viewed as a new program designed to strengthen economics understanding among students in grades K–9. The project will operate for a three-year period beginning with the 19X4–19X5 school year and the organizational goals for the first year are as follows:

1. The project staff will establish an economic resource center, which will serve as a storage area for instructional units and other economic resource materials.
2. The project staff will develop a minimum of five instructional units focusing on basic economic concepts and will establish procedures for assessing student learning in relation to the unit content of each.
3. The project staff will hold at least four in-service training workshops intended to increase teacher knowledge of economic concepts and/or teacher competence in the teaching of economic concepts.

The first two organization goals will be completed during the first year; however, it is intended that both goals will be extended into the second and third years. The third goal takes on greater importance in the final two years as the project is expanded into other schools and classrooms and as more instructional units become available for use. In order to accomplish these organizational aims (and the related product and process objectives) for the initial year, the project requires a project director approximately half-time. If evaluation results for the first year prove positive, the project director position may be extended to full-time in the second and third years. The full-time secretary is to have managerial responsibility for the resource center and teacher released time is to be required in completing the five instructional units. The evaluation is to be done through a contract with a local university, with the project director and teachers assisting in the data collection and testing requirements.

Such information as this is needed for the administration to begin to define object costs for the initial year of project operation. This can be done according to a set of object categories that differ only slightly from those presented in Table 9–2; one such possible object cost breakdown is presented in Table 9–3. The sum total of direct cost projections for 19X4–19X5 is $51,192.02. Observe that just over 50 percent of this total cost is committed to salaries and employee benefits.

Those developing the budget presented in Table 9–3 will probably want to develop separate itemized listings of general supplies, library supplies, and instructional materials needed during the first year. Such listings can be helpful in convincing the outside funding source that project developers know the details of their program. If less detail is requested, the budget summary presented in Table 9–4 can be used. On the other hand, a slightly more detailed and multiyear presentation by organizational components is presented in Table 9–5. A few observations about these several budget presentations are worth mentioning.

1. In both Tables 9–4 and 9–5, a 3 percent indirect cost figure has been included. Consideration of indirect costs in the budgeting process is extremely important. No matter what the project or service, there are almost always certain costs that cannot readily be identified directly with the project or service under consideration. In most cases, these costs are relatively small in relation to the total and are not marginal in the sense that they would be eliminated should the project or service be terminated. For example, the heat and light

Table 9–3 Detailed Budget of Direct Costs for Montclair District Economics Project, 19X4–19X5 (by object cost categories)

Certificated Salaries	$15,933.60
Project Director @ 120 days @ $107.78 per day = $12,933.60 Budgeted at an average teachers salary ($19,400 annually). On a daily basis, this is 19,400/180 or $107.78 per day.	
Substitute Teacher Time @ 60 days @ $50.00 per day = $3,000.00 Ten days each allocated to the five instructional units and another ten days to release a high school economics teacher for work in the resource center. Benefits included in the $50.00 per day rate.	
Classified Salaries	7,185.60
Secretary @ 180 days @ $39.92 per day = $7,185.60 Budgeted at an Office Personnel III rate of $4.99 per hour of $39.92 per day.	
Employee Benefits	3,247.82
Certified at 14 percent of salaries = $1,810.70	
Classified at 20 percent of salaries =$1,437.12	
Supplies and Materials	1,900.00
General Supplies = $1,500.00	
Library Supplies and Postage = $400.00	
Instructional Materials	18,000.00
Acquisition of 1,200 individual items at an average cost of $15.00 per item	
Contracted Services	2,525.00
Evaluation Design = $1,400.00 Includes $1,200 for design and first-year results summary and $200 to assist with expert panel review process.	
Expert Panel Review = $500.00	
Outside Consultants = $625.00 For assistance with the in-service training classes.	
Travel	1,000.00
Includes local travel reimbursement and a single round trip to Washington, D.C., for the project director.	
Capital Outlay	1,400.00
Includes microfilm reader and filmstrip projector to be used in the resource center.	
TOTAL DIRECT COST	$51,192.02

costs needed to cover the economic resource center room in the project under consideration here are difficult to identify in a direct manner; neither would they go away entirely simply by eliminating the project, particularly if the room to be used is a vacant classroom in an operating school facility. Therefore, it makes considerable sense to identify these costs as indirect to the project. All too often, school districts plan projects of this type without considering the types of additional demands these special projects may place on central functions such as maintenance, curriculum supervision, personnel selection, payroll, and data processing. Yet, to delineate all of these costs as direct to the project or service would entail considerable and perhaps needless guesswork. It usually works best to include most of these items in a single indirect cost estimate. In the case of projects covered by outside funding, a portion of these indirect costs is generally contributed by the local school district in an in-kind contribution to the project. Whether or not this is done, it is generally helpful

Table 9–4 Budget Summary by Object Cost for Montclair District Economics Project, 19X4–19X5

Object Category	*Amount*
Certificated Salaries	$15,933.60
Classified Salaries	7,185.60
Employee Benefits	3,247.82
Supplies and Materials	1,900.00
Instructional Materials	18,000.00
Contract Services	2,525.00
Travel	1,000.00
Capital Outlay	1,400.00
Direct Cost	$51,192.02
Indirect Cost (3 percent)*	1,535.76
TOTAL COST	$52,727.78

*Intended to cover costs of payroll, resource center space and utilities, and occasional consultant assistance from the district.

(as in Tables 9–4 and 9–5) to specify major factors included in the indirect cost figure, as this gives the reader some basis for evaluating the reasonableness of the figures used.

2. Budgeting a project over a multiyear period, as in Table 9–5, is extremely helpful. It provides both the sponsoring district and any outside funding agents with an overview of the entire project and reduces the likelihood of a false start. Schools too often start programs without carefully examining their probable cost implications for the future; this can result in a needless waste of time and effort. In addition, a multiyear budgeting permits project developers to address the flow of funds across the several project components over time. This is observed in Table 9–5, where the phasing of the several project components is presented. Notice in this case that the importance (and cost) of the "resource center" and "instructional unit development" activities tapers off in the second and third years of the project but the "in-service training" takes on more importance in the later years.

3. The most important thing achieved in this type of budget detail is the ability to communicate more clearly the exact organizational requirements associated with the project. It gives the reader confidence in the fact that project leaders have thought through the exact ways in which they will allocate money to the accomplishment of project goals. Note an example of this type of communication in the presentations in Table 9–3 on certificated salary and contract services. Under certificated salaries, observe that a high school economics teacher will be released a total of ten days to assist in the organization of

Table 9–5 Budget Summary by Organizational Component for Montclair District Economics Project (in dollars)

	19X4–19X5	*19X5–19X6*	*19X6–19X7*	*TOTAL*
Direction/Evaluation	12,917.70	32,110.28	30,868.61	75,896.59
Resource Center	25,631.62	10,728.42	8,255.95	44,615.99
Instructional Unit Development	8,123.20	—	—	8,123.20
In-service Training	4,519.50	7,548.45	12,285.26	24,353.21
Direct Cost	51,192.02	50,387.15	51,409.82	152,988.99
Indirect Cost (3 percent)*	1,535.76	1,511.61	1,542.29	4,589.66
TOTAL COST	52,727.78	51,898.76	52,952.11	157,578.65

*Intended to cover costs of payroll, resource center space, and utilities, and occasional consultant assistance from the district.

the economics resource center. Also, under contracted services, note that outside consultants will be used in assisting with the in-service training classes. Since neither of these elements has been described in prior information about the project, the budget presentation in this case communicates important new information about intended activities.

ADMINISTRATION AND EVALUATION OF THE BUDGET

Once prepared, the budget represents a spending plan that must be administered to see that expenditures at least roughly match those predicted at the beginning of the budget period. This is true whether we are dealing with the ongoing school program or a special project similar to the economics project discussed in the previous section. In cases where revenues are uncertain, they too must be monitored to assure that the expenditure schedule as originally planned will be supported at the required level. Beyond this administration of the budget comes evaluation of the extent to which programs and activities are meeting the goals of the organization. It is this final evaluation activity that permits closure of the budget cycle, as the evaluation should assist in establishing the planned expenditures for the following fiscal period.

A budget is administered through accurate record keeping and a review of various budget and financial status reports which will be examined in Chapter 10. The focus here is on the budget evaluation process and special attention is directed to communicating program results to the community and using these results as an evaluation tool in the budgeting process. Part of the problem in communicating program results to the public stems from problems in implementing program evaluation systems in schools, which typically have conflicting and overlapping goals among the several programs. Even recognizing these problems, however, school building administrators could do much better in communicating the outcomes of various school activities to the general public and in involving the public in the planning of school budgets based on these outcomes.

The schematic presented in Figure 1–4 and the models for consensus building suggested in Chapter 2 can be used effectively in achieving this improved communication about the result of school programs. As a matter of fact, this communication is likely to be at its best in those situations where there exists a close match between the action-program planning and the evaluation activities of the school. Budgets do represent priorities of the school community and it is only as these budgets are committed to the programs most desired by these same school communities that one can expect to achieve school support. Two trends having important implications for budgeting in schools today are zero-based budgeting and the sharing of test and evaluation results with the general school community.

Zero-Based Budgeting

Zero-based budgeting calls for annual review of all programs from ground zero. It is, at least in theory, the strongest evaluation measure that could be used in the budget process. While its recent popularity in both business and government settings was no doubt triggered by a 1970 Harvard Business Review article detailing a successful application at Texas Instruments, the antecedents of zero-based budgeting have been with us for some time.[12] The term was coined by E. Hilton Young in 1924, when he wrote that budget managers should "justify from zero."[13]

[12]See Peter A. Pyhrr, "Zero-Base Budgeting," *Harvard Business Review* 48 (November–December 1970): 111–121.

[13]The earliest history of zero-based budgeting, including this reference by E. Hilton Young, is summarized in A. E. Buck, *The Budget in Governments of Today* (1934), p. 172.

Six years before the article on Texas Instruments' success with zero-based budgeting, the U.S. Department of Agriculture announced that "a new concept has been adopted for the 1964 agency estimates; namely, that of zero-based budgeting. This means that all programs will be reviewed from the ground up and not merely in terms of changes proposed for the budget year" (Connors, p. 250).

Jimmy Carter, in his 1976 campaign for the presidency, promised to implement zero-based budgeting as a means of reducing federal spending. Carter's success in reducing federal spending can be questioned, but few would deny the increased popularity of zero-based budgeting and sunset legislation, which are viewed synonymously by most.[14]

Looking at the history of zero-based budgeting, it appears to be more of an attitude toward budget evaluation than it is a new system or plan of budgeting. Donald Thomas, superintendent of schools in Salt Lake City, emphasized this point in speaking about experiences with budget review in the Salt Lake City School District: "Zero-based budgeting is not complicated. All that is required is a yearly review of each program. Is the program needed? Is it effective? Does it contribute to the board of education objectives? Can it continue under a reduced budget? These are the questions to ask about every program each year" (Thomas, p. 86).

One should not, however, expect that budgets of very many programs will be reduced to zero. Even those agencies of the federal government cited during the Carter administration for most effective use of zero-based budgeting did not succeed in cutting overall programs below the 88 percent level. It is willingness to look seriously at the program's future and without direct reference to previous appropriations that makes zero-based budgeting different from other approaches to budget evaluation.

The business model of zero-base budgeting, which requires the development and ranking of decision packages, is not easily applied to education.[15] Many more of the decision packages in public education are required by state law or some other external regulation; hence, the emphasis in education is not likely to be on total elimination of programs but rather on alternative approaches to their implementation. Decision packages, or program plans as they might more appropriately be termed in the school context, will still be rank ordered much as in the business model; however, the process of rank ordering will be likely to involve more public input than would be characteristic of a business application.[16]

According to its opponents, a major liability of zero-based budgeting is the additional paperwork required by the process. There is little question that building and defending a budget from zero rather than as a simple extension of last year's appropriation will require additional paperwork; it will also, however, encourage needed consideration of program outcomes as they relate to school building and school district goals. This potential gain would seem to offset the additional paperwork, particularly if the paperwork itself can be used as a vehicle for getting the total school community involved in reviewing program outcomes and in establishing future direction for the school. Suggestions for accomplishing this community review were discussed at length in chapters 1 and 2 of this text.

[14]Sunset legislation refers to the fact that the sun will set on programs judged to be unsuccessful. This is quite obviously what should also happen through the use of zero-based budgeting procedures.

[15]Decision packages form the foundation of zero-based budgeting. A *decision package* as used here is essentially a set of objectives to be accomplished by a given program or service along with a description of resource and cost requirements needed to accomplish those objectives. For examples of the decision package and its use in zero-based budgeting, see Peter A. Pyhrr, *Zero-Base Budgeting* (1973), pp. 37–77. Specific suggestions for its application in education are found in Eugene T. Connors, Herbert Franklin, and Connie Kaskey, "Zero Base: A New Look at Budgeting for Education," (1978), pp. 256–259.

[16]The rank ordering of decision packages is ideally based on some analysis of probable program outcomes. In this sense, it is similar to the cost-effectiveness analysis described earlier in this chapter.

Use of Test Scores in Budget-Planning Process

Both school administrators and school support groups have traditionally questioned the merits of releasing test results for individual school districts. Even more questions have been raised about publishing test scores for individual schools. This resistance to sharing test information, while still present today, has softened considerably and many former opponents are actually involved in sharing test information with their respective communities.

Several reasons can be given for this reduced opposition to sharing test results. There is, of course, the expected support for such sharing in communities that consistently score well on tests. In some cases, these communities have been sharing such information for years. Beyond this, however, school leaders have become more accepting of the fact that sharing test results can, if handled properly, lead to constructive development of reasonable school goals. It can also be used as a springboard to the development of more useful evaluation tools at the local school level. Finally, there is an increased understanding that schools are not alone in the determination of school achievement. As a result of Head Start, Title I, and bilingual programs, the public has become increasingly aware that such variables as family environment, family income, and family education level play a very large role in a student's academic progress. Although students in the several educationally deprived categories can be aided by these remedial programs, few persons expect them as a group to achieve on a par with students coming from families and communities that traditionally have provided strong support for education. Once the general public is more understanding of the complex school and community factors involved in test-score comparisons, there is less chance that the scores will be used in ways that will harm the education of students or unfairly reduce staff morale and commitment.

Since sharing test scores is now a general practice in many areas, it is all the more important that administrators, whether in low- or high-achieving schools, aid in assuring broader public understanding of the complex factors associated with schools and testing. It is my conviction that this kind of understanding is achieved, not by attempting to withhold the test information, but rather by seeing that it is communicated carefully and in full recognition of the many factors that have an impact on school performance.

Beyond the need to give both community and school leaders a broader understanding of testing and its complexities, there is a set of suggested guidelines for releasing test scores on individual schools:

1. Ideally, results should be reported over a series of years and should be accompanied with a statement of what the results mean. Composite scores are not as useful as the separate scores for mathematics concepts, reading, spelling and so forth.
2. Along with these test results, there should be reported school comparisons on certain social and community factors such as education level of adults, percent of students from poverty families, qualification level of teachers, and percent of minority students.
3. The existence of special groups of students and/or special programs in each school should be communicated along with the test scores.
4. If there is a likelihood of public misunderstanding, the announcement should be accompanied by a public meeting or series of meetings designed to explain and discuss the test-score comparisons.

Administrators must learn to use test-score comparisons, whether done on a statewide, district, or even local school basis, as a beginning step toward planning with the community. This is why the series of results by specific areas as called for in Item 1 above is crucial. Only when a sequence of scores can be related meaningfully to a set of activities designed to affect those same scores can the test itself be a useful tool in budget planning and evaluation.

SUMMARY

Budgeting was described as a process that substitutes planning for chance in the financial operation of schools. The overall budget process involves three steps: (1) preparation of the budget or spending plan, (2) adoption and administration of the budget, and (3) evaluation of budget results. The role of the building administrator in accomplishing these three steps varies, depending on the size of the district and the degree of decentralization built into the budgeting process. In this chapter, attention was focused on those budgeting concepts and skills most frequently required in planning and controlling program costs at the building level.

The budget and accounting system used in schools and other public agencies is best described as a fund system. This term stems from the use of separate budgets and accounting records in each of the school district funds. Though the funds specified for use in the several states vary and are often given different names, they almost always include a general fund, a capital projects or building fund, a debt-service fund, and a student activity fund. Administrators involved in the budgeting process should be familiar with the revenue and expenditure categories used in their particular state and school district and should develop skill in estimating revenue and expenditure amounts in accordance with these categories.

Both line-item and program budgeting techniques were reviewed in this chapter and administrators were advised to select the best features of each in designing a budgeting procedure for their own building. Administrators were also urged to compile a careful evaluation of budget results at the end of each budget cycle and to consider the most stringent review of the zero-based-budgeting technique when applicable. The utilization of staff, student, and community input in the budget-review process was stressed throughout. The action-program planning activities described in Part I of this text are appropriate for use in this important review process.

QUESTIONS AND PROBLEMS ON CHAPTER 9

1. Four types of funds are identified in the text. These are the general, capital projects, debt-service, and student activity funds. Select any state or school district and determine for that state or school district which of these funds are a part of the basic accounting and budgeting system. Also, describe any special funds that cannot be classified as one of the four described in the text.
2. Select any two local school districts and compare the amount of budget control available to building principals in those two districts. Be certain in your comparison to examine both salary and nonsalary expenditure categories and also review policies on carry-over of unused budget capacity from one fiscal period to the next.
3. For the same two districts in Question 2 above, what object-of-expenditure categories are used and how do these objects compare with those recommended in U.S. Office of Education, *Financial Accounting* and presented in Table 9–2?

4. Using the sample object, function, and program classifications of Table 9–2, supply the proper coding for each of the following expenditure items:
   a. Library books for the regular instructional sequence at Meeker Junior High.
   b. Outside legal advice on a handicapped student problem at the cental office.
   c. Dental benefits for the eighth-grade teacher at Columbus Junior High.
   d. Computer terminal for the intermediate grades at Gooding Elementary.
   e. Salary for the counselor at Interlake High.
   f. Medical supplies for the nurse's office at Horizon View Elementary.
5. Critique the budgeting procedures of a single elementary or secondary school, making certain in the critique to comment on provisions for staff and parent participation in the budgeting process. (It would be useful in preparing the critique to talk with selected staff and parent leaders of the school community and to consider their reactions to some of the issues discussed in the text.)
6. Consider the budget presentation of Table 9–3 and assume a need to cut the budgeted direct cost from $51,192.02 to $45,050.
   a. What amount is saved by the reduction of one day for the project director?
   b. Assuming the reduction to $45,050 is to come solely from the project director's salary, what number of days for that position can be accommodated in the revised budget?
   c. How many of the project director days lost in Part b can be reinstated by cutting the number of individual instructional materials to 1,000 and the secretary's contract to 176 days?
7. Refer to the 19X4–19X5 budget presented in Tables 9–3 and 9–4, and respond to each of the following:
   a. What increase in indirect and total cost would be required if the project director's salary were to be budgeted at $20,000 rather than $19,400?
   b. If the total cost of the project were to be $53,900, what would the direct cost figure be assuming that indirect cost remains at 3 percent of the direct cost figure?
   c. How many extra contract days for the secretary could be accommodated assuming that the total budget is increased to $53,900 as in Part b and the project director's salary is budgeted at $20,000 as in Part a?
8. Examine the literature on zero-based budgeting and then develop two decision packages that might be used as part of a school budgeting process using the zero-based format.
9. Using the literature on cost-benefit analysis:
   a. Explain briefly cost-benefit analysis as used in making public policy decisions and the reasons why cost-effectiveness (a truncated version of cost-benefit) is much more likely to apply to budget-development activities in the school setting.
   b. Show how the cost-effectiveness technique might be used by the school principal in making a budget decision or recommendation.
10. Identify a particular school and a special program that might appropriately be added to the services provided within that school. Place yourself in the position of principal of this school and develop a proposal (appropriate for review by a governmental agency or foundation) for funding the special program. The proposal should include at least the following components:
    - Brief description of the school district and school in which the special program is to be carried out, including some statement of need for the special program.
    - Description of the special program and its intended outcomes.

- ◦ Budget identifying projected costs associated with each major component and/or phase of the project.
- ◦ Supporting cost data (e.g., salary schedules, travel and per-diem rates) as needed to explain budget figures.

11. Select a set of actual test scores for several elementary or secondary schools in a specific school district and write a letter that might accompany the distribution of these test scores to the patrons of the district.

CHAPTER 10
REPORTING FINANCIAL STATUS IN SCHOOLS

Most school districts are required to file at least an annual financial report with the state education department. In most cases, monthly budget-status reports are also prepared. These reports show the relationship of actual revenues and expenditures to those budgeted at the beginning of the fiscal year. The budget figures of reference here are developed as part of budget documents prepared and adopted at a public board meeting prior to initiating any expenditures. As mentioned in Chapter 9, the budget is a plan for the spending of anticipated resources and it must be constantly monitored to determine the extent to which budgeted revenues and expenditures are being realized. Just as separate budgets are made for each of the school district funds (e.g., general, student activity, and debt-service), so also are separate financial status reports prepared for these several funds.

BUDGET-STATUS REPORTS IN SCHOOLS

Because school principals are most likely to be involved with the general fund and the student activity fund, it is appropriate to begin in Table 10–1 with a simplified version of a general-fund budget-status report for the University Place School District.[1] This particular sample status report is similar in format to the reports likely to be received on a monthly basis by building principals; however, two major differences should be noted. First, the building-level budgets usually include only the expenditure section of this report, as buildings are generally given an allocation by the district at the beginning of the fiscal year. While this allocation is of course based on expected district revenues, the building administrator does not usually become involved in monitoring the district revenue calculations on a month-to-month basis. A second major difference relates to the object-of-expenditure categories used in this district budget-status report and those likely to be found in the building administrator's financial report. In Chapter 9, it was mentioned that most building principals have dollar control over only the nonsalary items. Hence, the "salaries" and "employee benefits" objects would generally not be used on the budget-status reports for building and program administrators.

It is important, now that we have identified these two differences, to comment on use of budget-status reports of the type presented in Table 10–1. The most obvious use is in monitoring the match between expected (or budgeted) figures and actual figures to date. In Table 10–1, note that as of January 31, 19X2, the school district had realized 44.4 percent of the budgeted revenues and had spent only 41.7 percent of the budgeted expenditures.[2]

Table 10–1 University Place School District Budget Status Report for General Fund—January 31, 19X2

Revenues (by source):	*Budget*	*Year-to-Date*	*Balance*	*Percent Received*
Local Taxes	$ 3,478,935.00	$1,782,837.32	$1,696,097.68	51.2
Other Local Taxes	791,185.00	319.328.46	471,856.54	40.4
State Funds	5,653,286.00	2,396,961.84	3,256,324.16	42.4
Federal Funds	929,733.00	278,929.24	650,803.76	30.0
Payments from Other Districts	18,529.00	5,476.33	13,052.67	29.6
TOTAL REVENUES	$10,871,668.00	$4,783,533.19	$6,088,134.81	44.0

Expenditures (by object):	*Budget*	*Year-to-Date Expenditures*	*Encum-brances*	*Unencum-bered Balance*	*Percent Expended or Encum-bered*
Salaries	$ 7,908,035.00	$2,730,983.92	$ 42,531.75	$5,134,519.33	35.1
Employee Benefits	896,732.00	298.257.18	5,492.36	592,982.46	33.9
Purchased Services	425,125.00	135,526.27	48,321.42	241,277.31	43.2
Supplies and Materials	757,483.00	575.687.45	35,481.27	146,314.28	80.7
Capital Outlay	864,245.00	592,181.32	24,522.38	247.541.30	28.6
Other Objects	99,010.00	74,142.08	1,486.12	23,381.80	76.4
TOTAL EXPENDITURES	$10,950,630.00	$4,406,778.22	$157,835.30	$6,386,016.48	41.7

[1]University Place District is a hypothetical school district with a high school for grades 9–12, a middle school with grades 6–8, and four K–5 elementary feeder schools. It is assumed to be using a slight modification of the revenue and expenditure classifications presented in Tables 9–1 and 9–2 respectively.

[2]The 41.7 percent in this case includes both year-to-date expenditures (items that have been received and for which payment has been made) and encumbrances (items that are on order but not yet received). It is important to remove these encumbrances from the budget figure in arriving at the unemcumbered balance or the amount remaining to be spent.

Although revenues are running ahead of expenditures (on a percentage basis) at this point in the school year, no judgment can be made regarding this state of affairs without knowing something more of the revenue and expenditure flows actually projected for a school system of this type. If, for example, in prior years 52 percent of projected revenues had been realized by this particular date, the apparent 44 to 41.7 percent advantage for revenues may in fact represent a problem with revenue flows for the 19X1-19X2 school year.

Whatever the overall percentage of revenues realized on any given date, the year-to-date revenue pattern is probably most useful when analyzed according to the separate revenue sources. In Table 10–1, we see that revenues from the several sources differ substantially in the portions realized as of January 31, 19X2. Perhaps a check should be made on each of these sources to see that the estimates are still reasonable based on experience in prior years and any information that may have become available since the original estimates were made.

A budget-status report of the type more likely to be used at the building level is found in Table 10–2. Here the budget allocation is divided according to program or departmental areas and a separate accounting of both expenditures and encumbrances is given for each of the areas. In this particular school, in most of the teaching areas (including mathematics, language arts, science, and social studies), the staff members utilize the "general" program designation for their budgeting activity. Presumably, there is some internal system for allocating textbooks and supply monies to teachers in these several subject areas from the general program budget. Note in Table 10–2 that the general category accounts for just over half of the total budget allocation for the school. The general budget in this case of Sunset Middle School contains a contingency fund that can be used to cover overexpenditures in any of the other areas. This may have to be used to support the art program for the remainder of the 19X1–19X2 school year, as the art area is already $48.15 over the budget allocation.

Just as in the earlier case, the budget-status report of Table 10–2 is used by the budget administrator in monitoring expenditures on at least a monthly basis throughout the school year. The administrator charged with budget responsibilities at Sunset Middle School will have discussed with the art teacher the budget status in that area prior to January 31, 19X2. Perhaps there is some understanding that the art teacher, having made a large equipment purchase earlier in the school year, will be allowed for this year only to utilize some portion of the general budget allocation. If such arrangements have not been made, art department spending will have to be halted immediately, at least until some budget adjustment can be

Table 10–2 Sunset Middle School Budget Status Report January 31, 19X2

Program Area	*Budget Allocation*	*Year-to-Date Expenditures*	*Encum-brances*	*Unencum-bered Balance*	*Percent Expended or Encum-bered*
General	$18,221.00	$13,123.43	$ 844.76	$4,252.81	76.7
Art	5,215.00	5,187.97	75.18	[48.15]	100.9
Music	2,143.00	985.40	43.24	1,114.36	48.0
Home and Family	3,432.00	3,012.19	—	419.81	87.8
Industrial Education	4,563.00	3,143.78	156.14	1,263.08	72.3
Physical Education	1,854.00	1,526.55	87.26	240.19	87.0
Total	$35,428.00	$26,979.32	$1,206.58	$7,242.10	79.6

Included here are purchased services, supplies and materials (including textbooks), and equipment. Salaries and employee benefits are budgeted separately on a districtwide basis. Numbers in brackets [ ] are negative.

arranged. It is generally easier to make internal budget adjustments among the categories as listed in Table 10–2 than to attempt to arrange for a budget extension. Typically, the controlling budget figure in Table 10–2 is the $35,428 and the building administrator is allowed to make adjustments across the various categories whenever the educational program is served by these adjustments.

As a means of controlling to this budgeted amount of $35,428, the building principal may find it helpful to periodically complete a worksheet of the type presented in Table 10–3. Note here the advantage of historical data from the immediate past year and from the preceding three years. This suggested worksheet permits a separate accounting for the one-time and ongoing types of expenditures. This is often important in isolating unusual one-time purchases that sometimes distort the figures for a single budget period. The administrator in the case of the Table 10–3 worksheet was apparently required to alter both the ongoing and one-time expenditure patterns of the prior year just to end the year with a $200 balance. The sort of prediction capability provided by this type of worksheet is extremely important in planning year-end balances for both district and school-building budgets.

One common concern raised in school budgeting at the building level is the disposition of any underexpenditure for a particular fiscal period. In the case of Table 10–3, what happens to the projected year-end balance of 200? In some schools, underexpenditures are lost and budgeting starts from zero at the beginning of each fiscal period. As schools move

Table 10–3 Sunset Middle School Budget Worksheet

Date January 31

	19X1–19X2	*Prior Fiscal Year*	*Average of Three Prior Fiscal Years*
1. Budgeted	35,428.00	32,803.00	30,094.00
2. Year-to-Date Expenditures and Encumbrances	28,185.90	23,782.18	22,329.36
3. Percent Expended or Encumbered	79.6	72.5	74.2
4. Unencumbered Balance	7,242.10	9,020.82	7,764.64
5. Year-to-Date Expenditures and Encumbrances			
5.1 One-time	3,420.92	1,560.26	1,782.22
5.2 Ongoing	24,764.98	22,221.92	20,547.14
6. Remaining Expenditures and Encumbrances			
6.1 One-time	420.14*	1,035.73	1,126.85
6.2 Ongoing	6,621.96*	7,452.91	6,155.69
7. Year-End Balance	200.00*	532.18	482.10

*Figures to be supplied as part of the expenditure projection for the remainder of the fiscal period. All other figures are available from prior accounting records.

toward greater decentralization in the budgeting process, this inability to carry unused expenditure allocations from one year to the next needs to be reexamined. Many schools today do permit some carry-over of underexpenditures in school building budgets to the next fiscal period. This possibility for budget carry-over encourages more responsible school management; it helps to avoid the traditional problem of thinking the entire budget should be spent before someone decides to take it away.

The budget reports of Tables 10–1, 10–2, and 10–3 are just samples of the many reports designed to aid district and building administrators in discharging their responsibilities for financial management. The concern of this chapter is that the administrator gain an appreciation for the several types of fiscal reports available for use in monitoring and reporting the financial health of the school system. Gaining this appreciation will require some understanding of the accounting system used in schools and firsthand experience in developing selected financial reports from summary accounting information. Subsequent sections of this chapter along with the questions and problems included at the conclusion should aid in accomplishing these several aims.

ACCOUNTING PROCEDURES IN PUBLIC SCHOOLS

School accounting is necessary for the purposes of providing accurate financial information and fiscal accountability. It is hoped that this financial information can be presented in a timely manner that permits its use in decision making. In most states, all except the very smallest school districts are required to maintain a double-entry accounting system. The accounting equation used as a basis for this double-entry accounting system is slightly different from that used in the private or business sector. There is also some difference in the types of assets recorded in the various accounts.[3] In addition, private business generally utilizes "accrual" accounting, wherein income and expenses are recognized at the time the income is earned and the expense incurred. In school district accounting, the revenues are usually not recognized until actually received in cash and the expenditures must be recognized on the books at the time the good or service is incurred or received and not postponed until the time payment is made. This latter approach is sometimes called the "modified accrual" system.

Basic Principles of Accounting

Despite these several differences, the basic accounting entries (debits and credits) are generally handled the same way in both private and governmental accounting. Governmental accounting begins with the equation:

$$\text{Assets} - \text{Liabilities} = \text{Fund Balance}$$

or

$$\text{Assets} = \text{Liabilities} + \text{Fund Balance}$$

It is perhaps easiest to explain this equation by thinking in terms of a person's checking account as the sole asset. Assume that this checking account has a beginning balance of

[3]Private or commercial accounting uses the equation "Assets = Liabilities + Equity." In public schools, the equation reads "Assets = Liabilities + Fund Balance." The asset accounts in private-sector accounting include plant and equipment; in public or governmental accounting, the assets are generally limited to cash, inventory, investment, and receivable accounts.

$2,000 but bills for dormitory rental ($250) and a personal debt ($150) are pending. Rewriting the above accounting equation to fit this particular situation results in:

	Assets (Checking Account)	=	Liabilities (Debts)	+	Fund Balance (Amount Available for Future Purchases)
Beginning Status(B)	2,000	=	400	+	1,600

The equation balances, as the fund balance is seen to have $1,600. Essentially, the double-entry accounting system is a way of keeping this equation balanced with every transaction. This is illustrated by using the system to account for five different events or transactions as follows:

1. Pay off the $250 dormitory rental obligation or debt.
2. Deposit a $1,000 paycheck.
3. Get car repaired for $100 but delay payment for 30 days.
4. Purchase and pay for a $70 tire on car.
5. Pay off the $100 debt for car repair.

These events are recorded on a set of T-accounts, which are structured in a way that forces the basic accounting equation always to remain balanced. To understand the structuring of these T-accounts, begin by defining "debit" and "credit" to be the left and right sides of the T, respectively. By defining debit (or left side) as an increase in asset accounts and credit (or right side) as an increase in the liability and fund-balance accounts, the equation can then be kept balanced by always entering debits and credits of equal magnitude for each transaction.

Notice that the T-accounts (shown below) begin with equal debit and credit entries and each of the five transactions involves debit and credit entries of equal magnitude.

	Assets		=	Liabilities		+	Fund Balance	
	Debit Increase	Credit Decrease		Debit Decrease	Credit Increase		Debit Decrease	Credit Increase
(B)	2000				400			1600
(1)		250		250				
(2)	1000							1000
(3)					100		100	
(4)		70					70	
(5)		100		100				

These transactions have been recorded as described below:

(B) This represents the beginning status of accounts. Note that the 400 represents a liability from the very beginning.

(1) The decrease in the checking account occurs in paying off the dormitory rental, which is also represented by a decrease in the liability account.

(2) Both the checking account and the fund balance or net worth of the individual are increased at the time of receiving and depositing the paycheck.
(3) The liability is increased by incurring this debt for the car repair but the checking account will not be reduced until the bill is actually paid. Since the debt for the car repair does represent a decrease in net worth of the individual, the debit to fund balance is necessary.
(4) Both the asset and fund-balance accounts are decreased by the tire purchase.
(5) When the debt for car repair is actually paid off, the checking account and liability accounts must both be decreased by the amount of the debt.

To see that the maintenance of equal debit and credit entries is equivalent to keeping the equation balanced, observe that a credit entry in the asset (or checking) account represents a decrease and can therefore be counterbalanced in the basic accounting equation by a debit entry in the liability or fund balance, either of which is also a decrease. Note that transactions 1, 4, and 5 above each represent this type, whereby reducing both sides of the equation by equal amounts maintains the balance. A similar balance of the equation is achieved in transaction 2, except here the debit or increase to the asset account is offset by the credit or increase to the fund balance. The third type of entry is where the corresponding debit and credit entries occur to different accounts on just one side of the equals sign. This is illustrated by transaction 3, where the credit or increase to liabilities is offset by the debit or decrease to fund balance.

A more standard procedure for filling in T-accounts is to label each individual debit and credit entry with the transaction number and to then determine the status of each account just prior to the monthly reporting period. This is accomplished for the checking account illustration as shown below.

Assets	
(B) 2000	(1) 250
(2) 1000	(4) 70
	(5) 100
2580	

Liabilities	
(1) 250	(B) 400
(5) 100	(3) 100
	150

Fund Balance	
(3) 100	(B) 1600
(4) 70	(2) 1000
	2430

Note on completion of the transactions that assets (checking account in this case) has $2,580 of which $150 is still owed for the personal debt. This means that the fund balance or net worth of the individual has increased exactly $830 over the beginning point. The increase can be explained as the difference between the $1,000 paycheck (transaction 2) and

Table 10–4 University Place School District Balance Sheet for General Fund September 1, 19X1

Assets		*Liabilities and Fund Balance*	
Imprest Funds	$ 625	Vouchers Payable	$ 26,382
Cash	1,194.079	Accrued Expenses	773,478
Warrants Outstanding	[910,432]	Reserve for Inventory	32,499
Investments	756,003	Fund Balance	244,797
Due from Other Funds	4,382	*TOTAL LIABILITIES AND FUND BALANCE*	$1,077,156
Inventory	32,499		
TOTAL ASSETS	$1,077,156		

All figures are to the nearest dollar to simplify the arithmetic calculations. Numbers in brackets [ ] are negative.

the $100 and $70 obligations incurred for the car repair (transaction 3) and tire (transaction 4), respectively.

Application of Basic Accounting Principles to School Context

It is now possible to apply the basic accounting equation and the way in which it is kept balanced to the school situation. Begin with the sample account status at the beginning of a fiscal period as recorded in Table 10–4. A glossary of terms explaining the different accounts and a set of debit/credit entries for some of the more common transactions is included in Appendix 6. The aim here is to show how a series of financial transactions is handled within the accounting system and to indicate the way in which the system can be checked at any time to assess the financial status of the organization.

A list of typical financial transactions for the University Place School District and the related debit and credit entries are recorded in Table 10–5. These transactions are assumed to have occurred during the first month of the fiscal period. The posting of these debit and credit entries is shown in Appendix 7. The following comments on the numbered transactions of Table 10–5 should be helpful, especially to those with little or no background in accounting.

Table 10–5 Sample Journal Entries for University Place School District General Fund (transactions described following entries)

Transaction Number	*Accounts*	*Debit*	*Credit*
1	Estimated Revenues	10,871,668	
	Fund Balance	78,962	
	Appropriations		10,950,630
2	Cash	1,685,735	
	Revenues		1,685,735
3	Warrants Outstanding	826,540	
	Cash		826,540
4	Investments	500,000	
	Cash		500,000
5	Encumbrances	825,000	
	Reserve for Encumbrances		825,000
6	Vouchers Payable	14,382	
	Warrants Outstanding		14,382
7	Accrued Expenses	675,492	
	Warrants Outstanding		675,492
8	Due from Other Funds	20,000	
	Warrants Outstanding		20,000
9	Cash	15,763	
	Revenues		15,763
10	Expenditures	32,564	
	Warrants Outstanding		32,564
	Reserve for Encumbrances	32,564	
	Encumbrances		32,564

Table 10–5 (continued)

11	Inventory	17,000	
	Warrants Outstanding		17,000
12	Expenditures	21,029	
	Inventory		21,029
13	No Entry	—	—
14	Expenditures	626,432	
	Warrants Outstanding		626,432
	Reserve for Encumbrances	626,432	
	Encumbrances		626,432

Description of Transactions

1. The budget for the fiscal year beginning on September 1, 19X1, includes estimated revenues of $10,871,668 and an appropriation (or estimated expenditure) of $10,950,630.
2. Property tax revenues amounting to $1,685,735 are received by the district and deposited in the cash account.
3. Notice is received that $826,540 worth of warrants have been redeemed at the county treasurer or bank.
4. The board of education approves investment of $500,000 in a 180-day note bearing interest of 9 percent.
5. Purchase orders totaling $825,000 are issued by the district business office.
6. Warrants totalling $14,382 are issued for amounts previously accrued and approved in voucher format.
7. Accrued expenses (mostly payroll) of $675,492 come due and warrants are issued for the total amount.
8. A $20,000 loan is made in warrant form to the student-body fund. This loan is made for a period of 90 days and carries an interest rate of 7 percent.
9. Interest payments of $15,763 on investments are received and deposited.
10. Warrants are issued for $32,564 worth of expenditures, which were previously encumbered for the same amount.
11. Additional lunchroom inventory of $17,000 is purchased by warrant.
12. A physical inventory reveals that actual inventories are $28,470 and this is reflected in the inventory account. No attempt is made at this time to adjust the reserve for inventory to reflect this lesser amount.
13. A $50 item is purchased from the imprest funds.
14. Warrants are written to pay for $626,432 of goods and services previously encumbered for the same amount.

Transaction 1.

This particular budget entry follows school board approval of the revenue and expenditure budgets for the fiscal period. This approval comes just prior to the beginning of the fiscal period, as no expenditures can be made until the budget has been approved by the school board. It should be noticed in the particular example of Table 10–5 that the expected revenues fall exactly $78,962 short of the anticipated expenditures. This difference is made up by a debit (or reduction) to Fund Balance. In some situations where it is preferred that the fund-balance account itself not be affected by the budget entry, this particular debit is applied to a separate contra account to the Fund Balance. In either case, the adjustment to

Fund Balance is effectively reversed at the end of the fiscal period when the budget entry is taken off the books.

Transactions 2, 9.
These entries show a revenue gain that will eventually be reflected in an increase in Fund Balance. This increase will occur at the end of the year when revenues and expenditures are closed out into Fund Balance.

Transaction 3.
Whether the school district does its own banking or goes through another agent (e.g., county treasurer), the reduction in cash must be recognized at the time notice of redemption is received.

Transaction 4.
Only the principal of the investment is recorded as an asset. The interest payment of $22,500 (4½ percent of $500,000) will be received as revenue at the end of the 180-day period.

Transaction 5.
The encumbrances of $825,000 represent a temporary reservation of the Fund Balance; hence, it is necessary to establish a reserve for encumbrances. This entry is reversed off the books at the time the good or service is received and the payment made.

Transaction 6.
The items purchased with these funds were received and charged as expenditures in the previous fiscal period. Hence, at this point, cash position and the appropriate liability account are both reduced.

Transaction 7.
Often there will be separate accounts for "salaries payable" and "payroll deductions and taxes payable." These separate accounts are not used in this particular illustration.

Transaction 8.
It is generally possible to lend money to other funds so long as the interest paid is similar to rates available from other potential lending agents. In this particular case, a corresponding entry in the student-body fund would debit cash and credit a "due to other funds" liability.

Transactions 10, 14.
Expenditure transactions of this type involve two debit and two credit entries. The debit to Expenditures will, at the end of the fiscal period, be closed out, thus resulting in a reduction in Fund Balance. The reversal of the originating encumbrance entries is necessary to avoid counting the items as both expenditures and encumbrances at the same time.

Transactions 11, 12.
Items purchased for inventory are generally expended at the time they are used rather than when purchased. In this case, the difference between the amount in the inventory account and the actual physical inventory is debited to expenditure. The Reserve for Inventory account could also be adjusted as low as $28,470 at the time of the physical inventory; however, such adjustments are not necessary. Reserve for Inventory should always be set at a level exceeding or equal to the actual physical inventory.

Transaction 13.

The Imprest Funds or petty cash account is generally not debited or credited except when its actual size is increased or decreased. At the time that purchases from imprest funds are approved by the school board, the fund itself is reimbursed and this generally results in a debit to Expenditures and a corresponding credit to Warrants Outstanding.

The trial balance following completion of these several transactions is presented in Table 10–6. The fact that the debit and credit entries each total $14,596,214 assures us that the basic accounting equation is still in balance. Much more information can be gained from a review of these trial balance figures. Most important is an update on the status of revenue and expenditures in relation to budgeted amounts. This can be seen by comparing selected accounts as follows:

Estimated Revenues	$10,871,668
Revenues	[1,701,498]
Balance (Rev.)	$ 9,170,170
Appropriations	$10,950,630
Expenditures	[680,025]
Encumbrances	[166,004]
Unencumbered Balance (Exp.)	$10,104,601

The use of brackets [ ] here designates subtraction and is justified because the account has an opposite balance to that with which it is compared. For example, the Revenue account in Table 10–6 shows a credit balance and it is therefore subtracted from the Estimated Revenues account having a debit balance. The above listing of budgeted and actual figures is similar to that presented earlier in Table 10–1. This type of analysis is available at any point during the school year by comparing debit and credit balances in the appropriate accounts.

Table 10–6 University Place School District Trial Balance for General Fund (as of September 30, 19X1)

Account	*Debit*	*Credit*
Imprest Funds	$ 625	
Cash	1,569,037	
Warrants Outstanding		$ 1,469,762
Investments	1,256,003	
Due from Other Funds	24,382	
Inventory	28,470	
Vouchers Payable		12,000
Accrued Expenses		97,986
Reserve for Inventory		32,499
Fund Balance		165,835
Encumbrances	166,004	
Reserve for Encumbrances		166,004
Estimated Revenues	10,871,668	
Revenues		1,701,498
Appropriations		10,950,630
Expenditures	680,025	
	$14,596,214	$14,596,214

Trial balance reflects beginning status as shown in Table 10–4 and the financial transactions of Table 10–5. T-accounts showing this beginning status and the several transactions are found in Appendix 7.

One also obtains from the trial balance an immediate status report on cash position by observing the relation between Cash and Warrants Outstanding. It appears in this particular case that if all warrants were redeemed immediately, the school district would still have $99,275 cash in the bank. It is advisable to assess future cash flows (primarily from anticipated revenues and investment turnover) to be certain the cash will be there to cover expenses. When this is not the case, expenditures must be stopped or some type of borrowing will be required.

As a final observation on the amounts recorded in the trial balance, we note that the Fund Balance has been reduced since the beginning of the year from $244,797 to $165,835, a total reduction of $78,962. This represents the difference between appropriations and estimated revenues in the initial budget entry. In actuality, the Fund Balance has been increased by $1,021,473, which is the excess of actual revenues over actual expenditures, but this latter increase is generally made only at the end of the year or at such other time as a balance sheet is created.[4] If original estimates are correct, one would expect this Fund Balance adjustment at the end of the 19X1–19X2 fiscal period to be closer to the $78,962 reduction mentioned above.

Formal Reporting in the School Context

A number of financial reports can be generated using the trial balance as a base of information. Some of these reports require more detailed breakdowns of revenue or expenditure accounts or further debit/credit adjustments in the accounts; others can be taken directly from the trial balance presented in Table 10–6. Four reports commonly used by governmental agencies, including schools, are included here.

The first of these reports is the budget-status report. A sample is presented in Table 10–7. This particular budget-status report is less detailed in revenue and expenditure categories than the earlier budget-status reports of Tables 10–1 and 10–2, but it does show revenue and expenditure patterns for a two-year period. This sort of comparison is often helpful in spotting possible problem areas and is a very useful monitoring device for administrators.

Another area of vital concern in the financial management of schools is the cash flow.

Table 10–7 University Place School District Budget Status Report for General Fund as of September 30

REVENUES	*Budgeted*	*Year-to-Date Revenues*	*Balance*	*Percent of Revenues Received*
19X0–19X1	10,004,433	1,630,309	8,374,124	16.3
19X1–19X2	10,871,668	1,701,498	9,170,170	15.7
EXPENDITURES AND ENCUMBRANCES	*Budgeted*	*Year-to-Date Expenditures and Encumbrances*	*Balance*	*Percent Expended and Encumbered*
19X0–19X1	10,136,470	1,243,987	8,892,483	12.2
19X1–19X2	10,950,630	846,029	10,104,601	7.7

The figures used for the 19X1–X2 school year come directly from the trial balance report of Table 10–6.

[4]Based on figures in Table 10–6, the Fund Balance account could also be increased another $4,029 by adjusting the Reserve for Inventory to the current inventory level of $28,470. This would be done by debiting Reserve for Inventory and crediting Fund Balance the indicated amount of $4,029.

Table 10–8 University Place School District Change in Net Cash and Investment Balance for General Fund (as of September 30, 19X1)

Net Cash and Investment Balance (September 1, 19X1)		$1,040,275
Net Change in Cash Since September 1, 19X1		315,628
Add: Revenues	1,701,498	
Deduct: Expenditures	[680,025]	
Deduct: Decrease in Liabilities[a]	[689,874]	
Deduct: Increase in Noncash Assets[b]	[15,971]	
Net Cash and Investment Balance (September 30, 19X1)		$1,355,903

[a]Decreases in the Vouchers Payable and Accrued Expenses accounts represent loss of cash not accommodated in the Expenditure account. These items were actually expended in a prior fiscal period and cash is just now being disbursed to cover these liabilities.

[b]This increase in noncash asset accounts (Due from Other Funds and Inventory) represents a deduction from cash and must therefore be recognized as part of the change in cash and investment position.

Since revenues come in at various times during the school year, it is sometimes necessary to borrow to meet payroll requirements. Good financial management also requires that excess cash be invested whenever possible. Cash-flow analysis for a given school district or school will depend on revenue/expenditure patterns, interest rates, and local preferences, but it is sometimes desirable to analyze the changes occurring in cash position between two points of time. One such report is found in Table 10–8. This report, called the "Change in Net Cash and Investment Balance," is useful in establishing the reasons for change in cash position between any two points in time. Note that the change as reported in Table 10–8 is based on the balance of realized revenues and expenditures and adjustments to liability and noncash asset accounts. These latter adjustments are explained in footnotes to the report.

Two additional reports are sometimes helpful in governmental agencies. These are the "Balance Sheet" and the "Analysis of Change in Fund Balance." (A beginning balance sheet for University Place School District was presented in Table 10–4.) Most generally these two reports are compiled only on completion of the fiscal period, as they require a number of closing debit/credit entries. Because the procedures used in preparing these two reports are the same regardless of time of completion, it is possible to present the "Balance Sheet" and "Analysis of Change in Fund Balance" reports for September 30, 19X1. Prior to completing these reports, it is necessary to clear all budgetary and control accounts and add to the fund balance the excess of revenues over expenditures. In relation to the University Place Trial Balance of Table 10–6, this is accomplished by the following debit/credit entries with C1, C2, C3 referring to successive closing entries:

		Debit	Credit
(C1)	*Reverse the original budget entry*		
	Appropriations	10,950,630	
	Estimated Revenues		10,871,668
	Fund Balance		78,962
(C2)	*Remove all encumbrances from the books*[5]		
	Reserve for Encumbrances	166,004	
	Encumbrances		166,004
(C3)	*Place excess of revenues over expenditures in fund balance*		
	Revenues	1,701,498	
	Expenditures		680,025
	Fund Balance		1,021,473

[5]The encumbrances represent items that have been ordered but not yet received; hence, they are usually reinstated at the beginning of the next fiscal period. They must, therefore, be considered part of the budgeted expenditures for the next period.

If these three closing entries are applied to the Trial Balance accounts in Table 10–6 and/or the T-accounts of Appendix 7, the only accounts with remaining balances are those appearing in the Balance Sheet of Table 10–4; hence, the updated Balance Sheet is presented in Table 10–9 and the sizable increase in the Fund Balance is examined in Table 10–10. Notice in Table 10–9 that the basic accounting equation, Assets = Liabilities + Fund Balance, is still in balance. The entire change in Fund Balance (from $244,797 on September 1 to $1,266,270 on September 30) is explained by the balance of revenues over expenditures; hence, a formal report of the type included in Table 10–10 is probably not needed in this instance. If, however, other direct adjustments to Fund Balance were to be made (e.g., adjusting the Reserve for Inventory[6]), this report would sometimes be useful in understanding the total pattern of change in financial capacity between two points in time.

Since the fund balance is such an important concept in school district accounting, some additional comment on its meaning may be useful at this point. Some think of fund balance as being similar to the concept of equity or net worth as used in the basic accounting equation of commercial accounting. While it is true that fund balance, including its several reserve portions (e.g., Reserve for Inventory in Table 10–9), represents the assets remaining on the books after all the liabilities have been paid, the fact that many assets of the school organization are not carried on the basic accounting records suggests some caution in interpreting the Fund Balance as the equity or net worth of the organization. Examples of assets not included in the school balance sheet are facilities, equipment, and land. Each of these assets is usually included on the books of the commercial or private organization; hence, the term "net worth" is more appropriately used in private-sector accounting.[7]

A wide variety of financial statements can be used in explaining aspects of the school operation. Certain of these may be produced routinely in school districts and others utilized for special purposes. Some reporting formats may be developed to deal with specific questions of importance in a given school district at a particular point in time. An extensive

Table 10–9 University Place School District Balance Sheet for General Fund—September 30, 19X1

Assets		*Liabilities and Fund Balance*	
Imprest Funds	$ 625	Vouchers Payable	$ 12,000
Cash	1,569,037	Accrued Expenses	97,986
Warrants Outstanding	[1,469,762]	Reserve for Inventory	32,499
Investments	1,256,003	Fund Balance	1,266,270
Due from Other Funds	24,382	*TOTAL LIABILITIES AND FUND BALANCE*	$1,408,755
Inventory	28,470		
TOTAL ASSETS	$1,408,755		

[6]This particular adjustment could be made by a debit of $4,029 to Reserve for Inventory and a corresponding credit to Fund Balance. The Reserve for Inventory can be viewed as a portion of the Fund Balance set aside to cover a nonliquid asset and the balance in this Reserve for Inventory should therefore not be allowed to fall below the actual amount held in Inventory.

[7]Even in private-sector accounting, some argue that the asset values typically used on land, facilities, and equipment are totally unrealistic. This is due primarily to their being carried at historical purchase price. The justification for including fixed assets on the balance sheet in private accounting is based largely on the potential of utilizing depreciation for a tax advantage.

Table 10–10 University Place School District Analysis of Change in Fund Balance—General Fund

Beginning Fund Balance (September 1, 19X1)		$ 244,797
Revenue/Expenditure Transations		1,021,473
Add: Revenues	1,701,498	
Subtract: Expenditures	680,025	
Ending Fund Balance (September 30, 19X1)		$1,266,270

list of the more common financial statements used in governmental agencies can be found in other reference sources.[8]

ACCOUNTING FOR STUDENT-BODY FUNDS

Most school districts manage student-body financing in a separate fund. Much of the revenue in these student activity funds has historically come from private fund raising by students. Many educational leaders advocate increasing use of public tax monies to finance the student activities program; yet, prime revenue sources today include student fees, student store proceeds, gate receipts for athletic events, and profits from candy or magazine sales. The question of whether some of these fund-raising efforts are appropriate in a society where free public education is guaranteed in the state constitution has been debated extensively over the past fifty years. In 1940, an Education Policies Commission report claimed that the imposition of student fees was contributing to the relatively high dropout rates in schools.[9] While the fees referred to in this particular report included fees for textbooks and general supplies in addition to those for student activities, there is little question but that participation in selected student activities has been and still is discouraged in some situations by the imposition of student fees.

Trends in Student-Body Financing

Recently, court cases and legal opinions in a number of states have cautioned school districts against the use of student fees for items that are "reasonably related to a recognized academic and educational goal of a particular school system."[10] There is of course some disagreement among educators and the lay public as to which programs are related to legitimate educational goals. Recognizing these uncertainties and as an alternative to doing away completely with fees for student activities, some school districts have opted to set up systems that provide support to those students who require financial aid for participation. One such example is the Fairfax County, Virginia, school system. In 1976, the board of education in that community set aside $66,000 for students requiring assistance for participation in the activities program.[11]

[8]Numerous samples of both final and interim reporting formats are found in Edward S. Lynn and Robert J. Freeman, *Fund Accounting, Theory and Practice* (1974), pp. 739–769. Samples are also found in accounting manuals published by various state departments of education and in the U.S. Office of Education publication *Financial Accounting: Classifications and Standard Terminology for Local and State School Systems,* Handbook II, rev. (Washington D.C.: U.S. Government Printing Office, 1973), pp. 167–174.

[9]See John K. Norton, *Education and Economic Well-Being in American Democracy* (1940).

[10]This phrasing came from a 1972 decision by the Supreme Court of the state of Montana and is reported in E. Edmund Reutter, Jr., and Robert R. Hamilton, *The Law of Public Education, 1973 Supplement* (Mineola, N.Y.: The Foundation Press, 1973), p. 38.

[11]For details on this situation in Fairfax County, Virginia, read *Education U.S.A.* (January 1976), p. 106.

The rationale for supporting a greater share of the student activity program through public tax funds is that student activities are very much a part of the regular school program and should therefore be funded through general public taxation rather than through student fees. Such fees, opponents claim, are an inappropriate application of the benefit principle of taxation. These persons argue that there is no more reason to charge for attending the school dance or school play than for the English or speech class. Some have suggested that the term *extracurricular* itself is a misnomer since the curriculum by definition should include all educational activities sponsored by the school.

Despite these strong arguments for increasing public tax support for student activity programs, it is likely that a significant portion of the funding for student activities will continue to be generated through entry fees, ticket sales, and so forth. This means that building administrators must carefully monitor both revenues and expenditures, which necessarily involves concern for specific accounts (e.g., mathematics club, basketball, sophomore class) as well as totals. In most cases, these monitoring procedures will be dictated by accounting practices specified by the state. In many states, the local school board will be expected to approve budgets prior to the beginning of each fiscal period and both internal and external auditing of student body funds is recommended.[12] In most respects, financial accounting procedures will match those described earlier for the general fund.

Generally, student-body funds will be handled either on a cash basis (items are expended at the time they are actually paid rather than when received) or through a system that can be easily monitored to prevent the creation of a negative fund balance, which is deemed undesirable because it means current and reliable assets may not be of adequate size to cover the liabilities associated with the fund. The monitoring to assure a positive fund balance is fairly easily handled by making adjustments in the fund balance with each revenue or expenditure transaction rather than at the end of the fiscal period as in the previous example.[13]

Another important difference with student-body funds is the involvement of the students themselves in the budget- and expenditure-approval process. Student activity funds are increasingly viewed as being managed for and by students and this attitude is reflected in procedures for financial control established in many states. Often, at the secondary level, students are expected to approve the student activity budgets and some representative of the student body is asked to approve each and every expenditure to make certain it is in fact included within the intended budget appropriation. While these funds are still public monies and are therefore under the legal control of the board of education, it seems entirely appropriate that elected student representatives be involved to a considerable extent in their management and control.

---

[12]For a comprehensive treatment of recommended internal audit provisions, the reader is directed to S. Fred Hawkins, ed., *Internal Audit Guide for Student Activity Funds,* pp. 1–16.

[13]With the modified accrual system recommended for most school district funds, revenue is not recognized until received in cash, but expenditures must be recognized (i.e., either paid or accrued as a liability) at the time the good or service is received. This means the Fund Balance can be reduced without impacting cash; hence, the continual updating of fund balance under a modified accrual system requires revenue and expenditure contra accounts. Examples of journal entries using these contra accounts are found in Table 10–13. The use of these contra accounts essentially converts the modified accrual system into a cash accounting system. A detailed explanation of the various bases for accounting—accrual, modified accrual, and cash—is beyond the scope of this text; however, the reader will find such an explanation provided in Charles G. Stolberg, ed., *School Accounting, Budgeting, and Finance Challenges,* pp. 4–6.

Accounting for and Reporting on Student Activity Financing

Our aim in this section is to see exactly how one specific accounting system can be applied to the management of student activities. To accomplish this end, the student activity fund of Sunset Middle School of the University Place School District will be used. The beginning balance for this student activity fund is presented in Table 10–11; revenue and expenditure projections for the 19X1–19X2 school year are found in Table 10–12. Notice in Table 10–12 that expenditures are estimated to exceed revenues by $550 ($7,500 – $6,950); and in the absence of any predicted change in accrued liabilities, we expect the ending net cash and investment balance to be the same $550 ($4,469 – $3,919) less than the beginning net cash and investment balance. It should also be observed that the general student body provides $4,200 of the projected $6,950 in revenues for the 19X1–19X2 school year. This amount represents approximately 60 percent of the total and is presumably raised primarily through the sale of student activity tickets.

In Table 10–13 a set of transactions (including appropriate debit and credit entries) occurring the first month of the 19X1–19X2 school year is presented. If these particular transactions were processed in the financial accounting system, the trial balance at the end of the month would be as presented in Table 10–14. The reader may desire to check these trial balance accounts by actually carrying out T-account balancing of the type illustrated in Appendix 7. Because the Fund Balance in Table 10–14 has already been adjusted for each revenue and expenditure transaction and the budget entry had no effect on the Fund Balance,[14] a balance sheet can be prepared without closing entries of any kind. Such a balance sheet for the Sunset Middle School on September 30, 19X1, is found in Table 10–15.

The usual budget control information is available directly from the Trial Balance of Table 10–14:

Estimated Revenues	$6,950
Revenues	[4,127]
Balance (Rev.)	$2,823
Appropriations	$7,500
Expenditures	[889]
Encumbrances	[650]
Unencumbered Balance (Exp.)	$5,961

Table 10–11 Sunset Middle School Balance Sheet for Student Activity Fund (September 1, 19X1)

Assets		*Liabilities and Fund Balance*	
Imprest Funds	$ 500	Accounts Payable	$ 626
Cash	1,168	Contracts Payable	250
Warrants Outstanding	[526]	Fund Balance	3,593
Investments	3,327	*TOTAL LIABILITIES AND FUND BALANCE*	$4,469
TOTAL ASSETS	$4,469		

[14]The budget adjustment to the Fund balance was made to a special account called "Appropriated Fund Balance." By reversing the same budget entry at the end of the fiscal period, we are able to maintain the budget control provided by Estimated Revenue and Appropriations accounts without having a direct impact on the Fund-Balance account itself.

Table 10–12 Sunset Middle School Student Activity Fund Budget Profile for 19X1–X2

Activity	*Beginning Net Cash and Investments*	*Revenues*	*Transfers*	*Expen-ditures**	*Ending Net Cash and Investments*
General Student Body	$2,450	$4,200	[2,535]	$2,025	$2,090
Athletics	1,126	550	1,378	2,150	904
Classes	450	325	275	600	450
Clubs	443	1,625	1,132	2,725	475
Payments from Other Districts	—	250	[250]	—	—
	$4,469	$6,950	—	$7,500	$3,919

*This figure is technically different from disbursements in the sense that some things are expended in one fiscal period but disbursed in a following fiscal period. This is accomplished by accruing a liability at the time the good or service is delivered rather than making immediate payment; hence, in subtracting expenditures to arrive at "Ending Net Cash and Investments," the expenditure accrual patterns are assumed to be essentially the same in 19X1–X2 as they were in the prior year. Revenues under this modified accrual system of accounting cannot be accrued but are recognized only when received in cash.

If Sunset Middle School realizes the additional projected revenue balance of $2,823, the unencumbered balance of $5,961 is available as a base for future expenditures in the 19X1–19X2 fiscal period. Even if the revenue falls short of the projected amount, the full unencumbered balance can still be used if the school is willing to reduce the fund balance carry-over into the following year.

Two aspects of the Balance Sheet of Table 10–15 require comment. First, there exists a large Investment balance on September 30, 19X1. With the recent high interest rates, the return on these investments can become an important source of revenue in both general and student activity funds. While school districts are usually restricted to investments in government notes and other low-risk securities, efficiently managed, these funds have become a substantial and highly visible source of school revenue in the past few years. The flow of revenues and expenditures in the typical school district never exactly matches and this difference can be used to advantage in many situations. In the specific example of Sunset Middle School, observe that an early sale of student activity tickets permitted a $1,500 increase in investments between September 1 and September 30. An average investment balance of even $2,000 over an entire school year can easily represent over $100 in additional revenue to the Sunset Middle School student activity program.[15]

It should be stressed again that the balance sheet rarely includes all possible assets of the fund in question. In the specific case of the Sunset Middle School Balance Sheets of Tables 10–11 and 10–15, no inventory items have been included. Neither are any equipment items shown. Most student activity programs will have at least some inventory items, particularly if student stores are operated within the student activity program. This omission of selected assets from the accounting system means that the theoretical net worth of the student activity program is generally greater than that reflected in the balance-sheet accounts. The accounting system for student body funds is primarily a means of managing the use of cash and other liquid assets in relation to a budget plan and the inclusion of all assets in the balance sheet serves no real purpose in that management process.

[15]At 6 percent, the revenue generated by a $2,000 investment is $120 per year. Most school districts can do considerably better than 6 percent, particularly if the investment program is combined for the several different funds of the district and/or for several different school districts.

Table 10–13 Sample Journal Entries for Sunset Middle School Student Activity Fund (transactions described following entries)

Transaction Number	*Accounts*	*Debit*	*Credit*
1	Estimated Revenues	6,950	
	Appropriated Fund Balance	550	
	Appropriations		7,500
2	Imprest Funds	500	
	Warrants Outstanding		500
3	Cash	3,612	
	Revenues		3,612
	Revenue Contra	3,612	
	Fund Balance		3,612
4	Accounts Payable	310	
	Warrants Outstanding		310
5	Investments	2,500	
	Cash		2,500
6	Warrants Outstanding	546	
	Cash		546
7	Encumbrances	849	
	Reserve for Encumbrances		849
8	Cash	1,040	
	Revenues		40
	Revenue Contra	40	
	Fund Balance		40
	Investments		1,000
9	Contracts Payable	200	
	Cash		200
10	Encumbrances	650	
	Reserve for Encumbrances		650
11	No Entry	—	—
12	Cash	475	
	Revenues		475
	Revenue Contra	475	
	Fund Balance		475
13	Expenditures	865	
	Warrants Outstanding		865
	Fund Balance	865	
	Expenditure Contra		865
	Reserve for Encumbrances	849	
	Encumbrances		849
14	Expenditures	24	
	Warrants Outstanding		24
	Fund Balance	24	
	Expenditure Contra		24

Table 10–13 (continued)

Description of Transactions:

1. The budget for the fiscal year 19X1–19X2 is entered into the accounting records. As indicated in Table 10–12, the budget calls for revenues of $6,950 and expenditures of $7,500.
2. The Imprest Funds account is increased to $1,000.
3. Proceeds from student activity tickets are deposited in a local bank. These proceeds amount to $3,612.
4. Payment for $310 worth of supplies delivered and expended prior to the beginning of the 19X1–19X2 fiscal period is made by warrant.
5. Approval is gained to invest $2,500 in a 180-day note. The annual interest rate on this note is 7½ percent.
6. Notification is received that $546 in warrants has been redeemed by the bank.
7. Purchase orders for aerospace club models total $849.
8. The final semiannual interest payment is received on a $1,000 note held by the Student Activity Fund. The annual interest rate on this note is 8 percent. The money is not reinvested but is deposited in the regular bank account.
9. The final payment of $200 on a three-year contract for a cash register in the student store is made.
10. Purchase orders for $650 worth of supplies are processed.
11. Decorations for the skating party totalling $24 are paid from the imprest funds.
12. Proceeds from the skating party are $475 and these are deposited in the Student Activity Fund.
13. The aerospace club models in transaction 7 above are received along with a bill for $865. The bill is paid by warrant.
14. The imprest fund is reimbursed by warrant for the amount of the payment in transaction 11 above. This reimbursement is approved in advance by the Board of Education.

Table 10–14 Sunset Middle School Trial Balance for Student Activity Fund (as of September 30,19X1)

Account	*Debit*	*Credit*
Imprest Funds	$ 1,000	
Cash	3,049	
Warrants Outstanding		$ 1,679
Investments	4,827	
Accounts Payable		316
Contracts Payable		50
Fund Balance		6,831
Appropriated Fund Balance	550	
Encumbrances	650	
Reserve for Encumbrances		650
Estimated Revenues	6,950	
Revenues		4,127
Revenue Contra	4,127	
Appropriations		7,500
Expenditures	889	
Expenditures Contra		889
	$22,042	$22,042

Table 10–15 Sunset Middle School Balance Sheet for Student Activity Fund (September 30, 19X1)

Assets		*Liabilities and Fund Balance*	
Imprest Funds	$1,000	Accounts Payable	$ 316
Cash	3,049	Contracts Payable	50
Warrants Outstanding	[1,679]	Fund Balance	6,831
Investments	4,827	*TOTAL LIABILITIES AND FUND BALANCE*	$7,197
TOTAL ASSETS	$7,197		

PROBLEMS OF REPORTING FISCAL STATUS IN SCHOOLS

Most often, the fiscal reporting practices of schools are designed to conform with federal and/or state mandates. Unfortunately, these formats sometimes utilize terminology that is extremely difficult for the nonaccountant to understand. The program or function categories mandated in state reports may also conflict with the way in which local school patrons tend to look at their own school programs or the complexities of matching revenues and expenditures to fiscal periods may result in total confusion for taxpayers. The school administrator at both the central office and building levels must be sensitive to these problems and must use a certain amount of creativity in formulating reports for public consumption. Often it is desirable to formulate special program or function codes within the accounting system just to monitor costs that are particularly sensitive in a given community. It is also useful to present financial reports in combination with reports on educational accomplishment. Such reports, when intended for consumption by the general public, should include only summary financial information and should avoid great detail. Summary charts and graphs can often communicate needed information, thus avoiding the confusion associated with state-mandated financial reports. Many of the reports required by the state and federal governments are intended to aid government budget analysts and/or auditors and their use with the general public and even local school boards should be handled with caution. In general, if an explanation of terms is required in interpreting the report or if a particular report addresses questions of minimal interest to the local citizenry, it should probably not be distributed for public use.

At the building level, the requirements of fiscal reporting can be used as a means of providing very practical training for student body officers and members of the student council. The administrator who understands the accounting concepts covered in this text can utilize the reporting requirements within the student body activity fund to introduce accounting concepts to students. Selected students at both the junior and senior high levels will become sufficiently interested in these concepts that they will seek an active part in preparing summary financial reports for use by the student council. Such experiences may also be used as practical application of concepts taught within the business department of the school. Student government in our secondary schools is often criticized for its lack of realism. If the school can educate young people in the techniques used in properly accounting for public monies and then provide opportunities to apply this learning, greater realism in the educational program will likely be achieved.

Reporting is the final phase of the budget cycle, as it is through the reporting process that budget results are evaluated and budget parameters for the following fiscal period are formulated. It is also here that the school addresses the important cost-effectiveness questions that serve as an ultimate guide in the allocation of public monies. The way in which these cost-effectiveness judgments fit in with the goal-based planning at the school building level were detailed in the first part of this text and a schematic of this planning process was shown in Figure 1–4.

SUMMARY

In this final chapter, the reader is provided background information on the financial accounting system used in monitoring revenues and expenditures in school systems. Samples of accounting entries associated with the most common financial transactions are presented and these are applied to general and student-body program funds of a hypothetical district. These two funds are used because they are most likely to be encountered by administrators at the building level.

An important part of financial accounting in schools is the development of financial status reports. Among the more important of these are the budget status report, the trial balance, the balance sheet, and the change in net cash and investment balance. Administrators should become skilled at reading these reports and summarizing the important information for staff members and the public. Both district- and building-level administrators are urged to seek ways of matching information obtained from financial records with reports on educational accomplishment. This important relationship is almost always on the minds of school board members, student council representatives, and other legislative groups when making decisions and it is best that their decisions be structured with reliable evaluation data whenever possible.

This evaluation data and a clear understanding of school district goals should be combined with cost information to make the crucial cost-effectiveness judgments required as part of budget preparation. Questions regarding the viability of organizational goals and related action programs are therefore very much a part of the fiscal-reporting and budget-review processes. The perceptive administrator will find ways to combine these concerns with the total budgeting and financial reporting system. The goal-based planning model presented in Part I will assist administrators in completing this connection among goals, activities, accomplishments, and costs. The design of budgeting and accounting systems that aid rather than frustrate this connection remains one of the major challenges facing administrators at all levels of the school system.

QUESTIONS AND PROBLEMS ON CHAPTER 10

1. In the basic accounting equation used in school systems, the term fund balance replaces "equity" or "net worth." Explain the meaning of the term fund balance and why it is the preferred term in governmental accounting.
2. Explain the difference between each of the following pairs of terms:
   a. Appropriation and expenditure
   b. Estimated revenue and revenue
   c. Liability and encumbrance
   d. Accrual and modified accrual systems of accounting
   e. Program and object
   f. Trial balance and balance sheet
3. Using as a guide the sample journal entries of Table 10–5 and the descriptive material in Appendix 6, indicate appropriate debit/credit entries for each of the following transactions. (Do not make adjustments to fund balance as part of the revenue and expenditure entries.)
   a. Revenues of $2,000 are received from a federal grant.
   b. The imprest funds cash account is increased by $500.
   c. Warrants are issued for $1,500 in expenditures that had been previously encumbered for $1,450.

d. A $40 purchase is made from imprest funds.
e. Notice is received that $1,300 worth of warrants has been redeemed at the county treasurer or bank.

4. In one recent school year, student stores in secondary schools of the United States sold over a million dollars worth of candy. Some students have been known to sell free lunch tickets in order to purchase candy from the student store. Since profits from such sales are used to support band, drill team, and club activities in the schools, administrators and teachers have been reluctant to move for elimination of such sales. What alternatives are available to raise needed revenues for the school extracurricular programs and what are your thoughts about current practices in fund raising? What recommendations would you make for funding the extracurricular programs in the local schools?

5. Consider the trial balance presented at the conclusion of Appendix 6.
a. What percentage of estimated revenues and expenditures had been realized at the time of preparing this trial balance?
b. What closing entries would be required prior to preparing a balance sheet showing the current status of the fund? (The current status as requested here must show a fund balance based on actual rather than estimated revenues and expenditures.)
c. The fund balance following the closing entries in Part b is $282,700. This represents a substantial increase over the $45,600 beginning fund balance. What factors account for this increase?
d. Prepare a current balance sheet for the fund and one that reflects the closing entries in Part b.

6. Prepare a set of T-accounts for the purpose of posting the beginning balance-sheet accounts and transactions for the Sunset Middle School student activity fund. (The beginning balances and transaction journal entries are found in Tables 10–11 and 10–13, respectively.)
a. Post the beginning balances and all transactions to T-accounts using the format of Appendix 7 as a guide.
b. Show that the ending balances in each account match those presented in the trial balance of Table 10–14.
c. Suppose that in Transaction 13 the student body does not pay the bill for the aerospace club models at this time but rather sets up a liability for the payment to be made at a future date. In this situation, how will Transaction 13 be modified and what journal entry would be required later at the time of payment?
d. Based on the trial balance of Table 10–14, prepare all entries as if it were time to close out the fiscal period. (Normally, the closing entries requested here would be completed on August 31, 19X2, the closing date for the fiscal period.)

7. The following balance sheet for a school district general fund has been presented for review:

ASSETS		LIABILITIES AND FUND BALANCE	
Imprest Funds	$1,000	Warrants Outstanding	$4,000
Cash	11,000	Accounts Payable	500
Inventory	850	Reserve for Inventory	400
Due to Other Funds	[400]	Fund Balance	7,550
Total	$12,450	Total	$12,450

a. What items in this statement seem inappropriately placed in the balance sheet?
b. The Fund Balance appears to be overstated. Explain why this might be so and what debit/credit entry could be used to correct this problem?
c. Present a revised balance sheet with proper placement and amounts for all items.

8. The following is a year-end (19X0) trial balance before closing entries for a particular student activity fund:

	DEBIT	CREDIT
Imprest Funds	500	
Cash	1,160	
Warrants Outstanding		125
Investments	2,000	
Revenue Contra	4,100	
Estimated Revenues	4,200	
Fund Balance		1,710
Appropriated Fund Balance	300	
Encumbrances	200	
Accounts Payable		325
Contracts Payable		1,500
Reserve for Encumbrances		200
Revenues		4,100
Appropriations		4,500
Expenditures	4,170	
Expenditure Contra		4,170

a. What was the Fund Balance at the beginning of the 19X0 fiscal period? Explain.
b. What was the "unencumbered balance of expenditure appropriations" at the end of 19X0?
c. What closing debit/credit entries must be made to close out the books for 19X0?
d. Prepare a year-end balance sheet for 19X0.
e. If we assume that encumbrances existing at the end of 19X0 are to be included in the 19X1 budget appropriation, what specific debit/credit entry will be required early in 19X1 to accomplish this inclusion?

9. The beginning balance sheet for a given student activity fund is as follows:

ASSETS		LIABILITIES AND FUND BALANCE	
Imprest Funds	$ 300	Vouchers Payable	$ 700
Cash	1,200	Fund Balance	3,600
Warrants Outstanding	[200]	Total Liabilities and Fund Balance	$4,300
Investments	3,000		
Total Assets	$4,300		

The particular accounting system utilized with this fund requires that the budget entry have a direct effect on Fund Balance and the revenue and expenditure transactions do not directly affect the Fund Balance until the close of the fiscal period. The budget for the current fiscal period calls for anticipated revenues of $4,500 and an appropriation for expenditures of $4,800.

a. Indicate the proper debit/credit entries for each of the following transactions:
   (1) The budget as specified above is recorded in the proper accounts.
   (2) Revenues of $3,500 are realized through sale of student activity cards and these are deposited in the Cash account.
   (3) Approval is gained for investing $2,500 in a 180-day note. A warrant is issued to cover this investment, which carries an 8 percent interest rate.
   (4) Band uniforms estimated to cost a total of $2,200 are ordered.
   (5) A dance band is paid $175 with a check drawn on imprest funds.
   (6) Interest earnings of $120 are realized on investments existing at the beginning of the budget period. These investments remain intact and only the interest is received in cash.
   (7) Payment by warrant is made on a $300 voucher payable that existed at the beginning of the fiscal period.
   (8) The warrant for the investment (in Number 3 above) has been redeemed.
   (9) The band uniforms are received along with a bill for $2,275. The bill is paid by warrant.
   (10) Imprest funds is reimbursed by warrant for the dance band payment.
   (11) Notification is received that both principal and interest earnings on the 180-day note (referred to in Number 3 above) has been received and deposited in the Cash account.
   (12) The warrant for the band uniforms has been redeemed.
   (13) A donation of $30 is received from the PTA.
b. Post the entries in Part a to a set of T-accounts and prepare a trial balance.
c. Based on this trial balance, indicate the percent of budgeted revenues and expenditures that have been realized.
d. Specify the debit/credit entries that would first be required to close the books and prepare a balance sheet for the fund assuming that it is closed at this particular point.
e. Prepare a report showing the change in net cash and investment balance since the beginning of the fiscal period.

10. A year-end trial balance for the general fund of a school district is as follows:

	DEBIT	CREDIT
Imprest Funds	3,500	
Cash	626,355	
Warrants Outstanding		157,840
Investments	71,022	
Due from Other Funds	3,240	
Inventory	365,438	
Taxes Receivable	1,426,422	
Vouchers Payable		124,326
Accrued Expenses		8,984
Reserve for Inventory		370,000
Reserve for Taxes Receivable		1,426,422
Fund Balance		192,778
Encumbrances	5,413	
Reserve for Encumbrances		5,413
Estimated Revenues	11,456,986	
Revenues		11,682,432
Appropriations		11,362,904
Expenditures	11,372,813	

a. What was the Fund Balance at the beginning of the fiscal period? (Assume here that no adjustments affecting the Fund Balance have been made to any of the reserve accounts during the fiscal period.)

b. Three additional journal entries are made before closing entries. Adjust the above trial balance for these three entries into the accounting system:

(1) Taxes in the amount of $310,438 are received in cash and are deposited in the Cash account.

(2) A $75 warrant covering a prior year expenditure is canceled and an appropriate adjustment in Fund Balance is made.

(3) A physical inventory reveals an amount of $359,445. Adjustments to both the Inventory and Reserve for Inventory accounts are made to reflect this amount.

c. Complete the necessary closing entries and prepare a year-end balance sheet for the fund.

d. Prepare a report showing the "Analysis of Change in Fund Balance." (Table 10–10 presents a sample of this report; however, adjustments for other than revenue/expenditure transactions will be necessary in this particular case.)

11. Some school districts encumber salaries at the beginning of each fiscal period (or at the time the salaries are obligated by contract). Explain the rationale for doing this and discuss problems such a practice might present in attempting to explain reports of the type presented in Table 10–7.

12. The actual cash position for University Place School District (as presented in Table 10–6) might be modified as follows:

ANALYSIS OF CASH
(as of September 30, 19X1)

Net Cash	99,900
Goods and Services Encumbered	[166,004]
Overpayment of State Apportionment to District	[45,845]
Unrestricted Cash	[111,949]

a. What accounts were accumulated to arrive at the Net Cash of 99,900?

b. What new information (i.e., information not available in Table 10–6) is presented in this modified Analysis of Cash statement?

c. In reviewing the account status in Table 10–6, what are possible sources of cash to cover this negative "unrestricted cash" position?

APPENDICES
BIBLIOGRAPHY
INDEX

APPENDIX 1

STRATEGIES AVAILABLE FOR ANALYZING GOAL PREFERENCES AND FOLLOW-UP ACTION STATEMENTS

In Chapter 1 of the text, three phases or steps in analyzing goal preferences in a school or a school system are identified. These include (1) examination of goal preferences, (2) analysis of current goal satisfaction, and (3) development of action statements relating to goal preferences. Alternative strategies exist for accomplishing each of these three phases of planning and some of the more promising are outlined here.

EXAMINATION OF GOAL PREFERENCES

Preferences can best be accomplished through some type of rating scheme. By far the simplest is a rank ordering of the designated goal list; however, this has the disadvantage of assuming an equal-interval scaling of goal importance from top to bottom. This assumption is highly suspect and is not consistent with what we know about individual goal preferences. Some people may place one or two goals far above the others in importance and are unable to indicate this set of preferences using a simple rank order procedure.

A more flexible point-allocation system as used with the Phi Delta Kappa "Model Program for Community and Professional Involvement," is a preferred method in situations where greater variation in the goal ratings is to be encouraged. Mean ratings using this particular method in one goal-setting experience are presented in Attachment A. Each respondent was allowed a total of 45 points to be distributed over the 18 goal statements. This represents an average rating of 2.5 points for each goal.

Other reasonable alternatives for the rating process include five- or seven-point scaling for each of the goal statements or a type of Q-sort procedure. The five- or seven-point scale has the advantage of permitting independent ratings of importance on each of the goal statements but is likely to result in lesser variation in group ratings for the several goals. This is true because respondents will tend to utilize only the upper end of the rating scale for most of the goals.

A Q-sort design does not permit the diversity in individual responses seen in the point-allocation system used with the Phi Delta Kappa goals program but rather assumes a particular distribution of importance ratings for each individual respondent. It has the advantage of being fairly easy to explain to a group of citizens. The particular forced-choice Q-sort model of Attachment B was used in connection with the nationwide Task of Public Education survey in 1958. Note that the forced distribution in this case was a seven-point scale with only one goal receiving the highest rating. The total point allocation for the sixteen goal statements is 64 (or $7 \times 1 + 6 \times 2 + \ldots + 1 \times 1$) and, to complete the survey, the individual respondent sorts the sixteen statements (listed under Task of Public Education in Figure 1–5 of the text) into the spaces indicated in Attachment B.

Since this first phase of examining goal preference is generally only an introductory step leading to the identification of some set of action programs for the school district and/or school, selection of a particular method of ranking goals is not crucial. It is probably best to discuss the several approaches with the designated steering committee members and let them make the decision as to the method to be used.

ANALYSIS OF CURRENT GOAL SATISFACTION

Quite often, goals rated by a group of citizens, staff, or students as being most important are also those they view as being least adequately addressed at the present time. While this tendency seems to operate in relation to the "importance" and "quality" ratings in Attachment A (e.g., citizens rated "develop skills in reading, writing, speaking, and listening" the most important of the goal statements and rated the quality of present programs in relation to this goal statement thirteenth in rank order), it cannot necessarily be assumed to be the case. It may be that a particular high-priority goal is being met in a satisfactory manner at the present time and it would make little sense to apply greater attention to that area. This points up the necessity of examining the results of the goal-preference inventory to decide which of the goals need attention in future planning by the school or school district. This examination is likely to be less objective than the establishment of goal preferences (as both citizens and staff are likely to know more about their own preferences than they are about how well the schools are doing or even can do in relation to those preferences); however, it is nonetheless an essential step in the process of planning in relation to the goal clarification activity.

In public schools, this analysis of current goal satisfaction is probably best based on the viewpoints of patrons of the school district. It is important that these judgments be made on an informed basis and it is therefore necessary that the school district make available the information needed for judging the services currently provided by schools. It is suggested that this include not only a review of the usual follow-up studies of graduates and

Attachment A Phi Delta Kappa Goals Profile

Goal Statement[a]	Rating of Importance[b] by:						Quality of Present Programs[c] as perceived by:					
	Citizens		Staff		Students		Citizens		Staff		Students	
	Mean	Rank	Mean	Rank	Mean	Rank	Mean	Rank	Mean	Rank	Mean	Rank
Develop skills in reading, writing, speaking and listening (#4)	4.43	1	3.63	3	2.86	6	7.56	13	7.84	11	10.20	1
Gain general education (#18)	4.00	2	3.75	2	4.43	1	8.00	9	8.56	7	10.11	2
Develop desire for learning now and in the future (#11)	3.57	3	2.75	7	3.43	2	7.37	16	7.12	17	7.63	16
Learn to respect and get along with people with whom we work and live (#8)	3.34	4	2.13	10	2.86	7	8.33	6	7.75	13	8.83	9
Develop pride in work and feeling of self-worth (#16)	3.43	4	3.88	1	2.57	10	7.22	17	7.03	18	8.00	14
Learn how to examine and use information (#6)	3.14	6	3.00	5	2.86	7	7.51	15	7.43	14	8.69	10
Develop good character and self-respect (#17)	3.00	7	3.63	3	2.00	12	7.74	12	7.15	16	7.74	15
Learn about and try to understand changes that take place in the world (#3)	2.29	8	3.00	5	1.57	15	8.48	5	7.81	12	9.43	5
Understand and practice democratic ideas and ideals (#5)	2.14	9	1.88	12	1.00	18	9.07	3	9.18	3	9.40	6
Practice and understand the ideas of health and safety (#13)	2.00	10	1.88	12	1.71	14	9.33	1	9.65	1	9.91	3
Learn to be a good citizen (#1)	1.86	11	2.25	8	1.86	13	8.07	8	7.96	9	8.57	11
Learn how to respect and get along with people who think, dress and act differently (#2)	1.86	11	2.13	10	2.43	11	8.85	4	7.96	9	8.29	13
Develop skills to enter a specific field of work (#9)	1.86	11	1.88	12	3.43	2	7.18	18	8.59	6	6.82	18
Understand and practice the skills of family living (#7)	1.71	14	1.63	17	2.57	9	9.25	2	8.75	5	9.34	7
Learn how to use leisure time (#12)	1.71	14	2.25	8	1.29	17	7.77	11	8.00	8	9.74	4
Appreciate culture and beauty in the world (#14)	1.71	14	1.88	12	1.57	15	8.18	7	9.00	4	8.84	8
Gain information needed to make job selection (#15)	1.43	17	1.38	18	3.29	4	7.59	14	9.32	2	7.34	17
Learn how to be a good manager of money, property, and resources (#10)	1.43	17	1.88	12	3.00	5	7.96	10	7.18	15	8.57	11

[a] This particular profile represents Coupeville School District of Coupeville, Washington, in January 1974. Goal statements listed here are in order of priority as rated by the citizen group. Numbers in parentheses following each statement correspond to the number of the goal statement as listed in Figure 1–3 of the text.

[b] Each respondent distributed 45 points over the 18 goal statements, with no single goal statement receiving more than 5 points.

[c] The quality ratings were based on a 15-point scale with 15 being high and 1 being low. A score of 8 is considered an average quality rating.

Attachment B Q-Sort Design for Task of Public Education Survey Conducted by Midwest Administration Center, University of Chicago

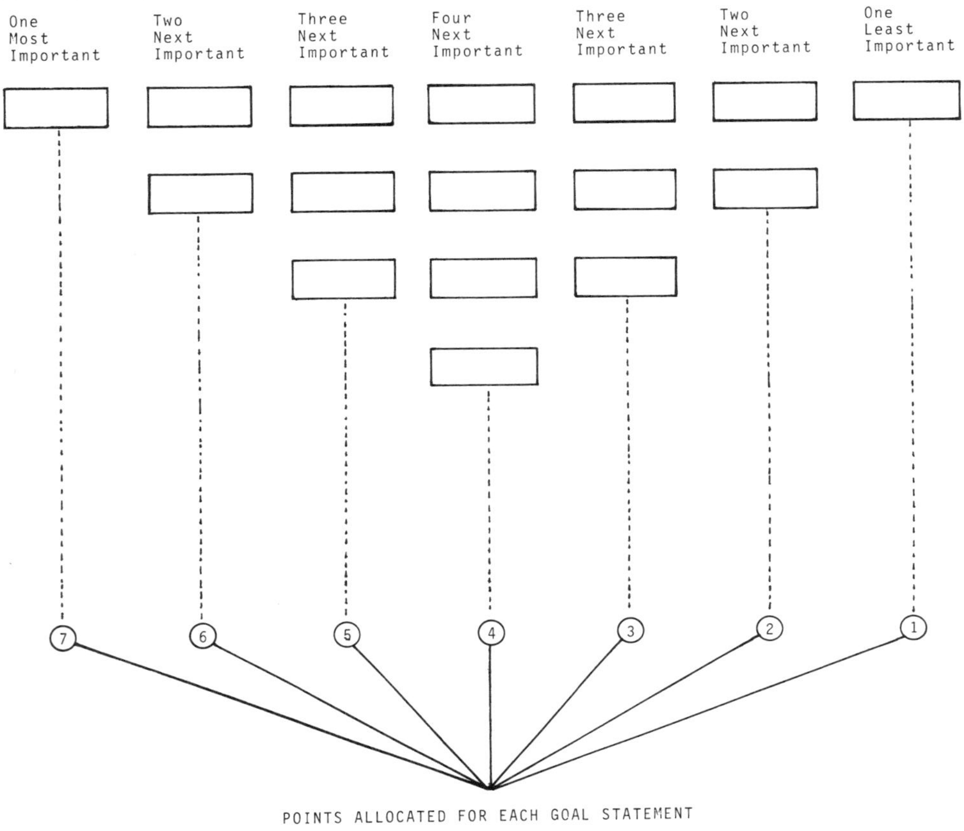

One Most Important	Two Next Important	Three Next Important	Four Next Important	Three Next Important	Two Next Important	One Least Important
7	6	5	4	3	2	1

POINTS ALLOCATED FOR EACH GOAL STATEMENT

comparative test scores but the opportunity to view classrooms in action and to discuss programs with a cross section of teachers and students. This judgment on current levels of goal satisfaction should also be made with an understanding of any state or federal regulations that might relate to the accomplishment of certain goals. For example, it would be unrealistic to expect that a goal of "teaching foreign languages and comparative cultures at the elementary level" would have been satisfied to any great extent if the legislature that is providing most of the funding for the schools had eliminated the teaching of foreign language at that level. At least the local district would have to consider this factor in analyzing the difficulties to be faced in making a future commitment to this goal statement.

The result of this phase is a list of goal and/or subgoal areas that can be used to develop future plans for the school or school district. Essentially, this represents a needs statement that forms the basis of future staff action. It is likely that the plans developed from this needs statement will entail the addition or deletion of certain program elements as well as changes in emphasis within existing programs. These plans are discussed at length in Chapter 2 of the text and involve citizens only in a review capacity. The actual implementation of these plans will be part of the input given citizens at some future time when they are again directly involved in the clarification and ranking of goals.

DEVELOPMENT OF ACTION STATEMENTS RELATING TO GOAL PREFERENCES

The results for the first two phases provide a background for the more detailed development of future plans for the school and/or school district. There is little question but that the staff could take the priorities judged to need greatest attention in the future, that is, the result of phase two, and develop a reasonable implementation plan to be shared with citizens at a later point; however, cutting off the collective citizen, staff, and student effort at this point would be unsatisfying to many of the participants. Citizens have invested a great deal of time in arriving at goal priorities stated in student outcome or product terms. It is likely that some of these citizens have very definitive ideas of how these products might best be achieved. In the absence of an exacting educational technology, it is unfair to the citizens and the school district not to consider their contributions regarding the way in which some of the priority goals might best be achieved.

Apart from suggested ways of accomplishing specific priority goals, it is also important to note that the goal clarification work discussed here has been limited to product-type statements. Some people feel strongly about processes of interaction taking place in schools and there needs to be some way to make these concerns known to the professional staff, even when these process preferences are not directly related to goal priorites of the school community. For example, some may feel that it is important for special programs to be offered for gifted students, even if this provision does not relate specifically to one of the high-priority goal statements. Conversely, it is doubtful that many people would approve of permitting elementary students to smoke on the school grounds, even if it could be shown that such smoking had a positive effect on their attitude toward cognitive learning tasks. Recognizing these strong process and organizational preferences among citizens is an important part of the goal clarification process and is most appropriately accomplished during this third phase of analysis.

One reasonable procedure is simply to let the citizen group make action statements to guide the staff in its more detailed planning effort. These action statements might be divided along the lines already suggested, namely, those preferred processes that relate to certain high-priority goal statements and those that exist as preferences without reference to the listed goal statements. A sample of such action-program statements follows:

ACTION/PROCESS STATEMENTS RELATING TO HIGH-PRIORITY GOALS

Goal: Develop skills in reading, writing, speaking, and listening

1. The school should establish a special reading laboratory to provide help for students reading below level.
2. The school district should expect students to exhibit a specific level of competence in writing as a condition for receiving the high school diploma.
3. Speaking should be given greater emphasis in the junior high school language arts programs and students should be required to give at least two five-minute speeches per semester.

Goal: Develop positive self-image in every student

1. The school should abolish the letter grading system and substitute a system that is less damaging to student self-concept.
2. The school counselor should talk with every student at least once each year and make program changes in those cases where the student is being asked to perform beyond his or her present ability.

ACTION/PROCESS STATEMENTS UNRELATED TO SPECIFIC GOALS

1. The educational system should employ more members of minority groups in key positions in the administration.
2. A wide variety of learning options should be established in subject areas and in individual courses.
3. Teachers should make a greater effort to demonstrate interrelationships between the various subjects offered in the school.
4. The school district should develop and implement an aggressive public information program.

APPENDIX 2

BUILDING MASTER SCHEDULE FOR UNIVERSITY HIGH SCHOOL

University High School is an existing senior high with 175, 150, and 150 students, respectively, in grades ten, eleven, and twelve. The staff is interested in moving toward a more elective language arts program in grades eleven and twelve. Students under this revised organization, rather than taking the usual English 10–11 sequence required by state graduation requirements, take a standard English 10 course followed by at least two semester electives selected from the several options—Language of Minority Opinion, Creative Writing, American Literature, Language of Laughter, and Language of Belief. An inventory taken in late spring showing the student course requests is listed in Attachment A. These requests reflect fall term registration only.

Special consideration should be given to the fact that the Distributive Education and Art Studio classes listed in Attachment A are double-period classes with all other classes meeting a single period each day. In proceeding with the schedule-building process, it is

Attachment A Student Course Requests for University High School

Courses	Grade Level			
	10	11	12	Total
English 10 (28)	175	--	--	175
Creative Writing (28)	1	38	14	53
Language of Laughter (28)	--	23	28	51
American Literature (28)	2	15	10	27
Lang. of Minority Opinion (28)	4	30	20	54
Language of Belief (28)	1	22	19	42
Distributive Education (24)	--	--	21	21
Typing 1 (28)	47	18	14	79
Typing 2 (28)	18	26	3	47
Advanced Typing (24)	--	21	16	37
Shorthand (24)	6	17	1	24
Bookkeeping (30)	4	7	16	27
Advanced Shorthand (24)	--	3	14	17
Speech (30)	131	15	15	161
Debate (15)	6	4	2	12
Advanced Debate (15)	--	7	4	11
Drama (24)	3	6	9	18
Advanced Drama (24)	--	1	3	4
Journalism (26)	13	9	1	23
Annual (20)	1	10	7	18
World History (28)	10	11	3	24
U.S./World History (28)	--	143	2	145
Anthropology (26)	--	4	5	9
Psychology (26)	2	2	7	11
American Government (30)	--	1	62	63
Contemporary Problems (30)	--	2	85	87
Basic Art (28)	2	23	30	55
Art Studio (28)	--	5	13	18
Latin I (28)	15	19	1	35
Latin II (28)	3	4	4	11
Spanish I (28)	30	22	4	56
Spanish II (24)	5	28	8	41
Spanish III (24)	--	2	4	6
French I (24)	43	27	4	74
French II (24)	3	35	10	48
French III (24)	--	6	11	17
German I (28)	23	4	--	27
German II (24)	--	18	2	20
Basic Home Economics (24)	65	4	1	70
Fashion Design (24)	1	6	8	15
Home Economics Projects (24)	--	15	52	67
Band (50)	10	9	12	31
Chorus (40)	14	8	13	35
Algebra I (30)	27	2	--	29
Geometry (32)	72	44	9	125
Algebra II (30)	--	73	21	94
Fundamental Math (30)	19	1	2	22
Math Analysis (26)	--	2	21	23
Biology (28)	75	12	9	96
Chemistry (26)	--	19	28	47
Physics (26)	--	5	19	24
Electronics (24)	4	7	6	17
Woodwork (28)	--	12	14	26
Driver Training (13)	52	22	2	76
Boys P.E. 10 (40)	85	2	--	87
Girls P.E. 10 (40)	78	1	--	79
Advanced Boys P.E. (35)	--	13	50	63
Advanced Girls P.E. (35)	--	3	27	30
Total	1050	888	766	2704

Numbers in parentheses are suggested class-size limitations. No class should exceed this suggested limitation and no class can be offered with fewer than ten students. Drama/Advanced Drama and Spanish II/Spanish III may be taught as combination classes in order to meet this class-size limitation.

Attachment B Faculty Assignments for University High School

Teacher	*Assignment*
Cook	Typing 2, Advanced Typing, Shorthand, Advanced Shorthand
Dodd[a]	Band, Chorus
Engelson	Basic Art, Fashion Design, Art Studio
Esmoris	Typing 1, Typing 2, English 10
Estep	Woodwork, Electronics, Biology, Physics
Flynn	Advanced Boys P.E., Driver Training
Hall	English 10, Language of Belief, Lang. of Minority Opinion
Johnson	Basic Home Economics, Home Economics Projects
Kuehn	Geometry, Algebra II, Math Analysis
Lackman[b]	Journalism, Annual, Debate, Advanced Debate
Marshall[c]	Basic Home Econ., Spanish I, Spanish II, Spanish III
Molitor	Speech, Bookkeeping, Distributive Education
Morgan	U.S./World, German I, German II
Parker[d]	Speech, Drama, Advanced Drama
Ronhaar[e]	Fundamental Math, Driver Training, Chemistry
Russell	Boys P.E. 10, Driver Training
Sabol	English 10, American Literature, Language of Laughter
Schindele	Algebra I, Algebra II, Geometry
Shean	Latin I, Latin II, Contemporary Problems, Psychology
Sutherland	English 10, Creative Writing
Tucker	Girls P.E. 10, Advanced Girls P.E., Biology
Turpen[f]	French I, French II, French III
Warner	U.S./World, Contemporary Problems
Wiese	French I, World History, American Government

[a]Teaches only two classes at University High. These classes must be scheduled fifth and sixth periods.

[b]In addition to the four classes listed, Mr. Lackman serves as lunchroom supervisor during fourth period. His planning period is scheduled during third period.

[c]Because of the limited enrollment in Spanish III, Ms. Marshall teaches one Spanish II/Spanish III combination.

[d]Because of the limited enrollment in Advanced Drama, Mr. Parker teaches a single Drama/Advanced Drama combination.

[e]Mr. Ronhaar has planning in both fifth and sixth periods and teaches only four class hours. As a substitute for a fifth class he receives a special assignment for coordinating accreditation activities.

[f]Ms. Turpen prefers to accept six classes of instruction rather than exceed the limit of 24 students in French I.

helpful to know that each student in University High School signs up for all six class hours with the exception of a few students (mostly seniors) who have completed their course requirements for graduation and have a job of some kind. No study halls are provided for such students and they have an early release or late arrival arrangement with the school. Also helpful in building the best possible schedule is the faculty assignment possibilities as presented in Attachment B.

The other essential element required in developing the master schedule is the conflict matrix. This is included as Attachment C. The conflict matrix shows the combinations of course registrations and can help minimize conflicts for individual students. No consideration need be given to room assignments in this particular problem. Utilizing the collective information provided in Attachments A, B, and C, the reader is now prepared to proceed with building the master schedule. As an aid in getting started, it might be helpful to utilize the initial course placements prescribed in Attachment D.

There are obviously many reasonable master schedules given the conditions stated here (including the starting point of Attachment D), but the reader may find it helpful to consult the sample schedule of Attachment E as representing one satisfactory solution. Note that

Attachment C Conflict Matrix for University High School

	English 10	Creative Writing	Lang. Laughter	Amer. Literature	Lang. Min. Opin.	Lang. Belief	Typing 1	Typing 2	Adv. Typing	Shorthand	Adv. Shorthand	Bookkeeping	Dist. Educ.	Speech	Debate	Adv. Debate	Drama	Adv. Drama	Journalism	Annual	World History	US/World	Anthropology	Psychology	Amer. Govt.	Cont. Problems
English 10	175	1	-	2	4	1	47	18	-	6	-	4	-	131	6	-	3	-	13	1	10	-	-	2	-	-
Creative Writing	.1	53	3	1	4	2	4	5	6	1	-	4	2	4	-	2	3	-	2	3	-	37	-	1	6	7
Lang. Laughter	-	3	51	2	2	1	3	2	12	5	2	3	3	5	1	3	1	1	1	1	2	23	2	1	12	15
Amer. Literature	2	1	2	27	1	2	1	2	4	2	1	2	-	2	-	1	1	1	1	2	1	15	1	1	6	4
Lang. Min. Opin.	4	4	2	1	54	1	2	4	7	2	2	2	7	5	3	1	2	1	2	3	2	29	1	-	9	11
Lang. Belief	1	2	1	2	1	42	5	4	3	3	3	4	2	4	1	-	1	-	2	4	2	22	2	1	8	10
Typing 1	47	4	3	1	2	5	79	-	-	-	-	4	-	22	3	1	2	-	7	5	8	18	2	2	6	8
Typing 2	18	5	2	2	4	4	-	47	-	-	-	2	-	15	2	1	1	-	2	1	3	26	1	2	1	2
Adv. Typing	-	6	12	4	7	3	-	-	37	5	5	5	4	2	-	-	1	-	1	-	-	21	-	-	8	8
Shorthand	6	1	5	2	2	3	-	-	5	24	-	-	-	4	1	-	1	-	1	-	1	17	-	-	1	-
Adv. Shorthand	-	-	2	1	2	3	-	-	3	-	17	3	-	2	-	-	2	1	1	1	-	3	-	1	6	8
Bookkeeping	4	4	3	2	2	4	4	2	5	-	3	27	2	1	1	-	1	-	1	-	1	7	-	-	7	8
Dist. Educ.	-	2	3	-	7	2	-	-	4	-	-	2	21	1	-	-	-	2	2	1	-	-	-	1	9	11
Speech	131	4	5	2	5	4	22	15	2	4	2	1	1	161	-	-	2	-	10	1	9	15	1	1	7	8
Debate	6	-	1	-	3	1	3	2	-	1	-	1	-	-	12	-	1	-	1	1	1	4	1	1	2	-
Adv. Debate	-	2	3	1	1	-	1	1	-	-	-	-	-	-	-	11	-	1	1	-	1	7	-	1	1	2
Drama	3	3	1	1	2	1	2	1	1	1	2	1	-	2	1	-	18	-	1	1	-	6	-	1	3	6
Adv. Drama	-	-	1	1	1	-	-	-	-	-	1	-	2	-	-	1	-	4	-	1	-	1	-	-	-	2
Journalism	13	2	1	1	2	2	7	2	1	1	1	1	2	10	1	1	1	-	23	1	-	9	-	1	1	-
Annual	1	3	1	2	3	4	5	1	-	-	1	-	1	1	1	-	1	1	1	18	1	10	1	-	3	3
World History	10	-	2	1	2	2	8	3	-	1	-	1	-	9	1	1	-	-	-	1	24	11	-	1	2	1
US/World	-	37	23	15	29	22	18	26	21	17	3	7	-	15	4	7	6	1	9	10	11	145	3	2	1	3
Anthropology	-	-	2	1	1	2	2	1	-	-	-	-	-	1	1	-	-	-	-	1	-	3	9	-	2	3
Psychology	2	1	1	1	-	1	2	2	-	-	1	-	1	1	1	1	1	-	1	-	1	2	-	11	3	4
Amer. Govt.	-	6	12	6	9	8	6	1	8	1	6	7	9	7	2	1	3	-	1	3	2	1	2	3	63	-
Cont. Problems	-	7	15	4	11	10	8	2	8	-	8	8	11	8	-	2	6	2	-	3	1	3	3	4	-	87
Basic Art	2	11	16	2	10	9	7	4	2	3	1	2	2	3	-	-	2	-	1	2	1	22	1	2	13	16
Art Studio	-	2	3	1	2	1	2	1	1	-	-	-	-	-	1	-	-	1	1	-	-	5	-	-	6	6
Latin I	15	2	4	1	5	3	3	2	-	-	-	1	-	13	1	-	-	-	2	-	1	19	-	-	-	1
Latin II	3	2	1	2	1	1	1	1	-	-	-	1	-	3	-	1	-	-	-	1	3	4	1	-	2	2
Spanish I	30	2	3	2	3	4	7	4	1	3	1	1	-	29	2	-	-	-	2	-	1	21	-	-	1	3
Spanish II	5	6	5	2	4	5	5	3	2	2	2	3	2	6	-	1	4	-	1	2	2	27	-	-	3	5
Spanish III	-	1	1	1	-	1	2	-	-	-	-	-	-	-	-	1	-	-	-	-	2	2	-	-	2	4
French I	43	3	5	3	5	6	7	4	4	2	2	2	-	38	-	-	2	-	1	2	2	25	-	-	2	2
French II	3	7	8	3	4	7	9	5	5	2	2	2	-	5	1	2	3	-	2	2	3	34	2	-	4	6
French III	-	4	2	1	-	2	1	-	-	-	-	1	1	2	-	2	-	-	-	1	-	5	1	1	5	6
German I	23	-	-	1	-	1	1	3	-	-	-	1	-	22	1	-	-	-	1	-	1	4	-	-	-	-
German II	-	2	1	1	1	3	3	2	1	2	-	1	-	1	-	3	-	1	-	2	2	18	1	-	1	1
Basic Home Econ.	65	-	1	2	-	-	17	8	1	2	-	-	-	61	1	1	2	-	3	-	4	4	-	2	-	1
Home Ec. Proj.	-	17	12	6	17	7	8	5	11	3	8	2	6	2	-	-	5	-	4	4	1	12	1	2	18	32
Fashion Design	1	5	2	1	2	1	3	-	2	-	1	-	-	1	-	-	1	-	2	1	-	6	-	1	4	4
Band	10	3	2	-	4	3	4	2	3	1	1	2	2	7	-	2	2	-	1	2	1	8	-	1	5	7
Chorus	14	3	3	2	8	2	6	2	8	2	2	1	4	9	1	-	1	1	1	1	-	8	-	2	4	9
Algebra I	27	-	1	1	-	-	5	3	-	-	-	-	-	24	1	-	1	-	1	-	2	2	-	-	-	-
Geometry	72	12	6	4	11	9	26	18	5	11	4	2	-	55	3	2	4	-	2	4	4	42	2	1	3	6
Algebra II	-	22	13	8	16	11	10	13	12	8	5	9	2	3	2	3	1	-	2	4	3	67	3	2	8	13
Math Analysis	-	3	2	1	-	1	2	1	1	-	-	-	1	-	2	4	-	-	-	-	3	1	1	-	7	14
Fund. Math	19	-	-	1	1	1	3	-	-	-	-	-	-	12	-	-	1	-	1	-	1	1	-	-	-	1
Biology	75	2	4	3	4	2	23	17	9	13	2	4	-	46	3	-	4	1	3	2	5	12	3	1	4	5
Chemistry	-	4	3	3	11	9	9	3	2	3	3	2	1	8	1	4	-	-	1	2	3	16	2	2	12	16
Physics	-	1	2	1	7	6	4	2	-	-	-	2	-	5	1	3	-	-	1	3	2	3	1	-	4	14
Electronics	4	2	3	1	2	1	2	-	-	-	-	2	-	3	-	-	-	-	-	-	-	6	1	1	2	4
Driver Training	52	7	4	3	3	1	10	7	2	3	1	2	-	40	2	-	3	-	2	1	2	22	1	-	1	1
Woodwork	-	2	1	-	3	4	3	1	-	-	-	5	1	7	-	-	-	-	-	-	-	11	-	-	4	10
Boys PE 10	85	-	-	-	-	-	22	7	-	-	-	3	-	60	4	-	-	-	6	1	6	-	-	1	-	-
Girls PE 10	78	-	1	2	-	-	25	11	-	6	-	1	-	66	2	-	3	-	7	-	4	-	-	1	-	-
Adv. Boys PE	-	22	13	6	11	5	1	3	-	-	-	6	2	5	-	-	1	-	2	2	3	13	-	1	25	32
Adv. Girls PE	-	4	7	7	4	1	2	6	5	4	-	-	1	2	-	-	3	-	1	2	1	3	-	-	5	10

Attachment C Conflict Matrix for University High School (continued)

Latin I	Latin II	Spanish I	Spanish II	Spanish III	French I	French II	French III	German I	German II	Basic Home Econ.	Home Ec. Proj.	Fashion Design	Band	Chorus	Algebra I	Geometry	Algebra II	Math Analysis	Fund. Math	Biology	Chemistry	Physics	Electronics	Driver Training	Woodwork	Boys PE 10	Girls PE 10	Adv. Boys PE	Adv. Girls PE
15	3	30	5	-	43	3	-	23	-	65	-	1	10	14	27	72	-	-	19	75	-	-	4	52	-	85	78	-	-
2	2	2	6	1	3	7	4	-	2	-	17	5	3	3	-	12	22	3	-	2	4	1	2	7	2	-	-	22	4
4	1	3	5	1	5	8	2	-	1	1	12	2	2	3	1	6	13	2	-	4	3	2	3	4	1	-	1	13	7
1	2	2	2	1	3	3	1	1	1	2	6	1	-	2	1	4	8	1	1	3	3	1	1	3	-	-	2	6	7
5	1	3	4	-	5	4	-	-	1	-	17	2	4	8	-	11	16	-	1	4	11	7	2	3	3	-	-	11	4
3	1	4	5	1	6	7	2	1	3	-	7	1	3	2	-	9	11	1	1	2	9	6	1	1	4	-	-	5	1
3	1	7	5	2	7	9	1	1	3	17	8	3	4	6	5	26	10	2	3	23	9	4	2	10	3	22	25	1	2
2	1	4	3	-	4	5	-	3	2	8	5	-	2	2	3	18	13	1	-	17	3	2	-	7	1	7	11	3	6
-	-	1	2	-	4	5	-	-	1	1	11	2	3	8	-	5	12	1	-	9	2	-	-	2	-	-	-	-	5
-	-	3	2	-	2	2	-	-	2	2	3	-	1	2	-	11	8	-	-	13	3	-	-	3	-	-	6	-	4
-	-	1	2	-	2	2	-	-	-	-	8	1	1	2	-	4	5	-	-	2	3	-	-	1	-	-	-	-	-
1	1	1	3	-	2	2	1	1	1	-	2	-	2	1	-	2	9	-	-	4	2	2	2	2	5	3	1	6	-
-	-	-	2	-	-	-	1	-	-	-	6	-	2	4	-	-	2	1	-	-	1	-	-	-	1	-	-	2	1
13	3	29	6	-	38	5	2	22	1	61	2	1	7	9	24	55	3	-	12	46	8	5	3	40	7	60	66	5	2
1	-	2	-	-	-	1	-	1	-	1	-	-	-	1	1	3	2	2	-	3	1	1	-	2	-	4	2	-	-
-	1	-	1	1	-	2	2	-	3	1	-	-	2	-	-	2	3	4	-	-	4	3	-	-	-	-	-	-	-
-	-	-	4	-	2	3	-	-	-	2	5	1	2	1	1	4	1	-	1	4	-	-	-	3	-	-	3	1	3
-	-	-	-	-	-	-	-	-	1	-	-	-	-	1	-	-	-	-	-	1	-	-	-	-	-	-	-	-	-
2	-	2	1	-	1	2	-	1	-	3	4	2	1	1	1	2	2	-	1	3	1	1	-	2	-	6	7	2	1
-	1	-	2	-	2	2	1	-	2	-	4	1	2	2	-	4	4	-	-	2	2	3	-	1	-	1	-	2	2
1	3	1	2	2	2	3	-	1	2	4	1	-	1	-	2	4	3	3	1	5	3	2	-	2	-	6	4	3	1
19	4	21	27	2	25	34	5	4	18	4	12	6	8	8	2	42	67	1	1	12	16	3	6	22	11	-	-	13	3
-	1	-	-	-	-	2	1	-	1	-	1	-	-	-	-	2	3	1	-	3	2	1	1	1	-	-	-	-	-
-	-	-	-	-	-	-	1	-	-	2	2	1	1	2	-	1	2	-	-	1	2	-	1	-	-	1	1	1	-
-	2	1	3	2	2	4	5	-	1	-	18	4	5	4	-	3	8	7	-	4	12	4	2	1	4	-	-	25	-
1	2	3	5	4	2	6	6	-	1	1	32	4	7	9	-	6	13	14	1	5	16	14	4	1	10	-	-	32	10
1	-	2	3	1	4	3	8	1	5	1	12	3	-	2	6	11	20	3	1	9	2	-	1	4	3	-	1	10	4
-	-	-	-	-	-	2	-	-	1	-	5	2	3	2	-	1	3	-	-	1	2	-	1	-	-	-	-	3	2
35	-	-	-	-	-	1	1	-	-	5	3	-	1	1	3	18	12	2	-	17	7	2	3	8	-	9	4	2	2
-	11	-	-	-	-	-	-	-	-	1	-	-	1	-	-	2	3	1	-	3	4	1	1	4	-	-	2	1	-
-	-	56	-	-	-	1	-	-	-	9	7	1	2	1	5	31	17	1	2	16	11	6	2	10	3	19	10	1	1
-	-	-	41	-	1	-	-	-	-	2	6	1	3	1	-	9	23	1	-	8	9	3	3	6	2	3	2	8	7
-	-	-	-	6	-	-	-	1	-	-	-	-	1	1	-	-	3	-	-	1	2	-	-	-	-	-	-	-	-
-	-	-	1	-	74	-	-	-	1	21	16	3	7	4	8	26	20	2	-	15	11	6	-	14	1	24	16	6	3
1	-	1	-	-	-	48	-	1	-	2	7	1	3	3	-	19	11	4	2	9	9	6	-	2	-	1	2	12	9
1	-	-	-	-	-	-	17	-	2	-	6	1	1	-	-	2	4	3	-	-	2	-	1	2	1	-	-	8	3
-	-	-	-	1	-	1	-	27	-	11	-	-	3	2	3	8	-	1	-	4	3	-	2	11	-	18	5	2	-
-	-	-	-	-	1	-	2	-	20	-	8	1	-	3	-	2	-	5	-	-	-	7	-	5	-	-	-	8	4
5	1	9	2	-	21	2	-	11	-	70	-	-	2	4	2	17	2	-	2	20	-	-	1	13	-	-	59	-	-
3	-	7	6	-	16	7	6	-	8	-	67	2	1	3	-	3	8	4	-	4	7	1	-	-	-	-	-	-	11
-	-	1	1	-	3	1	1	-	1	-	2	15	-	-	-	1	2	2	-	3	3	-	-	1	-	-	1	-	2
1	1	2	3	1	7	3	1	3	-	2	1	-	31	-	2	5	9	3	3	2	-	1	1	-	-	9	1	2	2
1	-	1	1	1	4	3	-	2	3	4	3	-	-	35	4	3	8	1	3	-	1	1	-	-	3	8	6	-	1
3	-	5	-	-	8	-	-	3	-	2	-	-	2	4	29	-	-	-	-	5	5	-	2	7	-	21	4	-	-
18	2	31	9	-	26	19	2	8	2	17	3	1	5	3	-	125	-	-	-	22	12	-	2	37	5	44	24	4	1
12	3	17	23	3	20	11	4	-	-	2	8	2	9	8	-	-	94	-	-	3	9	-	10	11	13	-	-	18	5
2	1	1	1	-	2	4	3	1	5	-	4	2	3	1	-	-	-	23	-	-	3	19	3	-	3	-	-	1	-
-	-	2	-	-	-	2	-	-	-	2	-	-	3	3	-	-	-	-	22	16	-	-	6	12	-	12	5	2	1
17	3	16	8	1	15	9	-	4	-	20	4	3	2	-	5	22	3	-	16	96	-	-	-	2	-	41	26	1	-
7	4	11	9	2	11	9	2	3	-	-	7	3	-	1	5	12	9	3	-	-	47	-	-	1	-	-	-	-	-
2	1	6	3	-	6	6	-	-	7	-	1	-	1	1	-	-	-	19	-	-	-	24	2	1	-	-	-	-	-
3	1	2	3	-	-	-	1	2	-	1	-	-	1	-	2	2	10	3	6	-	-	2	17	-	-	3	-	2	-
8	4	10	6	-	14	2	2	11	5	13	-	1	-	-	7	37	11	-	12	2	1	1	-	76	9	28	20	-	-
-	-	3	2	-	1	-	1	-	-	-	-	-	-	3	-	5	13	3	-	-	-	-	-	9	26	-	-	24	-
9	-	19	3	-	24	1	-	18	-	-	-	-	9	8	21	44	-	-	12	41	-	-	3	28	-	87	-	-	-
4	2	10	2	-	16	2	-	5	-	59	-	1	1	6	4	24	-	-	5	26	-	-	-	20	-	-	79	-	-
2	1	1	8	-	6	12	8	2	8	-	-	-	2	-	-	4	18	1	2	1	-	-	2	-	24	-	-	63	-
2	-	1	7	-	3	9	3	-	4	-	11	2	2	1	-	1	5	-	1	-	-	-	-	-	-	-	-	-	30

both total and grade-level student distribution by period are indicated on this sample schedule. This distribution seems to present a workable base for satisfying the student course requests summarized in Attachments A and C.

Attachment D Master Schedule Worksheet for University High School

TEACHER	PERIOD					
	1	2	3	4	5	6
Cook		Shorthand	Advanced Shorthand			
Esmoris						
Hall		Plan				
Lackman			Plan	Lunch Supervision	Debate	Advanced Debate
Molitor					Distributive Education	Distributive Education
Parker	Plan			Drama Adv. Drama		
Sabol		Plan				
Sutherland		Plan				
Dodd	--	--	--	--		Chorus
Engelson	Art Studio	Art Studio				
Johnson						
Marshall		Spanish II/III				
Morgan	Plan			German I		
Shean						
Turpen				French III		
Warner						
Wiese	World History					
Estep				Physics	Woodwork	Electronics
Flynn	Plan					
Kuehn						Plan
Ronhaar					Accreditation Planning	Plan
Russell						Plan
Schindele						
Tucker						

Attachment E Sample Master Schedule for University High School

TEACHER	PERIOD					
	1	2	3	4	5	6
Cook	19 Adv. Typing 0 11 8	24 Shorthand 6 17 1	17 Adv. Shorthand 0 3 14	23 Typing 2 9 13 1	19 Adv. Typing 0 11 8	Plan
Esmoris	23 Typing 2 9 13 1	25 Eng. 10 25 0 0	27 Typing 1 16 6 5	Plan	27 Typing 1 16 6 5	27 Typing 1 16 6 5
Hall	25 Eng. 10 25 0 0	Plan	27 Minority Opinion 2 15 10	27 Minority Opinion 2 15 10	21 Lang. of Belief 0 11 10	21 Lang. of Belief 0 11 10
Lackman	23 Journalism 13 9 1	18 Annual 1 10 7	Plan	Lunch Supervision	12 Debate 6 4 2	11 Adv. Debate 0 7 4
Molitor	27 Speech 22 3 2	27 Bookkeeping 4 7 16	Plan	27 Speech 22 3 2	21 Distributive Education 0 0 21	21 Distributive Education 0 0 21
Parker	Plan	27 Speech 22 3 2	27 Speech 22 3 2	22 Drama Adv. Drama 3 7 12	27 Speech 22 3 2	27 Speech 22 3 2
Sabol	25 Eng. 10 25 0 0	Plan	26 Lang. of Laughter 0 12 14	25 Eng. 10 25 0 0	27 American Literature 2 15 10	26 Lang. of Laughter 0 12 14
Sutherland	27 Creative Writing 1 19 7	Plan	25 Eng. 10 25 0 0	27 Creative Writing 1 19 7	25 Eng. 10 25 0 0	25 Eng. 10 25 0 0
Dodd	---	---	---	---	31 Band 10 9 12	35 Chorus 14 8 13
Engelson	18 Art Studio 0 5 13	18 Art Studio 0 5 13	28 Basic Art 1 12 15	28 Basic Art 1 12 15	Plan	15 Fashion Design 1 6 8
Johnson	Plan	23 H.E. Proj. 0 5 18	23 H.E. Proj. 0 5 18	23 H.E. Proj. 0 5 18	23 Basic H.E. 21 2 0	23 Basic H.E. 21 2 0
Marshall	23 Spanish II 5 18 0	24 Spanish II/III 0 12 12	28 Spanish I 15 11 2	Plan	23 Basic H.E. 21 2 0	28 Spanish I 15 11 2
Morgan	Plan	24 U.S./World History 0 24 0	24 U.S./World History 0 24 0	27 German I 23 4 0	20 German II 0 18 2	24 U.S./World History 0 24 0
Shean	29 Contemp. Problems 0 1 28	11 Psychology 2 2 7	11 Latin II 3 4 4	18 Latin I 8 9 1	18 Latin I 8 9 1	Plan
Turpeh	19 French I 11 7 1	24 French II 2 17 5	19 French I 11 7 1	17 French III 0 6 11	19 French I 11 7 1	24 French II 2 17 5
Warner	29 Contemp. Problems 0 1 28	24 U.S./World History 0 24 0	24 U.S./World History 0 24 0	29 Contemp. Problems 0 1 28	Plan	24 U.S./World History 0 24 0
Wiese	24 World History 10 11 3	21 American Government 0 0 21	21 American Government 0 0 21	19 French I 11 7 1	21 American Government 0 0 21	Plan
Estep	Plan	25 Biology 19 3 3	25 Biology 19 3 3	24 Physics 0 5 19	26 Woodwork 0 12 14	17 Electronics 4 7 6
Flynn	Plan	32 Advanced Boys P.E. 0 7 25	13 Driver Training 9 4 0	13 Driver Training 9 4 0	32 Advanced Boys P.E. 0 7 25	13 Driver Training 9 4 0
Kuehn	23 Algebra II 0 18 5	23 Math Analysis 0 2 21	31 Geometry 18 11 2	31 Geometry 18 11 2	31 Geometry 18 11 2	Plan
Ronhaar	13 Driver Training 9 4 0	22 Fund. Math 19 1 2	24 Chemistry 0 10 14	24 Chemistry 0 10 14	Accreditation Plan	Plan
Russell	29 Boys P.E. 10 28 1 0	13 Driver Training 9 4 0	29 Boys P.E. 10 28 1 0	29 Boys P.E. 10 28 1 0	13 Driver Training 9 4 0	Plan
Schindele	23 Algebra II 0 18 5	29 Algebra I 27 2 0	Plan	31 Geometry 18 11 2	23 Algebra II 0 18 5	23 Algebra II 0 18 5
Tucker	25 Biology 19 3 3	40 Girls P.E. 10 39 1 0	30 Advanced Girls P.E. 0 3 27	Plan	25 Biology 19 3 3	40 Girls P.E. 10 39 1 0
TOTALS	424 (1) 177 142 105	474 (2) 175 146 153	479 (3) 169 153 152	464 (4) 178 143 143	484 (5) 188 152 144	424 (6) 168 161 95

APPENDIX 3

COMPUTER PROGRAM FOR COURSE TALLY AND CONFLICT MATRIX

The BASIC program listing of Attachment A has two parts. First is the program itself, written in BASIC language (Version 3.4), and second is the sample data file. This particular version of the program is limited to ten courses but it can be expanded by simply extending the dimension statements and modifying the printed output formats. The program presented here is designed for batch processing; however, with minor adjustments, it can be adapted to interactive data input. The course tally and conflict matrix generated by this particular program listing are presented following the sample data file.

The printout of Attachment B is exactly as generated by the program listing (including sample data file). Notice in the sample data file a total of seven classes are offered and all but one of the six students signs up for the allowable five classes. This one student is signed up for only four classes. This is of course why the total student course enrollment is 29 instead of 30 on the program output of Attachment B.

Attachment A Program and Data File Listing

```
00100 REM THIS PARTICULAR PROGRAM GENERATES A SIMPLE TALLY AND
00110 REM CONFLICT MATRIX.  AS WRITTEN, THE PROGRAM IS LIMITED TO
00120 REM TEN COURSES.  DATA STATEMENTS BEGIN AT LINE 1500 AND
00130 REM PROCEED WITH SCHOOL NAME, COURSE NUMBERS, NUMBER OF COURSE
00140 REM REQUESTS PER STUDENT, AND THE ACTUAL REQUESTS MADE BY THE
00150 REM STUDENTS.  ANY STUDENT TAKING FEWER COURSES THAN THE
00160 REM DESIGNATED NUMBER MUST HAVE ZERO PLACEHOLDERS IN THE
00170 REM COURSE REQUEST LISTING.
00180 DIM T(10,10),A(11),A$(10),D(10),B$(10),C$(10)
00190 FOR I=1 TO 10
00200 FOR J=1 TO 10
00210 T(I,J)=0
00220 NEXT J
00230 NEXT I
00240 READ N$
00250 L=0
00260 FOR I=1 TO 11
00270 READ A(I)
00280 IF A(I)=0 THEN 00310
00290 L=L+1
00300 NEXT I
00310 FOR I=1 TO L
00320 READ A$(I)
00330 NEXT I
00340 N=0
00350 READ S
00360 REM WHEN NO MORE STUDENT COURSE REQUESTS ARE REMAINING IN DATA
00370 REM FILE, CONTROL TRANSFERS TO LINE 730 AND THE TWO REPORTS--
00380 REM COURSE TALLY AND CONFLICT MATRIX--ARE PRINTED.
00390 NODATA 00730
00400 C=0
00410 FOR I=1 TO S
00420 READ D(I)
00430 IF D(I)=0 THEN 00460
00440 C=C+1
00450 NEXT I
00460 N=N+1
00470 REM WHEN STUDENT REQUESTS A LISTED COURSE, THE SEQUENCE NUMBER
00480 REM OF THAT COURSE IS IDENTIFIED AS "M" AND ITS CONFLICTS WITH
00490 REM OTHER COURSE ARE THEN RECORDED.  THIS RECORDING PROCESS
00500 REM TAKES PLACE IN LINES 640-700.  IF A NONLISTED COURSE
00510 REM IS REQUESTED, THIS FACT IS PRINTED OUT AND THE PROGRAM
00520 REM TERMINATES.
00530 FOR I=1 TO C
00540 M=0
00550 FOR J=1 TO L
00560 IF D(I)<>A(J9 THEN 00590
00570 M=J
00580 GOTO 00640
00590 NEXT J
```

Attachment A Program and Data File Listing (continued)

```
00600 PRINT USING  00610,D(I),N
00610 :     IMPROPER NUMBER FOR COURSE ## FOR STUDENT ###.
00620 PRINT "       PROGRAM TERMINATED."
00630 GOTO 01390
00640 FOR K=1 TO C
00650 FOR J=1 TO L
00660 IF D(K)<>A(J) THEN 00690
00670 T(M,J)=T(M,J)+1
00680 GOTO 00700
00690 NEXT J
00700 NEXT K
00710 NEXT I
00720 GOTO 00390
00730 FOR J=1 TO L
00740 S=LEN(A$(J))
00750 IF S>10 THEN 00790
00760 C$(J)=A$(J)(1:8)
00770 B$(J)=""
00780 GOTO 00810
00790 B$(J)=A$(J)(1:8)
00800 C$(J)=A$(J)(9:16)
00810 NEXT J
00820 PRINT USING  00830,N$
00830 :COURSE TALLY FOR <########################
00840 PRINT
00850 PRINT
00860 T=0
00870 PRINT "        COURSE                     ENROLLMENT"
00880 PRINT
00890 FOR I=1 TO L
00900 PRINT USING  00910,A(I),A$(I),T(I,I)
00910 :    [##] ################    ###,###
00920 T=T+T(I,I)
00930 PRINT
00940 NEXT I
00950 PRINT USING  00960,T
00960 :          TOTAL                  ###,###
00970 FOR I=1 TO 6
00980 PRINT
00990 NEXT I
01000 PRINT USING  01010,N$
01010 :CONFLICT MATRIX FOR <########################
01020 MARGIN 130
01030 PRINT
01040 PRINT
01050 Q=26
01060 FOR J=1 TO L
01070 PRINT TAB(Q);"[";A(J);"]";
01080 Q=Q+9
01090 NEXT J
```

Attachment A Program and Data File Listing (continued)

```
01100 PRINT
01110 Q=24
01120 FOR J=1 TO L
01130 PRINT TAB(Q);B$(J);
01140 Q=Q+9
01150 NEXT J
01160 Q=24
01170 PRINT
01180 FOR J=1 TO L
01190 PRINT TAB(Q);C$(J);
01200 Q=Q+9
01210 NEXT J
01220 PRINT
01230 PRINT
01240 FOR I=1 TO L
01250 PRINT USING  01260,A(I),A$(I);
01260 :[##]>################
01270 Q=27
01280 FOR J=1 TO L
01290 PRINT TAB(Q);T(I,J);
01300 Q=Q+9
01310 NEXT J
01320 PRINT
01330 PRINT
01340 NEXT I
01350 FOR I=1 TO 5
01360 PRINT
01370 NEXT I
01380 PRINT "END OF PROGRAM"
01390 STOP
```

SAMPLE DATA FILE

```
1500 DATA IMAGINATION HIGH SCHOOL
1501 DATA 1,2,3,4,5,6,7,0
1502 DATA MATH ANALYSIS
1503 DATA SPANISH
1504 DATA GEOMETRY
1505 DATA WORLD HISTORY
1506 DATA CHEMISTRY
1507 DATA ENGLISH
1508 DATA BUSINESS MACHINES
1509 DATA 5
1511 DATA 1,2,4,5,6
1512 DATA 2,3,4,5,6
1513 DATA 1,3,5,6,7
1514 DATA 2,3,5,6,0
1515 DATA 4,3,6,1,7
1516 DATA 1,2,3,5,6
```

Attachment B Program Output

```
COURSE TALLY FOR IMAGINATION HIGH SCHOOL

        COURSE                  ENROLLMENT

    [ 1] MATH ANALYSIS               4

    [ 2] SPANISH                     4

    [ 3] GEOMETRY                    5

    [ 4] WORLD HISTORY               3

    [ 5] CHEMISTRY                   5

    [ 6] ENGLISH                     6

    [ 7] BUSINESS MACHINES           2

         TOTAL                      29
```

CONFLICT MATRIX FOR IMAGINATION HIGH SCHOOL

	[1] MATH ANA LYSIS	[2] SPANISH	[3] GEOMETRY	[4] WORLD HI STORY	[5] CHEMISTR	[6] ENGLISH	[7] BUSINESS MACHINE
[1] MATH ANALYSIS	4	2	3	2	3	4	2
[2] SPANISH	2	4	3	2	4	4	0
[3] GEOMETRY	3	3	5	2	4	5	2
[4] WORLD HISTORY	2	2	2	3	2	3	1
[5] CHEMISTRY	3	4	4	2	5	5	1
[6] ENGLISH	4	4	5	3	5	6	2
[7] BUSINESS MACHINES	2	0	2	1	1	2	2

END OF PROGRAM

APPENDIX 4

MONITORING TIME UTILIZATION

The first step in analyzing administrative time utilization is a careful assessment of current practice, which is most helpful when approached with certain hypotheses about current time-utilization problems or at least certain areas of concern in relation to time use. These hypotheses or areas of concern are especially helpful in arriving at a set of descriptive categories to be used in the time-monitoring process. One specific set of categories used in a national survey is presented in Table 5–2 of the text; however, these categories are not likely to be of much use to an administrator who is concerned about such common problems as "excessive time on the telephone," "drop-in conferences with staff," or "not enough time for classroom observations." Unless these areas of concern are specifically identified as a focus for time-monitoring activities, there is little chance that any reliable reading on current time-utilization patterns can be obtained.

This importance of the specific categories used in monitoring time is perhaps best illustrated by comparing three sets of categories as follows:

Set A
1. Mail and filing (including dictation)
2. Independent planning and reading
3. Meetings/group planning
4. Conferring with individual staff members
5. Conferring with individual students
6. Public relations/social
7. Telephone calls
8. Personal growth and development
9. Travel
10. Other

Set B
1. Group meetings
2. Scheduled conferences
3. Drop-in conferences
4. Telephone calls
5. Preparing reports/planning
6. Correspondence (reading mail, dictating letters, etc.)
7. Classroom observations
8. Tracking information
9. Travel
10. Professional growth and development
11. Reviewing work of others
12. Other

Set C
1. Communicating with students
2. Communicating with parents
3. Communicating with building professional staff
4. Communicating with building classified staff
5. Communicating with administrators/teachers in other buildings
6. Communicating with central office personnel
7. Responding to mail
8. Classroom observations
9. Quiet planning activities
10. Professional growth and development
11. Travel
12. Other

Set A might be useful for an administrator who is interested in isolating the amount of time spent on independent planning and reading or on telephone calls. Set B does not do a particularly good job of isolating the independent planning and reading time (as Category 5 in Set B does not separate independent from group planning) but it could be used in examining the comparative time spent on scheduled versus drop-in conferences or in isolating the amount of time given to telephone calls or classroom observations of teachers. In the categories of Set C, we see an attempt to break communications down according to the group being communicated with. This might be useful for an administrator who is concerned about spending too much or too little time working with a particular client group. Set C also makes explicit provision for monitoring quiet planning time and could be used to assess the administrator's ability to protect such time as part of the regular working day.

An illustration using data provided by an elementary school principal shows how one of these sets can be used in monitoring time utilization in a given administrative position. The procedure suggested here calls for completing three separate forms; however, all forms or parts are not required in using the time-analysis procedure. The three parts, along with a sample time log, are presented as Attachments A and B to this Appendix.

In completing Part I of Attachment A the administrator is encouraged to give some thought to major goals and activities for the week and for each day. Section B of this goal identification process is essentially a daily To-Do List and should be helpful in keeping the daily activities focused on the most important tasks.

Part II is designed to encourage an advance review of time allocation across the specific set of categories selected. In the particular example included here, note that Set B is selected as the appropriate set of time categories. This is based on the principal's desire to see if "drop-in conferences" and "telephone calls" are occupying excessive amounts of time. Analysis of the time log (Part III) did, in fact, show this to be the case, as the principal preferred an allocation of 15 percent to these two areas but actually spent over 35 percent. With a conscious effort to reduce time spent in these two activities, this particular principal may be able to come closer to the preferred time allocation.

In Part III, the administrator summarizes the daily time allocations as recorded in the time log. Notice that this elementary principal put in a working week of 47¾ hours (2,865/60). As expected, there exists considerable fluctuation in time allocation from day to day due to the varying priority activities established for the different days. Because of these daily fluctuations, it is probably best for the administrator to maintain the time log for a full two-week period before reaching any firm conclusions about characteristic time-utilization patterns. The administrator should also avoid first and last days of school and other times that would not accurately reflect the general time-utilization patterns.

On the time log of Attachment B, it should be noted that the fifteen-minute intervals can be subdivided further. This will be required particularly for items such as telephone calls, which generally occupy less than the full fifteen-minute time segment. Most administrators using the time log find that time use needs to be recorded three or four times each day. The average administrator simply cannot remember the use of each fifteen-minute segment of time at the end of the school day; but can, with the help of the appointments calendar, remember such allocation over the past two or three hours.

Notice in the time log presented here that abbreviations are quite proper. Also, no matter what set of categories is used, there will always be activities that do not quite fit any of the designated descriptions. This is the reason an "other" category is almost always needed. In the particular case presented here, "other" was used primarily for "discussions over lunch in the faculty room" and "setting up for a PTA meeting." These latter items could, of course, be used as basic functional categories in a future time log.

Attachment A Suggested Form for Planning and Analyzing Time Utilization

PART I: IDENTIFY MAJOR GOALS AND/OR ACTIVITIES

A. Major Goals for Week

1. *Prepare for PTA speaker series*
2. *Set up procedures for hiring 5th grade teacher*
3. *Midyear observations/conferences for at least five teachers*
4.
5.

B. Goals/Activities for Each Day

	MONDAY	TUESDAY	WEDNESDAY	THURSDAY	FRIDAY
Planned Activities*	1. *Enrol. update* 2. *Meet with Fred (1)* 3. *Adv. Council* 4. *Obs. two teachers (3)* 5.	1. *Team problem* 2. *Conf. with two teachers (3)* 3. *PTA Newsletter (1)* 4. 5.	1. *Set up PTA (1)* 2. *Released time for teacher* 3. *Review bus problem* 4. *Complete position desc. (2)* 5.	1. *Obs./conf. two teachers (3)* 2. *Review bus problem* 3. *Conf. with Gorman (3)* 4. 5.	1. *Obs. two teachers (3)* 2. *Conf. with Gorman (3)* 3. *Bus Problem* 4. *Complete position desc. (2)* 5.
Completion Record**	1. *c* 2. *c* 3. *c* 4. *p* 5.	1. *p* 2. *c* 3. *c* 4. 5.	1. *c* 2. *c* 3. *p* 4. *p* 5.	1. *p* 2. *c* 3. *n* 4. 5.	1. *p* 2. *c* 3. *c* 4. *n* 5.

*Activities are scheduled for each day. When these scheduled activities relate to one of the weekly goals, this can be indicated by recording in parentheses the number of the goal statement in Part A.

**In each case, the activity is judged to be completed (c), partially completed (p), or not completed at all (n).

PART II: PREFERRED AND ACTUAL TIME ALLOCATIONS

Category	Preferred*	Actual**
1. *Group Meetings (3 or more persons)*	*6*	*11.0*
2. *Scheduled Conferences*	*14*	*9.2*
3. *Drop-in Conferences*	*8*	*19.6*
4. *Telephone Calls*	*7*	*17.9*
5. *Preparing Reports and Planning*	*15*	*4.3*

*This column is filled in prior to completing the time log. These estimates on preferred time allocation should be based, in part, on the projected goals/activities identified in Part I.

**These figures are based on the actual time allocation as computed in Part III.

Attachment A (continued)

6. *Correspondence(reading mail, dictating, etc.)*	10	1.9
7. *Classroom Observations(incl. follow-up conf.)*	15	15.4
8. *Tracking Information*	5	2.9
9. *Travel*	5	.5
10. *Professional Growth and Development*	6	1.3
11. *Reviewing Work Done By Others*	4	3.9
12. *Other*	5	12.2

PART III: ANALYSIS OF TIME LOG (in minutes)

CATEGORY	MONDAY	TUESDAY	WEDNESDAY	THURSDAY	FRIDAY	TOTAL	
						NUMBER	PERCENT*
1. *Group Meetings*	60	0	195	0	60	315	11.0
2. *Scheduled Conf.*	23	15	45	52	128	263	9.2
3. *Drop-in Conf.*	101	115	121	140	85	562	19.6
4. *Telephone Calls*	100	75	140	95	102	512	17.9
5. *Prep. Reports/Plan*	40	22	35	10	15	122	4.3
6. *Correspondence*	0	15	10	30	0	55	1.9
7. *Class. Obs.*	45	173	37	187	0	442	15.4
8. *Tracking Inf.*	33	7	17	18	8	83	2.9
9. *Travel*	0	0	0	0	15	15	.5
10. *Prof. Growth*	0	37	0	0	0	37	1.3
11. *Rev. Work of Other*	85	10	0	0	17	112	3.9
12. *Other*	53	86	135	53	20	347	12.2

*Percent figures are recorded in Part II where they can be compared with the "preferred" time allocation.

Attachment B Suggested Form For Time Log—using sample data for elementary principal

	TIME	MONDAY	C	TUESDAY	C	WEDNESDAY	C	THURSDAY	C	FRIDAY	C
REGULAR WORKING DAY	7:30							Duplicator Repair	12		
		Patterson/Faletto	3-7 2-8	Check on Heat Problem	12	Craig/Bus Problem	4	"	12		
	8:00	Faletto	2	"	12	Burnell	4	Wells	3		
		Begley/Quam	3-10 4-5	Call to Maintenance/Bulletin Review	4-5 11-10	Store	12	Nina B.	3		
	8:30	Begley	3	Warehouse Call Heat Problem	4-5 12-10	Patterson/Hartung	7-7 3-8	Nina B./Molnan	3-8 2-7		
		Wilson/Lomax	12-10 4-5	Bill Check/Heat Check	8-7 12-8	Nystrom/Kitchen	4	Cosley/Orig	8-8 3-7	Brown Call/Murphy	4-5 11-10
	9:00	Prepare Bulletin/Rose	5-10 4-5	Nystrom	3	S.W. Area/Levy Vote	4	H. Johnson	2	Bus Problem	1
		Wilson/Personnel Call	12-10 4-5	Lomax/Heat	10-7 12-8	Barb/Nat	8-7 3-8	"	2	"	1
	9:30	Nystrom on PTA	11	Wilson	7	Coffee	12	"	2	Begley	2-8 11-7
		"	11	"	7	Pugh	7	Murphy/Daryl S.	3-10 4-5	Coffee/Faith	12-10 4-5
	10:00	Begley/Portable Information	3-7 8-8	PTA Letter	5	Dexis/Nyre	4-5 3-10	Wright	7	Begley/Carmichael	12-7 8-8
		Nat Steen	3	Letter/Wilson	5-7 7-8	Home/S.W. Area	4	"	7	Carmichael	4
	10:30	Faculty Room	12	Lomax/Wilson	7	Brown	4	"	7	Carmichael/Bowns	2
		Rodis/Victor	4-5 3-10	Lomax/Wilson	7	Catshall	3	"	7	"	2
	11:00	Students	3	Wilson	2	Burnell/Price	4-5 3-10	B. Pinnick	7	"	2
		Student Council	3	Return Calls	4	Price/Andrews	3-10 4-5	A. Tang.	12	Begley/Skeen	1
	11:30	Sandy/Reading	4-5 8-10	Wright	7	PO Check/Andrews	8-10 4-5	Burnell/Ringstad	4	"	1
		Faletto/Gorman	11-7 12-8	Thoren	7	Maintenance	3	Wright	7	Travel to ESC	9
	2:00	Enrollment Information	8	"	7	PTA	3	J. Thoren	3	Sandy T./Wells	4-5 3-10
		PTA Announcement/Parent Call	11-10 4-5	"	7	Mary B.	4	Karn	3	Bowns	4
	12:30	Film Company	12-10 4-5	Faculty Room	12	D. Costey	2	"	3	Transport	4
		Lawrence/Clark	4	"	12	"	2	Playground	7	Sandy T./H. Gacek	4-12 12-3
	1:00	Nystrom/Murphy	4	Playground	7	J. Thoren	2	"	7	Elliott	2
		Student/ITIP	3-7 5-8	"	7	CIP	3	"	7	Allen/Cairns	2
	1:30	ITIP Obs.	5-7 7-8	West	7	CIP	3	Burnell/Ringstad	4	"	2
		"	7	Area Offices	4	Burnell/Report	4-5 5-10	J. Watson	7	Gorman	3
	2:00	"	7	Student Conf./N.E. Area	3-10 4-5	Position Desc.	5	"	7	Moore	3
		ITIP/Faith	7-7 11-8	N.E. Area Call	4	Burnell/Rel. Time	4-5 6-10	J. Thoren	7	Gliva	3
	2:30	Advisory Council	1	PTA News	6	Bus Session	7	Watson/Bus	7-7 12-8	Student Council	2
		"	1	Mail	10	S.W. Area Call/Letter	4-5 5-10	Burnell/Ringstad	4	Held	3
	3:00	"	1	Faith	10	PTA Preparation	12	Cosley/Wells	3	Gorman	3
		"	1	Galetti Call	4	"	12	Wilson	3	Grade Assgn.	5
	3:30	Janice R.	11	J. Thoren	3	"	12	Bagley/Murphy	4-5 3-10	Grove	2
		"	11	"	3	"	12	Memo to J. Brown	6	Burnell	4
	4:00	SW/Area	4	"	3	"	12	"	6		
		"	4	"	3	"	12	Sandy T./Home	8-10 4-5		
	4:30	Minutes of Advisory Council	5	"	3	"	12	Ringstad/ASB	4-5 5-10		
				"	3	PTA Speaker Series	1				
EVENING WORK ACTIVITIES	7:00					PTA Speaker Series	1				
						"	1				
	7:30					"	1			J. West	4
						"	1				
	8:00					"	1	Renee/Colleran	4		
						"	1	District Maintenance	4		
	8:30					"	1				
						"	1				
	9:00					"	1				
						"	1				
	9:30					"	1				
						"	1				

APPENDIX 5

COMPARABILITY OF PERCENT-EQUALIZING, DISTRICT-POWER-EQUALIZING, AND GUARANTEED-VALUATION PLANS OF DISTRIBUTION

In Chapter 8, mention was made of comparability of the three plans of District Power Equalizing (DPE), Percent Equalizing and Guaranteed Valuation. Several states currently employ a modification of one of these equalizing distribution plans. This particular presentation attempts to demonstrate the mathematical equivalence of the three plans and should help the reader to understand the interrelationship between the formulas used in connection with these same funding plans. In establishing equivalence for the plans, we begin with the percent-equalizing formula similar to that presented in the text:

$$S_i = C_i\left[1 - k\left(\frac{y_i}{y}\right)\right] \qquad (1)$$

where S_i = state aid per student in District i
C_i = total expenditure per student in District i
y_i = assessed value per student in District i
y = average assessed value per student for state
k = scaling factor representing local share of total expenditure support for a district of average wealth

First, notice that by expanding the formula, we can express the state aid in the ith district (S_i) as a total expenditure support level (C_i) less some multiple of the assessed valuation per student in that same district:

$$S_i = C_i - \frac{kC_i}{y} \cdot y_i \qquad (2)$$

Since the total support for education in the ith district (C_i) is equal to the sums of the state aid (S_i) and the local contribution, we conclude that this multiple of assessed valuation in Equation 2, namely, the term $(kC_i/y)y_i$, must be the local contribution to school support. We identify this term as L_i and observe that kC_i/y must be the local tax rate in District i which we name r_i. This observation that $r_i = kC_i/y$ is true simply because any expression that when multiplied by the assessed value gives L_i must necessarily be the tax effort or rate.

A second area of interest at this point is the explicit identification of k as representing the proportion of total expenditure support (C_i) covered by the local district in a community of average wealth. This is seen by beginning with the formula for L_i from Equation 2 above. We then equate y_i/y to 1, as it certainly would be in a community of average wealth:

$$L_i = k \frac{y_i}{y} \cdot C_i$$

or

$$L_i = k \cdot C_i \qquad (\text{when } \frac{y_i}{y} = 1)$$

Notice here that k is necessarily the percentage of total expenditure support (C_i) raised from the designated local tax in a district of average wealth. Having demonstrated these two important characteristics of the percent-equalizing formula in Equation 1 above, we can now show the equivalence between this percent-equalizing formula and the DPE table presented in Chapter 8.

EQUIVALENCE OF PERCENT-EQUALIZING AND DPE PLANS

Remembering from Equation 2 above that $r_i = kC_i/y$ (with r_i equal to the local tax rate under a percent-equalizing formula), we conclude that $C_i = (y/k)r_i$. Using this equation, we conclude that cost figures on a DPE-type tax table (at least one of the linear type) can always be structured as a set of multiples of y/k as follows:

TAX RATE	GUARANTEED LEVEL OF EXPENDITURE
.001	$y/k \times .001$
.002	$y/k \times .002$
.003	$y/k \times .003$
.	.
.	.
.	.
r	$y/k \times$ r

Using the values of $y = 95{,}625$ and $k = .45$ and adjusting for the fact that tax rates are actual (rather than dollars per thousand of assessed value), we arrive at the exact tax table used as a basis for Figure 8–5 in the text. Notice that each additional increment of tax rate generates another basic increment of cost, which in this example from the text is $212.50.

The equivalence of the percent-equalizing formula and the DPE tax table is demonstated now as we work backward from the table to compute the amount of state aid in a District i with an assessed valuation y_i. We begin with the assumption that state aid (S_i) is the total guarantee (C_i) less the amount raised by the local tax rate specified in the DPE tax table. This logic along with the fact that $C_i = (y/k)r_i$ (from the structure of the DPE tax table itself) permits us to essentially build the formula for state support directly from the DPE tax table:

$$\begin{aligned} S_i &= C_i - r_i \cdot y_i \\ &= C_i - \frac{k}{y}\ C_i \cdot y_i \\ &= C_i - C_i\left(k \cdot \frac{y_i}{y}\right) \\ &= C_i\left[1 - k\left(\frac{y_i}{y}\right)\right] \end{aligned}$$

Note that the derived formula for state aid using the DPE tax table is the same as Equation 1 and hence the two plans are demonstrated to be one and the same.

EQUIVALENCE OF PERCENT-EQUALIZING AND GUARANTEED-VALUATION PLANS

Before attempting to show equivalence between the percent-equalizing and guaranteed-valuation plans, there is need to explain in more detail the basic structure of the guaranteed-valuation plan. As currently used in several states, this plan essentially guarantees each district the expenditure level obtained by a particular assessed valuation per student. The budgetary requirements of the district are compared with this guaranteed assessed value to determine the required local tax rate. This computed tax rate is then applied to the local assessed value to determine the local contribution. The state picks up the difference between the total budgetary requirement and the amount raised locally.

As an illustration of this guaranteed-valuation plan, let us assume the state guaranteed valuation to be $212,500 per student and compute the state aid for a district having an assessed value of $75,000 per student. If this district decides on an expenditure level of $1,700 per student, we compute the required local tax rate by dividing the amount of the total budget ($1,700) by the guaranteed valuation ($212,500). Applying the resulting tax rate of .008 (or $8 per thousand) to the assessed value of $75,000 per student, we arrive at a local share of $600 per student. This means that state aid in this case will be $1,100 per student. Notice that the figures exactly match the DPE computation for District A illustrated in Figure 8-5. Using the same guaranteed valuation figure of $212,500 per student, one could compute the state share for District B, thus again demonstrating the same results from the particular DPE and guaranteed valuation models.

Since our interest here is in showing equivalence for the more general case, we begin with the generalized percent-equalizing formula presented earlier and show that the local tax rate using this formula is as described above for the guaranteed valuation plan. Starting with Equation 2, we compute the local tax rate (r_i) to be:

$$r_i = \frac{kC_i}{y} = \frac{C_i}{y/k}$$

Notice here that the local tax rate under the percent-equalizing formula is obtained by taking the total budget or expenditure support level (C_i) and dividing by the ratio of the average assessed value for the state (y) and the portion of total costs covered in a district of average wealth (k). It is reasonable to view this ratio, y/k as being a guaranteed local valuation inherent in the percent-equalizing formula. This is so because the total budget or expenditure support level (C_i) is the amount of money raised when a tax rate of r_i is applied to a valuation of y/k per student. Application of this tax rate is shown as follows:

$$r_i \cdot \frac{y}{k} = \frac{kC_i}{y} \bullet \frac{y}{k} = C_i$$

Note that y/k does indeed operate as a guaranteed valuation because any district willing to levy a tax rate of r_i, under the percent-equalizing formula, is assured an expenditure support level (C_i). Since this latter statement exactly describes the way in which the guaranteed valuation plan works, the equivalency of the two plans is established and y/k is the guaranteed valuation.

A more direct way of establishing equivalency of the two plans is to observe that, under the guaranteed valuation plan, the product of the local tax rate (r_i) and the guaranteed valuation (V) is equal to the total expenditure support level (C_i). Thus, $C_i = r_iV$. Solving for r_i, we conclude that the local tax rate under the guaranteed valuation plan is simply C_i/V. The total local contribution is therefore $C_i/V \bullet y_i$. Equating this local contribution to that associated with Equation 2 above for the percent equalizing formula, we then solve for V as follows:

$$\frac{C_i}{V} \cdot y_i = \frac{kC_i}{y} \cdot y_i$$

$$\frac{1}{V}(C_iy_i) = \frac{k}{y}(C_iy_i)$$

$$\frac{1}{V} = \frac{k}{y}$$

$$V = \frac{y}{k}$$

This indicates that the two plans are equivalent any time we set the guaranteed valuation (V) equal to the state average assessed valuation (y) divided by the scaling factor (k).

CONCLUSION

We have established equivalency between the percent-equalizing formula and each of the other two plans—DPE when the expenditure guarantees are tax rate multiples of y/k and guaranteed valuation when the guaranteed valuation itself is y/k. This means of course that under these conditions all three distribution plans are exactly the same. Because the DPE and guaranteed-valuation formulations are less complex than the formula for percent equalizing, most districts have tended to adopt the distribution plan under one of these two names.

APPENDIX 6

DESCRIPTION OF ACCOUNTS AND SAMPLE JOURNAL ENTRIES USING THE ACCOUNTS

Accounting for finances in the public schools requires double-entry bookkeeping procedures. The exact set of financial accounts is frequently specified by the education department in each state. In this Appendix, we describe only some of the more common financial accounts used by school districts. Attention here is limited to accounts used in the general and student-body funds. For a more definitive list of school district accounts, it is best to check the school accounting manual or a local school district business office in the particular state of interest. Following the description of these accounts is a listing of sample journal entries to be used in connection with these accounts. Only the most frequently encountered transactions are presented here; others can be found by consulting school accounting manuals prepared by the several states.

DESCRIPTION OF SCHOOL FINANCIAL ACCOUNTS

CURRENT ASSET ACCOUNTS

Cash

Currency, coin, checks, postal and express money orders and bankers' drafts on hand, or on deposit, with an official or agent designated as custodian of cash and bank deposits. Sometimes separate cash accounts are maintained by the school district and by the elected official who serves as the school district's banker. The county treasurer often serves in this latter role.

Imprest Funds

Money set aside for the purpose of paying small obligations for which the issuance of a formal warrant, voucher, or check would be too expensive and time-consuming.

Due from Other Funds

An asset account used to indicate amounts owed to a particular fund by another fund in the same unit for goods sold or services rendered. It is recommended that separate accounts be maintained for each interfund receivable.

Inventory

The cost of supplies and equipment on hand and not yet distributed to requisitioning units. An example would be food inventories to be sold in the school cafeteria or materials to be sold through the student store.

Investments

Securities and real estate held for the production of income in the form of interest, dividends, rentals, or lease payments. The account does not include fixed assets used in school district operations. Separate accounts for each category of investments may be maintained.

Taxes Receivable

These are taxes levied for local school support and represent an asset to the district. Often, separate receivables are set up for each tax year. A reserve for taxes receivable is established as part of the Fund Balance.

LIABILITY ACCOUNTS

Accrued Expenses

Expenses incurred during the current accounting period but not payable until a subsequent accounting period. This account is often used when salaries are paid for services rendered in a given school year but after the close of the fiscal period in which the services are delivered (e.g., salaries earned in the 19X1–19X2 school year but paid out in salary warrants after the beginning of the 19X2–19X3 fiscal period).

Vouchers Payable

Liabilities for goods and services received as evidenced by vouchers that have been preaudited and approved for payment but have not been paid.

Due to Other Funds

A liability account required when cash assets are borrowed from another fund. At the time the loan is paid back, the interest payment if any is recorded as an expenditure to the fund receiving the loan.

Warrants or Checks Outstanding

This account includes warrants (in the case when the county treasurer is the school district banker) or checks that have been issued by the school district but have not yet been redeemed by the bank or county treasurer (whoever actually supplies payment to the person). This account functions very much like the outstanding checks in relation to a personal bank account and it is therefore best viewed as a deduction from the cash account. The account is generally shown on the asset side of the balance sheet and as a contra account to the Cash Account.

BUDGETARY AND CONTROL ACCOUNTS

Encumbrances

This account designates obligations in the form of purchase orders, contracts, or salary commitments that are chargeable to an appropriation and for which a part of the appropriation is reserved. In an interim report, encumbrances are deducted along with the expenditures from the Appropriations account to arrive at the unencumbered balance of appropriations.

Reserve for Encumbrances

A reserve representing the segregation of a portion of the fund balance. This reserve is equal to the dollar amount of encumbrances.

Appropriations

This account records authorizations granted by the school board to make expenditures and to incur obligations for specific purposes. At the end of the fiscal period, this account is closed out and does not appear in reports prepared at the close of the fiscal period.

Estimated Revenues

The amount of revenue estimated to be received or to become receivable during the fiscal period. At the end of the fiscal period, the account is closed out and does not generally appear in a financial report prepared at the close of the fiscal period.

Fund Balance

The excess of the assets of a fund over its liabilities and reserves, except in the case of funds subject to budgetary accounting where, prior to the end of a fiscal period, it represents the excess of the fund's assets and estimated revenues for the period over its liabilities, reserves, and appropriations for the period. In some accounting systems, where a current fund balance is required, an adjustment to fund balance is made each time a revenue or expenditure transaction is made. Accomplishing this adjustment requires the use of expenditure contra and revenue contra accounts.

Reserve for Inventory

A reserve representing the segregation of a portion of a fund balance to indicate that assets equal to the amount of the reserve may be tied up in inventories of supplies not yet issued to requesting units.

Reserve for Taxes Receivable

This account is a portion of the fund balance and offsets the taxes receivable asset account. Property taxes levied during the fiscal period are credited to this account.

Expenditures

This account appears in the financial reports during the fiscal period and designates the total expenditures charged against appropriations during such period. The account usually has a debit balance and is used in some reports as a deduction from the Appropriations account to arrive at the unexpended balance of appropriations.

Revenues

This account designates an addition to assets during a given fiscal period in the form of cash that does not accompany the incurrence of liabilities or represent refund of previous disbursements. The account usually has a credit balance and appears only in a report prepared during the fiscal period. At the end of the fiscal period, the account is closed out and does not appear on a balance sheet prepared at the close of the fiscal period.

Appropriated Fund Balance

This is considered a part of the fund balance account and is used in situations where budgetary accounting is used but where the fund balance itself is not adjusted at the beginning of the fiscal period to reflect the balance of estimated revenues and appropriations for the year. The appropriated fund balance is closed out at the end of the year by simply reversing the budget entry (or entries) made to estimated revenues and appropriations during the fiscal period.

SAMPLE JOURNAL ENTRIES FOR FREQUENTLY ENCOUNTERED TRANSACTIONS

In this section, a number of sample journal entries are demonstrated in relation to a particular fund. We start with an opening entry and proceed with the more common transactions experienced in accounting for general operating expenses in a school district. A trial balance reflecting these sample transactions is presented following the list of transactions.

OPENING ENTRY

	Account	Debit	Credit
(1)	Imprest Funds	1,000	
	Cash	87,300	
	Warrants Outstanding		36,700
	Taxes Receivable	1,413,700	
	Due from Other Funds	42,000	
	Inventory	27,000	
	Encumbrances	50,000	
	Accrued Expenses		39,000
	Vouchers Payable		36,000
	Reserve for Taxes Receivable		1,413,700
	Reserve for Encumbrances		50,000
	Fund Balance		45,600

To record the opening entry at the beginning of the fiscal period. Notice that purchase orders of $50,000 from the prior fiscal period have been encumbered as part of this opening entry.

BUDGET ENTRY

	Account	Debit	Credit
(2)	Estimated Revenues	8,750,000	
	Fund Balance	15,000	
	Appropriations		8,765,000

To record the annual budget as adopted by the board of education. The separate account, called "Appropriated Fund Balance," can be debited here instead of the Fund Balance.

INVENTORY

	Account	Debit	Credit
(3)	Fund Balance	27,000	
	Reserve for Inventory		27,000

To establish the Reserve for Inventory at a level high enough to cover current inventory levels.

		Debit	Credit
(4)	Expenditures	1,600	
	Inventory		1,600

To record withdrawal of 1,600 in inventory items from stock.

		Debit	Credit
(5)	Expenditures	200	
	Inventory		200

To record reduction of Inventory account when a physical inventory reveals a book figure to be $200 above the actual stock.

		Debit	Credit
(6)	Inventory	700	
	Warrants Outstanding		700

To record the payment for $700 in additional inventory and supplies.

PROPERTY TAXES AND OTHER REVENUE SOURCES

		Debit	Credit
(7)	Taxes Receivable	450,000	
	Reserve for Taxes Receivable		450,000

To record a special tax levy expected to yield $450,000.

		Debit	Credit
(8)	Cash	840,000	
	Revenues		840,000
	Reserve for Taxes Receivable	840,000	
	Taxes Receivable		840,000

To record receipt of $840,000 in taxes receivable.

		Debit	Credit
(9)	Revenues	1,200	
	Cash		1,200

To record a $1,200 refund on property taxes collected in the current year.

		Debit	Credit
(10)	Cash	75,000	
	Revenues		75,000

To record receipt of $75,000 in aid for a federal project.

INVESTMENTS

		Debit	Credit
(11)	Investments	400,000	
	Cash		400,000

To purchase $400,000 in an investment yielding 6 percent annual interest. The credit is to "cash" rather than to "warrants outstanding" simply because the bank directly handles the investments in this particular case.

		Debit	Credit
(12)	Cash	82,400	
	Revenues		2,400
	Investments		80,000

To record sale of an $80,000 investment yielding 6 percent annual interest. Investment sold after six months and interest is figured at 3 percent of principal amount.

EXPENDITURES AND ENCUMBRANCES

		Debit	Credit
(13)	Encumbrances	325,000	
	Reserve for Encumbrances		325,000

To record the issuance of purchase orders for $325,000 in goods and services.

		Debit	Credit
(14)	Expenditures	215,000	
	Warrants Outstanding		215,000
	Reserve for Encumbrances	210,000	
	Encumbrances		210,000

To record payment of $215,000 in purchases that were initially encumbered at an estimated cost of $210,000.

(15)	Expenditures	35,000	
	Vouchers Payable		35,000

To record $35,000 in expenditures prior to the issuance of the warrant for payment.

(16)	Vouchers Payable	26,000	
	Warrants Outstanding		26,000

To record payment by warrant of $26,000 of purchases expended at an earlier time.

(17)	Warrants Outstanding	230,000	
	Cash		230,000

To record redemption of $230,000 in warrants.

(18)	Expenditures	400,000	
	Accrued Expenses		400,000

To record accrual of $400,000 in salaries and payroll. This recognizes the obligation without actually making the payment.

IMPREST FUNDS

(19)	Imprest Funds	500	
	Warrants Outstanding		500

To increase the imprest fund by $500.00

(20)	Expenditures	300	
	Warrants Outstanding		300

To record reimbursement of an imprest fund for audited disbursements totaling $300. This entry is made only after board of education approval of the disbursement.

DUE TO OR FROM OTHER FUNDS

(21)	Cash	22,000	
	Due to Other Funds		22,000

To record the borrowing of $22,000 from the Building Fund.

(22)	Due from Other Funds	18,000	
	Warrants Outstanding		18,000

To record the loan of $18,000 to the Student Activity Fund.

Trial Balance

	Total		*Balance*	
	Debit	*Credit*	*Debit*	*Credit*
Imprest Funds	1,500	-0-	1,500	—
Cash	1,106,700	631,200	475,500	—
Warrants Outstanding	230,000	297,200	—	67,200
Taxes Receivable	1,863,700	840,000	1,023,700	—
Due from Other Funds	60,000	-0-	60,000	—
Investments	400,000	80,000	320,000	—
Inventory	27,700	1,800	25,900	—
Encumbrances	375,000	210,000	165,000	—
Accrued Expenses	-0-	439,000	—	439,000
Vouchers Payable	26,000	71,000	—	45,000
Due to Other Funds	-0-	22,000	—	22,000
Reserve for Inventory	-0-	27,000	—	27,000
Reserve for Taxes Receivable	840,000	1,863,700	—	1,023,700
Reserve for Encumbrances	210,000	375,000	—	165,000
Fund Balance	42,000	45,600	—	3,600
Estimated Revenues	8,750,000	-0-	8,750,000	—
Appropriations	-0-	8,765,000	—	8,765,000
Expenditures	652,100	-0-	652,100	—
Revenues	1,200	917,400	—	916,200
	14,585,900	14,585,900	11,473,700	11,473,700

This trial balance is the result of Entries 1–22 as presented on the previous pages. An explanation of each entry or transaction is provided immediately following the presentation of the entry itself.

APPENDIX 7

TRANSACTIONS AND T-ACCOUNTS FOR SEQUENCE OF FINANCIAL ACTIVITIES IN UNIVERSITY PLACE SCHOOL DISTRICT

FINANCIAL TRANSACTIONS

This sequence of financial transactions is exactly the same as that presented in Table 10–5 of the text. These transactions are mounted on the T-accounts on the next page. The beginning status of all accounts is also shown on the T-accounts.

Description of Transactions:

1. The budget for the fiscal year beginning on September 1, 19X1, includes estimated revenues of $10,871,668 and an appropriation (or estimated expenditure) of $10,950,630.
2. Property tax revenues amounting to $1,685,735 are received by the district and deposited in the cash account.
3. Notice is received that $826,540 worth of warrants have been redeemed at the county treasurer or bank.
4. The board of education approves investment of $500,000 in a 180-day note bearing interest of 9 percent.

5. Purchase orders totaling $825,000 are issued by the district business office.
6. Warrants totalling $14,382 are issued for amounts previously accrued and approved in voucher format.
7. Accrued expenses (mostly payroll) of $675,492 come due and warrants are issued for the total amount.
8. A $20,000 loan is made in warrant form to the student-body fund. This loan is made for a period of 90 days and carries an interest rate of 7 percent.
9. Interest payments of $15,763 on investments are received and deposited.
10. Warrants are issued for $32,564 worth of expenditures, which were previously encumbered for the same amount.
11. Additional lunchroom inventory of $17,000 is purchased by warrant.
12. A physical inventory reveals that actual inventories are $28,470 and this is reflected in the inventory account. No attempt is made at this time to adjust the reserve for inventory to reflect this lesser amount.
13. A $50 item is purchased from the imprest funds.
14. Warrants are written to pay for $626,432 of goods and services previously encumbered for the same amount.

T-Accounts:

IMPREST FUNDS

	Debit		Credit
(B)	625		
	625		

CASH

	Debit		Credit
(B)	1,194,079	(3)	826,540
(2)	1,685,735	(4)	500,000
(9)	15,763		
	1,569,037		

WARRANTS OUTSTANDING

	Debit		Credit
(3)	826,540	(B)	910,432
		(6)	14,382
		(7)	675,492
		(8)	20,000
		(10)	32,564
		(11)	17,000
		(14)	626,432
			1,469,762

INVESTMENTS

	Debit		Credit
(B)	756,003		
(4)	500,000		
	1,256,003		

DUE FROM OTHER FUNDS

	Debit		Credit
(B)	4,382		
(8)	20,000		
	24,382		

VOUCHERS PAYABLE

	Debit		Credit
(6)	14,382	(B)	26,382
			12,000

RESERVE FOR INVENTORY

	Debit		Credit
		(B)	32,499
			32,499

INVENTORY

	Debit		Credit
(B)	32,499	(12)	21,029
(11)	17,000		
	28,470		

ACCRUED EXPENSES

	Debit		Credit
(7)	675,492	(B)	773,478
			97,986

APPROPRIATIONS

	Debit		Credit
		(1)	10,950,630
			10,950,630

ESTIMATED REVENUES

	Debit		Credit
(1)	10,871,668		
	10,871,668		

ENCUMBRANCES

	Debit		Credit
(5)	825,000	(10)	32,564
		(14)	626,432
	166,004		

EXPENDITURES

	Debit		Credit
(10)	32,564		
(12)	21,029		
(14)	626,432		
	680,025		

REVENUES

	Debit		Credit
		(2)	1,685,735
		(9)	15,763
			1,701,498

RESERVE FOR ENCUMBRANCES

	Debit		Credit
(10)	32,564	(5)	825,000
(14)	626,432		
			166,004

FUND BALANCE

	Debit		Credit
(1)	78,962	(B)	244,797
			165,835

BIBLIOGRAPHY

The numbers in brackets following each entry represent the part of the book and the specific chapter to which the entry applies, that is, the reference II-6 means that the item relates to material in Part II, Chapter 6. Certain references apply to more than one chapter or part of the book.

Allen, D. W. "First Steps in Developing a Master Schedule." *Bulletin of the National Association of Secondary School Principals* 46 (May 1962): 34–36. [II-4]

Anderson, Ronald D. "Formulating Objectives for Elementary Science (Part 1)." *Science and Children* 5 (September 1967): 20–23. [I-2]

Apple, Michael W. "The Process and Ideology of Valuing in Educational Settings." In *Educational Evaluation: Analysis and Responsibility,* edited by M. W. Apple, M. J. Subkoviak, and H. S. Lufler, Jr. Berkeley, Calif.: McCutchan, 1974. [II-6]

Austin, David B. and Noble, Gividen. *The High School Principal and Staff Develop a Master Schedule*. New York: Bureau of Publications, Teachers College, Columbia University, 1960. [II-4]

Baker, Eva L. "Effects on Student Achievement of Behavioral and Non-Behavioral Objectives." *Journal of Experimental Education* 37 (Summer 1969): 5–8. [I-2]

Barr, Richard H. *Principles of Public School Accounting*. Handbook II-B, rev. Washington, D.C.: U.S. Government Printing Office, 1980. [III-10]

Battersby, Albert. *Network Analysis for Planning and Scheduling*. New York: John Wiley, 1970. [II-3]

Benson, Charles S. *The Economics of Public Education*. 3d ed. Boston: Houghton-Mifflin, 1973. [III-7, 8]

Bereiter, Carl. *Must We Educate?* Englewood Cliffs, N.J.: Prentice-Hall, 1973. [I-1]

Bernstein, Richard J. *Praxis and Action*. Philadelphia: University of Pennsylvania Press, 1971. [II-6]

Bloom, Benjamin S., ed. *Taxonomy of Educational Objectives, Handbook I: Cognitive Domain*. New York: David McKay, 1956. [I-2]

Bridge, R. Gary; Judd, Charles M.; and Moock, Peter K. *The Determinants of Educational Outcomes*. Cambridge, Mass.: Ballinger, 1979. [II-6]

Bruner, Jerome S. "Education as Social Invention." *Saturday Review* 49 (19 February 1966): 70–72. [I-1]

Buck, A. E. *The Budget in Governments of Today*. New York: Macmillan, 1934. [III-9]

———. *Public Budgeting*. New York: Harper & Brothers, 1929. [III-9]

Burrup, Percy E. *Financing Education in a Climate of Change*. 2d ed. Boston: Allyn & Bacon, 1977. [III-7, 8]

Bush, Robert N. et al. "The High School Schedule." *School Review* 69 (Spring 1961): 48–59. [II-4]

Butts, R. Freeman, and Cremin, Lawrence A. *A History of Education in American Culture*. New York: Henry Holt, 1953. [I-1]

Campbell, Donald T., and Stanley, Julian C. "Experimental and Quasi-Experimental Designs for Research in Teaching." In *Handbook of Research on Teaching,* edited by N. L. Gage. Chicago: Rand McNally, 1963. [II-6]

Candoli, I. Carl, et al. *School Business Administration: A Planning Approach*. Boston: Allyn & Bacon, 1978. [III-9,10]

Clark, D. Cecil. *Using Instructional Objectives in Teaching*. Glenview, Ill.: Scott, Foresman, 1972. [I-2]

Cohn, Elchanan. *The Economics of Education*. 2d ed. Cambridge, Mass.: Ballinger, 1979. [III-9]

Commission on the Reorganization of Secondary Education. *Cardinal Principles of Secondary Education*. Bulletin 35. Washington, D.C.: U.S. Bureau of Education, 1918. [I-1]

Conant, James B. *The American High School Today*. New York: McGraw-Hill, 1959. [I-1]

Connors, Eugene T.; Franklin, Herbert; and Kaskey, Connie. "Zero-Base: A New Look at Budgeting for Education." *Journal of Education Finance* 4 (Fall 1978): 248–259. [III-9,10]

Cramer, Harold L., and Wehking, Robert J. *Charretting the Planning Process*. A report published by Project Simu-School: Center for Urban Education Planning, and funded by U.S. Office of Education, Title III, June 1973 (ERIC Document Reproduction Service No. ED 084 681). [I-2]

Cubberley, Ellwood P. *School Funds and Their Apportionment*. New York: Columbia University Press, 1906. [III-8]

Cyphert, F. R., and Gant, W. L. "The Delphi Technique: A Tool for Collecting Opinions in Teacher Education." *Journal of Teacher Education* 21 (Fall 1970): 417–425. [I-2]

Deal, Stephen. "Individual School Budgeting." *SLANTS* 21 (March 1980): 1–2. [III-8]

De Bono, Edward. *New Think*. New York: Basic Books, 1968. [I-2]

Dodge, Bernard J., and Clark, Richard. "Research on the Delphi Technique." *Educational Technology* 17 (April 1977): 58–59. [I-2]

Douglas, Harl R. *Modern Administration of Secondary Schools*. 2d ed. Boston: Ginn and Company, 1963. [II-4]

Drucker, Peter. *Management*. New York: Harper-Row, 1974. [I-1]

Duncan, D. J. and J. W. Peach "School-Based Budgeting: Implications for the Principal." *Education Canada* (Fall 1977): 39–41. [III-9]

Dyer, Henry S. "Discovery and Development Goals." *National Association of Secondary School Principals Bulletin* 51 (March 1967): 1–14. [I-1]

Education, U.S.A. Washington, D.C.: National School Public Relations Association, January 1976. [III-10]

Educational Policies Commission. *Education for All American Youth*. Washington, D.C.: National Education Association, 1944. [I-1]

———. *The Purposes of Education in American Democracy*. Washington, D.C.: National Education Association, 1938. [I-1]

Edwards, Allen L. *An Introduction to Linear Regression and Correlation*. San Francisco: W. H. Freeman, 1976. [II-6]

Eisner, Elliot. "Instructional and Expressive Educational Objectives: Their Formulation and Use in Curriculum." In *Instructional Objectives,* edited by W. James Popham. AERA Monograph Series on Curriculum Evaluation, no. 3. Chicago: Rand McNally, 1969. [II-6]

———, and Vallance, Elizabeth, eds. *Conflicting Concepts of Curriculum*. Berkeley, Calif.: McCutchan, 1974. [I-1]

Figers, Joseph, Jr. *The Arlington, Virginia Story*. A paper on Charrette sessions presented to the Council of Educational Facility Planners Southeastern Regional Workshop, April 1971 (ERIC Document Reproduction Service No. Ed 049 556). [I-2]

Furno, Orlando F., and Magers, Dexter A. "An Analysis of State School Support Programs," In *Perspectives in State School Support Programs,* edited by K. Forbis Jordan and Nebla H. Cambren-McCabe, Cambridge, Mass: Balinger Publishing, 1981. [III-8].

Gardner, Don E. "Five Evaluation Frameworks." *Journal of Higher Education* 48 (October 1977): 571–593. [II-6]

Garms, Walter I; Guthrie, James W.; and Pierce, Lawrence C. *School Finance*. Englewood Cliffs, N.J.: Prentice-Hall, 1978. [III-7, 9]

Gmelch, Walter H. "The Principal's Next Challenge: The Twentieth Century Art of Managing Stress." *The Bulletin of the National Association of Secondary School Principals,* February 1978. [II-5]

"Goals of Primary Education." *School and Society* 96 (Summer 1968): 295–296. [I-1]

Goertz, Margaret E.; Moskowitz, Jay H.; and Sinkin, Judy G. *Plain Talk About School Finance*. Washington, D.C.: National Institute of Education, U.S. Department of Health, Education, and Welfare, 1978. [III-8]

Gorman, Ronald H., and Baker, H. Kent. "Brainstorming Your Way to Problem-Solving Ideas." *Personnel Journal* 57 (August 1978): 438–440. [I-2]

Guilford, J. P. *Psychometric Methods*. 2d ed. New York: McGraw-Hill, 1954. [II-6]

Hager, James L., and Scarr, L. E. *It's About Time*. Kirkland, Wash.: Management Development Association, 1978. [II-5]

Hamilton, David et al., eds. *Beyond the Numbers Game: A Reader in Educational Evaluation*. Berkeley, Calif.: McCutchan, 1977. [II-6]

Hartley, Harry J. *Educational Planning—Programming—Budgeting*. Englewood Cliffs, N.J.: Prentice-Hall, 1968. [III-9]

Hassenger, Robert. "The Social Foundations of Education: What the Schools Should Do." *National Elementary Principal* 57 (January 1978): 82–86. [I-1]

Hawkins, S. Fred, ed. *Internal Audit Guide for Student Activity Funds*. Park Ridge, Ill.: Association of School Business Officials, 1981. [III-10]

Hennessy, Bernard C. *Public Opinion*. 3d ed. North Scituate, Mass.: Duxbury Press, 1975. [II-6]

Hentschke, Guilbert C. *Management Operations in Education*. Berkeley, Calif.: McCutchan, 1975. [II-3; III-9]

Herbert, John J. "Class Scheduling and Grade Reporting Aided by Marginally Punched Card System." *Bulletin of the National Association of Secondary School Principals*. 47 (February 1963): 129–137. [II-4]

Herzberg, Frederick. *Work and the Nature of Man*. New York: World, 1966. [II-5]

Holland, John L. *The Self-Directed Search/A Guide to Educational and Vocational Planning*. Palo Alto, Calif.: Consulting Psychologists Press, 1970. [I-2]

Holmes, T. H., and Rahe, R. H. "The Social Readjustment Rating Scale." *Journal of Psychosomatic Research* 11 (August 1967): 213–218. [II-5]

Holz, Robert E. "Generalized Academic Simulation Programs." A report on the scheduling project at Massachusetts Institute of Technology, 1963. [II-4]

Horowitz, Joseph. *Critical Path Scheduling*. New York: Ronald Press, 1967. [II-3]

House, Ernest R. "Assumptions Underlying Evaluation Models." *Educational Researcher* 7 (March 1978): 4–12. [II-6]

Howard, John H.; Rechnitzer, Peter A.; and Cunningham, D. A. "Coping with Job Tension—Effective and Ineffective Methods." *Public Personnel Management* 4 (September–October 1975): 317–326. [II-5]

Howe, Harold, II. "The Trouble with Educational Research." *National Elementary Principal* 56 (November–December 1976): 43–46. [II-6]

Ingram, Ruben L. "The Principal: Instructional Leader, Site Manager," *Educational Executive* 8 (May 1979): 23–25. [III-8, 9]

Johnson, Howard M. "Flexibility in the Secondary School." *Bulletin of the National Association of Secondary School Principals* 53 (October 1969): 62–72. [II-4]

Kimball, Roland B. "Six Approaches to Evaluating Teaching: A Typology." *National Association of Secondary School Principals Bulletin* 64 (March 1980): 41–47. [I-2]

King, Arthur R., Jr., and Brownell, John A. *The Curriculum and the Disciplines of Knowledge*. New York: John Wiley & Sons, 1966. [I-1]

Kirst, Michael W. "The Rise and Fall of PPBS in California." *Phi Delta Kappan* 56 (April 1975): 535–538. [III-9]

Knezevich, Stephen J. *Program Budgeting (PPBS)*. Berkeley, Calif.: McCutchan, 1973. [III-9]

———. "Program Budgeting Revisited: Reexamining Its Promise for the Enhancement of Educational Administration During the 1980s." *The Executive Review* 2 (1981):1–5. [III-9]

Krathwohl, David R.; Bloom, Benjamin S.; and Masia, Bertram B. *Taxonomy of Educational Objectives, Handbook II: Affective Domain*. New York: David McKay, 1964. [I-2]

Kuttner, Monroe S. *Managing the Paperwork Pipeline*. New York: John Wiley & Sons, 1978. [II-5]

Lakein, Alan. *How to Get Control of Your Time and Your Life*. New York: Times Mirror, 1973. [I-1, II-5]

Levin, Betsy, ed. *Future Directions for School Finance Reform*. Lexington, Mass.: Lexington Books, 1974. [III-8]

Likert, Rensis. *Human Organization*. New York: McGraw-Hill, 1967. [II-5]

Lindvall, C. M., ed. *Defining Educational Objectives*. Pittsburgh: University of Pittsburgh Press, 1964. [I-2]

Linstone, Harold A., and Turoff, Murray, eds. *The Delphi Method*. Reading, Mass.: Addison-Wesley, 1975. [I-2]

Lynn, Edward S., and Freeman, Robert J. *Fund Accounting: Theory and Practice*. Englewood Cliffs, N.J.: Prentice-Hall, 1974. [III-9, 10]

McAshan, Hildreth H. *Writing Behavioral Objectives: A New Approach*. New York: Harper & Row, 1970. [I-2]

McCleary, Lloyd E., and Thompson, Scott D. *The Senior High School Principalship*, vol. 3. Reston, Va.: National Association of Secondary School Principals, 1979. [II-5]

MacKenzie, R. Alec. *The Time Trap*. New York: Anacom, 1972. [II-5]

Mager, Robert F. *Preparing Instructional Objectives*. Belmont, Calif.: Fearon, 1962. [I-2]

Manasse, A. Lorri. "Effective Principals: Effective at What?" *Principal* (March, 1982): 10–15 [I-1, II-5]

March, James G. "Analytic Skills and the University Training of Educational Administrators." *Education and Urban Society* 6 (August 1974): 382–427 [I-1]

Maslow, Abraham. *Motivation and Personality*. 2d ed. New York: Harper & Row, 1970. [II-5]

Maxwell, James A. *Financing State and Local Governments*. Washington, D.C.: The Brookings Institution, 1969. [III-7]

Morrison, Henry C. *School Revenue*. Chicago: University Chicago Press, 1930. [III-7]

National Advisory Council on Bilingual Education. *The Fourth Annual Report of the National Advisory Council on Bilingual Education 1978–1979*. Prepared by Inter-American Research Associates, Inc., of Rosslyn, Virginia, 1979. [III-7]

National Commission on the Reform of Secondary Education. *Reform of Secondary Education*. New York: McGraw-Hill, 1973. [I-1]

National Education Association. *Report of the Committee of Ten on Secondary School Studies*. New York: American Book, 1894. [I-1]

Nie, Norman H. et al. *Statistical Package for the Social Sciences*. 2d ed. New York: McGraw Hill, 1975. [II-6]

Norton, John K. *Education and Economic Well-Being in American Democracy*. Washington, D.C.: Educational Policies Commission, 1940. [III-10]

NOW. A newsletter. Washington D.C.: National Education Association, 12 June 1978. [I-2]

Nunnally, Jum C. *Educational Measurement and Evaluation*. New York: McGraw-Hill, 1972. [II-6]

Odden, Allan, and Augenblick, John. *School Finance in the States: 1980*. Denver: Education Commission of the States, 1980. [III-8]

———; Berne, Robert; and Stiefel, Leonna. *Equity in School Finance*. Denver: Education Commission of the States, 1979. [III-8]

Oldman, Oliver, and Schoettle, Ferdinand P. *State and Local Taxes and Finance*. Mineola, N.Y.: Foundation Press, 1974. [III-7]

Oncken, William, Jr., and Wass, Donald L. "Management Time: Who's Got the Monkey?" *Harvard Business Review* 52 (November–December, 1974): 75–80. [II-5]

Ovard, Glen F. "Daily Computer Scheduling." *Bulletin of the National Association of Secondary School Principals* 58 (March 1974): 113–118. [II-4]

Owens, Thomas R., and Evans, Warren D. *Program Evaluation Skills for Busy Administrators*. Portland, Ore.: Northwest Regional Education Laboratory, 1977. [II-6]

Payne, Stanley L. *The Art of Asking Questions*. Princeton, N.J.: Princeton University Press, 1951. [II-6]

Pechman, Joseph. *Federal Tax Policy*. 3d ed. Washington, D.C.: The Brookings Institution, 1977. [III-7]

———, and Olsner, Benjamin, A. *Who Bears the Tax Burden*. Washington D.C.: The Brookings Institution, 1974. [III-7]

Perrow, Charles. *Complex Organizations*. Glenview, Ill.: Scott, Foresman, 1972. [I-2]

Peters, R. S. *Authority, Responsibility, and Education*. London: George Allen & Unwin, 1959. [I-2]

Phi Delta Kappa National Study Committee on Evaluation. *Educational Evaluation and Decision Making*. Itasca, Ill.: F. E. Peacock, 1971. [II-6]

Pierce, Lawrence C. "Emerging Policy Issues in Public Education." *Phi Delta Kappan* 58 (October 1976): 173–176. [III-9]

Plowman, Paul B. *Behavioral Objectives*. Chicago: Science Research Associates, 1971. [I-2]

Popham, W. James. *Educational Evaluation*. Englewood Cliffs, N.J.: Prentice-Hall, 1975. [II-6]

———. *The Uses of Instructional Objectives*. Belmont, Calif.: Fearon, 1973. [I-2]

Potts, Vernon, and Kemper, Ray. "Micro-Mini Units for Junior High Schools." *Clearing House* 48 (May 1974): 530–532. [II-4]

Provus, Malcom. *Discrepancy Evaluation*. Berkeley, Calif.: McCutchan, 1971. [II-6]

Pyhrr, Peter A. *Zero-Base Budgeting*. New York: John Wiley & Sons, 1973. [III-9]

Raths, Louis E.; Harmin, Merril; and Simon, Sidney B. *Values and Teaching: Working with Values in the Classroom*. Columbus, Ohio: Charles E. Merrill, 1966. [I-1]

Ribeaux, Peter, and Poppleton, Stephen E. *Psychology and Work*. London: Macmillan, 1978. [II-5]

Rivlin, Alice M. *Systematic Thinking for Social Action*. Washington, D.C.: The Brookings Institution, 1971. [III-9]

Rogers, Daniel C., and Ruchlin, Hirsch S. *Economics and Education: Principles and Applications*. New York: Free Press, 1971. [III-9]

Saville, Anthony. *Instructional Programming: Issues and Innovations in School Scheduling*. Columbus, Ohio: Charles E. Merrill, 1973. [II-4]

Scriven, Michael S. "The Methodology of Evaluation." In *Perspectives of Curriculum Evaluation*, edited by Ralph W. Tyler, Robert M. Gagne, and Michael Scriven. AERA Monograph Series on Curriculum Evaluation, no. 1. Chicago: Rand McNally, 1967. [II-6]

Shane, Harold G. *The Educational Significance of the Future*. Bloomington, Ind.: Phi Delta Kappa, 1973. [I-1]

Snyder, Phillip C., and Hogan, Earl E. *Cost Accountability for School Administrators*. West Nyack, N.Y.: Parker, 1975. [III-9]

Soltis, Jonas F. *An Introduction to the Analysis of Educational Concepts*. 2d ed. Reading, Mass.: Addison-Wesley, 1978. [I-2]

Stokey, Edith, and Zeckhauser, Richard. *A Primer for Policy Analysis*. New York: W. W. Norton, 1978. [III-9]

Stolberg, Charles G., ed. *School Accounting, Budgeting, and Finance Challenges*. Park Ridge, Ill.: Association of School Business Officials, 1981. [III-10]

Suchman, Edward A. "Action for What? A Critique of Evaluation Research." In *The Organization, Management, and Tactics of Social Research*, edited by Richard O'Toole. Cambridge, Mass.: Schenkman, 1970. [II-6]

Tanner, Daniel. *Secondary Education*. New York: Macmillan, 1972. [I-1]

Thomas, Donald. "Budget Cutting: Lessons from Experience." *American School and University*, November 1977, pp. 855–875. [III-9]

Thompson, Mark S. *Benefit-Cost Analysis for Program Evaluation*. Beverly Hills, Calif.: Sage, 1980. [III-9]

Tidwell, Sam B. *Financial and Managerial Accounting for Elementary and Secondary School Systems*. Chicago: Research Corporation of Association of School Business Officials, 1974. [III-10]

———. *Public School Fund Accounting*. New York: Harper & Brothers, 1960. [III-10]

Time Management. Operations Notebook No. 8 of the Association of California School Administrators, January 1974. [II-5]

Tyler, Ralph W. *Basic Principles of Curriculum and Instruction*. Chicago: University of Chicago Press, 1950. [I-2; II-6]

Tuckman, Bruce W. Evaluating Instructional Programs. Boston: Allyn and Bacon, 1979. [II-6]

U.S. Office of Education. *Financial Accounting: Classifications and Standard Terminology for Local and State School Systems*. Handbook II, rev. Washington, D.C.: U.S. Government Printing Office, 1973. [III-9]

Van Dusseldorp, Ralph A.; Richardson, Duane E.; and Foley, Walter J. *Educational Decision Making Through Operations Research*. Boston: Allyn & Bacon, 1971. [II-3]

Weiss, Carol H. *Evaluation Research*. Englewood Cliffs, N.J.: Prentice-Hall, 1972. [II-6]

Weldy, Gilbert R. *Time: A Resource for the School Administrator*. Reston, Va.: National Association of Secondary School Principals, 1974. [II-5]

Wiley, W. Duane, and Bishop, Lloyd K. *The Flexibly Scheduled High School*. West Nyack, N.Y.: Parker, 1968. [II-4]

Woodring, Paul. "Subject Matter and the Goals of Education." *Educational Forum* 24 (May 1960): 417–419. [I-1]

Worthen, Blain R., and Sanders, James R. *Educational Evaluation: Theory and Practice*. Worthington, Ohio: Charles A. Jones, 1973. [I-2; II-6]

INDEX